Computer Science, Technology and Applications

snova
New York

Computer Science, Technology and Applications

Computational Arts and Creative Products: Languages, Spaces and Practices
Alessandra Micalizzi, PhD (Editor)
ISBN: 979-8-89530-426-6
eBook ISBN: 979-8-89530-499-0

Blockchain Technology for Healthcare Applications: Challenges, Privacy, and Securing of Data
Ahmed J. Obaid, PhD,
Vinod Kumar Shukla, PhD,
Soumi Dutta, PhD, Abhishek Bhattacharya, PhD
and Satyajit Chakraborti, PhD (Editors)
ISBN: 979-8-89530-132-6
eBook ISBN: 979-8-89530-359-7

Cognitive Connections: Unleashing the Potential of Interactive Technologies
Yogesh Kumar Rathore, PhD,
Shweta Bansal, PhD,
Suman Kumar Swarnkar, PhD,
Vishal Sharma, PhD
and Saroj Pandey, PhD (Editors)
ISBN: 979-8-89530-157-9
eBook ISBN: 979-8-89530-310-8

Thinking Machine
Ping Zhu
ISBN: 979-8-89530-203-3
eBook ISBN: 979-8-89530-274-3

Accessible Technology for People with Disabilities, Older Americans, and Veterans
Willis S. Roland (Editor)
ISBN: 979-8-89530-232-3
eBook ISBN: 979-8-89530-254-5

Cybersecurity: Improvements Needed, National Strategy, and Operational Technology
Sander T. Karlsen (Editor)
ISBN: 979-8-89530-101-2
eBook ISBN: 979-8-89530-201-9

Ensemble Machine Learning: Advances in Research and Applications
M. A. Jabbar, PhD,
Loveleen Gaur, PhD and Abdelkrim Haqiq, PhD (Editors)
ISBN: 979-8-89530-101-2
eBook ISBN: 979-8-89530-201-9

More information about this series can be found at
https://novapublishers.com/product-category/series/computer-science-technology-and-applications/

Jessica Andrews
Editor

Big Data, Big Impact

Navigating Competition, Privacy, and Reform

snova
New York

Library of Congress Cataloging-in-Publication Data

ISBN: 979-8-89530-538-6 (Hardcover)
ISBN: 979-8-89530-565-2 (eBook)

Published by Nova Science Publishers, Inc. † New York

Contents

Preface

As nearly every aspect of our society and economy has moved online, vast amounts of digital data are being collected about us—data that spans everything from who we are, to what we like, to who we communicate with, and even what we do. While this mass data collection has some valuable and productive applications, it also poses profound risks.

What happens to our basic autonomy as individuals when both the government and private companies can amass detailed profiles about us, using that information to predict and, potentially, manipulate our behavior? What are the implications for our economy when some of the most popular online products and services depend on opaque data collection and personalization? And what does it mean for our democracy when these data practices shape public discourse and influence the flow of news and information?

Chapter 1

Big Data, Big Questions: Implications for Competition and Consumers*

Committee on the Judiciary

Tuesday, September 21, 2021

United States Senate Subcommittee on Competition, Policy, Antitrust, and Consumer Rights, Committee on the Judiciary

Washington, DC.

The Subcommittee met, pursuant to notice, at 2:51 p.m., in Room 226, Dirksen Senate Office Building, Hon. Amy Klobuchar, Chair of the Subcommittee, presiding.

Present: Senators Klobuchar [presiding], Blumenthal, Lee, Hawley and Blackburn.

Also Present: Chair Durbin, Senators Padilla and Cruz.

Opening Statement of Hon. Amy Klobuchar, a U.S. Senator from the State of Minnesota

Chair KLOBUCHAR. Okay. We've been joined by my friend and colleague, Senator Lee, so we're ready to begin the hearing. I call to order the hearing of

---

* This is an edited, reformatted and augmented version of HearingBefore the Subcommittee on Competition Policy, Antitrust and Consumer Rights of the Committee on the Judiciary United States Senate, Serial No. J–117–35, dated September 21, 2021.

In: Big Data, Big Impact: Navigating Competition, Privacy, and Reform
Editor: Jessica Andrews
ISBN: 979-8-89530-538-6

the Subcommittee on Competition, Policy, Antitrust, and Consumer Rights on Big Data, Big Questions: Implications for Competition and Consumers.

Good afternoon, and before we begin, the Chair of the Committee can only be here for the first few minutes. It was very important to have him here and as we would give Senator Grassley the same due, we will—I asked Senator Durbin if he could say a few words before I begin.

Opening Statement of Hon. Richard J. Durbin, a U.S. Senator from the State of Illinois

Chair DURBIN. Thank you very much, Senator Klobuchar, and to our witnesses and my colleague Senator Lee for giving me this opportunity to say a few opening words about the scope and unrestricted nature of big data collection.

In 2018, we had an extraordinary hearing with the head of Facebook, Mr. Zuckerberg. He faced 42 Senators who had questions for him because of overlapping jurisdiction of the Committees. It was an ordeal that went on for some period of time. I was somewhere in the middle of the pack. The question I asked him was very basic. "Would you mind sharing with us the name of the hotel you stayed in last night?" After a kind of embarrassed and awkward pause, he said, "No." I said, "Well, would you mind sharing with us the emails that you've sent out in the last 24 hours and who you sent them to?' He said, "No." I said, "Really isn't that the issue we're getting down to, privacy? Am I right to say there's a line I'm going to draw, and you can't cross it legally to invade my space and invade my privacy?"

In today's world, information is economic power. Companies are using it to make more money. I share the concerns of my colleagues that have enabled the collection of too much information by selected few giant companies. There could be benefits and efficiencies to big data, but there are cost and impact. These cost and impact affect everyone, including our children.

I introduced the Clean Slate for Kids Online Act because I was concerned with the amount of data collected and stored on our children and grandchildren. Every click a child makes on the internet leaves a trail of personal data that can last a lifetime.

Companies that market online products and apps geared toward children are accumulating massive amounts of personal data, and the kids never had the chance to even consider giving informed consent.

My bill would give every American enforceable legal right to demand that internet companies delete all personal information collected about a person when she was—he or she was under the age of 13. Kids deserve the right to request a clean slate once they've grown up and are old enough to appreciate the consequences of data collection. This bill gives them a basic privacy protection. It's one aspect of data collection that can be manipulated and impacted on consumers and competition.

Today's hearing is an important part of that effort to shine light on big data collectors.

I thank Senator Klobuchar and Senator Lee.

Chair KLOBUCHAR. Thank you very much, Chairman Durbin. I wanted to make clear that this hearing is one of a series of hearings that Senator Lee and I are conducting, our bipartisan review of America's competition issues. I thank my staff, as well as Senator Lee and his staff, for helping to plan the hearing.

Today we're going to be talking about how competition is affected and threatened by the use of big data. Big data is at the core of our modern economy, as Senator Durbin so well pointed out, powering targeted advertising and driving artificial intelligence to select what products and services we are shown online and increasingly offline as well.

In this hearing, we'll explore the companies that control the data, the state of competition and barriers to entry, and the effects of big data on consumers, their choices, and their privacy.

I'd like to be clear about what we mean when we say big data. Technology companies such as Google, Facebook, and Amazon collect an enormous amount of information, as Senator Durbin pointed out, about our daily activities in real time. They know what we buy, who our friends are, where we live, work and travel, and more.

In fact, their very business models, their very business models were set up around getting that information and then using it to profit. Through services such as Google's Gmail and Facebook's Instagram, though those services are offered to us for free, these companies and advertisers use the data they collect about us to sell to other companies. In the end, you can't get around the fact. We are the product. We are the product that makes the companies money.

Big tech companies are not the only ones keeping tabs on all of us. Data brokers including Kinesso and its sister company, Acxiom, also buy, process, and sell massive amounts of personal information about consumers, and they've actually been doing it since before we even knew what the internet was. They collect information from the Department of Motor Vehicles, from public records, from our grocery store loyalty cards, and even from other data brokers.

Today they also buy our browsing histories, and guess how much money we make, and what religion we practice. This data has immense competitive value and the way that it is collected and used has important impacts on consumers.

I'll give you an example. The simple act of a consumer visiting a utility company's website to pay a monthly gas bill allowed dozens of companies to profit off of her, for the most part, without her knowledge.

Facebook and Google are likely to know about that consumer paying her bill even though they had nothing to do with the transaction. If the gas company runs advertisements on Facebook as many do, Facebook would have trackers embedded on the gas company's website. If the consumer, if she uses the world's most popular web browser, Chrome, Google would know what websites she visited.

Both companies collect and analyze this kind of information, building a detailed profile of the consumer and giving advertisers access to our online, for a price of course, but not something she gets paid.

At the same time, data brokers like Acxiom are buying and selling data from utility providers, so they also potentially know that she paid her gas bill, and they pair that information with her other purchasing habits, location data, financial information, family details, and their guesses about her race and gender. They sell this kind of information to governments, advertisers, healthcare companies, and others.

Just a few years ago, Acxiom had a partnership with Facebook to combine their data for advertisers and share the profits. At that time, Facebook would have supplied the consumer's online activities and Acxiom would have provided her offline activities, and advertisers could use them both to show her ads. Facebook ended that program in 2018, raising questions about whether massive technology companies now have so much data that they don't need to buy from data brokers.

In today's hearing, we will discuss how this kind of control over enormous data affects competition. While data-driven targeting can filter out things we don't want, show us products that might be of interest, and help some small businesses reach new customers, it also functions as a gatekeeper to important services and opportunities.

We talk a lot in this space, as Senator Durbin did, about the privacy concerns, and obviously, there's big concerns about that. I've been a longtime advocate for privacy legislation, Federal privacy legislation. I think its time has long come, and I know we are look ing at focusing some resources into these privacy issues in the bill that's currently being debated in the Senate.

We also have to look at another piece of this, and that is that there are real threats to fair competition from these massive data sets and the artificial intelligence inferences that these companies make based on them.

For example, after years of complaints and a Federal lawsuit, Facebook is reportedly still disproportionately showing job ads for mechanics to men and for pre-school nurses to women. That distorts labor markets, and it doesn't help us get to where we need to be to be able to recruit people for these jobs.

We also see the control that big data has serious implications for healthy competitive marketplaces. Data can be a barrier to entry. Unless you have a lot of it, you may not be able to reach consumers successfully. The big data allows you to target ads, to create algorithms that others who might want to be entering the market can't do if they don't also have the data. It can be another way that powerful internet gatekeepers maintain control of how small businesses reach customers and earn outsized profits from that control. The impact of big data should also play an important role in merger analysis. As dominant digital platforms try to acquire other companies with massive troves of consumer data, the antitrust agencies must place greater emphasis on determining the competitive impact of obtaining even more data through mergers.

This is why I talk about that our laws have to be as sophisticated as the markets that we today operate in. We all want opportunities for new and innovative companies to emerge and for new markets to develop.

When big data inhibits competition by allowing those who have it to block access to markets for those who do not, we need to step in and fix it. This means enforcing our existing antitrust laws to their fullest extent to protect competition. It means updating our antitrust laws for the modern economy, just as we've done centuries past.

It's like every 50 years or so, we do a major update. The time has long passed for today's tech world.

My bill, Competition and Antitrust Law Enforcement and Reform Act, would do so by updating the legal standard to prohibit harmful mergers and anticompetitive conduct, shifting the burden to dominant companies to prove that their acquisitions and, most significantly here, their exclusionary conduct doesn't threaten competition.

We also have to make sure that our antitrust enforcers have the resources to do their jobs. They can't take on the biggest companies and some of the most complex conduct the world has ever seen with duct tape and band-aids.

Senator Grassley and I, with the support of this Committee, got our bill through to update the merger fees which will bring in over $100 million for both agencies. It has passed the Senate. We are waiting action in the House. We have every reason to believe we'll get it done.

There's more we can do not only in the reconciliation bill before us, but in the year-end budget to make sure these agencies have what they need.

We also need competition reform specifically targeted at tech. These are things like issues of interoperability. We've been talking about app stores recently. There's a major bill on that, bipartisan, that's been introduced, as well as bills targeting discriminatory conduct with tech companies.

As we explore paths forward, we see that the dynamics of data mining are already changing. In recent months, Apple rolled out an update that lets iPhone and iPad users decide whether they want to be tracked online by Facebook and other apps. That was a major good change. What happened? What do we know so far? Early reports indicate consumers have overwhelmingly opted out of being tracked. More than 75 percent, Senator Lee, decided not to be tracked on apps or their Apple devices when they were posed that simple straightforward question.

As we push for increased consumer privacy, we must make sure that monopolists don't fool us into handing over all control of our data to them at the expense of fair competition. We must both fight monopolies and protect consumer data. Guess what? We can do both things at once.

I don't want us to not realize this brave new world we are in, where having the data at all completely advantages certain companies who are the gatekeepers and makes it much more difficult to have a competitive market.

I will now turn it over to Ranking Member Lee. Thank you.

Opening Statement of Hon. Michael S. Lee, a U.S. Senator from the State of Utah

Senator LEE. Thank you, Chairwoman Klobuchar. I like the band-aids and duct tape analogy. I knew a guy named Fred Trent who used to say, "If you have a spool of baling wire, a roll of duct tape, and a pair of vice grips, you can fix anything."

Chair KLOBUCHAR. Okay.

Senator LEE. I'm sure he wasn't talking about antitrust laws. Yes.

Chair KLOBUCHAR. Maybe not this. Yes. Thank you.

Senator LEE. I think the title of today's hearing is an apt one, as big data does itself by its very nature present big questions, although the answers might not always be what we expect.

On the one hand, data is increasingly valuable and it's often essential to developing and improving technologies that'll power our economy through the rest of the 21st century. These technologies obviously have a bearing on consumer markets and retail markets, but they also make enormous contributions to national security and national defense and likely influence global strategic thinking in countless ways.

At the same time, as more and more data about us is collected, the risks of unauthorized disclosure increase considerably. The more valuable and the more useful our data becomes the more companies will do to obtain it, and the more we can start to expect more intrusions into our privacy.

Privacy, too, can be weaponized to entrench market incumbents and provide them with the convenient pretext for excluding competition and, in some cases, evading it altogether.

I see several key considerations going forward. The first is the value of our data. Viewing user data as a form of payment for online services is no longer just a theory. It's how the companies themselves, and how many antitrust enforcers, view the market. It's time for lawmakers and for the public to catch up, and we need to reframe our understanding and our expectations of supposedly free online services. To realize that they're not, in fact, free at all, but they come at the cost. A cost that's often opaque, unstable, and significantly greater than we may realize.

The second consideration, which flows naturally from the first, is the need to reinforce our ownership and our control over our data. When we recognize the value of the data that we provide for companies like Google and Facebook in exchange for their services and realize the massive imbalance in bargaining power the consumers have had—had up until this point, it should compel us to take greater care that our data is truly ours, that we have the ability to meaningfully consent to its use and to revoke that consent.

Each of these will help to promote competition in markets that rely heavily on data by forcing companies to compete for the quality of services offered in exchange for our data and for the right to continue using our data.

Speaking of data and product quality, it's often claimed that better data will mean better services. That depends entirely on how the data are put to use. Intrusions on our privacy are an obvious threat to quality, but so too are the more insidious threats like those uncovered recently by the Wall Street Journal about Facebook. It may be that the most pressing question when it comes to data access in aggregation is not whether it's entrenching monopolies, but whether it's leading big tech firms to act with flagrant disregard for the effects of their businesses on society at large.

Finally, we should be reticent to immediately embrace concerns that focus merely on the bigness of data access or aggregation. Data is not a finite resource. It's constantly being generated by innumerable sources, and no one company could likely ever control all data necessary to its or a competitor's business.

Moreover, punishing companies for obtaining the data sets necessary to achieve economies of scale and scope smacks of penalizing success, and it's not something we should be doing.

In the name of tearing down all barriers to entry, will we next demand that market incumbents share their trade secrets, their expertise, and their intellectual property with competitors?

All these questions and more should make for a deeply interesting and informative discussion, both at today's hearing and in the years to come. I look forward to it. Thank you, Madam Chairwoman.

Chair KLOBUCHAR. Thank you very much, Senator Lee. I'm going to introduce our witnesses now. Some are remote, some are here with us.

Steve Satterfield. Mr. Satterfield is a vice president on the Public Policy Team at Facebook. He leads a team responsible for developing and advocating for the company's positions on privacy and data related regulations. Prior to joining Facebook, he worked at Covington & Burling as a privacy lawyer.

Markham Erickson. Mr. Erickson leads Google's Centers of Excellence, a global team of subject matter experts focused on the application of law and policy with respect to technology and the internet. Prior to joining Google, Mr. Erickson was a partner at Steptoe & Johnson.

Sheila Colclasure. Ms. Colclasure is the global chief digital responsibility and public policy officer at IPG Kinesso. She is responsible for leading the global data policy and digital responsibility strategies at the company. She previously worked at the sister company, the data broker Acxiom as its global chief data ethics officer in public policy executive. She also served as staff assistant here in the United States Senate. I always like to add that when they do.

John Robb. Mr. Robb is an author and podcaster with The Global Guerrillas Report. He is alumnus of the United States Air Force Academy and Yale University. He previously served in uniform as a pilot and with the Special Forces. He is also the author of the book, "Brave New War."

Charlotte Slaiman has been with us in the past. Ms. Slaiman is the competition policy director at Public Knowledge, a nonprofit dedicated to promoting freedom of expression and open internet, and access to affordable communications. Prior to joining Public Knowledge, she served as an attorney with the FDC, and here in the Senate as a legislative aide.

We thank you, and if the witnesses could please stand and raise your right hand, including our remote witnesses.

[Witnesses are sworn in.]

Chair KLOBUCHAR. I will now recognize the witnesses for five minutes of testimony each, and why don't we begin with you, Mr. Satterfield. Thank you.

Statement of Steve Satterfield, Vice President of Privacy and Public Policy, Facebook, Menlo Park, California

Mr. SATTERFIELD. Thank you. Chairwoman Klobuchar, Ranking Member Lee, and Members of the Subcommittee, good afternoon, and thank you for the opportunity to be here today. My name is Steve Satterfield, and I'm vice president of privacy and public policy at Facebook, where I focus on developing and sharing the company's perspectives on data regulation globally.

I appreciate the Subcommittee's interest in the topics of today's hearing and the work that you all do to ensure the competitiveness of American markets and to shape data policy. I believe Facebook has an important perspective here given the substantial contributions we've made to the technology sector in the nearly 20 years since our founding.

We believe that many of the concerns expressed by Congress and other stakeholders with respect to privacy and content moderation can be addressed by appropriate legislation, and we stand ready to be a productive partner in those efforts.

As you know, our company is currently facing multiple lawsuits, including those brought by the Federal Trade Commission and a number of State Attorneys General, and that will limit what I'm able to address today. I assure you we want to be helpful where we can, and I look forward to our discussion.

Like many services, Facebook helps people share, connect, communicate, or simply find entertaining content. Each day, millions of Americans use Facebook to connect with people and businesses, to share and view a wide range of content, to join communities of interest, and to set up fundraisers for good causes, among many other things.

All of these activities support our mission to give people the power to build community and bring the world closer together. The data helps make all of this possible.

At Facebook, we use and analyze data responsibly to provide personalized user experiences. We also use data to improve our products, to provide measurement, analytics, and other business services; to promote safety, integrity, and security; to communicate with people who use our services; and to research and innovate for social good, including by connecting and lifting up marginalized communities and addressing humanitarian crises.

Data also helps us show people better and more relevant ads, which keep Facebook free. It lets advertisers reach the right people, which benefits more than ten million businesses and non-profits. For the data people trust us with, we recognize that we have an important responsibility to protect it, and we work around the clock to help protect people's accounts, and we build security into every Facebook product.

We offer a number of tools that provide people transparency and control over the data we receive, and we've steadily made improvements to the privacy protections and controls we offer. We also have a variety of tools to help users understand the data Facebook has about them. We're always working to develop technologies that enhance the way people connect and communicate, and data is key to that work. We know that if we don't keep innovating and improving, we'll fall behind.

When Facebook started, we faced established competitors, including AOL and MySpace, with lots of user data that didn't protect them from competition. Success comes from creating products users value and enjoy, not from how much data you have.

As our CEO, Mark Zuckerberg has explained, we believe that strong and consistent competition is vital because it ensures the playing field is level for all. Facebook competes hard because we're up against other smart and innovative companies. We know that our future success is not guaranteed, especially in the global tech industry defined by rapid innovation and change.

Technological innovation has created an ever more competitive environment, and we invest heavily in our products and services to stay relevant, competitive, committing more than $18 billion to research and development last year. We're proud of our record and will continue to focus on building and updating our products to give people the best experiences possible.

Thank you and I look forward to your questions.

[The prepared statement of Mr. Satterfield appears as a submission for the record.]

Chair KLOBUCHAR. Thank you very much, Mr. Satterfield. Next up, Markham Erickson of Google.

Statement of Markham Erickson, Vice President of Government Affairs and Public Policy, Google, Washington, DC

Mr. ERICKSON. Chairwoman Klobuchar, Ranking Member Lee, and distinguished Members of the Subcommittee, thank you for the opportunity to appear before you today.

My name is Markham Erickson, and I'm a vice president of government affairs and public policy at Google, where I oversee a global team of subject matter experts focused on the application of law and policy to technology and the internet.

Data should be used to make consumer's lives better by improving the quality and diversity of products and services available, while protecting user's privacy and giving them control.

In my testimony, I will describe how Google uses and protects data, the safe data mobility empowers consumers and boosts competition, that data alone does not guarantee better products for consumers.

Data plays an important role in making Google products and services people use every day functional and helpful, and we are committed to treating that data responsibly and protecting privacy with strict protocols and innovative technologies. Google combines industry-leading technology with insights from data to develop products that help people find directions, build businesses, and search for information.

On an individual level, what data is collected and how it is used depends on how each person uses our services and how they manage their privacy controls. Data is one element of our ads business where it helps us connect people with relevant advertisements. Advertising is Google's main source of revenue, and it enables us to make many of our flagship—flagship products available for free to billions of people around the world.

The ads shown are often informed by a search query or page content, but they can also be based on a user's interest or their personal data, if their privacy settings permit. We do not sell our users' personal information to advertisers or to anyone. Our business relies on ensuring our user's trust, specifically in how we use and protect their data. We work to maintain that trust by offering industry-leading controls to manage privacy. Three billion users visit Google accounts every year, where they can review and change their privacy settings and delete data stored with their account.

We constantly innovate to improve privacy across our products and on our platforms. For example, Privacy Sandbox is a collaborative initiative that aims to build a more private and secure web, because many publishers and advertisers rely on online advertising to fund their websites and connect with consumers. We will continue to partner with the industry, civil society, and governments to get this balance right.

In addition to our work to advance privacy-preserving technology, we contribute data and expertise to the broader ecosystem. Data portability empowers consumers to choose services or online platforms based on quality and individual preference, not because they're locked in.

Since 2011, Google Takeout has enabled users to easily move their content to competing services with more than one billion gigabytes exported from Google products. Additionally, through our leadership in the data transfer project, Google makes it easier for other companies to provide tools that let users seamlessly move data between online services.

We are also proud of our contributions to the open-source community. Many of the larger successes in the machine learning ecosystem have come from data that is openly available on the web. Senators, data by itself does not guarantee better and more and more successful products. Rather, it is the investment, innovation, and methods that matter, not just the amount of data that a company may have. Cutting edge technology or new ideas allow companies, new companies, to succeed, sometimes without any data at all. New entrants such as Zoom, Snapchat, Spotify, Pinterest, and many others, they've all become successful because they provide an innovative product, not because they have access to data from established companies.

Our focus is continually improving our products, and our greatest source of innovation comes from extensive research and development. Last year alone, we spent over $27.6 billion on research and development, which is nearly ten times what we spent in 2009.

At Google, we are committed to protecting data through privacy, security, and user control, and improving our products in a way that ensures more consumer choice and competition. We will continue to engage with policymakers and regulators, as well as other stakeholders, to support thoughtful regulation that encourages innovation and protects consumers. For example, we have long supported Federal privacy legislation in the United States, and we encourage to Congress to enact such legislation.

Thank you for the opportunity to discuss our work with you today, and I welcome your questions.

[The prepared statement of Mr. Erickson appears as a submission for the record.]

Chair KLOBUCHAR. Thank you very much Mr. Erickson. Next up, Ms. Colclasure.

Statement of Sheila Colclasure, Global Chief Digital Responsibility and Public Policy Officer, IPG Kinesso, Little Rock, Arkansas

Ms. COLCLASURE. Chairwoman Klobuchar, Ranking Member Lee, Members of the Committee, good afternoon. Thank you for the opportunity to speak today.

I'd like to make several key points about the importance of fair and open data use, the intersection of data privacy laws and Federal competition practices, and their potential impact on today's connected marketplace.

First, responsible companies are ready for a comprehensive Federal data privacy law that is good for citizens and good for America. I work for Kinesso, a subsidiary of the Interpublic Group of companies or IPG, one of the largest and most data-driven advertising agency holding companies in the world. We strongly support a national privacy law.

IPG's business is built on four pillars of consumer trust: accountability, fairness, safety, and transparency. We work hard with our industry partners to instill these values throughout data-driven advertising.

Second, in today's economy, any privacy law, functionally, will be a competition law, whether a legislature intends it to be or not. America needs a future-fit national privacy law and appropriately applied antitrust policy.

In our connected marketplace, both of these have data availability, use, and control at their core. A Federal privacy law should be people-centered and ensure data is used to serve people. Limiting who can collect, control, and use data won't work. A privacy law that restricts who can collect data would give data control and, thus, market control to a few companies and unavoidably weaken competition. As we have seen in other jurisdictions, market power belongs to whoever controls the data.

A Federal privacy law should preserve data sharing for beneficial and innovative purposes, while making companies responsible and accountable for harmful uses. Similarly, competition policy should ensure that companies with better technology, better ideas, and innovation, but which may not have adequate data of their own, are not foreclosed from the marketplace. A company shouldn't have to create a first-party platform to compete.

Today's connected marketplace increasingly is dominated by companies who thrived thanks to ready access to consumer data. National laws that in effect limit data to just a few dominant players risks putting more power in those few players' hands. In our data- intense economy, overly restrictive data use and sharing laws preclude robust competition, vibrant innovation, and the possibility of the small company finding and competitively serving its audience. We emphasize how essential data availability, open data flow, and fair uses of data are to innovation, competition, and a vibrant market of connected participants.

Federal privacy law and competition law should provide for responsible and accountable data sharing so that everyone can compete. We urge you to consider the effect of mergers on who controls the consumer data value change and, thus, on competition. An analysis of the growth of the major online platforms shows the role that acquisitions have played in the development of dominant data positions. To protect people, the fair use of their data, and support a robust, trustworthy, and competitive connected marketplace, Federal law should promote fundamental privacy rights for citizens and enable responsible accountable use and sharing of consumer data by commercial enterprise. This allows the market to continue to provide a wide array of benefits to people, including things like safer online payments, ready access to business and consumer credit, access to free content and platforms, and cost-effective and efficient advertising for all, especially small business and new market entrants.

We at IPG have built accountability and responsible data practices into everything we do. We believe that corporate America is ready to responsibly collect and share consumer data and be accountable for its actions in doing so. We encourage the Committee to protect the fair and open use of data as fundamental to competition. We urge the Committee to help develop a Federal privacy law that is future-fit for the digital age and protects consumers and enables a connected marketplace in which all participants can compete fairly, so long as they engage in safe and accountable data use and sharing.

I thank the Committee for its attention and look forward to your questions.

[The prepared statement of Ms. Colclasure appears as a submission for the record.]

Chair KLOBUCHAR. Thank you very much. Next up, John Robb.

Statement of John Robb, Author, the Global Guerrillas Report, Acton, Massachusetts

Mr. ROBB. Thank you so much for the invitation. I'm a bit of an outlier here; I'm not a lawyer. Big data and the AI's that are articulated are clearly already valuable. They'll become more valuable over time as they're integrated into all of the products and services that will be sold in the next 20 or 30 years.

Unfortunately, there isn't a clear approach to how to deal with this big data in the marketplace. Currently, there is three major methods of actually dealing with data. We have it in China, where they have incorporated this big data into their national security and implemented a national security totalitarian state. You have in Europe, who's suppressing the aggregation of big data through privacy laws, basically turning it into something to be destroyed rather than embracing it. That'll affect their economic capabilities long term, reducing the capabilities to even produce high-quality products in the future, but, you know, it does award them better social stability. And then we have the U.S., which is still, you know, up in the air. We're still trying to decide what to do with it. If you use a framework on the economic model for the United States, the way we're treating data right now is very feudal. It's basically a feudal system where you have the corporations are acting as, you know, the lords and owners of the data, and they farm people for their data as they traverse their platforms. That's clearly not sustainable over the long term. You know, it will create, you know, wealth inequalities as big data and its AIs move toward the center of the economy. That, you know, that will also create the social instability.

The solution to that is the same solution we used to eradicate feudalism in the past, is that data ownership—is to give people ownership over their data so they can exercise ownership privileges associated with it and reap the benefits for having that ownership. That means taking data off the big platforms and putting it into a central repository, you know, that's controlled by the owner of the data, where it can be pooled with others and then resold or lent to organizations that will make use of it, build AIs that are useful in a variety of different ways.

It doesn't always have to be commercial. It could be open source efforts, it could be non-commercial university development, but putting the consumer, putting the individual in the driver's seat changes the whole equation. It could also be a source of royalties and revenues for that individual, driving their personal prosperity forward. It's a different way to approach it. It does destroy the data directly through privacy, but it allows them to benefit from data as it moves forward.

There's also a strong tie between big data and these AIs to the national security component that's going to come into all of this tangentially. I don't think people would fully appreciate how much things have shifted over the last 20 years. All of the technologies that are needed to implement a national security data-driven surveillance state have leapt forward substantially, and that most of the shift has occurred within the context of the corporate development. We've seen a shift from what governments used to be only able to do to now corporations are only able to do it.

China has embraced that, and they're using those corporations to gather the data, create the tools, and control their society.

The problem here in the United States is that there aren't any natural limiting factors to prevent that from happening here. We don't have any protections against the overreach in the corporate realm. We don't have any—like we do against Government overreach. We don't have any free speech rights. We don't have any rights of access. We don't have the ability to resolve disconnection, because disconnection in the modern environment can radically reduce your ability to operate in the world.

We need a set of digital rights that we can exercise over—to protect us against any kind of overreach at the corporate side.

Thanks.

[The prepared statement of Mr. Robb appears as a submission for the record.]

Chair KLOBUCHAR. Okay, very good. Thank you. Next up, Charlotte Slaiman, with Public Knowledge.

Statement of Charlotte Slaiman, Competition Policy Director, Public Knowledge, Washington, DC

Ms. SLAIMAN. Chairwoman Klobuchar, Ranking Member Lee, thank you so much for the opportunity to testify today on behalf of Public Knowledge, a nonprofit working in the public interest for over 20 years.

I'm Charlotte Slaiman, competition policy director at Public Knowledge. Gatekeeper power is at the root of big tech's competition problems. Experts, policymakers, and advocates the world over have identified gatekeeper power, sometimes bottleneck power, sometimes strategic market status, as the power that dominant digital platforms have over other businesses' ability to reach their customers.

Right now, big tech has the power, over us and our data, and we need to protect both users and a competitive market with new laws and rules to promote fair competition against them. Until we have a real choice to leave these platforms if we're not happy with them, they won't have the incentive to win us over, and we'll continue to miss out on disruptive innovations that challenge the status quo. I want to take this opportunity to highlight important legislation that I think can help to address the underlying power dynamics that have led us here. Interoperability, data portability, and delegatability are the privacy-protective ways to neutralize the power that big data confers upon dominant digital platforms.

Right now, if I'm frustrated with how Facebook treats my data, I don't really have the option to leave, because my friends and family, the businesses, groups, and even schools I need to communicate with are on Facebook. Interoperability would allow competition to flourish by letting users communicate across platforms.

Look to the Access Act for a model of implementing interoperability to maximize competition and protect privacy. These platforms can abuse their gatekeeper power to freeze out would-be competitors from the market. One of the tools for that anticompetitive discrimination is big data. Gatekeeper platforms can put their own products first on the page, give them the best attention-grabbing design, and point users away from companies that pose a competitive threat. While this offends our basic notions of fairness, this behavior would be difficult to stop using our existing antitrust laws.

We need a nondiscrimination law to reliably stop it. I'm so glad to see news reports that Chairwoman Klobuchar is working on just such a bill here in the Senate. There's a strong model in the American Choice and Innovation Online Act from Chairman David Cicilline in the House.

Strict limitations on mergers by dominant digital platforms and giving our Federal antitrust enforcers the ability to sue to break up vertically integrated dominant digital platforms are also important parts of how we can address gatekeeper power. The Platform Competition and Opportunity Act and the Ending Platform Monopolies Act are strong examples of how these tools could work. These four bills were recently endorsed by a bipartisan group of 32 State attorneys general.

App stores and operating systems preference their own products when it comes to communication with the user and to data. The Open Apps Market Act zeros in on the gatekeeper role that app stores play.

Purposeful narrowing of our antitrust laws by the courts have left big business with a license to engage in a host of anticompetitive conduct. A myopic focus on price and other easily quantifiable effects leaves out important innovation and consumer choice harms that antitrust is supposed to address.

Chairwoman Klobuchar's Competition and Antitrust Law Enforcement Reform Act would help reign in the power of big data by updating the legal standards for blocking mergers and stopping exclusionary conduct. Competition is not a panacea for the challenges of big data. We also urgently need new privacy laws to protect users and a digital regulator to comprehensively address the policy questions surrounding digital platforms.

A comprehensive Federal privacy law can be procompetitive by creating a level playing field for dominant incumbents and new entrants alike.

For decades, Washington has taken the perspective that we need to let digital businesses run wild to see what great innovations they might come up with, but today, unscrupulous data practices and consolidated power have led us to a place that isn't anyone's dream of what the internet was supposed to be.

These largely unregulated platforms have been allowed to amass powerful gatekeeper roles where they need not fear competition or Government intervention. For users to really have control, we need to have a real choice to leave these platforms. We need real competitors, and we need switching to be easy. To get those things, we need new laws and rules to promote fair competition on and against gatekeeper platforms like Google and Facebook.

Congress has already done the laudable work of introducing a series of bills to combat these harms. The best time to pass them was 10 years ago, but the second-best time is now.

Thank you.

[The prepared statement of Ms. Slaiman appears as a submission for the record.]

Chair KLOBUCHAR. Okay, very good. All right. Why don't we start out, Mr. Satterfield, Mr. Erickson, Facebook, and Google both collect data about consumers to enable targeted advertising, which is the principal way I believe your companies make money. How important is consumer data to each of your companies? You can start Mr. Satterfield.

Mr. SATTERFIELD. Thank you, Chairwoman Klobuchar. The way that we look at it is success comes from building great products and not from how much data you have.

Chair KLOBUCHAR. Okay. Is—just if you could just straightforward answer the question, how important is consumer data to your company and your profit model?

Mr. SATTERFIELD. Data's important, you know, to connect people to relevant experiences. That includes showing them relevant ads, but again I'd say that you know, the success that we've had has come through building great experiences and not from the amount of data that we collect.

Chair KLOBUCHAR. Mr. Erickson, how do you answer that for Google?

Mr. ERICKSON. Thank you, Senator, for the question. At Google, we provide a means for people to find relevant information and helpful information on the internet, and to do that we have to understand what they're looking for. Anyone can use our products for free without providing or storing any personally identifiable information with us. We provide transparent mechanisms for users to understand how their data is being collected and how their data is being used, and meaningful tools to give consumers the ability to see the data that is stored in their account and to make choices like delete the data, or use one of our auto-delete tools to set up regular cadences where information, such as their search history or viewing history or location history if they've opted in to location history, can be regularly deleted.

We've also, as I mentioned in my testimony, since 2011, have created tools to give consumers the ability to take the data that they provided to us and move it to a competitor's site. We don't want users to work to engage with Google because they feel locked in because their data is with us. We want them to be able to go to the services and the technologies that suit their needs based on a competitive dynamic rather than any sense of lock-in.

Chair KLOBUCHAR. Okay. Why don't we go to you, Ms. Slaiman. I was just looking at some Twitter feed. Someone just reported that they were talking with a few friends on one of the sites, going back and forth online about being a female politician a while back, including a TV make-up artist for some reason, and this person said they referred to me as inimitable online, and within an hour they got an online ad for Chanel Inimitable mascara, linking the TV make-up artist comment with their adjective. Is that possible? I don't know if this is true or not, but I'm just saying this is what's happened to me, and how important is the data to these companies? They've kind of gave round around about answers here. What does it mean for other platforms trying to compete if they don't have the data?

Ms. SLAIMAN. I think the data is very important. I appreciate what the other witnesses have said, that there is also a role played by their innovative engineers. I think that's absolutely right, but the data is important, and that's why we're concerned about whether it's being treated competitively or not. You know, I think the relevant ads are not always what is best for us. It's what's best for the platform, and sometimes that lines up with what's best for us, and sometimes it doesn't.

We need to make sure that we have protections for users and for the competitive marketplace when we're looking at that problem. Chair KLOBUCHAR. Mr. Satterfield, along the same lines, last quarter Facebook publicly reported that its advertising revenue per users in the U.S. and Canada was $51.58. I want to ask you a few questions about that.

The comparable number for Europe was only $17.08. In Asia, it's $4.13. The rest of the world, you reported advertising revenue per user of about $3.00. Why is the value of a user in the U.S. worth so much more than the rest of the world, especially when we're comparing ourselves to comparable countries in Europe?

Mr. SATTERFIELD. Senator, I think there are a lot of factors that go into those average revenue per user numbers.

Chair KLOBUCHAR. Okay. I just—that's not really an answer though, man. That's the beginning of an answer, so.

Mr. SATTERFIELD. What we're doing is we're breaking down revenue per region according to the number of folks that we serve in those regions. That's what's reflected in the numbers that you're describing.

Chair KLOBUCHAR. Okay. Why don't we go to you, Mr. Robb? Do you think Facebook should pay all of its U.S. users $51.58 for Facebook's use of their data, which we now know, it's in their re- cent fiscal report? Maybe the individual profit centers, which is all of us, should actually get the money back?

Mr. ROBB. If you own the data, you would at least be able to compare offers and get paid for its usage. I don't think you'd get the full amount, obviously, but then——

Chair KLOBUCHAR. Right. Maybe there'd be a discount, but you could get a good chunk of it just like you do when you, you know, when you're a consumer and—they—you go and buy something or you sell something, is probably the better example.

Mr. ROBB. That's correct.

Chair KLOBUCHAR. Mr. Robb, when companies collect data about us and either sell it or use it to target us with ads, we aren't just the consumer or the user anymore. We really have to start thinking about this because I think when we get on these platforms, we, you know, can have fun, people do business, but they don't realize every single second they're on there, they are creating profits, but they are not reaping the benefit.

We are, in fact, our data is a commodity, but consumers as I know it aren't getting enough in return, and I've discussed the idea of somehow putting a tax on the data for these companies to pay. You have written about paying people for their data.

In your opinion, what is the strongest argument for ensuring that the tech companies have to pay for the consumer data that they collect and use, and if Facebook and Google had to pay for using consumer data, how do you think their behavior would change?

Mr. ROBB. Okay. The most compelling argument is that it would change the perspective people have on data if they were in—if they had ownership rights over it. By unlocking it by, you know, through ownership, you don't just limit the data to what—that Facebook collects or Google collects to what they can do with it. You then open it up to what all of these other companies can actually do with it, and they can generate revenue. You know, people in control of their data, people who have ownership of their data, they will be more willing to give more and if they can set permissions in terms of how it's used, they'll feel comfortable with it. They'll feel like they're participating in the economy rather than being observers or being treated as resources. It's a complete face shift. It's not even comparable to what we have now.

Chair KLOBUCHAR. Okay. I thought it was just so interesting. I'll go back to you, Mr. Erickson, Mr. Satterfield, my last questions here. I just thought it was interesting, when Apple unleashed the power of allowing people to opt out, that 75 percent did that, because I think it's probably because they did it in a pretty straightforward way. Because I know I tried to do it sometimes, and then I'm on some site and I don't know if I've opted out, and it's really complicated for people, or they make me opt in to try to do something, and I can't figure it out, and you're just trying to order something online.

Mr. Erickson, you've spoken about putting consumers' privacy preference first and giving them the ability to change what is collected and used about them. I understand how you think that protects user privacy, but from a competition policy perspective, it seems like we look beyond what benefits an individual user. Even if millions of consumers give you permission to collect and use their data, shouldn't we be concerned about the competitive impact of your exclusive access to their data, which you use to compete with companies that don't have that data? Do you want to answer that, Mr. Erickson, first?

Mr. ERICKSON. Sure. Thank you, Senator, for the question. At Google, we do want to make sure that consumers first understand how their data is being collected and how their data is being used, and we do want to give them meaningful choice about their use of their data.

Unlike Facebook, the user can use Google services for free. They do not need to establish an account or provide any personally identifiable information to Google. We never sell personally identifiable information about our users, even when they do sign in. They can delete that information at any time.

Most users, when they're using online services, are providing similar information, if not the same information, to multiple online services, so in that regard, the data's really—the data's really non-rivalist from a competition standpoint. It's easily gotten by other companies that want to purchase data from, for instance, data brokers, or other entities, but I think the key here for us is to put users in a position where they have meaningful choices and meaningful control about the use of their particular data.

Chair KLOBUCHAR. Okay. Do you want to take a crack at that one, Mr. Satterfield, from Facebook's perspective?

Mr. SATTERFIELD. Yes. Thank you. Just to be clear, Facebook services are also free. To your question, Chairwoman Klobuchar, you know, the statistics are so interesting right now. The average user has something like 46 apps that they're using every month. There's more than 100 apps on the average person's phone. People are sharing more data in more places than they ever have been before. We think that there's a lot of data out there that's being used for innovative purposes, including to show people ads.

Chair KLOBUCHAR. Do you think they all know that they're sharing their data on all those apps?

Mr. SATTERFIELD. Senator, we hope so. We think transparency and controls are core values of ours, though we think that they should be core values of other companies as well.

Chair KLOBUCHAR. No, I just—if you could answer though, do you think that they know they're sharing that data? Do you think that they all know that?

Mr. SATTERFIELD. On Facebook, Madam Chairwoman, they do. I'm confident of that. There's core values of ours. We invest a lot in providing transparency and control. I think with respect to other companies, this is an area where Congress could intervene, make sure they do. Transparency and control could be core components of a Federal privacy legislation.

Chair KLOBUCHAR. Okay. I'm going to just ask just one followup because I really want a turn for Ms. Slaiman. Do you think that's true, that they all know this? Do you think we need—and by the way, the companies are now coming to us saying they want privacy legislation after opposing it, various iterations of it, after all the States have started to get into the act, which is kind of a pattern we've seen in other areas here, but do you want to respond to this quickly? Then I should let Senator Lee ask some questions.

Ms. SLAIMAN. Yes. I'm sure there are many users who do not know that they are sharing the data. I also think even if they know about the data that they're sharing, it's quite complicated to understand what that data can be used for. That data can be used to figure out additional information about you, so a user may be making a decision to share some data, not realizing what that data actually could tell a company about who they are and their preferences.

I also think I want to respond to the point that Mr. Erickson made about Google doesn't sell your data. I think it's important to keep in mind that Google has within them the capacity to fully exploit your data without ever selling it because they have the advertising system. Within this one large vertically integrated company, they can both collect the data and fully exploit it to advertise to you, so the necessity for selling isn't there, and it can still be exploiting it just as effectively.

Chair KLOBUCHAR. Okay. Thank you very much. Senator Lee.

Senator LEE. Thank you. Mr. Satterfield, I'd like to start with you. I want to start by asking you about some recent reports about Facebook. The first is from Geoffrey Fowler at the Washington Post. He did a deep dive into Facebook's collection of user data, including revealing that Facebook's own financial modeling estimates that Facebook's estimates of its user data is worth an average of $164 per user per year. This would seem to confirm my own view and that of several State attorneys general, including my home State attorney general, Sean Reyes, in Utah, that Facebook isn't actually a free service, as you suggested a moment ago, but rather it's one that we pay for with our data. What's concerning is that there's so little transparency in the transaction, and you've sort of confirmed that now moments ago by saying that it is completely free. I am never told what my data is worth. You're not even acknowledging that it is worth anything or that there's any kind of a transaction involved here. What I get in return is always subject to change. You change systems by which posts are reviewed, what's prioritized, what deprioritized.

It's basic antitrust law that you look for symptoms. You look for signs. One pretty consistent sign of monopoly power involves the ability to set prices and control output. What could be a better example of that very thing than Facebook's ability to demand data from its users, as it does, without telling them its value or even acknowledging that it has a value at all, while providing a service whose quality, whose features, whose terms of service, in terms of use, are subject to change at any moment and they do frequently change at any moment?

Can you answer that question for me?

Mr. SATTERFIELD. Thank you, Senator. You know, respectfully, I think we see things differently. We don't see data as something that people give us in exchange for providing our services. We see data as something that we use to provide the service to them, to provide value to them.

Senator LEE. Okay, so you disagree with the assumption that when you're—when there's a service out there that purports to be free, you are the product. You are sort of what's being served. I mean, I get your point. Nobody's paying out of pocket with money. They're not paying in literal coins or virtual tokens to go on there, but you are in fact a for-profit business enterprise. You are in fact profitable, and you do that because there's something of value. I think we're quibbling here over sort of nonsensical distinctions between literal payment, which I didn't say, nor did I imply.

I guess I'd ask you to answer the question, accepting the premise that I think all the rest of us in this room and pretty much every other American would acknowledge exists, which is the premise that your service is—well, it purports to be free. It is in fact paid for in the sense that people contribute their time, they give their time, and with their time you acquire data. You're able to monetize that. With that understanding, I'm asking you, it is a basic principle of antitrust law that one sign of monopoly power is the ability to set prices and control output. With that premise, what's your response to that? About the fact—I'm asking what better example could one find, once one accepts this premise, than that of Facebook's ability to demand data from its users without telling them the value of that data and without a service—when dealing with a service, whose quality and whose features and whose terms of service are subject to change at any moment and often do.

Mr. SATTERFIELD. Senator, you know, again, respectfully, that's just not how we think about data and how we use data to provide value to people.

Senator LEE. All right. All right, I get it. That's not how you think about it. It's clear to me you don't want to answer that, whatever. I was throwing you a bone there to try to allow you to engage in a dialog.

We'll move on to the next question. The Wall Street Journal released a series of bombshell reports last week on internal Facebook documents that revealed shocking, absolutely stunning lapses in Facebook's ability to protect Facebook's consumers, its users, from being harmed by using its platforms. This too looks like the behavior of a monopolist, a monopolist that's so sure that its customers have nowhere else to go that it displays a reckless disregard for quality assurance, for its own brand image, and even just being honest with its users about the obvious safety risks that it's subjecting its users to, particularly its teenage users.

In light of these reports doesn't it look to you like Facebook lacks competition?

Mr. SATTERFIELD. Senator, thank you. The Journal series that you're referencing raises, you know, really serious and important questions. I think it misses the mark in terms of what we're trying to do in the matters that it describes. These are——

Senator LEE. How does it miss the mark? How does it miss the mark any more than revelations years ago about tobacco companies concealing the dangers of tobacco? How is that missing the mark any more than the revelations about tobacco and what tobacco companies knew about what they were doing to their own users?

Mr. SATTERFIELD. Senator, I think what's being discussed in these articles are issues that we have identified ourselves and that we're attempting to work through as a company. This is research that we're doing ourselves in order to identify gaps and issues and to address them to make our platforms safer.

I think these are self-identified issues, and these are internal deliberations that are dedicated to one thing, which is making the platform a safer place for the people who use it.

Senator LEE. Ms. Slaiman, I'd like to turn to you. In your testimony, you advocate for updating the antitrust laws to tackle problems like big data. It seems to me that we have to first try to enforce the laws we have, which I think in most circumstances are more than up to the task, if in fact we will utilize them. If in fact, we will utilize the law and enforce the law. The reason we haven't used antitrust law to address many of the problems in big tech has everything to do with things that could be accomplished with the law. In other words, it's not just because the courts have said no. It's not because enforcers have taken these things repeatedly to the courts and the courts have smacked them down. That hasn't been the case. It's rather been because our antitrust enforcers simply didn't bring the cases to begin with.

Look at the Obama administration. President Obama's antitrust enforcers let Google off the hook after a two-year monopolization investigation, ignoring—ignoring rather specific, rather conclusive staff recommendations to sue. They failed to stop Facebook from buying Instagram and failed to stop Facebook from buying WhatsApp, nascent competitors that they acquired at the time, and they failed to stop Google from buying its way to dominance of digital advertising.

Moreover, in the last year of the Trump administration alone, just the last year of that administration, the Trump administration, which finally filed cases against Google and against Facebook that the Obama administration had turned down, the FTC blocked 27 mergers. So far in 2021, the FTC, now supposedly run by antitrust hawks eager to protect competition, has filed just seven merger cases, one of which is the case against Facebook and five of which were filed in fact by the outgoing Trump administration.

Can't we agree that the problem with antitrust law isn't just the law but lacks antitrust enforcement?

Ms. SLAIMAN. Thank you, Ranking Member Lee. We absolutely need to improve antitrust enforcement. I believe it will be very important to improve the antitrust laws as well, but there have been lapses in enforcement.

I think there are some situations where the antitrust enforcers have correctly identified that the law wasn't there for them, but there absolutely are also cases that they missed that I wish they had brought. Improving antitrust enforcement is definitely an important part of this effort.

Senator LEE. Mr. Erickson and Mr. Satterfield, I want to ask both of you this question. The Wall Street Journal and the New York Times, they reported about a year ago that Google and Facebook had entered into an agreement to partner together with regard to digital advertising.

Setting aside the question of whether data can be a barrier to entry, shouldn't we at least be concerned when two companies with possibly the greatest access to user data secretly agree not to compete with each other for the primary way in which that data is to be used, which is digital advertising?

We'll start with you first, Mr. Erickson.

Mr. ERICKSON. Thank you, Ranking Member Lee. At the time of that agreement, we publicly announced Facebook's participation in our open bidding platform, as well as 25 other companies that are participating in that platform. We thought it would be useful to publishers and accretive to publishers where we'd have multiple ad networks competing for the publisher's inventory, and having large ad networks like Facebook benefits consumers. There's no truth to the allegation that these—our auction system is somehow rigged in Facebook's favor. If they provide the highest, bid they'll win. If they don't, they'll lose, but at the end of the day, those 25 companies which Facebook is one of them, creates more competition and more demand for the publisher's inventory.

Senator LEE. Okay. You're saying that just one of them, you're just two of those companies. You are in fact the two biggest, arguably the two biggest companies with access to this much data. You don't see that there's any antitrust implication associated with this?

When two companies with possibly the greatest access to user data, agree not to compete with each other when it comes to digital advertising, you see no antitrust implications for that?

Mr. ERICKSON. Yes, Senator, respectfully, that's not the agreement. There is no prohibition for Facebook to provide their ad network and compete on other auction systems. Competing on Google's auction system with other ad networks creates actually more competition and more competitive dynamics, which ends up benefiting the publishers who are selling their inventory.

Senator LEE. Mr. Satterfield, my time's expired. Can you respond to that same question?

Mr. SATTERFIELD. Senator, I don't have anything to add to what Mr. Erickson said. You know, we compete hard. We compete fairly. We did so here as well.

Senator LEE. Oh, wow. I'm not surprised to hear that you don't think there's anything unseemly. We'll get back to that later. My time's expired. Thank you.

Chair KLOBUCHAR. Very, very good, Senator Lee. I was off in the other anteroom doing another hearing, and I can see you used your time well.

With that, we turn it over to Senator Blumenthal, and we've also been joined by Senator Hawley and Senator Cruz. Senator Blumenthal.

Senator BLUMENTHAL. Thanks, Madam Chair. I want to thank both you and our Ranking Member for holding this hearing. I hope it will be the beginning or maybe another step in an effort to forge a bipartisan effort on privacy law. I've been working with one of our colleagues, Senator Moran, on a draft for quite some time. We have come very close, and I am very hopeful that we'll continue to make progress because this issue of privacy is one of the central ones of our time.

There's no question as you, Madam Chair, have pointed out so well that data is the source of pay and power to these companies. It is not only a source of vast revenue; it is also the fulcrum of dominance and the ability to prevent others from entering the market, and the companies have learned how to do it very adroitly and have adapted to the challenges that have been put to them by the kinds of answers that we've seen today.

I want to return to those issues that my colleagues have raised so well. First, let me just ask a few questions about the Wall Street Journal investigative report that was published last week showing the heinously destructive impact of Instagram on teens. The simple fact of the matter is that Facebook has known for years that Instagram is directly involved in an increase in eating disorders, mental health issues, and suicidal thoughts, especially for teenage girls. Despite that horrifying risk, Facebook is now dead set on pushing Instagram to even younger children.

Far from being transparent about this danger, as Mr. Satterfield just attempted to represent, Facebook in fact has been blatantly deceptive and disingenuous about it.

Last month, on August 4th, Senator Blackburn and I wrote to Mark Zuckerberg and asked him specifically about this issue. We asked, and I am quoting, ''Has Facebook's research ever found that its platforms and products can have a negative effect on children's and teens' mental health or well-being, such as increased suicidal thoughts, heightened anxiety, unhealthy usage patterns, negative self-image, or other indications of lower well-being?''

It wasn't a trick question. It preceded the published reports in the Journal. We had no idea about the whistleblower documents that were ultimately revealed. Facebook dodged the question. Quote, "We are not aware of a consensus among studies or experts about how much screen time is too much," end quote. We are not aware. Well, we all know now that that representation was simply untrue. Internal documents reported on by the Wall Street Journal demonstrate that Facebook has known for years that Instagram harms children and young people. For years, Facebook studies have found clear links between Instagram and mental health problems. It was common knowledge in the company, so the response was a clear attempt to mislead Congress and misinform parents. I ask that the Wall Street Journal report of September 14, by Georgia Wells, Jeff Horwitz, and Deepa Seetharaman be made a part of the record, Madam Chair.

[The information appears as a submission for the record.]

Chair KLOBUCHAR. It will be. Thank you.

Senator BLUMENTHAL. Thank you. The comparison to big tobacco made by Senator Lee is entirely apt. I know something about big tobacco because I sued big tobacco and I remember the revelation of the documents that showed big tobacco not only knew but had done experiments proving that cigarettes cause cancer. They had denied it for years. They had the knowledge about the damage done to people who smoke.

My question to you, Mr. Satterfield, is, why did Facebook misrepresent its research on mental health and teens when it responded to me and Senator Blackburn?

Mr. SATTERFIELD. Senator, thank you. Respectfully, I don't agree with that characterization, but I do understand the frustration and concern that we're hearing about these reports. The safety and well-being of the teens on our platform is a top priority for the company. We're going to continue to make it a priority. This was important research. We're proud that we did it, and we're going to continue to, you know, study these really important issues.

Senator BLUMENTHAL. Why did you conceal it?

Mr. SATTERFIELD. Senator, we didn't make it public as we don't with a lot of the research we do because we think that that's an important way of encouraging free and frank discussion within the company about hard issues.

Senator BLUMENTHAL. Do you have more research that shows the destructive effect of your platform on teens?

Mr. SATTERFIELD. Senator, I'm not aware of any other research on teens. I don't work on these issues. I work on privacy and data. Senator BLUMENTHAL. Are you not aware in the same way that the company responded that it was not aware when, in fact, it knew about the research?

Mr. SATTERFIELD. Senator, I apologize. I'm not familiar with the context of that letter or what went into the response. You know, what I can tell you is that we think it's important to be having a dialog with Congress on these issues, and we're prepared to work with you and your team going forward.

Senator BLUMENTHAL. Will you work with me and my team by appearing on September 30 at a hearing that we've invited you to do?

Mr. SATTERFIELD. Senator, I know our folks have been in touch with your staff, you know, to discuss that. It's something that I think we're discussing right now.

Senator BLUMENTHAL. We are discussing it right now. I'm asking you for a commitment that your company will send a high-ranking, qualified, and knowledgeable representative to that hearing on September 30. Senator Blackburn and I are, respectively, the Ranking Member and Chairman, but it includes Senator Klobuchar and Lee. They are Members, as well. We need to hear from someone who's capable of answering these questions, and it should be next week. Will you commit to have someone at that hearing?

Mr. SATTERFIELD. Senator, we're going to follow-up promptly on this. We know these are incredibly important issues, and we want to work with you and your staff going forward. We'll follow-up promptly.

Senator BLUMENTHAL. Mr. Satterfield, I just want to point out to you that your company, contrary to what you've just told this Committee, is continuing with this really unfortunate charade. Vice President Nick Clegg doubled down on the misleading statement, in fact, this weekend, when he said the research is, quote, "Still relatively nascent and evolving," end quote. According to one of these studies, Facebook found 13 percent of British users and six percent of American users traced a desire to kill themselves to Instagram. How is it not misleading to tell this Committee that the research is unclear if, according to your own research, tens of thousands of teens have suicidal thoughts directly because of Instagram? Don't you think you owe us an explanation next week?

Mr. SATTERFIELD. Senator, I appreciate the concerns. I do, and I do think that Nick was accurate in his op-ed. What I can tell you is that we can commit to working with you and your staff going forward on these issues.

Senator BLUMENTHAL. Has Facebook ever conducted research that found Instagram was more toxic to teens than another—other social media platform?

Mr. SATTERFIELD. Senator, I'm not aware of that but these, again, these aren't issues that I work on at the company. You know, we're happy to follow-up with you and your staff.

Senator BLUMENTHAL. Will you follow-up next—the September 30th by having someone at that hearing who can tell us the answer? By the way, the answer is that you have found Instagram is more toxic than Snap and TikTok. It's more of a Facebook problem. Your own research has shown it. I'd like somebody to come provide an answer, an explanation next September 30th.

Mr. SATTERFIELD. We're going to get back to you promptly, Senator. I can commit to that.

Senator BLUMENTHAL. I want to ask about another area but perhaps I should wait until I hope we'll have a second round?

Chair KLOBUCHAR. Yes, we will. We will.

Senator BLUMENTHAL. Thank you.

Chair KLOBUCHAR. Thank you. Thank you so much, Senator Blumenthal. Next up, Senator Hawley, then Senator Ossoff, and then you, Senator Cruz, if it works. Thank you.

Senator HAWLEY. Thank you, Madam Chair, and thank you, Senator Lee, also for holding this hearing. Thanks to the witnesses for being here. This is such an important topic. Mr. Satterfield, let me just pick up where Senator Blumenthal left off. Can I just ask you a fundamental question? Are teenagers safe on any of your platforms?

Mr. SATTERFIELD. Senator, we're working really hard to make that the case.

Senator HAWLEY. They're not now?

Mr. SATTERFIELD. Senator, we are investing a lot in safety and integrity across all of our platforms. We've invested billions of dollars.

Senator HAWLEY. Are you concerned, though, that teenagers are currently subject to all kinds of potential predators, the social effects—I mean, you're saying you hope that they'll be safe on the platforms? Are they not safe now?

Mr. SATTERFIELD. Senator, I think it's our responsibility to invest the resources that we need to make sure that these things don't happen. You know, that's why we're investing billions of dollars in protecting the integrity of our platforms.

Senator HAWLEY. By "these things" do you think things like this, let me read you a few quotes. "Thirty-two percent of teen girls said that when they felt bad about their bodies, Instagram made them feel worse." Quote, "We make body image issues worse for one in three girls," end quote.

New quote, "Teens blame Instagram for increases in the rate of anxiety and depression. This reaction was unprompted and consistent across all groups."

Or how about this? "Teens who struggle with mental health say that Instagram makes it worse."

Or how about this? "Social comparison is worse on Instagram." Or about this? "Aspects of Instagram exacerbate each other to create a perfect storm when it comes to body issues, identity, depression, anxiety."

That doesn't sound like a very safe platform to me. Those, of course, are all from your own internal research. What do you have to say about that?

Mr. SATTERFIELD. Senator, again these aren't issues that I work on but I—we do have teams that are working across all of those issues, body image, well-being, and so forth. We're investing, you know, we're doing research like this so that we can identify gaps and address them. We're going to continue to do so.

Senator HAWLEY. Will you make the research public?

Mr. SATTERFIELD. Senator, again, you know generally the way that we approach research is that we keep it confidential to encourage free and frank discussion about it internally. It's—keeping it confidential actually enables us to——

Senator HAWLEY. Sounds like a no to me.

Mr. SATTERFIELD [continuing]. Ask hard questions about these really important issues.

Senator HAWLEY. I haven't been in the Senate that long, but this sounds like that's a no. Let me try again. You've already done the research. This research is completed. You've done it, you know the results, you know the data. You've actively misled Congress for years now. You've deliberately misled Senators as recently as just a month ago. Senator Blumenthal was just telling—putting on the record. You have the research. Will you make it public? Yes or no?

Mr. SATTERFIELD. Senator, I—respectfully, I'd strongly reject, you know, those characterizations. The issue of greater transparency around the research——

Senator HAWLEY. Let's try answering my question. Will you release the research? Yes or no?

Mr. SATTERFIELD. Senator, it's something we're looking into, how to provide greater transparency with appropriate context around the research—

Senator HAWLEY. Right. What would the appropriate context be, exactly? What's the context for 32 percent of teen girls saying that they feel worse when they use Instagram? Is there context that I'm missing there? What is it that parents need to know? What's the context, exactly? I'm intrigued by that statement.

Mr. SATTERFIELD. Senator, I mean, I think it's the broader view of what the potential impact of services could be on folks, and I think that the—

Senator HAWLEY. Oh, like maybe the things that Instagram does is positive that outweighs all of the terrible effects that it has on teen girls and others. Is that what you're talking about, your benefits? Let me ask you this. How much money does Instagram make for Facebook every year?

Mr. SATTERFIELD. Senator, I don't know the answer to that.

Senator HAWLEY. How much money do you make from teens being addicted to Instagram every year?

Mr. SATTERFIELD. Senator, I wouldn't agree with that characterization.

Senator HAWLEY. How much money do you make from your teen users every year?

Mr. SATTERFIELD. Senator, I don't know the answer to that question.

Senator HAWLEY. I bet it's a lot. I'll give it to you for the record. I think the—we all know what's really going on here. You won't release the research because this is a cash cow for you. You won't answer our questions because you make a gob of money on this. I mean, it's the whole reason Mark Zuckerberg wanted to get Instagram in the first place, right? I mean, back in 2012, Mark Zuckerberg wrote to his own chief financial officer that buying Instagram will give us time to integrate their dynamics before anybody else can get close to their scale. We know why Facebook bought Instagram. It was to get rid of a competitor, to gobble up all the data. Now they've done that. Now, it's making teenagers sick and destroying their mental health, but, you know, hey, it's lucrative. It's really—it's amazing. How about this?

Will you commit to suspending any efforts to develop the Instagram Kids product that would target children under the age of 13?

Mr. SATTERFIELD. Senator, we know that tweens are online, and, you know, we want them to have an experience that is a good one, that is a healthy one like we have with——

Senator HAWLEY. Like the one that teenage girls are having on Instagram right now, that kind of experience?

Mr. SATTERFIELD. Senator, respectfully, these are issues that we take incredibly seriously that we're investing in. You know, there is no more important priority than the safety and well-being of the people who use our products.

Senator HAWLEY. [Laughter] I really can't believe you're saying that. I mean, really, I've listened—I've listened to Facebook and these other big tech companies before these Committees for years, and I guess it's two years, although it feels like 20, and you always dissemble. You always mislead, but I can't believe that, given the research that you have conducted, that you can sit there and say that teens' health and security and safety's your top priority.

Clearly, it's not. You won't share any of the data. You're stonewalling every Member of this Committee. What about this? Will you at least commit to keeping behavioral advertising out of any product that a kid can access?

Mr. SATTERFIELD. Senator, we think that, you know, advertising is potentially very valuable. We have made changes with respect to teens under 18, limitations around the ability of advertisers to use our products to reach them.

Senator HAWLEY. Let's see. You won't reveal the research. You won't restrict your advertising. You won't pull back on plans to target children under the age of 13 with this platform, which you know is toxic for so many teenagers, especially female teenagers, and yet their health and well-being is your top priority. Do I—have I got that right? Did I miss any part?

Mr. SATTERFIELD. Senator, I'm not sure I said any of that. What I would say is, again, these are incredibly important issues to the company. We're committed to having a constructive dialog with Congress about them, and we're going to continue to invest heavily in them at the company.

Senator HAWLEY. I'm sure you'll invest heavily in it. I have absolutely no doubt about that. That I think is probably the truest statement you've made today. I have no doubt you will continue to pour money into Instagram as long as you can extract money from it and from the teenagers whom you are, quite frankly, exploiting. Here's just a final question for you. Why should—why should you be able to advertise to teenagers at all? I mean, given all the dangers inherent in collecting their data, which is what you're doing on Instagram, why should you be able to advertise to teenagers?

Why shouldn't we prohibit that?

Mr. SATTERFIELD. Senator, as you know advertising supports our service. We do think that additional protections for teenagers are appropriate. We put those in place. We're going to continue to look into ways to keep teenagers safe on our services while being able to support them with advertising.

Senator HAWLEY. Mr. Satterfield, the truth is you and I both know is that your product isn't safe. Your platforms aren't safe. They're dangerous. You know it, we know it. You stonewalled us. You've stonewalled the public. It's time for some accountability, and all I can say is accountability is coming.

Thank you, Madam Chair.

Chair KLOBUCHAR. Thank you very much, Senator Hawley. Before I turn it over to Senator Ossoff, I just want to—something when I was asking my questions that could lend some information to you here.

Facebook publicly reported that last quarter its revenue, advertising revenue per user, which I presume includes teens in the U.S. and Canada, was $51.58 per user. I guess just to follow-up, Mr. Satterfield, do you have the breakdown for teens versus the rest that we could get, maybe not today, but later?

Mr. SATTERFIELD. Senator, the only breakdown I'm aware of is the one you referenced, which is the average revenue per user.

Chair KLOBUCHAR. Does that include Instagram? Is it company- wide?

Mr. SATTERFIELD. Senator, I believe it's company-wide.

Chair KLOBUCHAR. Okay. All right. Senator Hawley compared it to some of the other countries which were a lot less than our country, so we'll have to be looking into that. How much revenue they make with that?

I'll turn it over to Senator Ossoff.

Senator OSSOFF. Thank you so much, Madam Chair. The first question please for you, Ms. Colclasure, does Acxiom or any other IPG company provide services to entities outside of the United States based upon or linked to data about U.S. persons?

Ms. COLCLASURE. Thank you, Senator, for your question. Of course, I'm at Kinesso and formerly at Acxiom, and a part of the IPG family. Acxiom data, we at Acxiom and at Kinesso both, we do have clients that are multinationals, and we have clients that operate in other markets around the world, and part of the services we provide are data-enabled services, marketing, and advertising services, so, yes.

Senator OSSOFF. Thank you. Do Kinesso, Acxiom, or other IPG companies provide data-connected services or services based on or related to data about U.S. persons to Federal agencies, State or local law enforcement, or any other public sector actors in the United States?

Ms. COLCLASURE. Of course, again, I'm speaking about Acxiom. Acxiom does have, and shortly to be retired, an identity authentication product, which is made up of regulated data and provided for regulated service and that is—we call that our risk product suite, and it solves things like know-your-customer obligations that financial services have—that we're actually exiting that business shortly and concentrating on marketing and advertising.

Senator OSSOFF. Is that the only product or service that you sell to any public sector entity in the United States?

Ms. COLCLASURE. We do other things like marketing and advertising data-enabled services. Like we supported an Ad Council advertising campaign to help get information out to help with the pandemic. Another example I can think of is we helped the American Red Cross when the Hurricane Katrina hit New Orleans several years ago. We helped get data to them for some marketing communications to go out and find audiences so they could learn about help and services from the American Red Cross.

We have a few other campaigns like that that I am aware of. Does that help?

Senator OSSOFF. Thank you, Ms. Colclasure. Do many IPG entities provide any services or have any financial relationships, direct or indirect, with any agencies or clients at the Department of Defense, in the intelligence community, or in Federal, State, or local law enforcement?

Ms. COLCLASURE. It is not an area of concentration, and I don't know the answer right off. I feel like I would——

Senator OSSOFF. Is that for the record?

Ms. COLCLASURE. Yes. I do not know the answer right off, but I promise I will go and research it and get you an answer so that I can be certain. Of course, there may be confidentiality issues that I'll have to navigate if we do have those sorts of contracts. I'm glad to go research and get you an answer.

Senator OSSOFF. Just to be clear, Ms. Colclasure, you are not personally aware and have never heard of any financial relationship between an IPG entity and the Department of Defense, the U.S. Intelligence Community, or any Federal, State, or local law enforcement entity?

Ms. COLCLASURE. I do know that Acxiom—of course, I'm not at Acxiom now, and Acxiom historically has had some relationships with some of that community, but I do not have the knowledge to share at this—but I'll research it for you.

Senator OSSOFF. What are you aware of? What do you recall?

Ms. COLCLASURE. We do have some—we did, again I'm not in command of the knowledge because I'm not at Acxiom now, but there are some Governmental agencies that we have worked with, most of it, like the Veterans Administration, was advertising and trying to do outreach to their veterans' community, so rather than fish around, if you might allow me, Senator, I'll go and research and get you an exactly right answer, if that would be OK?

Senator OSSOFF. Thank you. Do any IPG entities have direct or indirect financial relationships or provide any services or products to any foreign governmental entities?

Ms. COLCLASURE. Not to my knowledge.

Senator OSSOFF. Will you please double-check, for the record?

Ms. COLCLASURE. I certainly will. Certainly.

Senator OSSOFF. Thank you. How does Acxiom or how do other IPG entities engaged in their activities obtain device identifiers, such as IMEI or IMSI numbers?

Ms. COLCLASURE. At Acxiom and at Kinesso, of course, we operate in the digital advertising and marketing space, and we run a unified ethical framework as the basis for our data governance program. When we either source data, we undergo a due diligence process. I always like to say not all data's the same, and not all data uses are the same. Some of the data, like device IDs, that is a connecting piece of data that we use to enable and activate digital advertising campaigns on behalf of our clients. It may be that it flows in from one of our connected partner ecosystem providers, like an advertising network or a publisher, and we sit in the middle as a connector. That is typically how the data flows.

Does that help answer?

Senator OSSOFF. Do you place any limitations? Does Acxiom or any IPG entity place any limitations on the form, category, type, of entities to whom you'll sell services?

Ms. COLCLASURE. Absolutely, Senator. Thank you for that question. We do. As I mentioned, we use what's called a unified ethical frame for our data governance program. We practice an accountability-based, data-governance program.

Senator OSSOFF. Which plans—forgive me, but my time is limited. Which types of entity specifically will you not license data to or provide services to?

Ms. COLCLASURE. We—they have to be a legitimate commercial enterprise. We don't provide data to individuals or data-enabled services to individuals. It is to commercial entities for a legitimate ethical purpose. We judge the data use in context via our privacy impact assessment process. We check it off against legal requirements, regulatory requirements, coregulatory requirements. We do a harm detection and prevention test, and then very important to all of us, we do a fairness test. I mentioned in my opening remarks that we're people-centered, and that is we design from people outwards, from the engineering layer outward.

Senator OSSOFF. Ma'am, my time is limited. I appreciate the elaboration of that policy. Let me ask you this question? Does any IPG entity or has any IPG entity provided any service or sold any product to private investigators?

Ms. COLCLASURE. No. A very long time ago there was one business that Acxiom owned that we divested that did serve PIs, but that might have been 10 or 15 years ago. The answer's no, today.

Senator OSSOFF. Which firm was that?

Ms. COLCLASURE. It was—it was Acxiom-owned. We had acquired an entity. We operated it for a few years, and then we sold it, and I apologize, I cannot recall the name right now.

Senator OSSOFF. Thank you, ma'am. Madam Chair, I may return for a second round if we have the opportunity. I yield.

Chair KLOBUCHAR. Excellent. Senator Blackburn.

Senator BLACKBURN. Thank you, Madam Chairman. Ms. Slaiman, let me come to you first. I know that you're aware that Senators Blumenthal,

Klobuchar, and I filed the Open Market App Store Bill so that we could address Google and Apple and their stranglehold on that app market. Very quickly, how do Apple and Google's data practices factor into this app store and how they limit the use there, and do they incentivize the app store developers to continue the monopoly over—over this market that they have?

How are they manipulating that marketplace, very quickly?

Ms. SLAIMAN. Thank you so much, Senator Blackburn. We were so glad to see the introduction of the Open App Markets Act. I think that's going to be really important, not just for big data but for gatekeeper power writ large when it comes to app stores.

In particular, with regard to big data, I think the app stores and the operating systems have this privileged position where they can treat users, decisions about their data, differently, based on whether the app is owned by the app store company or the operating system company, or whether it's a competitor.

One thing that's really important is to make sure that those are being treated the same so that we have a level playing field for competition.

Senator BLACKBURN. I think that's important and that privileged position that they exercise is important to note. You've mentioned the gatekeeper property and how that would apply to other applications, whether it is publishers and other forms of content development. I think that this is an important bill that we get passed in on the record.

Very quickly on filter bubbles, and I know you've mentioned that—how do you address—how do you think we could address the filter bubbles and the platforms' secret algorithms, if you will, that really, kind of manipulate that consumer experience online?

Ms. SLAIMAN. One of the ways that big data is used is to decide what products to show the users. The platforms, again, are in this gatekeeper role where they're making those decisions. A lot of times that's based on an algorithm that is fed by data that they're collecting from users.

Those decisions about which products to show to users, which services to offer to users, those are decisions that the platform gets to make, and that's limiting the options that a user sees.

Senator BLACKBURN. Yes. I think that the Open Apps Market Act gives us that footing, as I said, that gatekeeper role to begin to address that so that the consumer, online consumer, has a more private and a more genuine experience, and we're looking forward to getting that bill passed. Thank you for those comments on that, because I agree with you. I think the implications we're going to see are writ large in the industry.

Mr. Satterfield, if I may come to you for just a moment. As you're aware, Senator Blumenthal and I have kind of been doing a deep dive on what you're doing with this data that you're collecting on teenagers. From working with whistleblower and from the data that we've seen, basically reams of data at this point, we are concerned about this amount of data that you are keeping on teens. Basically, what you're doing is building a virtual presence, a virtual you, of these teenagers. Do you think that is a violation of the Children's Online Privacy Act, the fact that you're tracking and following and building these files on these children?

Mr. SATTERFIELD. Senator, no. We're complying with the law. We do think it's really important to provide protections around teens' experiences on our services. These are things that we've been investing in. We've been consulting with third-party experts so that we do this thoughtfully and——

Senator BLACKBURN. Okay. Who are the third-party experts that you're consulting with? Because when we talk to teachers, to parents, to pediatricians, to psychologists, and when we look at the data that you have collected from teens and the changes that they have recommended that you make to your platform, it's like you're turning a blind eye to that because you're chasing a dollar. Why don't you bring some clarity to bear on that?

Mr. SATTERFIELD. Senator, this isn't something that I work on at the company. I'm happy to get back to you with more on the experts, and I'd say that——

Senator BLACKBURN. You know, if you're the VP——

Senator LEE. Still going.

Senator BLACKBURN [continuing]. On privacy and public policy, one would think that you probably were in meetings and that you would have a stakeholder position in what your company chooses to do on that issue. Are you not involved in these discussions of privacy and how to protect this data, and thereby how to protect the virtual you of these children and teens that are using your platform?

Mr. SATTERFIELD. Senator, yes, of course. I was talking about, you know, safety experts, experts on well-being and such. Yes, of course, I'm involved in privacy issues, including privacy issues that affect the teens on our platform.

Senator BLACKBURN. Do you have any plans in the works to use the data that you have collected, the data that teens gave you, the information they gave you when they participated in your mental health survey? Are you going to use that to put protections in place for these teens on your site? Yes or no?

Mr. SATTERFIELD. Senator, all of the research that we do, you know, informs the decision-making in the company. It's certainly something that we'll take into account as we're——

Senator BLACKBURN. The decision-making that you are exercising shows that you're making decisions that allow you to be more profitable, not that you're making decisions that are based on the welfare of that child. Why do you collect so much data on your users if you do not use it to improve the user experience? You're not using it to protect children or to improve the user experience, so for the record, why don't you tell us what you're using this data for?

Mr. SATTERFIELD. Senator, we are using the data that we collect when people use our services to improve their experience. That's our——

Senator BLACKBURN. Why would teens that took your mental health survey say—why would older teens say, "We're advising our younger siblings not to use Instagram, not to be a part of this online community?" Because they feel like you're not following what they're asking you to do. What are you using the data for? Are you using it for micro-targeting, to go in and target advertising? Are you using it to feed them—to push them further down paths if they click on one something then you keep feeding them more of that? Why don't you, for the record, tell us what you're using this data for? You've got reams of it.

Mr. SATTERFIELD. Senator, when it comes to the data that we collect when people use our services, you know, we do a couple of things. We use that data to provide the service. We use it to improve the service, to provide enhanced experiences, as you were saying.

Senator BLACKBURN. Tell me what improvements you have made that would keep teens healthier and safer. Give me three examples of things you've done that would keep teens healthier and safer as they use your platform.

Mr. SATTERFIELD. Senator, with respect to Instagram, we have made changes to the ways in which adults can contact potentially younger users. We've made changes to the way in which people can comment, and we've made changes that are designed to address potential bullying and harassment. In comments, we've made resources available on well-being and body image issues. We've made a number of investments over the years that address these kinds of issues.

Senator BLACKBURN. Do you nibble around the edges, or are you aggressive? Are you going to stop allowing human traffickers, sex traffickers, drug traffickers, to use your platform, whether it's in the U.S. or other countries? Is that the kind of improvement that you're making?

Mr. SATTERFIELD. Senator, respectfully, absolutely not. There's no place on Facebook for——

Senator BLACKBURN. It happens.

Mr. SATTERFIELD [continuing]. Activities like that.

Senator BLACKBURN. It happens. There's a Mexican drug cartel that's been on your platform. You didn't take them off.

Mr. SATTERFIELD. Senator, that organization was designated and banned on our platform, if what you're referring to is the organization from the Wall Street Journal article.

Senator BLACKBURN. You know, I have to tell you—and I have grandchildren, I have two grandsons and a granddaughter. My grandsons are 12 and 13, and my granddaughter is a year old. I tell my grandsons all the time that they cannot trust you all with their information. I think what you have done to a lot of these children is inexcusable. I think the fact that you collect this data, you monetize that data, you benefit from that data, and then knowing you have this data, don't you think parents would have liked to have known that this was taking place on your site? I do. I think it is unfortunate that you all have hesitated to answer the questions that Senator Blumenthal and I have. We do look forward to having a representative from your company come next week and answer the questions that we have in our hearing. Madam Chairman, we look forward to hearing more from Google and Apple about the Open Market Apps Bill. With that, I will yield back my time.

Chair KLOBUCHAR. Thank you very much, Senator Blackburn.

Second round, Senator Blumenthal.

Senator BLUMENTHAL. Let me just say, Mr. Satterfield, if you fail to have someone here on September 30th, there can be only one reason, that you're continuing the concealment. Let me just be very blunt. You've been sent here to defend the indefensible, but at some point, Mr. Zuckerberg should get the message, ''Houston, we have a problem.'' Better to be here on September 30, than continue to evade responsibility. I thank my colleague Senator Blackburn for putting it so succinctly and so eloquently.

I just want to point out that behind the numbers and the perhaps seemingly abstract questions there are real human beings, young women and men who are deeply hurt by these images, the focus on body images, on self-worth that comes along with those images. In one study of teens in the U.S. and the UK, according to the Journal article, Facebook found that more than 40 percent of Instagram users who reported feeling unattractive, said the feeling began on the app, and about a quarter of the teens who reported feeling not good enough said the feeling started there, and many felt in quotes, "addicted" to the app and felt that they were deprived of self-control.

Again, the analogy to big tobacco is undeniable. It's an analogy, not an exact comparison, but the exploitation of that kind of attraction, even addiction, I think is reprehensible. I really do hope that you understand that there is a certainty here, which is accountability is coming, as Senator Blackburn has said and Senator Hawley put it exactly. Accountability is coming, and it will be bipartisan.

I want to shift to the issue that Senator Blackburn also raised, our bipartisan bill, the Open App Markets Act would set robust rules to promote competition and strengthen consumer protection. I am proud that this bill is bipartisan. I want to thank my colleague Senator Klobuchar for her leading role in this area and she is a co-sponsor of the bill. It's received wide support, as was mentioned earlier, from consumer groups, antitrust experts, and app developers. Ms. Slaiman, I especially appreciate your reference to it, and the support that Public Knowledge has provided for the bill. Two companies, Google and Apple, have gatekeeper control of the dominant app stores that allow them to dictate the terms for everyone. Their duopoly allows them to set the terms and they do. If app developers don't like the terms, there is nowhere for them to go.

That is what we call a broken market.

Not even Facebook is immune to Google and Apple's gatekeeper control, big as Facebook is, powerful as it is, it's not immune. Apple has blocked the Facebook Gaming app from the app store at least five times, and it has prohibited other cloud gaming services from becoming available on the app store. Apple has also forced Facebook to remove a notice informing consumers about the so- called Apple tax, that is the infamous 30 percent rent fee that they extract from digital goods and services. The little guy is as much a victim as the big guys like Facebook.

The Open Markets—Open App Markets Act would protect developers' ability to offer competitive prices, tell consumers about lower prices, and give consumers the right to make their own decisions about the apps they install. That's what's called competition, and a free market, or at least freer than it is now, and it would mean that Facebook and others don't have to pass the Apple tax on to consumers and small businesses.

It would mean that iPhone users could sideload Facebook Gaming directly on to their phones if Apple continues to block the app. These are basically pro-consumer and pro-competition rules.

Mr. Satterfield, would Facebook support Congress setting fair, clear, enforceable rules on app stores that would prevent Apple and Google from using their gatekeeper power to extract excessive rents and block competition like what happened to you and your app, Facebook Gaming?

Mr. SATTERFIELD. Senator, thank you. Our team is looking at the bill, and we're providing feedback through the, you know, the normal channels. You know, we're continuing to work with you and the other co-sponsors and providing that feedback.

Senator BLUMENTHAL. What are the normal channels?

Mr. SATTERFIELD. We're communicating with your staff and others.

Senator BLUMENTHAL. Okay. Let me point out, in case it isn't obvious, and I think it is, that Facebook really should support these kinds of rules if it is in favor of competition and open markets and not just for you, but for others.

Mr. Erickson, Apple has claimed that if we allow consumers to make their own decisions, all sorts of really horrible or terrible things are going to happen. Unlike Apple, Google has allowed sideloading and better developing access on Android from the very start. Given Apple's alarming claims, would you characterize everyone's Apple phone as insecure or vulnerable to cybersecurity risk, because that's what Apple says will happen if we eliminate the Apple tax of 30 percent?

Mr. ERICKSON. Senator, thank you for your question. If I may step back for a minute, we share the values that you and Senator Blackburn have that consumers should be able to choose the lawful applications, to download those, and that there should be competition in this marketplace. We're taking a look at your legislation as well, and we'll be happy to engage with you going forward.

The Android ecosystem, no, we do believe we provide a very safe and secure ecosystem for our app developers to reach a global audience of billions of users in 190 countries, and that's not undermined by allowing consumers to be able to download applications outside of the app store or to sideload those applications.

Senator BLUMENTHAL. You do believe Android is secure?

Mr. ERICKSON. Senator, yes.

Senator BLUMENTHAL. Let me just close this round of questioning, because I know my colleagues may have other questions. I cannot help but make this observation about the action just over the last weekend by Google and Apple, at the behest of Vladimir Putin, to censor their apps. In fact, censor apps that were used to organize democratic protests in Russia. Apple has taken down thousands of apps from its app store at China's request. Almost a third of them relate to human rights, and it includes Hong Kong protests and LGTBQ rights.

You know, in a tweet I analogized what's going on here to Neville Chamberlain and the attempt to appease Germany. I view it as very much the same kind of appeasement of Vladimir Putin and the Communist Party in China. I think it was Winston Churchill who said about Neville Chamberlain that he had to choose between dishonor and war. He chose dishonor and he got war. In fact, he got both.

At the end of the day, you're not going to appease these totalitarian dictators. Not even Apple or Google or any of the big tech companies are going to win by appeasement when it comes to human rights. I think that it's pandering. It's craven pandering, and it undermines our national interest, and I yield the floor, Madam Chair.

Chair KLOBUCHAR. Thank you very much, Senator Blumenthal.

Senator Lee is next.

Senator LEE. Thank you very much. My next question is for Mr. Robb. Mr. Robb, what are the ramifications of our personal data having become the method of payment for so many online services?

Mr. ROBB. It's a loss of control, loss of income, and, you know, we're looking at the snapshot right now of the tech industry, and we're looking at—we're focusing in on marketing and the big players that exist today, but this is going to evolve. You know, I've been in the tech industry for decades, and I started on the internet 25 years ago, and that was well before Facebook and Google even existed.

The same thing's going to happen in the next 20-30 years, is that this data is going to persist, and we need to give individuals control of that data so they can learn how to exercise their control, set permissions on how it's used, and make money on commercial apps that actually use it to build products and services.

You know, changing the dynamic here——

Senator LEE. What if anything can we do to reassert our ownership and our control over our own data?

Mr. ROBB. I think the key way to do that is to get the data off of the platforms that are aggregating it, and then putting it into a central repository that's managed by the individual, and if they do that, they're in control. They're the focal point where actually combining that data and who's using it, rather than having it sold by third parties to third parties or—and combined in ways that they don't have any jurisdiction over.

By putting the, you know, the individual at the center of the equation, you know, it makes life more complicated, but it's an essential thing for us to move forward and be able to do this successfully long-term. Otherwise, we're going to be caught in this, you know, privacy trap. I mean, privacy's fine, but it really is just destruction of data and limitations on—rather than actually solving the problem at root.

Senator LEE. Are third-party brokers like Acxiom an obstacle or are they an aid to consumers trying to regain control of their data? Mr. ROBB. The fact that they're combining data from multiple sources, they're actually acting in opposition to what individuals should—should be able to do. If you have the individual at the center of the equation, you don't need an Acxiom. We don't need a data broker. I mean, they can cut deals directly with them. They might even be managing the data repository. You know, it seems like—you know, we don't have a data repository now, and it seems, you know, fanciful to even think in terms of that, but I mean, we can build it. I mean, we can set the standards for how that would operate. We can lay out those standards and have companies actually compete to deliver on those standards, just like we built the web, just like we built so much of what we have in terms of web architecture.

You know, data aggregators can do business with individuals, but they can't be a substitute for them.

Senator LEE. Mr. Erickson, I'd like to turn to you next. In the last year, Google announced that it would stop servicing third- party cookers—cookies in the Chrome browser. Google's announcement said that the purpose of this was to protect consumers and to protect their data.

Left unsaid was how this could impact Google's ad tech competitors, and also left unsaid was the amount of information that Google collects from consumers—the browser data, location data, app usage data, financial transaction data, et cetera.

Tell me, how is it that consumers are any more protected if Google collects this data and your competitors can't? Can you help me understand that?

Mr. ERICKSON. Senator, thank you for the question. Yes, I can try. With the announcement that we made you rightfully point out that we would stop supporting intrusive tracking technologies like third-party cookies. We made the announcement in an effort to chart a course for a more privacy-enhancing web. We did not unilaterally withdraw our support for that but rather wanted to engage in a thoughtful conversation with advertisers, with publishers that rely on an ad-supported ecosystem to be able to function their websites or to reach consumers. We want to engage with regulators and governments and other stakeholders to explore more privacy- protective technologies, those are the intrusive technologies.

Senator LEE. Sir, I'm not sure you're grasping my question. You're at least not answering it. I appreciate that you're wanting to have a thoughtful conversation. I appreciate that you include this was in your business interest, and it may well have been. That's totally within your right. What I'm asking you to explain is your apparent assertion that consumers are any more protected if you collect that data and your competitors can't.

Mr. ERICKSON. Senator, so——

Senator LEE. That is your assertion, right? I mean that is the assertion that you made in that announcement. You said you're not going to service the third-party cookies in the Chrome browser, and——

Mr. ERICKSON. I'm sorry. Senator LEE. Go ahead.

Mr. ERICKSON. Senator, we think the advertising ecosystem can thrive without having privacy-intrusive technologies like tracking devices or third-party cookies. The data that users—we are transparent with the collection practices that we have and the uses of our data, and we want to give consumers, and we do give them meaningful choice over the uses of their data, including to decide that they don't want to see targeted ads and relevant ads. They can choose not to see those or to mute ads that appear on third-party sites. There's many, many advertisers in the ecosystem. The access to data from consumers can be gotten from data brokers and other providers, so we don't think—the data in that regard is not viable. The data that consumers may provide with us are often provided to other online actors as well, and some of these companies are some of the biggest companies in the world. You implicitly raised a very important point, which is as we see regulators around the world push us and others, rightfully so, to have more privacy-protective technologies and to chart a course through a more privacy-centric web. There are competitors out there that are urging competition authorities to have us make more personally identifiable information released to the ecosystem.

We think that—we want to engage in these conversations. We think we can have a privacy-centric web while ensuring consumer choice and competition, and that publishers and advertisers will continue to be able to have a business model that allow them to provide their websites and services to consumers in the way they do today.

Senator LEE. Okay, yes, I understand that. Look, I get the fact that you can always point to areas where things could get worse. Mandatory disclosures of personally identifying information on the web or otherwise. It is rather significant here that these things that you're talking about, steps that you've taken to exclude would- be competitors from the marketplace in circumstances in which Google's happy to provide advertisers with an alternative making them more dependent on Google, or it does in pretty much your bottom line.

Ms. Slaiman, do you agree with Google's statement? Are consumers better off with only Google being able to collect these types of data?

Ms. SLAIMAN. No, I don't agree with that statement. I don't think that users' privacy is improved, and I think it's a problem for competition. I really think we're being presented here with a false choice. There's another alternative, which is that some of this data should not be tracked at all.

Senator LEE. Sounds like you agree with my reluctance to accept the premise that people are safer because of this. I just realized I'm dangerously over time. Chairwoman Klobuchar has been very indulgent. I apologize. Thank you.

Chair KLOBUCHAR. Thank you. Next up Senator Cruz. Thank you.

Senator CRUZ. Thank you, Madam Chair. Mr. Satterfield, my questions will be for you. Last week, the Wall Street Journal ran a damning article entitled, "Facebook Knows Instagram Is Toxic For Teen Girls, Company Documents Show." The tagline below it was quote, "Its own in-depth research shows a significant teen mental health issue that Facebook plays down in public."

I know about this article because my wife, Heidi, who reads the Journal every day said, "You need to read this article now." I read it word for word.

All of us know that these products are addictive and that companies like Facebook design them in this way in order to maximize addiction, to capture eyeballs, which captures data, which is then used to sell advertising. For years, Facebook has been publicly insisting that its products aren't harmful and particularly that they're not harming teenagers.

We now know that was a lie. Facebook knew that its products, and specifically Instagram, was destroying the lives of far too many teenage girls. Facebook knew this because Facebook conducted its own studies into how Instagram affected young users and found that Instagram is harmful to a sizable percentage of them.

In fact, a slide from 2019 summara—summarizing this research said quote, "We make body image issues worse for one in three teen girls." Another Facebook slide said quote, "Teens blame Instagram for increases in the rate of anxiety and depression." Another slide said quote, "Teens who struggle with mental health say Instagram makes it worse." Most egregiously, one presentation said that among teens who reported suicidal thoughts, 13 percent of British users and 6 percent of America's users traded—traced their desire to kill themselves to Instagram.

This should've made Facebook stop dead in its tracks and ask what in the hell you were doing. Instead, Facebook publicly downplayed the risk to young users and committed to push, to make sure more at-risk teenage girls used Instagram because more users including more teenagers means more money, whatever the human cost.

This is appalling. The American people deserve a thorough investigation into Facebook's willingness and eagerness to mislead the public about the risks of their own products.

The Wall Street Journal article states that the research has been reviewed by top Facebook executives and was cited in a presentation given to Mark Zuckerberg.

Mr. Satterfield, is this accurate? Did Mark Zuckerberg have personal knowledge of this Facebook research?

Mr. SATTERFIELD. Senator, I don't know the answer to that question, but, you know, to your other points, I would strongly disagree with the notion that our products are unsafe. I strongly believe they are safe——

Senator CRUZ. Let me ask you. Did you have knowledge of this research, Mr. Satterfield?

Mr. SATTERFIELD. I'm sorry, Senator. I've read the Wall Street Journal article——

Senator CRUZ. Did you have knowledge of it before the Wall Street Journal article?

Mr. SATTERFIELD. Senator, I'm generally aware that we do research on our products.

Senator CRUZ. Are you familiar with this research?

Mr. SATTERFIELD. I wasn't familiar with this research outside of the context of the Journal article, no.

Senator CRUZ. Wait a second. Your title is vice president of privacy and public policy, and you had no idea about Facebook's own research showing that you're violating the privacy and destroying the lives of teenage girls. You didn't know about it? Is that what you're testifying today?

Mr. SATTERFIELD. Senator, we're a large company, we have a lot of teams working on a lot of different issues. I don't work on these issues, safety and well-being.

Senator CRUZ. You didn't know about it?

Mr. SATTERFIELD. I didn't. Other people did. We're happy to connect——

Senator CRUZ. You have zero knowledge whether Mark Zuckerberg knew about it or not?

Mr. SATTERFIELD. I—Senator, I don't know that. I don't know. Senator CRUZ. You knew you were coming to testify in this hearing. I'm going to guess you read the Journal article before you showed up to testify?

Mr. SATTERFIELD. Senator, I came here to testify on data issues and antitrust——

Senator CRUZ. Did you read the Journal article before you showed up to testify?

Mr. SATTERFIELD. Senator, yes, I've read the Journal article.

Senator CRUZ. Okay. Presumably, you prepared for today's testimony, yes?

Mr. SATTERFIELD. Yes, Senator, I prepared.

Senator CRUZ. Did that preparation involve enquiring whether the Wall Street Journal was accurate when it said Mark Zuckerberg was aware of this research?

Mr. SATTERFIELD. Senator, I can't get into the issues that we discussed during prep with my lawyers.

Senator CRUZ. Why not? You're here testifying on behalf of Facebook. I'm asking whether you inquired, whether the Journal was right, that Zuckerberg knew about this research? Did you inquire about it, or did you remain willfully blind and not want to know if Zuckerberg knew about it?

Mr. SATTERFIELD. Senator, respectfully, I'm here to testify about data and antitrust issues. I don't work on these issues. I'm happy to put you in touch with the folks that do——

Senator CRUZ. Again, you're the vice president of privacy and public policy and so putting in place policies that result in more teen suicides, that does not fall within your purview?

Mr. SATTERFIELD. Senator, I don't agree with that characterization. I work on privacy. There are many people that work on these issues at the company.

Senator CRUZ. Okay. Let's take the specifics of Facebook's research. I read a quote a minute ago, quote, "We make body-image issues worse for one in three teen girls." I didn't write that. Facebook wrote that. Is that an accurate statement?

Mr. SATTERFIELD. Senator, we do this research in order to inform hard conversations that we have at the company.

Senator CRUZ. I didn't ask why you did the research. I asked if the statement that was the result of your research is true?

Mr. SATTERFIELD. Senator, this is the research that was discussed in the Journal. This is research that we did internally.

Senator CRUZ. Was that a conclusion of your research? Yes or no?

Mr. SATTERFIELD. Senator, I'm aware of the Wall Street Journal article. I've read the Wall Street Journal article which discusses the research.

Senator CRUZ. All right. Let's try another conclusion. The Facebook research concluded that 13 percent of British users and 6 percent of American users trace their desire to kill themselves to Instagram. Is that a conclusion of your research?

Mr. SATTERFIELD. Senator Cruz, respectfully, we have teams that work on these issues. I'm not on those teams. We would be happy——

Senator CRUZ. Respectfully, you're not answering the question. It's a simple binary question. Did your research conclude that or not? If it's not, show us the research that didn't conclude that? If it is, then the question is, "What's the culpability of a company that knows it is contributing to an expanding teen suicide?" Did your research conclude that six percent of American users trace their desire to kill themselves to Instagram? Yes or no?

Mr. SATTERFIELD. Senator, again, these aren't issues that I work on at the company. I'm happy to bring folks in for a briefing with you and your staff.

Senator CRUZ. I understand that you would prefer a briefing without the public being aware of it, but I'm the father of two girls, including a teenage girl. Let me ask you something. In your judgment, in the judgment of Facebook, is increased teen suicide an acceptable business risk?

Mr. SATTERFIELD. Senator, of course not.

Senator CRUZ. Has Facebook quantified how many additional teenagers took their life because of your products?

Mr. SATTERFIELD. Senator, again, with respect, these aren't the issues that I work on. I came here today to talk about data and antitrust.

Senator CRUZ. Let me ask you. What would you say to the parents of a teenager who took her own life because of your products? What would you say when, two years ago, you had research that you conducted that concluded your products would contribute to and expand teen suicide? What would you say to a parent on behalf of Facebook who was facing that horrific tragedy?

Mr. SATTERFIELD. Senator, obviously losing a child to a tragedy like that is devastating. I have children. I take these issues incredibly seriously myself.

Senator CRUZ. Does Facebook?

Mr. SATTERFIELD. Of course, we do, Senator.

Senator CRUZ. Then what did you do differently? You got these results two years ago. What conduct changed? You don't get to say you take these issues seriously if you continue doing exactly the same and profiting off of—off of applications that are endangering the lives of teenage girls. What did you do differently because of this research?

Mr. SATTERFIELD. Senator, we did this research to inform our decision-making. We have consistently made——

Senator CRUZ. Did anything change?

Mr. SATTERFIELD [continuing]. Improvements to the product——

Senator CRUZ. Did anything change?

Mr. SATTERFIELD [continuing]. To address issues like well-being.

I would love to have a team come in——

Senator CRUZ. Did anything change?

Mr. SATTERFIELD. Senator, we've made changes to our products over the last, you know, 10, 12 years——

Senator CRUZ. Did anything change to reduce the risk of teen suicide because of your product? Did you read this research and say, "Oh, my God, this is horrifying. Let's change?" Did you do anything to change, or did you just say, "Hey, we're printing money so we're good with this?" Which one was it?

Mr. SATTERFIELD. Senator, I would love to have a team come and give you and your staff a full briefing on these issues. We have made significant—

Senator CRUZ. It's the American people who deserve a briefing.

Mr. SATTERFIELD [continuing]. To safety and security. I would love to share more about this with you with the folks who work on these things.

Senator CRUZ. The entire American people deserve to know the answers to these questions.

Chair KLOBUCHAR. Thank you very much. I'm going to finish up here with my second round of questions, and I want to bring us back to the subject of the hearing on data, because we have some major opportunities to move, right now, legislation that I think will be very helpful.

The first I've mentioned, which is right in front of us before the House, the bill that Senator Grassley and I have to modernize the merger filing fees. We also have opportunities in this budget in reconciliation, and you know, my view is—and I guess I'll ask you this, Ms. Slaiman. The President can appoint aggressive enforcers. He can issue executive orders which was great, but if we don't have the resources to take on the world's biggest companies, is it going to all work?

Ms. SLAIMAN. Right. I think you're absolutely right, Madam Chairwoman. We need more funding for our antitrust enforcement agencies. Obviously, that alone is not going to be sufficient so I'm glad that you're working on a lot of other important pieces of the puzzle as well, but that's an important one that we ought to be able to get done.

Chair KLOBUCHAR. Okay. Very good. Then we have not seen a lot of antitrust enforcement against mergers or anticompetitive conduct based on the issue raised by what this hearing has for the most part focused on, which is data. It's clear that big data does raise complex competition issues, but I'm doubtful that when you see some of these court cases recently that in my mind have gone in the wrong direction to begin with, but then we have this complex area of data and what that means for dominant carriers with no new laws or adjustment of laws. That's why the Competition and Antitrust Law Enforcement Reform Act that I introduced with Senators Leahy, Blumenthal, Booker, and many others would update our laws.

Could you talk about how this would help to address competition issues raised by big data?

Ms. SLAIMAN. Yes. Thank you so much, Madam Chairwoman. I think that's absolutely right that recently, and not so recently—it's been going on for decades now—that our antitrust laws have been narrowed and narrowed by these court decisions. So, now that we are facing the difficult challenges of big data, it's very difficult to bring a case, for example, where innovation harms are an important part of, you know, what the agencies are trying to argue. I think it will be incredibly helpful to have your legislation in place that updates the legal standard both for mergers and for exclusionary conduct.

Exclusionary conduct in particular is how a lot of these big data concerns are happening, and it has really been difficult to bring exclusionary conduct to cases, which is a broader problem beyond big data, but it's particularly relevant here.

Chair KLOBUCHAR. Maybe we could talk a little bit about that, you know, the relevance of it.

As we look at privacy legislation, and I know, Mr. Satterfield, you talked about privacy legislation, and in your written testimony and past blog posts you've written about the need for Congress to enact it that could create rules to govern how platforms should use, analyze, and share data. What restrictions do you think the U.S. Government should put on targeted advertising, both from a privacy and competition perspective, and should such legislation be limited to platforms like Facebook, Google, and Amazon, or should it apply to data brokers too?

Mr. SATTERFIELD. Thank you, Senator. We think the comprehensive privacy legislation is incredibly important for the Congress to take up and pass. In terms of who it should apply to, we think it should apply across the board to companies that process people's personal data. We think that it should have components like basic rights around your data, the rights to access, correct, delete and move your data to another service. We think that companies should be required to build internal processes to make sure that they're thinking about privacy when they build their products and services. I think that those are the basic components of the framework that we would advocate for.

Chair KLOBUCHAR. Anyone else like to comment on the rules the Federal Government should put in place to ensure the market for targeted advertising remains competitive, which is a little different than just privacy?

Ms. COLCLASURE. I'd like to jump in.

Chair KLOBUCHAR. Okay.

Ms. COLCLASURE. Say that I think we need an accountability-based law. We've been advocating for a Federal law for almost 20 years, and we believe it's very important for all Americans to have the same rights and for businesses to have predictability and certainty. The accountability construct is one that says it parses out, and this is especially important for digital advertising, that you should use data for benefit, for good purpose, and you are responsible and answerable, the accountability construct, for detecting and preventing harm.

I love what Senator Blumenthal said earlier, that data is an abstract of a person, and I believe it deserves all the dignity that we people should have. So when you process data, when you activate data for digital advertising, it's about fairness, not manipulation, and that's the way we govern data, and that's what we believe, and that's what we advocate for in addition to the basic rights. We parse privacy out. It's the right to an area of seclusion. Where can we as people be free, natural, unobserved humans? The right to agency. That's that choice, participation, control, access. Then the right to fair processing. That is the third piece of privacy and that is in the digital age.

The reality of digital is it's getting so complex people do not want to sit in front of a NASA space station control panel and say, "Yes, yes. No, no. Yes, yes." We have to get the defaults right, and it has to be that participants, all participants, are accountable for, "Do no harm" and "Do good things in service to people."

It is privacy by design. The computer code is the conduct. Thank you, Senator.

Chair KLOBUCHAR. Okay. Very good. Ms. Slaiman, you may want to add to that, but one of the goals of competition as to policy is to ensure there's a broad range of choices. If ads are targeted based on data companies have collected about each of us and the inferences they have made about our interest, does that raise concerns for you about consumers abilities to freely choose the products and services that are best for them, ranging from financial services, housing, healthcare, employment opportunities, and more, when some of them are being targeted because of their data that they didn't really know they shared compared to other competitors?

Do you want to address that?

Ms. SLAIMAN. Yes, that's something that we're very concerned about. I do think that creates an opportunity for anti-competitive discrimination. It also creates an opportunity for discrimination, racial discrimination, and gender discrimination, and we've seen instances of that happening, so I think these are very serious harms that we need to be addressing.

To focus on the anti-competitive discrimination, I do think in addition to the consumer choice limitations, we're also concerned about the impact that this has on businesses. If a business is assessed by one of these algorithms to not be popular with a certain category of users, that can make things incredibly difficult for them because of the power of these platforms, because they occupy that gatekeeper role. It's much different than if a brick-and-mortar grocery store decides not to show your product, you can go somewhere else. With these gatekeeper platforms that's not a practical real option for companies. There's a variety of harms I think that come from that.

Chair KLOBUCHAR. Mr. Erickson, what is your company doing to ensure that competition is not being distorted by your targeted advertising systems with Google?

Mr. ERICKSON. Senator, thank you for the question. I think primarily consumers need to have transparency over their data, how data is being used, and meaningful choices about the use of that data. On the Google platforms, we provide an easy way for consumers to see exactly what data is stored relative to their account. They can delete that data if they want to. They can also make changes to say they don't want behavioral advertising targeted ads to them. They don't want to see—they want to mute ads on third- party sites, so I think the important thing here is to ensure that consumers have transparency and that they have meaningful choice, and we think privacy legislation should reflect those values as well.

Chair KLOBUCHAR. Okay. Earlier in my opening, I talk about Apple recently rolling out an update to its users, prompting them to agree or opt out of being tracked from across the apps they use. Early indications, as I noted, suggest a lot of them are doing it, something like 75 percent. Has Google considered doing something similar, including for its Android operating system?

Mr. ERICKSON. Senator, thank you. Google has announced that they will—we will stop supporting privacy-intrusive tracking technologies, like third-party cookies. At the same time, we've opened up a dialog through our Privacy Sandbox initiative to have a discussion with advertisers, with publishers, with governments, on how the industry can move to more privacy-enhancing, privacy-protective business models that still allow small businesses, website owners, to be able to have an ad-supported business and provide free products and services to consumers.

Chair KLOBUCHAR. Through the initiative the Privacy Sandbox initiative, you've mentioned some of these changes that you made to your web browser, Chrome.

However, from a competition perspective these changes have raised concerns that Google will still have access to detailed data, but others won't. How do you respond to those concerns?

Mr. ERICKSON. Senator, when we announced that we would cease support of these intrusive tracking devices, the third-party cookies, we also announced that we would not substitute those for alternative tracking mechanisms, but rather the idea behind the Privacy Sandbox was try to move as an industry toward more privacy, secure technologies that would still support an ad ecosystem but in privacy-enhancing ways.

Chair KLOBUCHAR. Do you want to respond to that, Ms. Slaiman, and then I'll just ask you the last question here?

Ms. SLAIMAN. Thank you so much. The Privacy Sandbox creates a situation where Google is still getting the data. They may call that privacy because fewer companies are getting the data, but Google is still able to fully exploit that data.

I don't think that that is giving users more privacy.

Chair KLOBUCHAR. Okay. My last question of you is about, you know, I've asked you some questions on the record, later, on mergers and things like that, and my bill, but just a kind of broad question here, Ms. Slaiman. In your opinion, do we need new laws to fully address the competition issues raised by big data, or can we just live with what we've got? That's called a softball.

Ms. SLAIMAN. [Laughter] Thank you so much. We absolutely need new laws, and that's something that we're working very hard on. I think we need to use all of the tools at our disposal, so we need to increase enforcement with the current laws that we have. We need to push for rulemaking at the FTC with the current laws that we have, but at the same time, it is so important that we have improvements to the antitrust laws and sector-specific antitrust laws focused on big tech.

Chair KLOBUCHAR. Very good. I think that says it all. Do you want to add anything, Senator Lee? Oh, you do? Okay. Because we want to have a 4-hour hearing, not just three and a half, no. Go, I'm kidding. Go ahead.

Senator LEE. I can go for four and a half.

Chair KLOBUCHAR. No, that's okay. Why don't you just finish up here.

Senator LEE. I'll keep this brief. Mr. Satterfield, what's going to happen to the employees at Facebook involved in providing the leaked documents to the Wall Street Journal? Are they going to be retaliated against?

Mr. SATTERFIELD. Senator, I can't discuss H.R. issues in a public forum.

Senator LEE. Would it be appropriate for you to retaliate against them, assuming they broke no laws? Would it be appropriate for you to retaliate against them?

Mr. SATTERFIELD. No, Senator, of course not. Of course, it wouldn't be appropriate to retaliate against anyone.

Senator LEE. Will you issue a commitment to me that Facebook will not retaliate against them?

Mr. SATTERFIELD. Senator, yes. I'm happy to commit to that.

Senator LEE. That would be wonderful. Thank you. I appreciate that.

Chair KLOBUCHAR. Okay. I want to thank everyone for coming. There is a lot going on. We have a bill this week before the full Committee for markup on venues that Senator Lee and I have done together, the companion in the House. We have the funding bills and proposals that are very ripe for action right now. We have other bills that are tech-specific with Senator Blumenthal and Senator Blackburn and myself with the App Bill. We have interoperability proposals from the past, and then we have discrimination bills, anti-discrimination bills for exclusionary conduct and the like, that we're in the middle of right now, working on. The House, of course, has proposals, some similar to ours, some different, but we've been working closely with our counterparts, which is Representative Cicilline and Representative Buck.

Then also we have broader bills. We had a hearing on meatpacking and consolidation in the grocery area. We have a— which went—was very well attended with the full Committee here. Senator Lee and Senator Grassley have a broad bill on antitrust. I have another one with a number of co-sponsors. There are some similarities in the bill right, Senator Lee? Yes, there are.

We're also looking at that across industry lines about things that we can do that aren't just about tech, actually, that hit the fact that we're seeing consolidation across this country from everything from cat food to coffins.

It's not really good to end with the word coffin, so—although, you know, we're not too far from Halloween, but I just want to thank the witnesses and assure you that we continue to want to work with everyone, but we know we need change, that just keeping on going like we are and saying, "Everything is fine, and we trust you," and it's just not enough. You know, we're glad that these companies have been successful. We're glad they employ people, we truly are. I have a Fitbit. Senator Lee and I have compared some of our Fitbit data over the years. I'm not going to reveal that, although you guys already know it, so there.

And—but, at the same time, we believe in capitalism and encouraging capitalism and rejuvenating capitalism, and a lot of what's going on right now has the obvious privacy concerns, many of which you heard today with a lot of understandable emotion. But then there's also competition concerns that once you get so big and have so much dominance that there are these barriers to entry. They make it impossible to allow competition, and that, in turn, of course, in the long term allows for too much money in the same few hands. It allows for companies to start preferencing themselves, and while we've seen incredible developments in technology, we do not deny that, we'll never know of some of the new bells and whistles on privacy we might've seen if we didn't have Facebook buy Instagram or WhatsApp, if there'd been some control on that. It's one of the reasons that I support looking back in some of the most consolidating industries, just as we did during the days of the AT&T breakup, to figure out what we can do to make this area more competitive.

You're not going to find a more interested and energized Subcommittee than this one, as you could see from today, including some visitors that aren't even on the Subcommittee that we welcome. So, thank you.

We will keep the record open for—is it a week? Okay, very good.

Thank you to Mark and to Avery for their work, and Senator Lee and his staff. Do you want to add anything, Mike?

Senator LEE. Thank you.

Chair KLOBUCHAR. Okay. Thank you. The hearing is adjourned. [Whereupon, at 5:28 p.m., the Committee was adjourned.]. [Additional material submitted for the record follows.]

Witness List
Hearing before the
Senate Committee on the Judiciary
Subcommittee on Competition Policy, Antitrust, and Consumer Rights

"Big Data, Big Questions: Implications for Competition and Consumers"

Tuesday, September 21, 2021
Dirksen Senate Office Building Room 226
2:30 p.m.

Mr. Steve Satterfield
Vice President, Privacy & Public Policy
Facebook, Inc.
Menlo Park, CA

Mr. Markham Erickson
Vice President of Government Affairs and Public Policy
Google, Inc.
Mountain View, CA

Ms. Sheila Colclasure
Global Chief Digital Responsibility and Public Policy Officer
IPG Kinesso
Little Rock, AR

Mr. John Robb
Author
The Global Guerrillas Report
Acton, MA

Ms. Charlotte Slaiman
Competition Policy Director
Public Knowledge
Washington, D.C.

Sheila Colclasure
Testimony to the Senate Judiciary Committee Subcommittee on Competition Policy, Antitrust, and Consumer Rights Big Data, Big Questions: Implications for Competition and Consumers September 21, 2021

Executive Summary of Testimony

Sheila Colclasure is the Global Chief Digital Responsibility and Public Policy Officer for Kinesso, an IPG company. Sheila and IPG support national competition and data privacy laws that enable fair and open use of data, require accountability of companies that collect, process, share and use data, and ensure robust protection for individuals and their data.

Witness Background

As Global Chief Digital Responsibility and Public Policy Officer, Sheila leads the global data policy and digital responsibility strategies for Kinesso, ensuring that data and digital technology are used ethically and accountably across the enterprise and with its parent company, IPG, and their clients. This means ensuring data and technology are used in ways that serve people. She helps ensure practices operating at the leading edge of digital technology are consistent with principles of responsible, respectful, proportionate and fair data use. Sheila is responsible for public policy engagement with regulators, policy groups, clients and other key stakeholders globally, advocating for ethical advertising and marketing practices in ways that earn trust. She is an advisor on the development and deployment of Kinesso's data-driven and digital solutions and services. She is a trusted thought partner, advisor, and reputational champion for IPG companies.

Ms. Colclasure is a recognized global thought leader on applied data ethics, accountable data governance and human-centered digital responsibility. Sheila has extensive knowledge of laws and societal expectations governing the collection and use of information, with particular depth in the rapidly evolving data-driven advertising and marketing ecosystem. She is continuously sought out by policy makers, regulators and government agencies for her views on data integrity and how to address the complexity of operationalizing and harmonizing next-generation data governance for the global digital data-driven ecosystem. Sheila is a Presidential Leadership Scholar and was recognized by CSO as one of the "12 amazing women in security" (2017).

She is a frequent speaker and media interviewee and has advanced data leadership and policy with the marketplace, regulators and lawmakers in many fora, including the Department of Health and Human Services' Datapalooza, the Attorney General Alliance, Dublin Tech Summit, Global Data Transparency Lab, Information Accountability Foundation Digital University for Regulator Series, and Ibero-American Data Protection Network. Sheila has presented key talks at global events for the Consumer Electronics' Show, Forrester, adExchanger, International Association of Privacy Professionals,

Healthcare Information and Management Systems Society, Digital Advertising Alliance, American Bar Association and the Marketing Sciences Institute.

Sheila serves on the advisory board of the Information Accountability Foundation (IAF) and is corporate liaison to several industry standards-setting groups.

Testimony of Witness

1. Introduction of IPG

Kinesso, Acxiom and Matterkind, and our parent company, IPG, provide marketing services for many of the largest brands in the world. We believe that marketing done ethically, fairly and subject to accountability connects people to brand value, creates community, democratizes knowledge and access, and is a vital economic engine. This guardianship requires that marketing be done in a transparent, accountable, and trustworthy manner.

Taking a proactive approach to the ethical use of data is at the core of how we deliver products and services to our clients. We start with the application of the design principles of security, privacy, and ethical data use in the planning, engineering and deployment of our marketing products and services. This is our North Star, and our approach includes processes that facilitate security, compliance with data protection and privacy requirements, accountability, and the trusted use of data. We continuously seek ways to advance thought and practice leadership within the marketing and advertising industry.

2. The U.S. Economy Depends on Data for Innovation and Growth

a. Consumer Data and Technology Fosters Innovation, Transformation, and Growth

First and foremost, consumer data and technology are fundamental to the global economy. The United States is home to many of the most innovative data-driven and technology-enabled companies in the world. The U.S. is also home to large online ecommerce and social media platforms that combine the benefits of consumer data and technology, thereby changing the competitive landscape for publishers, advertisers and independent data providers. As data has become ever more central to the modern economy, multiple states in the US have adopted, or are considering, privacy laws that will significantly impact today's data-driven, competitive dynamics in ways that are both intended and unanticipated.

Rather than restricting consumer data usage in a manner that stifles innovation and picks economic winners and losers, we support national competition and data privacy laws that (i) enable fair and open use of data, (ii) require accountability of companies that collect, process, share and use data, and (iii) ensure robust protection for individuals and their data. It is vitally important for America to have national competition and data privacy laws that are well-balanced, future-fit, good for people, good for our economy, and good for America's globally competitive position. We cannot burden shift accountability to people, stifle innovation, or write laws that prevent fair, responsible, and accountable uses of data in critical ways that benefit American consumers and businesses alike.

For at least the past two decades, data driven companies in the U.S. have generated tremendous innovation, benefits for people, and benefits for our economy. Technological advances have improved Americans' lives, enabled consumers to perform more of their daily activities online, and created more access for people to products, goods, services, and knowledge. The connected marketplace and economy became even more vital to American people during the COVID-19 crisis. This shift from brick and mortar to connected commerce was enabled by data, and as a part of this acceleration, generated increasing amounts of data. Given the breadth and depth of the connected ecosystem, it is fair to say that the health of the data ecosystem, and fair competition within that ecosystem, are critical to maintaining the economic leadership position of the United States.

Just a few examples of the dynamic innovation and competition in the digital ecosystem include:

- Connected Advertising: Innovation requires companies to try new things. Independent data providers and technology companies pioneered Internet advertising as we know it today. They invented real time online ad space auctions and developed the technology, standards, and protocols on which those auctions run today, powering much of the consumer-driven internet. This is now estimated by Statista to be a $378 billion market and projected to reach $646 billion by 2024, shaped and led by U.S.-headquartered companies. This advertising market is also the engine that enables the distribution of much of the valuable content online, which has put more information in the hands of more people than ever before. Connected advertising and independent data enables small businesses to compete in the connected marketplace and enables new market entrants to find audiences for their products and services.

- E-Commerce and Digital Payments: Fraud-detection and identity-verification tools, which enable online commerce, rely on robust and accurate data to protect businesses and consumers. These tools enable consumers to safely conduct transactions and make payments whenever, wherever, and however they want, with confidence that their identity and wealth will not be commandeered by online fraudsters. At the same time, companies that sell their goods online and companies that manage online payments must be able to detect fraud and confirm the identity of the consumers with whom they are doing business. The combination of technology and the free flow of consumer data across the internet are critical tools both for online commerce and payments and for companies providing those goods and services.
- Personalized Marketing: U.S. companies developed the all-in-one solutions that enable speakers and organizations to communicate directly with consumers via email, text, and other digital channels. The defaults on how information about people is used must be set at "benefits on" rather than "benefits off," while also enabling consumers robust rights to transparency, choice, and other important controls over their data. Laws and regulations should support, rather than stifle or block the fair, open and accountable flow of information, payments and commerce, across the internet.

The combination of technology and consumer data allowed publishers to benefit from their own content, advertisers to benefit from tailored ad placement and campaign measurement, and consumers to benefit from the new products and services whose emergence and growth was accelerated through more personally relevant advertising and messaging. As the market evolved though, online ecommerce and social media platforms have become increasingly dominant in the technology aspects, audience aspects, and control of the online advertising marketplace that enables the connected marketplace. The size, volume and control of consumer data generated within their platforms may create natural limits on the ability of third parties to curate audiences, serve their own customers, and compete in and benefit from that marketplace.

b. Independent Data Providers Play a Key Role

Independent data providers play a key role in maintaining the competitive, vibrant, and innovative technology and data ecosystem the U.S. now enjoys. They collect consumer data from a variety of sources and make it available to other companies, subject to contractual protections, for responsible uses. This facilitates commerce and innovation that drives value for citizens and companies alike.

A good example of the power of combining consumer data and technology is customer relationship management (CRM) systems, which are virtually ubiquitous in corporate America. These systems allow companies to know who their customers are and manage customer needs and preferences on an individualized basis. Similar systems have been developed in other arenas (such as HR and marketing) to identify and communicate with individuals (who may be employees or prospects), manage their preferences and satisfy their requirements. Without accurate, robust and curated consumer data though, these technologies are unable to identify relevant individual citizens, develop appropriate communications for a particular citizen, and measure the effectiveness of those communications, while at the same time implementing the citizen's privacy, communications and data preferences.

3. Privacy Laws Should Be Drafted to Enhance the Flow of Responsibly Sourced Data Which Fosters Innovation and Competition

Regulatory approaches to privacy thus far have not considered the potential impacts of data use restrictions on competition. Instead, U.S. and EU privacy laws have taken a "pure privacy" approach, with the apparently singular goal of further restricting use of consumer data. Responsible data collection and use is critical for citizens. Such principles must be implemented in a manner that promotes innovation and competition. This is best explored by considering (a) why data is important for competitive markets, (b) the (perhaps unintended) anti-competitive consequences of laws that focus myopically on data use restrictions, and (c) U.S. merger policy that impacts data-driven markets.

a. Data Sharing is Key for Competition because Data is " Non-Rivalrous"

Data sharing is particularly important at the intersection between privacy and competition. Data is what economists call a "non-rivalrous good." Company A and Company B can use the same data set at the same time. It is fundamentally different than a physical asset, such as a pair of shoes – if one person is wearing the shoes, no one else can wear them.

The ability to share data, rather than limiting its use to only one entity, thus simultaneously supports both innovation and competition. Independent data providers, for instance, can provide accurate, lawfully gathered and maintained consumer data to multiple companies, for responsible, fair, and legitimate uses. Multiple companies, for instance, can draw on a consumer data set to reduce fraud, and use that same data to advertise useful products and services, resulting in better service to people, and better economic and communications results. Those companies then compete against one another, but only to the extent they each have sufficient access to consumer data with which to do so.

When dominant players are able to maintain exclusive control over vast amounts of consumer data, it tends to enhance their market power and create barriers to entry. Exclusive control over data can provide an incumbent with critical economies of scale and scope, allowing them to raise product quality and attract consumers at lower cost than competitors. In contrast, lack of access to that data constitutes a barrier to entry, expansion and innovation by smaller competitors. As the influential Stigler Committee on Digital Platforms observed in 2019, exclusive control over data tends to make the strong stronger and the weak weaker.[1]

Rules that unreasonably restrict the use or sharing of consumer data can exacerbate these concerns by transforming data into a rivalrous good. The General Data Protection Regulation adopted by the EU in 2018 (commonly known as the GDPR) gives preferential treatment to "first parties" – a company that collects consumer data directly from a consumer. The GDPR sets strict limits on beneficial consumer data uses by "third parties," such as companies that rely on consumer data they receive from independent data

---

[1] STIGLER COMM. ON DIGITAL PLATFORMS, FINAL REPORT at 40 (2019), available at https://research.chicagobooth.edu/-/media/research/stigler/pdfs/digital-platforms---committee-report--- stigler%20center.pdf ("Barriers to equivalent data resources, a side effect of not having the history, scale, or scope of the incumbent, can inhibit entry, expansion, and innovation. The same effects that drive the quality of digital services higher as more users join—a positive feedback loop—makes the strong stronger and the weak weaker.").

providers. The GDPR rules give the first parties control of consumer data. These are often larger and entrenched competitors who are given a major competitive advantage over third parties who may be smaller or nascent competitors. Under this regulatory approach, a company's position in the data ecosystem can perhaps outweigh its ability to innovate and provide better products and service.

b. The GDPR Experience Shows the Potential Negative Effects of Privacy Laws on Competition

The evidence is now in. The GDPR has harmed competition in the name of privacy protection. While it has increased protections for personal data in the EU, it has simultaneously undermined competition, and this has entrenched the dominant players in many online markets.

According to multiple observers, the GDPR helped the largest platforms become more dominant, while making it more difficult for smaller companies and new market entrants to survive. The Wall Street Journal,[2] Politico,[3] and the New York Times[4] have all reported that the GDPR primarily benefitted Google and Facebook, while hurting smaller competitors in the online advertising industry. A survey conducted by Ghostery and Cliqz, two providers of cookie-related services, found widespread belief that "Google is the biggest beneficiary of the GDPR," while third parties, such as smaller and mid-sized online advertising companies, were the biggest losers.[5]

Academic experts Michal Gal and Oshrit Aviv have written the most comprehensive study of the effects of GDPR on competition. They wrote in 2020:

> The GDPR creates two main harmful effects on competition and innovation: it limits competition in markets, creating more concentrated

---

[2] Nick Kostov & Sam Schechner, *GDPR Has Been a Boon for Google and Facebook*, WALL ST. J. (June 17, 2019), available at https://www.wsj.com/articles/gdpr-has-been-a-boon-for-google-and-facebook-11560789219.

[3] Mark Scott et al., *Six Months in, Europe's Privacy Revolution favors Google, Facebook*, POLITICO.COM (Nov. 23, 2018), available at https://www.politico.eu/article/gdpr-facebook-google-privacy-data-6-months-in-europes-privacy-revolution-favors-google-facebook/.

[4] *How Facebook and Google Could Benefit from the G.D.P.R.*, NEW YORK TIMES (Apr. 23, 2018), available at https://www.nytimes.com/2018/04/23/technology/privacy-regulation-facebook-google.html.

[5] Björn Greif, *Study: Google is the Biggest Beneficiary of the* GDPR, CLIQZ.COM (Oct. 10, 2018), available at https://cliqz.com/en/magazine/study-google-is-the-biggest-beneficiary-of-the-gdpr.

> market structures and entrenching the market power of those who are already strong; and it limits sharing between different collectors, thereby preventing the realization of some synergies which may lead to better data-based knowledge.[6]

After studying the effects of GDPR, Professors Gal and Aviv report that these limits on competition help explain "troubling empirical evidence regarding investment in EU data-driven markets following the adoption of the GDPR," finding that the new law has had unintended effects on competition, efficiency, and innovation.

The findings of Professors Gal and Aviv are consistent with the analysis that consumer data is a non-rivalrous good. Their position is that the GDPR limits data sharing between data collectors, blocking the useful sharing of data. They further assert that the GDPR limits competition in data markets, because the law entrenches the first parties in their position of market dominance.

In short, if privacy laws focus myopically on restricting data collection and sharing, while ignoring the potential effects on competition, they are likely to harm the very citizens they set out to protect by entrenching dominant players and undermining competition and innovation. Congress should consider privacy laws that permit beneficial forms of data sharing while (a) increasing transparency, (b) regulating sensitive or harmful uses of consumer data, and (c) imposing accountability on companies that collect, hold, and transfer data.

c. Mergers Can have Anticompetitive Effects in Data-Driven Markets

Mergers have been a key part of the strategy for many of the largest companies in the U.S., including the largest digital platforms, to achieve their current market position. For years, it appeared that regulators did not perceive that these acquisitions posed a threat to competition or innovation.

For example, in 2007, Google received antitrust clearance to purchase DoubleClick, then the market leader in display ads on the internet. Later, Facebook was permitted to purchase Instagram, before the latter could become a competitor at scale in the social media space.

There are, however, signs of change. Late last year, for example, the Federal Trade Commission (FTC) brought suit against Facebook, alleging that it maintained its monopoly in personal social networking through a years-long course of anticompetitive conduct, including its acquisitions of WhatsApp and

---

[6] Michael Gal & Oshrit Aviv, *The Competitive Effects of the GDPR*, 16 J. OF COMPETITION L. & ECON. 349 (May 18, 2020), available at https://academic.oup.com/jcle/article-abstract/16/3/349/5837809?redirectedFrom=fulltext.

Instagram.[7] And just last week, the FTC took two steps that suggest a renewed commitment to aggressively scrutinizing acquisitions in data-driven markets. First, the FTC released a report in which it analyzed a decade's worth of acquisitions by large digital platforms that were too small or otherwise exempt from reporting requirements under the Hart-Scott-Rodino Act.[8] FTC Chair Lina Khan explained that in light of the report's findings, the FTC will closely examine reporting requirements to close reporting loopholes that she said may have allowed certain deals to "fly under the radar."[9] Second, the FTC voted to withdraw the Vertical Merger Guidelines just over a year after they were published. In doing so, the majority of the Commission promised to offer a new framework for vertical merger analysis that better takes into account the features specific to digital markets, including the potential for transactions to enable firms to exclude rivals by "degrading interoperability, reneging on access policies, or gaming algorithms."[10]

And, as this Committee knows, there are also a variety of legislative proposals before Congress that would make significant revisions to U.S. merger laws, including some that revise the standards for merger reviews or even bar some transactions altogether.[11]

---

[7] A timeline of the FTC's action against Facebook, including links to the FTC's complaints, can be found at https://www.ftc.gov/enforcement/cases-proceedings/191-0134/facebook-inc-ftc-v.

[8] *See* Fed. Trade Comm'n, *Non-HSR Reported Acquisitions by Select Technology Platforms, 2010-2019: An FTC Study* (Sept. 15, 2021), available at https://www.ftc.gov/system/files/documents/reports/non-hsr-reported-acquisitions-select-technology-platforms-2010-2019-ftc- study/p201201technologyplatformstudy2021.pdf.

[9] *See* Fed. Trade Comm'n, *Remarks of Chair Lina M. Khan Regarding Non-HSR Reported Acquisitions by Select Technology Platforms*, Comm'n File No. P201201 (Sept. 15, 2021), available at https://www.ftc.gov/system/files/documents/public_statements/1596332/remarks_of_chair_lina_m_khan_regarding_non-hsr_reported_acquisitions_by_select_technology_platforms.pdf.

[10] *See* Fed. Trade Comm'n, *Statement of Chair Lina N. Khan, Comm'r Rohit Chopra, and Comm'r Rebecca Kelly Slaughter on the Withdrawal of the Vertical Merger Guidelines*, Comm'n File No. P810034 at 7 (Sept. 15, 2021), available at https://www.ftc.gov/system/files/documents/public_statements/1596396/statement_of_chair_lina_m_khan_commissioner_rohit_chopra_and_commissioner_rebecca_kelly_slaugh ter_on.pdf.

[11] *See, e.g.*, the Competition and Antitrust Law Enforcement Reform Act of 2021, S. 224, 117th Cong. (2021), available at https://www.congress.gov/bill/117th-congress/senate-bill/225/text; and the Trust- Busting for the Twenty-First Century Act, S. 1074, 117th Cong. (2021), available at https://www.congress.gov/bill/117th-congress/senate-bill/1074. For a bill introduced in the House, *see* the Platform Competition and Opportunity Act, H.R. 3826, 117th Cong. (2021), available at https://www.congress.gov/bill/117th-congress/house-bill/3826/ (would prohibit dominant platforms from acquiring competitive threats or engaging in acquisitions that would "increase or enhance" the platform's market position).

Countries such as Germany have already amended their competition laws to provide more flexibility to address data-related issues. In Germany, Facebook was not subject to merger review when it purchased WhatsApp. Even though Facebook paid $19 billion to acquire WhatsApp, the merger controls did not apply because of the low amount of revenue WhatsApp generated at that time. Since then, Germany has implemented changes to permit regulatory scrutiny of acquisitions at lower revenue thresholds.

Given the importance of data to the economy and to consumers, we welcome efforts by enforcers and Congress to carefully consider appropriate steps to ensure that competition in data markets is unfettered and vibrant and that future acquisitions do not improperly stifle new entry and innovation.

4. How Privacy Legislation Can Foster Innovation and Competition

We encourage the Committee to consider privacy and competition not as separate bodies of law, but instead to be interrelated. Privacy laws materially impact markets, so they should be drafted to foster innovation and competition, not simply to increase data control and potential resulting concentration.[12] Antitrust laws impact citizen privacy, so they should be drafted to protect citizens and require responsible and accountable uses of their data. America should focus on constructing future-prepared laws that support a fair, competitive, healthy, trustworthy, connected economy.

a. Accountability-Based Frameworks Support Innovation and Growth

Our economy depends in key part on companies' ability to readily access and share consumer data. We thus encourage the Committee to consider legislative approaches that do not severely restrict companies from collecting, using, or sharing consumer data. The economy is too complex, and consumer data practices are too multilayered, for statutes to pinpoint who should hold consumer data and who should not. That approach potentially determines

[12] Of significant note, the United Kingdom announced earlier this month that it was beginning a consultation process that would build on principles within the GDPR in order to "support vibrant competition and innovation to drive economic growth" and "maintain high data protection standards without creating unnecessary barriers to responsible data use." *See* United Kingdom Department for Digital, Culture, Media, and Sport, *Data: A New Direction* (Sept. 10, 2021), available at https://assets.publishing.service.gov.uk/ government/uploads/ system/uploads/attachment_data/file/1016395/Data_Reform_Consultation_Document Accessible_.pdf.

which companies can compete, unfairly entrenching companies with more consumer data with a superior competitive position.

Instead, we encourage the Committee to consider a more balanced approach that focuses on imposing accountability on companies that use citizens' data. Accountability-based frameworks regulate sensitive or potentially harmful uses of consumer data, while permitting the pro-competitive data collection and sharing the U.S. economy needs for innovation and growth. For example:

- Accountability can require holders of citizens' data to build internal governance programs for protecting data, such as (a) implementing internal privacy policies and controls, (b) designating data privacy officer(s), and (c) documenting Privacy Impact Assessments before engaging in activities that present heightened risks to citizens. Governance requirements can be scaled so that larger data holders are expected to have more robust governance in place.
- These frameworks can also require companies to contractually bind service providers and third parties that receive consumer data to specified protective obligations.
- Emerging practices that carry risk for citizens – such as algorithm development – can be subject to additional assessment and reporting requirements.
- Companies that hold consumer data and are not immediately visible to consumers, such as independent data providers, can register with a regulator to enable consumers to know who they are.

Accountability-based frameworks can also be supplemented with transparency rules and individual control rights that consumers can exercise. These can include rights to access their consumer data, delete that data, or opt-out of specified types of data sharing.

b. Now is the Time to Act

In closing, the right view of the intersection of data and competition should lead to the right outcome for a national privacy law. Congress has a critical window to act on privacy legislation. In January 2023, California's Privacy Rights Act (CPRA) as well as the new Virginia privacy law will go into effect, followed by the new Colorado Privacy Act in July 2023.[13] We expect more state privacy laws to pass next year. These statutes will significantly limit how consumer data can be collected and shared, and will have practical effects across our national economy. In particular, CPRA will make consumer data sharing more difficult for online advertising. Consumers will have a right to opt-out of all "sharing" of their consumer data for common types of online advertising. Further, CPRA suggests that companies that provide online advertising services may not be able to use customer data to improve their advertising services for all their customers.

These rules are likely to have GDPR-like anticompetitive effects. Companies that have large quantities of citizen data may be by largely unaffected by CPRA, since they do not have to "share" consumer data with anyone but themselves. But for smaller competitors, which are critical to a robust marketplace and the development of future innovative solutions, access to essential consumer data may be cut off. This would require advertisers, publishers and others to work with fewer, more dominant players in order to communicate and interact with consumers, likely in a more expensive manner – which leaves small businesses fewer options on how to reach out to consumers. That is not an outcome that is pro-consumer.

5. Conclusion

Consumer data and technology are critical to the national and international economy. We support the adoption of a well-balanced federal privacy law and competition laws and policies that provide critical protections for individuals and their data, and enable the responsible flow of consumer data among all accountable companies, in order to preserve and enhance the connected marketplace.

---

[13] For the California Consumer Privacy Act and/or California Privacy Rights Act, see Cal. Civ. Code § 1798.100 et seq. For the Colorado Privacy Act, see Colo. Rev. Stat. § 6-1-1301 et seq. For the Virginia Consumer Data Protection Act, see Va. Code § 59.1-571 et seq.

Written Testimony of Markham Erickson Vice President of Government Affairs and Public Policy, Google

Senate Committee on the Judiciary Subcommittee on Competition Policy, Antitrust, and Consumer Rights

"Big Data, Big Questions: Implications for Competition and Consumers" September 21, 2021

Chairwoman Klobuchar, Ranking Member Lee, and distinguished members of the Subcommittee:

Thank you for the oppotunity to appear before you today. My name is Markham Erickson. I am a Vice President of Government Affairs and Public Policy at Google. I have worked at the intersection of technology and policy for over 25 years, primarily in private practice where I had the oppotunity to work on issues that defined the evolution of the modern Internet. In my role at Google, I oversee a global team of subject matter expets focused on the application of law and policy to technology and the internet, including on issues related to data governance and competition.

We appreciate the topic of this hearing on the implications of data for competition and consumers. Data should be used to make consumers' lives better by improving the quality and diversity of products and services available,[14] while protecting users' privacy and giving them control over their data. In this testimony, I will describe (1) how Google uses and protects data; (2) how data mobility empowers consumers and boosts competition, including data potability and advancing open data; and (3) that data alone does not guarantee better products for consumers.

---

[14] For example: Doctors can use data to improve patient outcomes, scientists rely on data to better predict weather, and governments rely on data to monitor things like the impact of the COVID-19 pandemic. And brick and mortar retail businesses reduce costs and connect with and help consumers through the innovative use of data.

How We Use and Protect Data

Data plays an impotant role in making the Google products and services people use everyday functional and helpful. We are committed to treating that data responsibly and protecting privacy with strict protocols and innovative privacy technologies.

Google combines insights from data with industry-leading technology to develop products that help people find directions, grow their businesses, or search for information. Google provides information about the personal data we collect and how we use it—such as to provide better services—to our users and the public. We provide notice not just through our privacy policy,[15] but also through our work to actively inform individuals about data use in the context of the services themselves, helping to make the information relevant and actionable. On an individual level, what data is collected and how it is used depends on how each person uses our services and how they manage their privacy controls.

Data is one element of our advetising business, where it helps us connect people with relevant advetisements. Advetising is Google's main source of revenue, and enables us to make many of our flagship products, including Search and Maps, available for free to billions of people around the world.[16] Google's advetising platforms suppot businesses of all types and sizes by helping them reach customers. To give an example of what this means for small businesses, the owner of a local flower store, Studley Flowers in Rochester, New Hampshire said, "Google Ads has provided us with a cost-effective way to compete with the national flower delivery brands and their larger ad budgets. Additionally, it provides us with a way to make sure that when locals search for flowers, we stay top of mind against those larger brands. Our investment in Google tools has cetainly paid off, and we're excited to see what's next."[17]

Google also helps millions of website publishers earn advetising revenue on their sites and apps. The ads shown are informed by a search query or page content, but can also be based on a user's interests or other personal data if their privacy settings permit.[18] We do not sell our users personal information to advetisers, or to anyone else.

---

[15] https://policies.google.com/privacy?hl=en-US.

[16] https://about.google/intl/en_US/how-our-business-works/.

[17] https://partnertestimonials.withgoogle.com/?_ga=2.19953275.2136290102.1632085855-932915823.1630594247#q[15].

[18] https://howwemakemoney.withgoogle.com/.

Our business relies on ensuring our users' trust, specifically in how we use and protect their data. We do this in pat by offering industry-leading controls to manage privacy and empowering users to adjust what data is stored in their Google Account. Three billion users visit their Google accounts every year, where they can review and change their privacy settings and delete data stored in their account. For example, Google users can always turn off personalized ads[19] in their Account Settings[20] while still using Google products for free. And since 2019,[21] we have offered industry-leading auto-delete features that give our users the option to automatically delete data from their account, like their Search History. Stating in 2020,[22] new accounts auto-delete some account data by default after 18 months. We regularly prompt our users to review and manage their privacy and security settings with emails and promotions on the Google homepage.

We also invest in research and development of cutting-edge privacy and security engineering techniques that are applied in our products. We share a range of these innovative tools in open source formats, which are free for anyone—including competing companies—to use, benefitting the broader ecosystem. For example, Google's differential privacy library has been used by hundreds of developers around the globe to gain insight from data while protecting individual privacy.[23]

In addition to putting users in control, we keep their data secure by default. Every day, we block 100 million phishing attempts and 15 billion spam messages in Gmail and encrypt four billion photos.[24] Our free Safe Browsing[25] tool helps keep the rest of the Internet secure, automatically protecting more than four billion devices every day by showing warnings to users when they attempt to navigate to dangerous sites or download dangerous files.

We constantly innovate to improve privacy across our own products and on our platforms. This sometimes means finding ways to reduce the amount of personal information needed to achieve similar outcomes. For example, we recently announced Privacy Sandbox, a collaborative initiative that aims to help build a more private and secure web. Through the Sandbox initiative, we are working with the ads industry to develop new digital advetising tools that protect people's privacy and prevent covet tracking, while continuing to

---

[19] https://support.google.com/accounts/answer/465?hl=en&co=GENIE.Platform%3DDesktop.
[20] https://support.google.com/ads/answer/2662856?
[21] https://blog.google/technology/safety-security/automatically-delete-data/.
[22] https://blog.google/technology/safety-security/keeping-private-information-private/.
[23] https://developers.googleblog.com/2019/09/enabling-developers-and-organizations.html.
[24] https://blog.google/technology/safety-security/our-work-keep-you-safe/.
[25] https://safebrowsing.google.com/.

suppot an open and free Internet enabled by advetising. From the stat of this project, we developed these tools in an open manner, and sought feedback from industry patners, civil society, and governments. Because many publishers and advetisers rely on online advetising to fund their websites to connect with customers, getting this balance right is key to keeping the web open and accessible to everyone. We are proud of our work to apply innovative solutions that balance these interests.

Data Mobility Empowers Consumers and Boosts Competition

There are considerable options to use available data safely, including tools and resources from Google. Data can be transferred safely in two ways: personal information can be moved from one service to another based on a specific individual's instruction, and datasets can be shared safely as open data using appropriate privacy technologies.

Data Potability

Google has been a leader on data potability for over a decade, enabling our users to expot their data and take it to another platform. Google's approach to data potability is simple: the user comes first.[26] Data potability empowers consumers to choose services or online platforms based on quality and individual preference—not because they are locked in or because they can not move their data to alternatives.

Since 2011, Google Takeout[27] has allowed users to expot their data from over 70 Google products and download them in machine-readable formats so that they can be easily uploaded to another service. Takeout makes it possible for users to move their content to competing services,[28] so no one feels they have to continue using Google if they prefer a service of another company. Since our launch of Takeout, users have expoted more than one billion gigabytes from Google products.[29]

---

[26] https://publicpolicy.googleblog.com/2009/09/introducing-dataliberationorg-liberate.html.
[27] https://takeout.google.com/u/0/settings/takeout.
[28] https://support.google.com/accounts/answer/3024190?hl=en.
[29] https://www.regulations.gov/document?D=FTC-2020-0062-0011.

Additionally, through our leadership in the Data Transfer Project,[30] Google makes it easier for companies of all sizes to provide tools that let users move data between online services. The Data Transfer Project, a patnership among Google, Apple, Facebook, Twitter, Microsoft, and Smugmug, suppots the direct transfer of data between providers, allowing consumers to seamlessly and securely transfer their data directly from one provider to another, rather than downloading and re-uploading their content. The code available through the Data Transfer Project reduces the engineering work any individual company has to do to offer potability to their users.[31]

Data potability benefits both consumers and competition. Giving users control over their data through easy-to-use data expot tools boosts competition by reducing the burden of switching services. It paves the way for innovative and new oppotunities for service providers of all sizes, and empowers people to try new services and choose the offering that best suits their needs.

Advancing Open data and AI for All

Atificial intelligence (AI) is a transformative technology, and we are committed to making it accessible to more people and institutions. Google is a leader in releasing public data and tools that suppot advanced technological applications like machine learning (ML) and AI.

Many of the largest successes in machine learning have come from data that is openly available on the web. Google has released over 80 labeled datasets for ML researchers and developers to use.[32] For example, we open sourced the Open Images dataset to provide developers with geographically diverse images to suppot more inclusive results for underrepresented cultures in ML models. And through TensorFlow—an ecosystem of tools, programming libraries, and community resources—we are enabling developers from statups, large companies, and nonprofits to more easily use ML to build a variety of applications, from fraud detection in digital payments to online English grammar correction.[33] TensorFlow has more than 200,000 users and over 160 million downloads, and suppots over $15 billion in economic impact in industries including computer manufacturing and software publishing.

---

[30] https://datatransferproject.dev/.
[31] https://www.regulations.gov/document?D=FTC-2020-0062-0010.
[32] https://ai.google/tools/datasets/.
[33] https://www.tensorflow.org/.

In some cases, data that is already publicly available is hard to use because it is hard to find. Google has developed cutting edge tools to address this issue.[34] For example, Google pays for storage of, and provides public access to, public data available through Google Cloud Public Dataset Program.[35] Kaggle makes data science easier by providing all the code needed to leverage over 80,000 public datasets.[36] We also launched a search engine for datasets called Dataset Search.[37] Using a simple keywordsearch, users can discover datasets hosted in thousands of repositories across the Web.[38]

Google also makes insights from our data publicly available in privacy-safe formats, contributing to impotant research around the world. For example, Google Trends[39] was launched in 2006 and provides access to a largely unfiltered sample of actual search requests made to Google. It is anonymized (no one is personally identified), categorized (determining the topic for a search query), and aggregated (grouped together). Google Trends is a poweful tool for researchers, journalists, and civil society. There are more than 21,000 research papers on Google Scholar that cite Trends as a data source.[40]

During COVID-19, we have leveraged our expetise in open data and privacy to suppot governments, health officials, researchers, nonprofits, and others to understand the changing conditions around the pandemic. For example, Google provides a public repository of open-source data related to the global response to the novel coronavirus.[41] This includes epidemiology and health datasets, as well as data on government responses. We also share a privacy-safe version of Google's own mobility data. Google launched the COVID-19 Community Mobility Repots[42] in April of 2020.[43] These repots provide aggregated, anonymized mobility data. They use differential privacy to protect our user data, adding atificial noise to our datasets and enabling high

---

[34] https://www.blog.google/technology/ai/sharing-open-data/.

[35] https://cloud.google.com/solutions/datasets.

[36] https://www.kaggle.com/datasets.

[37] https://datasetsearch.research.google.com/help.

[38] With this data, computer vision researchers can train image recognition systems. Waze for cities (https://www.waze.com/en-GB/wazeforcities) datasets are to inform mobility projects and policies, from congestion to event-specific traffic controls. Alphabet's Waymo Open Dataset (https://waymo.com/open/about/) contains high resolution sensor data collected by Waymo self-driving cars to aid the research community in making advancements in machine perception and self-driving technology.

[39] https://trends.google.com/trends/.

[40] https://scholar.google.com/scholar?hl=en&as_sdt=0%2C5&q=%22google+trends%22&btnG=.

[41] https://cloud.google.com/blog/products/data-analytics/publicly-available-covid-19-data-for-analytics.

[42] https://www.google.com/covid19/mobility/.

[43] https://blog.google/technology/health/covid-19-community-mobility-reports/

quality results without identifying any individual person.[44] The repots have helped governments around the world understand how social distancing measures are influencing outcomes.

Companies of all sizes utilize code, tools, and knowledge sharing in open source platforms to suppot their product development. Google is one of the largest contributors to open source code to GitHub, a popular repository for software development tools.[45] In 2020, Googlers made more than 240,000 contributions to tens of thousands of projects on GitHub.[46] Google's open source work includes AI building blocks, data processing tools to process data including TensorFlow Privacy,[47] and models for language understanding and computer vision. All of these contributions make it easier for new and existing companies to develop and bring new products to consumers.

Data Alone Does Not Guarantee Better Products for Consumers

Consumers have many choices over where they share their data—and they can and do choose to share the same data with multiple providers. In our experience, data by itself does not guarantee better or more successful products. It is the investment, innovation, and method that matters most.

Cutting edge technology or new ideas allows new companies to succeed, sometimes without any data at all. New entrants such as Zoom, Snapchat, Spotify, or Pinterest have been successful because they provide an innovative product, not because they have access to data from established companies.

Conversely, having more data does not itself guarantee success. Many businesses have had access to data but have had products that struggled to succeed.

Drawing insights from raw or aggregated data, including publicly available data, is where a company can add paticular value to consumers and businesses. The process of using information and feedback to improve products and services is not unique to Google or the online world—it takes place across all sectors of our economy, where data helps firms improve and innovate and better serve consumers. It is what a company makes of the data,

---

44 https://support.google.com/covid19-mobility/answer/9825414?hl=en&ref_topic=9822927.

45 https://github.com/google.

46 https://opensource.googleblog.com/2021/08/metrics-spikes-and-uncertainty-open-source-contribution-duri ng-a-global-pandemic.html.

47 https://blog.tensorflow.org/2019/03/introducing-tensorflow-privacy-learning.html.

not how much data they have or use that determines their ability to innovate and succeed, and better serve their customers.

For example, data is just one component of what makes Google Search a useful product for users and businesses. To deliver Search results, Google's systems sot through hundreds of billions of webpages in our Search index to find the most relevant and useful results for our users. The publicly available web is an impotant data set to make that happen and we also have invested in indexing a wide range of information from images, books, research papers, and much more to help our users understand the world's information.[48]

We know we need to keep innovating to find new ways for Search to deliver more useful information faster and more conveniently to consumers. In 2020, we ran over 600,000 experiments that resulted in more than 4,500 improvements to Search.[49] Improving our product involves steps as seemingly simple as a synonym system that allows us to find relevant documents even if they do not contain the exact words a user typed. For example, a user may search for "change laptop brightness" but the manufacturer has written "adjust laptop brightness." Our systems understand the words are related and are able to connect users with the right content. This system took over five years to develop and significantly improves results in over 30% of searches across languages.[50]

Our focus on continually improving our products means that our greatest source of innovation comes from extensive research and development (R&D). Last year alone we spent $27.6 billion on R&D, nearly ten times what we spent in 2009.

Advancements in AI and machine learning increasingly suppot ways to minimize the use of data while continuing to deliver and improve helpful products people rely on every day. For example, Google has been a leader in federated learning, a machine learning approach that learns from a user's interaction with a given device while keeping all the training data on the device, so that the data does not need to be shared with a server.[51] More recently, Google published research on Entities as Expets AI,[52] that answers text-based questions with less data.

---

[48] https://www.google.com/search/howsearchworks/how-search-works/organizing-information/

[49] https://www.google.com/search/howsearchworks/how-search-works/rigorous-testing/

[50] https://www.google.com/search/howsearchworks/how-search-works/ranking-results/.

[51] https://ai.googleblog.com/2017/04/federated-learning-collaborative.html.

[52] https://venturebeat.com/2020/04/20/googles-entities-as-experts-ai-answers-text-based-questi ons-with-les s-data/.

Conclusion

We appreciate the oppotunity to share our views on the implications of data for consumers and competition.

We recognize policymakers and regulators are working to protect privacy while also considering arguments by those who contend that making more data available among competitors would increase competition. These complex discussions involve defining the types of data at issue, as well as identifying the types of services that use data, and the data necessary to make those services useful. We are encouraged to see some privacy and competition regulators conferring more formally to contribute their relevant expetise to the impotant questions being considered, for example when a privacy practice is being evaluated in an antitrust context. We will continue to engage with policymakers and regulators, as well as other stakeholders, to suppot thoughtful regulation that encourages innovation and protects consumers. For example, we have long suppoted federal privacy legislation in the U.S.[53]

We are committed to protecting data through privacy, security, and user control, and to continuing to improve our products in a way that ensures more choice and competition. We look forward to engaging with this Committee on these impotant issues.

Thank you for the oppotunity to discuss our work today.

John Robb

Making Big Data Work for Us

Global Guerrilla Special-Report

Senate Testimony September 2021

[53] https://blog.google/competition/#facts.

Big Data has become central to economic and social progress in the 21st Century.

Depending on what we do right now, Big Data and what it makes possible will be either a boon or a bane. Here's how to make it work for us, rather than against us.

Big Data is Essential

How we handle Big Data and what we build with it will determine how successful we are in the 21st Century.

- It is already immensely valuable, as evidenced by the valuations of the world'sbiggest tech companies. It will only become more so as corporations use it to train economy and society scale AI's.[54]
- Every product and service sold will eventually utilize this data *and* these AIs. Ifwe successfully harness the development of Big Data, it will drive economic prosperity and societal well-being well for decades to come.
- There are three major socioeconomic approaches to Big Data: China's centrally managed approach (sacrifice freedom for economic prosperity), Europe's opt-outprivacy approach (sacrifice economic prosperity for traditional social stability), and the corporate-led approach used by the US and most of the world (this path is up to us).

Data Ownership

If Big Data is valuable, how do we make it work for us? We start with a critical early reform: data ownership.

- The closest model for our current system is feudalism. Lords/ corporations own all of the data to build AIs of immense value.

[54] The AIs that are currently being developed aren't the human equivalent AIs of science fiction. They are closer to symbionts that live in the space between us, feeding off of the data we produce and providing services to us in return. It's useful to think of these AIs as an intelligent interface layer between us as individuals and everything else: other people, technological artifacts, our work, and the external world (increasingly as AR emerges).

Corporations farm us for our data both as private citizens and while at work.

- To cast off this feudal system, we should apply the same solution that worked in the past: ownership. In the past, that meant giving people the right to own land and exercise rights over its use. In our current situation, that means giving people the right to their data and exercise rights over its use.
- Data ownership works, in practice, by allowing people to aggregate their data safely, pool it with other people's data to increase its value radically, and generate benefits (royalties, services, etc.) by licensing its use by third parties.

Digital Rights

With Big Data, we run the risk of a long night of data-fueled oppression. Here's how to avoid that future.

- Big Data and the AIs derived from it are already being used to monitor and control societal discourse (and increasingly behaviors) in real-time, down to the conversational level. Worse, these big systems can punish infractions with bans that disconnect people from the myriad of online services that are now essential to modern life (think: disconnection as an open-air gulag).
- To avoid Big Data becoming a means of ubiquitous oppression, as we see elsewhere, we need digital rights. These rights would enumerate our freedoms. Of speech: what can't we say online in public or in private? Of association: when can you be banned, and when would algorithmic soft bans be permissible (you can publish, but nobody can see it)? Of resolution: requirements for the rapid notification of actions taken and the resolution of disputes.
- Big Data can create barriers to small business success. Small businesses suffer from the same problems as individuals -- from barriers to access (only the company store allows access, and it's terribly expensive) to data loss (the big data incumbents capture customer data to product mix data to customer service data and use it against the business). Therefore, we can adapt many of the remedies needed to protect individuals, to protect small businesses.

Digital Identity

To tie this all together, we need a new form of digital identity.

- Digital identity is in addition to anonymity and not a replacement for it. Digital identity will serve as a way to dampen the disruption we currently see online.
- Digital identity will serve as a means of exercising ownership rights over data (from claiming ownership to licensing it to collecting benefits).
- Digital identity will allow us to exercise our freedoms -- from rights of speech to rights of association to rights of speedy resolution of disputes.

The Global Guerrillas Report is a reader-supported research service that covers the intersection of warfare, technology, and politics. It is available for a modest pledge of support on Patreon: https://www.patreon.com/johnrobb

Hearing Before the United States Senate Committee on the Judiciary, Subcommittee on Competition Policy, Antitrust, and Consumer Rights
September 21, 2021

Testimony of Steve Satterfield
Vice President, Privacy and Public Policy
Facebook, Inc.

I. Introduction

Chairwoman Klobuchar, Ranking Member Lee, and members of the Subcommittee: good afternoon and thank you for the opportunity to be here today. My name is Steve Satterfield, and I am Vice President of Privacy and Public Policy at Facebook. I have been with the company for seven years. In my current role, I focus on developing and sharing Facebook's perspectives on data regulation globally.

I appreciate the Subcommittee's interest in the topics of today's hearing and the work that you all do to ensure the competitiveness of American markets. I believe Facebook has an important perspective on these issues, given the substantial contributions we have made to the technology sector in the nearly twenty years since our founding.

I also welcome the chance to engage on the topics of data and privacy. We believe that many of the concerns expressed by Congress and other stakeholders with respect to privacy issues can be addressed by appropriate legislation, and we stand ready to be a productive partner in those efforts. As we have said for some time now, we support updated rules of the road for the internet and privacy regulations that will set more consistent data protection standards that work for everyone.

Facebook provides many ways to communicate, discover, share, and connect with people, businesses, news, and entertainment. We also help millions of businesses reach and engage with their customers. To earn people's time and attention, we compete fiercely with many other services across the world.

Facebook respects the role of Congress in shaping our nation's competition policy and wants to be helpful where we can. We strongly believe that we are a force for good in the world, and I look forward to discussing our products with you. The reality, however, is that our company is currently facing multiple lawsuits, including those brought by the Federal Trade Commission and a number of state attorneys general, that limit what I will be able to address today. As we informed the Subcommittee well in advance of the hearing, the litigation process will necessarily limit the extent of my testimony. Nevertheless, we appreciate the invitation to participate in today's hearing, and I am glad to be able to share what I can.

II. Facebook Uses Data Responsibly

Like many services, Facebook helps people share, connect, communicate, or find interesting content. Each day, Americans use Facebook to connect with people, businesses, and other entities; share and view content, including videos, photos, livestreams, posts, and messages; read the news; join communities of interest; and set up fundraisers for good causes, among many other things. All of these activities support our mission to give people the power to build community and bring the world closer together, and data helps make all of them possible. We believe that our products are most useful when people can connect with what they care most about. People around the world choose to use our products not because they have to, but because they want to—because our products make their lives better.

At Facebook, we use data responsibly to provide personalized experiences. We also use information to, among other things, improve our products; provide measurement, analytics, and other business services; promote safety, integrity, and security; communicate with people who use our services; and innovate for social good, including by connecting and lifting up marginalized communities and addressing humanitarian crises. For example, Facebook's innovative use of data helps people to understand what is needed in the first hours of a disaster or the public conversation around a health crisis, information that is crucial to decision-making but previously was either unavailable or too expensive to collect in a timely manner.

Data also helps us show people better and more relevant ads, which keeps Facebook free. And it lets advertisers reach the right people, benefiting more than 10 million businesses and non-profits that use Facebook every day to advertise to those that might be interested in their product or cause. Our advertising platform can accommodate almost every budget, and we help advertisers reach their target audience and maximize their impact. Our advertising services have enabled numerous businesses to grow, create jobs, and more effectively compete, leading to more choice and better products for consumers.

We take very seriously our responsibility to protect the data people entrust us with. We also seek to ensure that the machine learning we use in processing people's data is applied in a responsible manner. We invest billions of dollars each year in people and technology to keep our platform safe, including protecting people's data. We work around the clock to help protect people's accounts, and we build security into Facebook products.

We further offer a number of tools that provide people transparency and control over the data we receive. Our approach is based on the belief that people should be able to control who can see what they share and how their data shapes their experience on Facebook. People can control the audience for their posts and manage how apps receive their data. They can choose people, Pages, Groups, and Events to connect to. They can provide feedback on posts they see on Facebook—feedback, for example, that they want to see less of a particular kind of post or fewer posts from a particular person or Page. They also have options to remove content they share from Facebook.

We have steadily made improvements to the privacy protections and controls we offer, and we continue to invest in building new privacy technology. Our goal is to be clear about how our apps work and give people control over their experience, so we've worked with policymakers, regulators, academics, civil society, businesses, and other stakeholders over the years to build tools that show people how their information is used and let them manage it. For example, people can tap Why Am I Seeing This Ad? on ads in News Feed to get more information and control over what they see going forward. This tool shows people reasons why they're seeing a certain ad, whether it's based on interests that matched them with the ad or actions they took on the business' website; and, where possible, people can see how that information was gathered. From there, people also have easy access to controls, like Ad Preferences, which lets them manage the ads they see, learn more about how ads work, and hide ads from specific advertisers or topics. And our controls aren't just for ads. We also offer tools like Manage Activity and Privacy Checkup so people can easily customize their overall experience on Facebook based on what's right for them. Millions of people use our Privacy Checkup tool each month.

We also offer a variety of tools to help users understand the data Facebook has about them. This includes the Access Your Information tool, which allows users to see information such as their recent activity, security and recent login information, advertisers they've interacted with, and more. And to provide more transparency and control around these practices, we have rolled out a way for people to manage their off-Facebook activity. Off-Facebook Activity lets people see a summary of apps and websites that send us information about their activity and allows them to disconnect this information from their account if they want.

At Facebook, we believe that if people share data with one service, they should be able to move it to another. Making it easy to move data to new services unlocks exciting opportunities. This is why we offer the Download Your Information tool, enabling people to download a copy of the information they share on Facebook in a format that is easy to view, or a machine readable format, which could allow another service to import it. Additionally, we participate in the Data Transfer Project, a collaborative effort with Apple, Google, Microsoft, SmugMug, and Twitter to build a common way for people to transfer this data between online services. The goal of this project has been to make it easier for users of services of any size to securely and directly transfer data from one service to another. Building on the Data Transfer Project's open-source framework, in 2020, we launched the Transfer Your

Information tool. We continue to build out the capabilities of this tool, and today it enables users to directly transfer their Facebook photos, videos, posts, notes, and events to a variety of relevant destinations that include WordPress, Blogger, Google Docs, Google Photos, Google Calendar, BackBlaze, Dropbox, Photobucket, and Koofr. We want to build practical portability solutions that can enhance participation across the digital ecosystem, and we continue to invest in adding new capabilities to strengthen our data portability offerings.

Of course, there are always risks when people transfer data online. Congress should set out clear rules on data portability so that we can continue to scale the tools we've built to better enable people to safely and securely move their data between services. Along the same lines, Congress could also create rules to govern how platforms should use, analyze, and share data for the public good.

We store the information that we receive in multiple data centers throughout the country and the world, and we strive to make these facilities climate-friendly. In fact, in 2011, Facebook was one of the first companies to commit to supporting its facilities with 100% renewable energy. Today, the company's U.S. data center fleet is supported by 100% renewable energy, and Facebook is on track to maintain this commitment for future data center developments and expansions.

Finally, it is important to note that our data analysis facilitates cooperation with law enforcement as they seek to protect us all. We have a long history of working successfully with the Department of Justice, the FBI, state and local law enforcement, and other government agencies around the world to address a wide variety of threats to our platform. We reach out to law enforcement when we see a credible threat of imminent harm. We contact federal, state, or local law enforcement depending on the specific circumstances of a threat. We also have robust processes in place to handle government requests we receive, and we disclose data in accordance with our terms of service and applicable law.

III. Facebook Innovates Constantly

We work constantly to improve our services and products, including by introducing fresh features and developing new ways for people and businesses to connect. Data is part of that effort.

When Facebook was first created, the site consisted primarily of text details about each user. Today, we offer a much wider variety of capabilities through the Facebook family of products and services. Facebook users can create new content, read news, broadcast or watch live video, play games, connect with businesses, buy and sell their own products, send and receive payments, organize groups and events, and raise money for important causes, among many other options. Like many services, WhatsApp provides free, secure communication, including voice and video calls. Instagram offers world-class tools to create and share content based not just on photos, but also videos, augmented reality, and more.

Providing the highest-quality features and best experience for consumers is at the heart of what we do. We offer innovative services that people use to connect and share with their friends, families, businesses, and wider communities. Our products also allow content creators to share their creativity and build community, entrepreneurs to grow their businesses, and non-profits to hit their fundraising goals, among other things.

When Facebook launched in 2004, it had no Photos, Like button, News Feed, Messenger, Events, Shops, or Rooms. As the ways people connect and share evolved over the years alongside rapid innovations in technology, we built new and better apps and services. In turn, many of the iconic features we pioneered have been adopted and improved upon by other companies. And the Facebook family today goes beyond software, with hardware products like Oculus and Portal.

We are always working to develop technologies that enhance the way people connect and communicate, and data is key to that work. We use the data that people entrust to us to pursue new products and features that people want, and we do so because we know that if we don't constantly keep innovating and improving, we will fall behind. When Facebook started, we faced established competitors—including AOL and MySpace—with lots of user data. That did not protect them from others building better products, as success comes from creating products users value and enjoy, not from how much data you have. Apps often rise from nothing to prominence very quickly.

IV. Facebook Competes Vigorously

Facebook as we know it today would not have been possible without laws that encourage competition and innovation. We've been successful because we've made risky bets, invested, innovated, and delivered value to people, advertisers, and shareholders. As the internet has grown over the last 25 years, the ways in which people share and communicate have exploded thanks to dynamic competition. The most successful platforms mature and adapt to people's changing preferences. Our products became popular for this very reason—we constantly evolve, innovate, and invest in better experiences for people against world-class competitors like Apple, Google, Twitter, Snap, Amazon, TikTok, Microsoft, and many more. We innovate and improve constantly because we have to in order to stay relevant.

As our CEO Mark Zuckerberg has explained, we believe that strong and consistent competition is vital because it ensures that the playing field is level for all. Facebook competes hard, because we're up against other smart and innovative companies. We know that our future success is not guaranteed, especially in a global tech industry defined by rapid innovation and change. The history of technology is often the history of failure, and even industry-leading tech companies fail if they don't stay competitive, hence our focus on delivering better services for people and businesses and competing as vigorously as we can within the rules.

We face robust competition in every aspect of our business, and we only succeed when we build things that people find valuable. Today, people have more choices at their fingertips than ever before. Near-constant technological innovation has created an ever-more competitive environment, and we invest heavily in our products and services to stay relevant and competitive, committing more than $18 billion to research and development last year.

And just as people choose to use Facebook, so too do millions of businesses—large and small— choose to use our free tools and advertising products. We compete for advertising dollars with other digital platforms, from Google to TikTok, and with other channels such as television, radio, and print. Businesses choose us because our apps and services deliver real value. We are proud of our record, and we will continue to focus on building and updating our products to give people the best experiences possible.

V. Conclusion

Facebook's success rests on our ability to bring value to people's lives, and that requires us to innovate constantly. In doing so, we responsibly use and analyze data to enhance user experiences and improve our products and services that allow people to connect and share what matters most to them, recognizing that if we don't keep improving, our many competitors will, and we will lose our users and advertisers. Thank you, and I look forward to your questions.

Testimony of Charlotte Slaiman[55] Competition Policy Director Public Knowledge Before the United States Senate, Committee on the Judiciary, Subcommittee on Competition Policy, Antitrust, and Consumer Rights

Hearing On: Big Data, Big Questions: Implications for Competition and Consumers

Washington, D.C., September 21, 2021

Chairwoman Klobuchar and Ranking Member Lee:

Thank you for the opportunity to testify today on behalf of Public Knowledge, a nonprofit working in the public interest for over 20 years. I'm Charlotte Slaiman, a former antitrust enforcer at the Federal Trade Commission and now Competition Policy Director for Public Knowledge. We fight for an open internet, free expression, and access to affordable communications tools for everyone. Achieving these goals is only possible through robust online competition free from the control of today's digital gatekeepers. This hearing smartly zeroes in on one of the key components of this power: data. Although Big Data is most often discussed in policy circles for its privacy implications, I am very pleased that this Subcommittee is focusing on Big Data in the context of antitrust and competition policy.

Data is everything to a platform. It is the lifeblood, the currency, and the fuel that drives Big Tech and many of the products they offer. Perhaps most importantly, data is a key component that platforms use to maintain their gatekeeper power. This should be a dynamic industry where innovation can flourish, but because of the hands-off approach policymakers have taken in the past, new disruptive innovators have not had a fair shot. This hearing marks an important step toward addressing that power, and until we do so, Big Tech will continue picking winners and losers in digital markets.

---

[55] I want to thank Alex Petros, Policy Counsel, for his support in preparing this statement.

Data & Gatekeeper Power

Gatekeeper power is at the root of the competition problems Big Tech presents. Expert economists and antitrust professors, policymakers here in the U.S. and abroad, and advocates the world over have identified gatekeeper power—sometimes "bottleneck power," or "strategic market status"—as the power that dominant digital platforms have over other businesses' ability to reach their customers.[56] As a result, these dominant digital gatekeepers also serve as the primary access point for key consumer data. These gatekeepers get to determine who can play the game in which they also compete. They have the incentive and ability to pick themselves as the winners of this game and pick potential competitive threats as the losers. These same gatekeepers can wield their superior access to data as a cudgel to ensure their gates remain closed—and they stay on top. We can't expect gatekeepers to give up their power just because it's the right thing to do. We need Congress to act to break open the gates and promote a competitive market.

Digital gatekeepers benefit from a triumvirate of market characteristics—network effects, economies of scope and scale, and the ability to control the choice architecture that influences user behavior.[57] We see network effects when users naturally flock to the most popular services as their utility from a service is directly related to how many other people use it. The fact that most of your friends are on Facebook's social network is probably what convinced you to join Facebook in the first place and what keeps you there now. The inherent economies of scope and scale in Big Tech's products also turbocharge gatekeeper growth. It can be difficult for new platforms to compete with dominant ones, yet once a new platform gets going, each additional user results in negligible costs for the platform and exponential benefits in terms of additional data. Finally, gatekeepers have complete control over the user interface—what users see when they access the platform—and can use that interface to push them towards certain choices.

---

[56] George J. Stigler Center for the Study of the Economy and the State, Committee for the Study of Digital Platforms Market Structure and Antitrust Subcommittee Report ["Stigler Report"] 32 (Jul. 1, 2019), https://www.chicagobooth.edu/-/media/research/stigler/pdfs/digital-platforms---committee-report---stigler- center.pdf; Digital Competition Expert Panel, *Unlocking digital competition* 59 (Mar. 13, 2019), https://assets. publishing. service.gov.uk/government/uploads/system/uploads/attachment_data/file/785547/unlockin g_digital_competition_furman_review_web.pdf.

[57] *See supra* Stigler Report, 7–8.

Big Data Fuels Anticompetitive Discrimination

The user interface of a digital gatekeeper has a much bigger impact than the interface of an average website or the layout of a physical store. Dominant digital platforms can pick winners and losers in the digital economy by prominently ranking someone at the top of a page or hiding someone's listing away after lots of scrolling. There are many other tools at their disposal, too. For example, some Google search results get to take up a lot of "real estate" on the search engine results page. These results can have images, bold type, or multiple clickable links to different parts of a website to really grab the user's attention. A user is much more likely to click on one of those results than one that's given fewer engaging features. Amazon chooses which retailer wins the coveted Buy Box (the "Buy Now" button that most users click on to actually buy a product), but Amazon also leverages clever site design to make it seem like the Buy Box is the only way for a customer to buy a particular product.[58] Most users don't even realize there are other sellers offering the same product due to this design feature.

How these design choices influence user decisions is called the "choice architecture."[59] It can be extremely effective and misused to trick customers, a phenomenon researcher have termed "dark patterns."[60] To understand and use these tools of discrimination to their greatest effect, the platforms are constantly running tests on us, the users. Based on what I click or don't click, dominant digital platforms can refine what they're doing to more accurately get the next person to click. This applies to influencing me to stay on Facebook longer, or to purchase a particular product on Amazon. Dominant platforms meticulously optimize their user interfaces to push us to behave in a platform's best interest. This could mean keeping us constantly engaged with a product or it might mean keeping us away from companies that could challenge gatekeeper dominance if they were given a fair shot on the platform.

The platforms also can choose winners and losers through the Big Data-driven algorithms they develop and use to determine which options they'll show to a user. Users may be harmed by the high degree of tracking and

---

[58] *See* Amazon Seller Central, *How the Buy Box Works*, https://sellercentral.amazon.sg/gp/help/external/help.html?itemID=37911&ref=efph_37911_cont_home

[59] Richard H. Thaler et al., *Choice Architecture*, SSRN (Apr. 2, 2010), https://papers.ssrn.com/sol3/papers.cfm?abstract_id=1583509.

[60] Sara Morrison, *Dark patterns, the tricks websites use to make you say yes, explained*, VOX (Apr. 1, 2021), https://www.vox.com/recode/22351108/dark-patterns-ui-web-design-privacy.

engagement needed to target these offerings.[61] They may also be harmed by seeing fewer options and by the assumptions the algorithm makes about us. What a platform's algorithm thinks you'll click on isn't always what's best. We as users could lose out on products we might actually want if our full range of short-term and long-term interests aren't adequately captured by these blunt algorithms. Platforms also offer behavioral targeting for use in perpetuating racial and gender discrimination. Federal enforcers have accused Facebook of targeting housing ads based on race, in violation of the Fair Housing Act.[62] Prospective employers can target their job ads at young men, leaving qualified older workers and women out in the cold.[63]

And this doesn't just harm users. Businesses trying to reach us through Google or Facebook will also suffer if they don't fit into the prescribed categories that the platforms expect based on the Big Data algorithms they deploy. If I haven't previously consumed much content from creators of color, Google and Facebook probably aren't going to show that to me.[64] If I haven't previously purchased foods Amazon deems "ethnic" they're probably not going to highlight those for me. Businesses assessed by the platforms to not be appealing to large groups of customers or to wealthy customers may be denied a chance at fair competition. If a grocery store declines to put a product on their shelves, that producer can go elsewhere. If Google decides your product won't be popular with the people in your city who can afford it, your business would be in much bigger trouble.

Even seemingly minor changes to these algorithms can have disastrous effects for small businesses. Facebook's infamous "pivot to video" was one such case.[65] Facebook determined that videos were getting more attention on their site, and started promoting video content much higher than other types.

---

[61] For an excellent review of the collateral damage to everyday life caused by this complex advertising ecosystem, *see* TIM WU, THE ATTENTION MERCHANTS: THE EPIC SCRAMBLE TO GET INSIDE (2016).

[62] Katie Paul, *U.S. Charges Facebook with racial discrimination in targeted housing ads*, REUTERS (Mar. 28, 2019),https://www.reuters.com/article/us-facebook-advertisers/u-s-charges-facebook-with-racial-discrimination-in-targeted-housing-ads-idUSKCN1R91E8.

[63] Ava Kofman & Ariana Tobin, *Facebook Ads Can Still Discriminate Against Women and Older Workers, Despite aCivil Rights Settlement*, PROPUBLICA (Dec. 13, 2019), https://www.propublica.org/article/facebook-ads-can-still-discriminate-against-women-and-older-workers-despite-a-civil-rights-settlement.

[64] *See* Chris Lewis, *Fighting the Free Speech Divide Requires Interoperability and Privacy Protection*, TECHDIRT (May 29, 2020), https://www.techdirt.com/articles/20200527/11104344587/fighting-free-speech-digital-divide-requires-interoperability-privacy-protection.shtml.

[65] Will Oremus, *The big lie behind the "pivot to video,"* SLATE (Oct. 18, 2018), https://slate.com/technology/2018/10/facebook-online-video-pivot-metrics-false.html.

Whole industries had to change their business models to keep up. In the news industry in particular, many writers were laid off to make room for hiring new video content teams.[66] Later, we found out that Facebook had misled advertisers and publishers. Video posts on Facebook actually were not receiving nearly the attention Facebook had claimed.

Google's search algorithm has its own esoteric preferences it thinks users prefer, like recipe blogs that have a cute (or annoying) little story you have to scroll through before you get to the actual recipe. This influences what small businesses do to "work the algorithm" to access users through the dominant platforms' gates.

Wielding Data Access as an Anticompetitive Weapon

Dominant platforms have strategically positioned themselves at internet bottlenecks. Many times, companies are forced to pay gatekeeper tolls to access customers and data. These tolls can take the form of monetary payments and/or unfair data sharing and access conditions that reinforce the platform data advantage. The penalties for not towing the gatekeeper line can end once-promising products or services.

For example, access to the Facebook network is a lifeline for upstart social networks. The strategic cutting off of that access for potential rivals is a pillar of the ongoing Federal Trade Commission's case against Facebook.[67] According to the FTC, Facebook retooled its network access as an "anticompetitive weapon"—only granting access to companies that agreed not to compete with Facebook or support its rivals. Potential competitive threats were cut off as they began to exhibit growth that could threaten Facebook. Soon after losing access to the Facebook network, these would-be rivals promptly folded, depriving consumers of services they otherwise might have enjoyed.

Finding out who is collecting your data is not as simple as the brand you see at the top of the page. You might be surprised to learn that it's actually Google and Facebook collecting your data instead. If you use Google to find

---

[66] Alexis C. Madrigal & Robinson Meyer, *How Facebook's Chaotic Push Into Video Cost Hundreds of Journalists Their Jobs*, THE ATLANTIC (Oct. 18, 2018), https://www.theatlantic.com/technology/archive/2018/10/facebook- driven-video-push-may-have-cost-483-journalists-their-jobs/573403/.

[67] Amended Complaint, Fed. Trade Comm'n v. Facebook, Inc., No: 1:20-cv-03590-JEB (D.D.C. Aug. 19, 2021).

a news article, you may end up not on the newspaper's website, but one of Google's Accelerated Mobile Pages (AMP). In that case, it's actually Google that gets to track my data, and if the newspaper wants to know which of their articles is getting the most readers, they need Google to "share" that data with them.[68]

In order to advertise to you, a lot of companies use third party cookies to track your web browsing activity. But most browsers have begun blocking third party cookies or have announced they will block third party cookies—including Google's Chrome browser. Some browsers, like Brave and Firefox, have taken the position that they will never enable passive tracking of their users. Google has not; they have implemented their "privacy sandbox" as an alternative to cookies. Now instead of third-party cookies doing the tracking, it's your web browser that is tracking you. Under their new system, Google has even more control over your personal data, because it is increasingly one of the only options for tracking people across the web. Third party cookies were bad for privacy. However, this new system from Google doesn't prevent tracking from occurring; but for many users it means Google is the only one able to do the tracking.[69]

As a user, I don't want to rely on Google's or Facebook's interpretations of privacy. We need comprehensive federal privacy legislation that protects users from Google's and Facebook's data collection and use just as much as it protects us from other companies.

Big Data is a Major Incumbency Advantage

Digital gatekeeper platforms also exhibit increasing returns to scope and scale, largely because of how the value of data increases so significantly when it's merged with other data. Twice as much data isn't just twice as good for a company, but many times more so. This is true both on an individual and a

[68] Competition & Mkts Auth., Online Platforms and Digital Advertising: Market Study Interim Report (2019) ¶ 5:252 ("Publishers... have concerns around restrictions on their ability to monetise these pages and their ability toaccess data generated from consumers' interaction with them.").

[69] *See* Cory Doctorow, *Fighting FLoC and Fighting Monopoly Are Fully Compatible*, ELECTRONIC FRONTIER FOUNDATION (Apr. 21, 2021), https://www.eff.org/deeplinks/2021/04/fighting-floc-and-fighting-monopoly-are-fully-compatible; Charlotte Slaiman, *Data Protection is About Power, Not Just Privacy*, PUBLIC KNOWLEDGE (Mar. 3, 2020), https://www.publicknowledge.org/blog/data-protection-is-about-power-not-just-privacy/.

group level. A company that is able to aggregate multiple sources of data on you will be much more powerful than one that is relegated to a single or few sources.[70] Think of a user fully integrated into the Google ecosystem. Google knows where you are by looking at your Android phone or your Google Maps app. They know what videos and shows you like from YouTube and YouTube TV activity. They know your interests from your Chrome web browsing and Google search history. All of this data can be merged together to build an in-depth profile about you and what you might be interested in right now. A company with just one of those sources of data can't predict your behavior as accurately.

Data from large groups of individuals is similarly more and more valuable with each new user added. Data about other users can fill in the few things a company doesn't know about you by looking at people who are similar to you on the data points they do have. If other white women my age who live in my neighborhood, work in Dupont Circle, and follow Epic Gardening on Instagram like something, Big Data analyzers can assume I will like it, too. Combining a variety of data points helps to more effectively influence users and discriminate between them.

The dominant platforms sometimes argue that data ages rapidly, so a new competitor could quickly amass the data needed to compete. This is theoretically true, but it is not just old data that today's dominant digital platforms control. Users are still today locked in to these platforms through their gatekeeper power, so the platforms continue to have access to ongoing data streams. These data streams can be used to continuously update algorithms to stay on top. They can also keep platforms updated about the users so as not to rely on just static or past data about them. This allows platforms to not just "know" their users, but see how their users change over time—often in response to the algorithms that platforms created using older user data. This cycle of collection, use, and iteration gives platforms significant power over their users.[71]

By taking advantage of the significant increase in the value of a data stream when it's merged with other data streams, vertically integrated and conglomerate firms like the dominant digital platforms can exacerbate barriers

---

[70] Tom Wheeler, *Big tech and antitrust: pay attention to the math behind the curtain*, BROOKINGS INSTITUTE (July 31, 2020), https://www.brookings.edu/blog/techtank/2020/07/31/big-tech-and-antitrust-pay-attention-to-the-math-behind-the-curtain/.

[71] *See, e.g.*, Will Oremus, *Facebook keeps researching its own harms — and burying the findings,* THE WASHINGTON POST (Sept. 16, 2021), https://www.washingtonpost.com/technology/2021/09/16/facebook-files-internal-research-harms/.

to competition. The wide variety of products Google offers gives an illustrative example. Google can see from my calendar and my email that I have a meeting coming up across town. Using Google Maps, it can tell me exactly when I should leave for said meeting. There are competitors that offer different navigation apps, calendars or email clients, but it's very difficult for a smaller company to offer all three. Simultaneously entering multiple markets to compete with multiple arms of the Google leviathan at once is called dual-market entry, a notoriously difficult feat according to antitrust economists.[72] Consumers could lose out on a better single product if innovative entrepreneurs are blocked from the market unless they can debut multiple great apps at the same time. This huge entry barrier is one way that vertical integration and conglomeration results in less competition against Big Tech and fewer options for consumers.

Finally, gatekeepers can prevent rivals from getting the data they need to effectively compete. This is perhaps best seen in the infamous episode of Google starving Bing of data it needed to effectively challenge its market power in online search.[73]

Solutions

Competition is not a panacea for the challenges of Big Data. We also urgently need new privacy laws to protect users, as well as a digital regulator to comprehensively address the policy questions surrounding digital platforms. We can't afford a race to the bottom on privacy with companies scrambling to maximally exploit consumer data. It's not the realm of antitrust or competition policy to decide what markets are just too harmful to people and, thus, not worth having at all. A comprehensive federal privacy law can be pro-competitive by creating a level playing field for dominant incumbents and new entrants alike.

At the same time, we need new laws and rules focused on promoting fair competition on and against dominant gatekeeper platforms to give back some real control to consumers and business users. Until we have a real choice to

---

[72] *See, e.g.*, U.S. Dept. of Justice & Fed Trade Comm'n, Vertical Merger Guidelines 7–8 (2020), https://www.ftc.gov/system/files/documents/reports/us-department-justice-federal-trade-commission-vertical- merger-guidelines/vertical_merger_guidelines_6-30-20.pdf.

[73] *See* CMA Report, *supra* note 13, at ¶ 24; Fiona Scott Morton & David Dinielli, Roadmap for a Monopolization Case Against Google Regarding the Search Market 37, OMIDYAR PROJECT (June 2020), https://omidyar.com/wp-content/uploads/2020/09/Roadmap-for-a-Monopolization-Case-Against-Google-Regarding-the-Search-Market.pdf.

leave these platforms if we're not happy with them, they won't care about doing what is in their users'—our—best interest. Thankfully, there's already a template for legislative change that could have a major impact on the power of Big Tech and Big Data. The package of antitrust bills focusing on Big Tech that recently passed through markup in the House Judiciary Committee represents a key piece of the solution, as does broad antitrust reform as Chairwoman Klobuchar has proposed here in the Senate. The recently introduced Open App Markets Act from Senators Blumenthal and Blackburn is also an important part of the reform solution. These solutions aren't mutually exclusive. Both sector-specific and economy- wide antitrust reforms are needed. I hope that we will see Senate companions to the House legislation, and a House companion to the Senate legislation.

Interoperability, Data Portability, and Delegatability

Interoperability, data portability, and delegatability are the privacy-protective ways to neutralize the power that Big Data confers upon dominant digital platforms. Right now, if I'm frustrated with how Facebook treats my data, I don't really have the option to leave because my friends and family, the businesses, groups, and even schools I need to communicate with are on Facebook.

Facebook is able to rest on its laurels and faces little incentive to innovate or actually protect my privacy. When the Stop Hate for Profit campaign last year convinced many advertisers and users to boycott Facebook because of their refusal to moderate hateful content on the platform, Mark Zuckerberg said he wasn't concerned, that they'll be back "soon enough."[74] He knows that other platforms can't compete because his network is so much larger. Interoperability would address these network effects and allow competition to flourish by letting users connect back to Facebook from a new competitor if they choose.

Data portability allows users to bring their data with them from a dominant platform to a competitor. For users, this helps address one of the high switching costs in leaving a platform. Think about how much time you've spent building out your social media presence—all the uploaded photos, comments, statuses, etc. If the only way to end your relationship with Facebook is to lose all this data, you may be wary about leaving. Portability also helps upstart competitors because when a customer chooses them over

---

[74] James Clayton, *Zuckerberg: Advertisers will be back to Facebook 'soon enough,'* BBC (July 2, 2020),https://www.bbc.com/news/technology-53262860.

the incumbent, the new platform gets not just a new user and the data they choose to share going forward, but also the past data they choose to port over from the incumbent. That should make dominant platforms fight harder to win your business and give new entrants more of a leg up. To be clear, data portability on its own will not be sufficient to jumpstart competition.

Delegatability allows users to designate a third party to manage their online interactions and account settings (including privacy settings) across multiple platforms. If interoperability and portability work as intended, we expect to see new entrants actually competing against some of these dominant platforms. Delegated services can simplify the process of interoperability across multiple platforms and help consumers receive the maximum benefit from it.

Thankfully, we have an excellent congressional blueprint in the form of the ACCESS Act, a bipartisan and bicameral bill with origins on this Subcommittee. What I love about the ACCESS Act is that it puts users in control and puts privacy first. If a user wants to move their data elsewhere or try out a new competitor they can. And the Act explicitly lays out detailed privacy protections such as giving the FTC explicit rulemaking authority over the privacy of relevant data, specifying that any data gleaned cannot be commercialized, and creating data minimization requirements. The ACCESS Act is an excellent example of a bill that couples massive benefits for both privacy and competition and should be passed as soon as possible.

Non-Discrimination

These platforms can abuse their gatekeeper power to freeze out would-be competitors from the market and one of the tools for that discrimination is Big Data. Gatekeeper platforms can put their own products first on the page, give them the best attention-grabbing design, and point users away from companies that might threaten their gatekeeper power. They can give their own services unfettered access to consumer data that they zealously guard from others. They can even misuse competitor data (data that the competitor must give as a condition of competing on the platform) to launch rival products or hamstring competitors.[75] While this offends our basic notions of fairness, without greater legislation and regulation this behavior would be very difficult to stop using our existing antitrust laws.

---

[75] *See* Makena Kelly, *Jeff Bezos can't promise Amazon employees don't access independent seller data*, THE VERGE(July 29, 2020), https://www.theverge.com/2020/7/29/21347083/jeff-bezos-amazon-tech-antitrust-hearing-jayapal- questioning.

A non-discrimination law like House Antitrust Subcommittee Chairman David Cicilline's American Choice and Innovation Online Act could help solve these tough problems. Dominant platforms would be prohibited from advantaging their own products and services or disadvantaging the products and services of their rivals or potential competitors. There are also specific prohibitions on using non-public data from a platform's business user to compete against them and impeding or restricting the portability or interoperability of business user data. The proposed law was written with data issues in mind and would target some of the most pernicious platform behaviors.

Merger Limitations

Today's Big Tech titans did not always grow organically, but through strategic acquisitions to fend off rivals and maintain their hold on their respective markets. Many times, a platform will acquire a company to integrate their data or data streams with the treasure trove of data the platform has already accumulated or data streams they already have access to. This feeds into the increasing returns to scope and scale that help entrench Big Tech market dominance. Efforts by advocates and enforcers to block or unwind these deals have been an uphill battle. We need our laws to better recognize the power that can come from conglomerating sources of data that may at first seem unrelated. Bills like Rep. Jeffries' Platform Competition and Opportunity Act would represent an important step forward. It would chill predatory acquisitions by dominant tech platforms and allow innovation and competition to flourish. Chairwoman Klobuchar's Competition and Antitrust Law Enforcement Reform Act of 2021 would also be a great help in this area. Amending the Clayton Act merger standard to ban mergers that "create an appreciable risk of materially lessening competition" and shifting the burden to the merging parties in certain instances would both help our overworked enforcers and stop the worst anticompetitive mergers from moving forward.

Structural Separation

Merging multiple data sources helps huge conglomerates know even more about us, so they can even more effectively manipulate and discriminate against us. It's important that antitrust enforcers have the ability to sue dominant digital platforms collecting data across multiple lines of business to separate off a line of business that's posing a conflict of interest. Rep. Jayapal's Ending Platform Monopolies Act would provide this needed tool to antitrust enforcers and sets forth the situations in which it can be used.

App Market Reforms

The Open App Markets Act is targeted at the worst abuses of dominant app stores, a notorious and narrow internet bottleneck. The bill would allow apps to use alternative payment systems and require the app store operator to give third parties fair access to device and software features. There is also a specific ban on using non-public data gleaned from an app to compete against the app. The bill requires operating systems to offer interoperability, including letting users choose third-party apps as defaults and use alternative app stores.

Broad Antitrust Reform

Purposeful narrowing of our antitrust laws by the courts have left big business with license to engage in a host of anticompetitive conduct. A myopic focus on price and other easily quantifiable effects leaves out important innovation and consumer choice harms that antitrust is supposed to address. It's well past time for our antitrust laws to receive a refresh. The Chairwoman's Competition and Antitrust Law Enforcement Reform Act of 2021 would help rein in the power of Big Data by updating the legal standards for blocking mergers and stopping exclusionary conduct. The bill also restores an appropriate definition of market power that goes beyond prices. Antitrust enforcers can bring in anticompetitive data practices as direct evidence of market power. The newly proposed Division of Market Analysis could also study data markets to improve enforcement.

Conclusion

For decades now, Washington has taken the perspective that we need to let digital businesses run wild to see what great innovations they might come up with. But today, unscrupulous data practices and consolidated power have led us to a place that isn't anyone's dream of what the internet was supposed to be. These largely unregulated platforms have been allowed to amass powerful gatekeeper roles in multiple markets, where they need not fear competition or government intervention. For users to really have control, we need to have a real choice to leave these platforms. We need real competitors and we need switching to be easy. To get those things, we need new laws and rules to promote fair competition on and against gatekeeper platforms like Google and Facebook. Congress has already done laudable work of introducing a series of bills to combat these harms. The best time to pass them was 10 years ago. The second-best time is now.

Senator Grassley
Questions for the Record – Big Data, Big Questions: Implications for Competition and Consumers
Sheila Colclasure, Global Chief Digital Responsibility and Public Policy Officer, IPG Kinesso

1. There is debate over whether Big Data should be regulated through the lens of consumer protection and privacy or whether antitrust laws should be used to address competition concerns with the collection of data. Do you have an opinion about the best approach to address this issue or should we be looking at a combination of different approaches?

Response to Senator Grassley

In our modern American economy, any data privacy law is also competition law. Both privacy and competition concerns have data availability, use, and control at their core. For businesses of all sizes, but especially small business and new entrants, access to data is the dependent factor on whether the business can compete or not. Companies may have better technology, better ideas, and innovation at their core, yet without access to data, they cannot compete.

Recently introduced data privacy legislation, as drafted, would have a catastrophic impact on competition because it restricts who can collect, control, and use data. This effectively picks winners and losers, consolidating market power into the hands of a few massive, Big Tech, data holders. In many ways, Big Tech is like a basic consumer utility, like water and energy. Big Tech has grown data-dominant relatively unimpeded, offering functionality to people that has become ubiquitous with our daily lives, giving these companies tremendous market power to gain consumer consent for the collection of their data.

There has been much debate about consumer consent versus other data regulatory approaches such as fair, open, and accountable data flow and use. While consumer consent is important, and a laudable goal, it alone is an insufficient model in the complex digital ecosystem of data infinity and tech certainty. Data is essential to all market players, especially small business, new business, and our innovators. By writing laws that grant control of data to a few companies that get to the consumer first, we create economic winners and losers. Such laws would effectively grant data access to some and deny it for others. This approach frustrates free and fair competition among all of the players in the ecosystem.

We are beyond the point where it is possible to pass a data privacy law that does not also – whether explicitly or by omission – affect competition. The reality is that today's connected marketplace is dominated by companies who were able to thrive and grow, thanks in part to ready access to consumer data. A comprehensive federal privacy law that in practical effect limits consumer data to just a few dominant players risks concentrating even more power in the hands of a few, giving more exclusive control of data about people to a few. In our data-intense economy, this precludes robust competition, vibrant innovation, and the possibility of the small company becoming connected, finding its audience, and serving its audience competitively. We emphasize the essential nature of data availability, open data flow, and fair uses of data to innovation, competition, and a vibrant ecosystem of connected market participants. We contend that a federal data privacy law and a competition law should be complementary and provide for responsible and accountable data sharing so that everyone can compete on a level playing field.

We urge the Committee to consider the effect that mergers have had on control of the consumer data value chain, and thus on competition. Traditional antitrust analysis has focused on the effect of mergers in a specific consumer-facing market, but the enhancement of dominant data positions plays a large role in the acquisition strategy of the dominant online platforms. We hope this Committee will recognize the essential nature of data to our entire connected economy and the ecosystem of companies that enable our connected marketplace.

In order to protect people, promote the fair use of their data, and support a robust, trustworthy and competitive connected marketplace, a federal privacy law should be drafted in a way that protects and enables competition. It should promote fundamental privacy rights for consumers and enable responsible and accountable use and sharing of consumer data by commercial enterprises. This allows the market to continue to provide a wide array of benefits to people including things like safer online payments, ready access to business and consumer credit, access to free content and platforms, and cost efficient and effective advertising for all, especially small businesses, and new market entrants.

We at IPG have built accountability and responsible data practices into everything we do. We believe that corporate America is ready to responsibly collect and share consumer data and be accountable for its actions in doing so.

We encourage the Committee to protect the fair and open use of data as fundamental to competition. We urge the Committee to help develop a federal privacy law that is future-fit for the realities of the Digital Age, protects consumers, and enables a connected marketplace in which all participants can compete fairly, so long as they engage in safe and accountable data use and sharing.

Senator Ossoff
Questions for the Record – Big Data, Big Questions: Implications for Competition and Consumers
Sheila Colclasure, Global Chief Digital Responsibility and Public Policy Officer, IPG Kinesso

1. Please list any instance where any IPG company provides or has ever provided products or services to any federal agency, or to any federal prime contractor or federal subcontractor for purposes of supporting a federal program, including the nature and value of the products or services provided. As part of this response, please describe the nature of Acxiom's 2019 contract with the United States Special Operations Command, including how Acxiom supports "Project Red Mouse." If necessary, submit a classified annex to the Committee on the Judiciary to ensure this information responsive to this question is complete.

At the outset, it is important to note that the Interpublic Group of Companies, Inc. (IPG) is a holding company compromised of roughly 90 different companies, the vast majority of which are creative advertising agencies. For purposes of these responses, I have limited my response to the two principal data and technology companies within IPG: Acxiom and Kinesso. Moreover, given the limited availability of some historical records, the resources that would be required to undertake a comprehensive search, and my desire to respond with confidence based on records that we do have, I have limited our investigation and responses to facts going back to 2017. Kinesso was launched in 2019 and so my responses specifically applicable to Kinesso go back to that date. With that understanding, I offer the following responses to the QFRs.

Response to QFR 1

Kinesso has not provided products or services to any federal agency or to any federal prime contractor or federal subcontractor for purposes of supporting a federal program. Acxiom has performed occasional work with federal agencies, such as analytic programs with the Department of Veterans Affairs, Office of Enterprise Integration (OEI). OEI's primary goal is to utilize data and analytics to develop insights that enable VA programs to better connect with veterans and strengthen the VA's delivery of services and benefits to veterans, their families, survivors, and caregivers. The accuracy and reliability of that data is critical to the success of the mission. Acxiom serves as a subcontractor to the prime contractor and provides Data Products and Information Services as part of that relationship. (Data Products and Information Services are defined in response to QFR 7 below.)

Acxiom provides consulting services to the United States Department of State Visa and Passport Analysis Branch (VPAB) in Diplomatic Security, pursuant to GSA Schedule 70. Our relationship began with a strategic consulting assessment focused upon information assets and resources related to VPAB's Investigative Management System (IMS). IMS is the central repository and user portal for all State Department investigative cases, predominantly visa and passport fraud. Acxiom's primary goal is to assist the State Department in making IMS a more accurate and complete investigation solution for its agents and analysts. Acxiom provides consulting services only and does not provide any Data Products or Information Services as part of that relationship.

Finally, Acxiom is not at liberty to confirm or deny the existence of any classified agreement or to discuss any other work the company may do on a classified basis for agencies of the United States Government. We recommend the Committee contact U.S. Special Operations Command or other appropriate resources within the United States Government if additional information is needed on any classified initiative.

2. Please list any instance where any IPG company provides or has ever provided products or services to any state or local law enforcement agency.

Response to QFR 2

Based on our investigation, neither Kinesso nor Acxiom has bid for, or provided any products or services to state or local law enforcement agencies since 2017.

3. Please list all bids for federal contracts submitted by any IPG company, even if such bids were unsuccessful. Specify the federal agency, the title and purpose of the bid, the products or services that were to be provided, and where applicable the estimated or suggested value of the contract(s).

Response to QFR 3

As there does not appear to be a public database or reliable comprehensive resource that tracks bidding on federal contracts, research for this question proved difficult. In addition to the work we perform for the Veterans Administration mentioned in Response to QFR 1 as a sub-contractor to Sierra7 (prior to that, the prime contractor was HMS Technologies, Inc.), we identified four additional bids to federal agencies:

Year	Agency	Purpose	Products/Services	Value	Bid Status
2018	DMDC	Identity Verification	Data and Data Processing	$275,000	Lost
2018	Login.gov	Identity Verification	Data and Data Processing	$25,000	Lost
2020	HHS	Digital Activation of Vaccine Campaign	Data and Data Processing	$625,000	Lost
2020	Defense Health Agency	Information Management	Consulting	$1.1 million	Lost

4. Please list all bids for contracts with state or local law enforcement agencies submitted by any IPG company, even if such bids were unsuccessful. Specify the agency, the title and purpose of the bid, the products or services that were to be provided, and where applicable the estimated or suggested value of the contract(s).

Response to QFR 4

As indicated in response to QFR 2, we did not find any instances where Acxiom or Kinesso bid on state or local law enforcement work since 2017.

5. Please describe any instance where any IPG company provides any product or service to any foreign governmental entity, foreign state-owned enterprise, or foreign political entity (e.g., foreign political parties, political candidates, or political campaigns).

Response to QFR 5

Kinesso in the US has not provided a product or service to any foreign government entity, foreign state-owned enterprise, or foreign political entity since 2019. Acxiom has performed small data enhancement projects (i.e., two projects for under $100,000 total), for a Caribbean tourism authority. A sister company, Acxiom Ltd. (UK), has provided information services to the UK Information Commissioner's Office (UK Data Protection Authority). We cannot rule out situations where Acxiom or Kinesso may have provided products or services to an entity that is wholly or partially owned by a foreign government (e.g., a national airline), however, no such entity was readily apparent while we performed our research.

6. Please describe any instance where any IPG company provides or has provided any product or service to any foreign or U.S. business for purposes of supporting that business' contract work on behalf of any foreign governmental entity.

Response to QFR 6

It is important to note that data ethics is integral to everything we do. For more than two decades, we have focused on the sources of our data, how it is used, and whether both of those complied with law and were consistent with our ethical data framework. We have extensive systems and policies and procedures in place to make sure that this is the case. While it is possible that one of our clients used our products and services for purposes for purposes of supporting its work on behalf of a foreign governmental entity, our investigation failed to identify any instance where we knew about this type of service when it was contracted for, and we have not identified any instance since 2017 where this occurred.

7. Please describe any relationship through which any IPG company receives personally identifiable data or any data pertaining to U.S. persons from federal, state, or local governments or government agencies. As part of this response, please describe whether data received includes information about the online presence of individuals, such as social media accounts.

Response to QFR 7

Kinesso does not directly license personally identifiable data or data pertaining to US persons from federal, state, or local governments or government agencies. Acxiom serves as the primary data sourcing entity for Kinesso.

Acxiom has two primary lines of business. The first line of business is referred to as "information services," which includes sophisticated database administration services to improve the useability of data that Acxiom's clients provide. The second line of Acxiom's business is data products, where Acxiom provides data to its clients for their (and in the case of an Acxiom data reseller, their end users'), internal use. Acxiom licenses public records such as voter records, hunting/fishing licenses, and real estate transactions, for its data products. All of this information is publicly available, and if its use is restricted in any way by a statute or by the licensor, we conform our use and distribution of that data with those restrictions and our own guidelines.

8. Please describe in detail the sources from which Acxiom or other IPG companies obtain unique device identifiers, including IMEI, IMSI, MAC addresses, or IDFA/Ad-IDs.

a) If you receive or obtain unique identifiers from commercial partners, please describe the means by which those partners obtained the identifiers.

Response to QFR 8

Acxiom and Kinesso collect Mobile Ad IDs (MAIDs) via a licensed file from SDK providers. We do not receive lat/long or IP addresses in combination with those MAIDs. We do not incorporate the MAIDs into any other product, but we do provide them to third parties as a data product. Consistent with our overall ethical data framework, we require that the source of this information represent and warrant their compliance with laws and applicable industry practices when they provide us the data and we have a program in place to confirm that their sources have not changed and these fundamental representations remain in place on an annual basis.

9. Please describe efforts by any IPG company to link unique device identifiers with the IP addresses of residential or commercial internet connections.

Response to QFR 9

Acxiom and Kinesso have not traditionally offered this type of product, nor do we currently have any commercial offerings where we link device identifiers to IP addresses. Given client interest and demand, we are exploring this potential opportunity from a commercial and regulatory perspective. If we decide to move forward and offer a commercial product that links unique device identifiers with IP commercial or residential addresses, it will be legal under all applicable laws and will also comply with our ethical data framework, which verifies the source and the intended use of the data on a client- by-client basis.

10. Please describe any products or services any IPG company offers to clients to enable them to see connections between personally identifiable data, such as SSN, home address, email address, or telephone number, and sensitive data, such as web browsing activity, web search history, or purchase history.

Response to QFR 10

Acxiom offers its "Real Identity" product, which performs a valuable function for Acxiom's clients. Real Identity allows Acxiom's clients to synchronize identity data (e.g., name, home and email address, and telephone number) used across the client's enterprise. By synthesizing and analyzing billions of customer transactions and interactions, both digitally and offline, Real Identity allows Acxiom's clients to build and maintain first-party identity graphs to recognize individuals and build deeper customer relationships across their full enterprise.

Importantly, this service is only used to build first party data graphs for our clients, the data flowing through this service is not added to any Acxiom third-party data graph. So, whether it is the client using the product on its own behalf or Acxiom providing those services as the client's processor, the client's own data or ethically sourced, third-party data licensed by our client is used to make these connections in accordance with the client's own privacy policy and the client's notice to consumers of the potential for re-identification.

Lastly, it is also important to state that Acxiom and Kinesso do not offer products or services to clients that enable them to see connections between personally identifiable data and sensitive data, such as SSN, web browsing activity, or web search history, that is not already in their possession. Acxiom does license consumer purchase behavior data that is associated to personally identifiable information. However, that data is categorical (e.g., clothing, hardware); not at an item/SKU level of granularity, nor is it associated to the specific location that the purchase was made.

11. Please describe any contractual limitations Acxiom places on entities' use or disclosure of data about individuals.

a) Does Acxiom monitor its clients for contract adherence? If so, how?
b) Has Acxiom or any other IPG company discovered or become aware of a contracting partner's contractual breach relating to personally identifiable information? If so, please describe any resulting actions taken by IPG or an IPG company.

Response to QFR 11

Acxiom's client contracts require clients to comply with all applicable laws and restrict the use of data and services for client to internal business purposes. Acxiom includes similar flow-down obligations through restrictions in its contracts with resellers and data brokers (so that their customers are subject to the same restrictions). This is central to how we conduct our business and how we have conducted it over the last three decades. It is part of our internal ethical data framework.

In addition to contractual restrictions, Acxiom has a due diligence team that confirms who our client are and what they do (to the extent, their business can be determined). That team also reviews compliance with our client contracts, including data use provisions in the contracts. It is impossible to confirm compliance with every client contract, so reviews are done on a systematic basis to sample compliance across our user base. We also follow up on any credible information we receive regarding potential non-compliance with our agreements.

Acxiom has business interactions with many clients that can be described as "high touch" and "long-term" information services. In these situations, Acxiom has a close working relationship with the particular client over a long period of time. These types of relationships afford greater visibility into the manner in which the client uses our products and services, allowing greater confidence regarding their compliance with contractual restrictions in those situations.

12. Other than its website, what steps does Acxiom take to alert consumers to their ability to opt out of the company's use of their data?

a) Do you treat opt-out requests from California residents differently than opt-out requests from residents of other state?
b) If so, please describe any differences in how Acxiom would treat data about a person from California after receiving an opt-out request, compared to how it would treat data about a person from another state who submitted an opt-out request.

Response to QFR 12

Acxiom provides CCPA rights to all individuals in the United States. Acxiom does not treat California residents differently from an opt out (or any other data rights perspective), than any other resident of the United States.

Acxiom works hard to provide as much educational information to consumers as possible. We have extensive information available on our website, but in addition, we promote consumer awareness in media interactions and in consumer oriented educational activities (e.g., conferences, seminars, and consumer group sponsorships).

Senator Tillis
Questions for the Record – Big Data, Big Questions: Implications for Competition and Consumers
Sheila Colclasure, Global Chief Digital Responsibility and Public Policy Officer, IPG Kinesso

1. The term "data" can have multiple meanings, which can sometimes generate confusion in policy discussions. How would you define "data" and "big data", as used in your written testimony?

a) How would you define consumer and user data, specifically what would be included and excluded from these definitions?
b) Would this include user uploaded videos, images, and text?
c) Would such content be considered part of the "user" data, even if it includes content that originates from other sources?
d) Does it include data in which intellectual property rights, including copyright, trade secret, trademark, or design rights, may subsist?

Response to Senator Tillis

The fact that humans use data in so many different ways is part of what makes legislating with respect to data issues so difficult. Policymakers generally want to preserve and foster beneficial data uses while limiting harmful ones. The unique purpose for which data is being regulated should help define the term – and different inclusions or exclusions may be needed within the scope of a single bill.

You specifically asked how I would define the term “data” “as used in my written testimony.” I was asked to testify about how my company competes in data-driven marketing as compared to others, specifically first-party platforms. The main data that matters for the purposes of that competition is not user-generated content, such as you describe above. Such data may be of interest to others, but not to us. However, user- generated digital history – product search information, for example – is useful for marketing, and therefore access to it is relevant to competition issues. Again, Congress should consider the purpose it intends to effectuate in determining the scope of defined terms.

Data may be protected by intellectual property rights in and of itself, or it may be processed by use of algorithms or processes that themselves constitute IP, in which case the resulting product may contain protectable IP. However, IP protections are not incompatible with any of privacy, competition and the enforcement of antitrust laws.

2. Your testimony advocates for an expansive view of competition law that would account for the flexibility to account for data-related issues, and advocates for the Committee to consider privacy and competition to be interrelated.

a) Would the same consideration be extended to other “big data” issues, such as intellectual property rights, cybersecurity, national security, data protection, and other issues?
b) How should antitrust law be tailored to appropriately account for privacy rights, or other legitimate concerns such as intellectual property rights?

Response to Senator Tillis

I did advocate for the Committee to consider privacy and competition to be interrelated, and in the context of the hearing, which related to S. 2992, I stand by that recommendation. I did not, and did not intend, to advocate for an expansive view of antitrust law, and therefore underscore my suggestion that the Committee "consider privacy and competition not as separate bodies of law, but instead to be interrelated." A better statement would be that in the context of this legislation, antitrust and privacy become interrelated. If Congress is going to regulate competition, it should consider the privacy implications of doing so, and vice versa. Congress should consider the other interests you mention, as well.

The ability to access data that consumers are making available about themselves is key to competition in today's markets. Legislation that would regulate competition in digital markets must recognize this, and so must legislation that would protect privacy by regulating use of consumer data.

3. Ms. Slaiman advocates for "a digital regulator to comprehensively [regulate] the policy questions surrounding digital platforms."

a) Do you agree that this is necessary?
b) Given the many issues beyond privacy and competition that address and implicate digital policy—including cybersecurity, national security, consumer rights, free speech, and intellectual property concerns—what existing agency would be the best situated, in your view, to carry out this role?
c) Is it important to you that the regulator should be politically accountable?

Response to Senator Tillis

We support enactment of a national privacy law, with enforcement by the FTC and state attorneys general. We also support resourcing the FTC appropriately to conduct this expanded mission. We do not have a position on whether it is necessary to have a regulator specific to digital platforms.

For privacy regulation, the best situated agency is the FTC, because it has developed experience and expertise. We do not oppose creation of a Bureau of Privacy in the FTC. Privacy regulation primarily impacts the commercial sector, and as a commercial regulator, the FTC is well-positioned. I would also add that, as demonstrated by the August 11, 2022, FTC Advanced Notice of Proposed Rulemaking, federal legislation is necessary to prevent FTC overreach and to ensure that the FTC develop rules pursuant to congressional authorization and consistent with congressional intent.

Senator Blackburn
Questions for the Record – Big Data, Big Questions: Implications for Competition and Consumers
Sheila Colclasure, Global Chief Digital Responsibility and Public Policy Officer, IPG Kinesso

It's imperative for the U.S. to get a national consumer privacy law in place – the EU and China have already done so. Given consumer concerns about how their data is being used online, what should that regime look like? What are the obstacles the United States faces in getting to that point?

Response to Senator Blackburn

While many proponents of a national privacy law point to the EU General Data Protection Regulation as a model for the United States, Congress can, and should, do better. Studies since the GDPR went into effect in 2018 make clear that the GDPR has had a severe negative effect on the European economic market, including suppressing competition and consolidating market power into the large gate-keeper technology platforms. See, e.g., "GDPR Cost Businesses 8% of Their Profits, According to A New Estimate," https://techmonitor.ai/policy/privacy-and-data-protection/gdpr-cost-businesses-8-of-their-profits-according-to-a-new-estimate. It is also clear that the GDPR has not been able to adjust to the rapid change of innovation. In part for these reasons, both the European Union and the UK are already considering a major overhaul of their GDPR legislation. "UK Pauses Data Reform Bill to Rethink How to Replace GDPR," https://techcrunch.com/2022/10/03/uk-data-reform-bill-replace-gdpr/. In fact, GDPR has had such anticompetitive effects that the EU has introduced five additional pieces of legislation to attempt to better govern the big gatekeepers and the realities of data and algorithms in the Digital Age. "A Europe Fit for the Digital Age," https://ec.europa.eu/info/strategy/priorities-2019-2024/europe-fit-digital-age_en. The EU's difficulties with GDPR demonstrate that it should not serve as model for the U.S. Contrary to GDPR, U.S. privacy legislation should protect data-driven business practices, while providing meaningful redress to Americans who suffer actual harm through violation of their privacy rights.

The U.S. should restore its leadership role on the global stage with a forward-thinking, future-fit approach. Congress should consider a bill that focuses on harm prevention and accountability. The law should prohibit certain uses of data that are per se unfair, such as fraud, unlawful discrimination, stalking, and harassment, and expressly permit the collection, sharing, and use of data for beneficial uses including advertising and marketing purposes. The policy principles championed by the Privacy for America coalition are incredibly instructive and should be fully adopted in any national privacy law. https://www.privacyforamerica.com. Additionally, the Information Accountability Foundation has developed model legislation, The FAIR and OPEN USE Act, that would be better for America and better for Americans.
https://secureservercdn.net/192.169.221.188/b1f.827.myftpupload.com/wp-content/uploads/2021/05/FAIR-and-OPEN-USE-Act-May-26-2021-1.pdf?time=1622546970.

The U.S. should also consider the model of Singapore, which has enacted a national privacy law that leads to accountability without unnecessarily hampering the flow of information or favoring certain market participants in the information economy over others. https://www.pdpc.gov.sg/Overview-of-PDPA/The-Legislation/Personal-Data- Protection-Act. The law, which was drafted in consultation with The Information Accountability Foundation and the Center for Information Policy Leadership addresses the practicalities of the digital future, and ensures robust, competitive and trustworthy economy. Essentially, the law says, “let data flow for beneficial uses, but be accountable to detect and prevent harms.”

In addition to adopting a harms-based approach, a federal privacy law must resolve two issues that are relatively unique to the U.S. system: state law preemption and the scope of any private right of action.

If federal privacy legislation is to ensure future a competitive digital economy, it must include a provision that broadly preempts recent and future state forays into the use of personal information for marketing and advertising. Given the importance of advertising to the U.S economy and the fact that advertising also directly subsidizes valuable services and free speech activities on the Internet, a comprehensive national privacy law should expressly indicate Congress’ intent to occupy the field. Without a strong preemption provision, the national law simply becomes yet another law that companies must navigate, creating uncertainty, operational inconsistencies, and administrative costs that are passed right back to consumers in the form of increased costs of goods and services and less access to knowledge, news, and the connected marketplace. The inevitable differences in these state level laws creates administrative and financial burdens that divert important resources that can be otherwise devoted to innovation and will substantially restrict companies' ability to grow.

More specifically, a well-drafted preemption provision would expressly preempt states and state subdivisions from adopting, maintaining, or enforcing a state law or regulation that relates to the subject matter of the national privacy law or any regulation promulgated by the national privacy law. Similarly, to remove any potential ambiguity, the national privacy law should explicitly reference and preempt the California Consumer Privacy Act, as amended by the California Privacy Rights Act, Cal. Civ. Code §1798.100 et seq., the Virginia Consumer Data Protection Act, Va. Code Ann. §59.1- 580 et seq., the Colorado Privacy Act, Co. Rev. Stat. 6-1-1301 et seq., the Utah Privacy Act, Utah Code Ann. §13-61-101 et seq., and the Connecticut act concerning personal data privacy and online monitoring, 2022 Ct. SB 6, as well as any regulations implementing those statutes.

The second major obstacle to a national privacy law is whether to include a private right of action, especially if that right includes statutory damages. As we saw with other state and federal statutes that include a private right of action with a statutory damage component, (e.g., the Fair Credit Reporting Act, the Telephone Consumer Protection Act, and the Michigan Video Rental Privacy Act), lawyers brought a number of class action cases seeking astronomical statutory damages even though the consumers objectively did not suffer actual harm. See, e.g., TransUnion v. Ramirez, 141 S.Ct. 2190 (2021).

Many companies are willing to accept a limited ability to sue to recover actual damages, provided the resulting privacy law includes a corresponding strong preemption provision. Without a correspondingly strong preemption provision, companies have continued exposure to causes of action under state law that likely include significant administrative penalties under those laws (e.g., the California Privacy Rights Act), as well as class action lawsuits for statutory damages under state laws. Such a situation is untenable and would undo any efforts by Congress to institute and enable digital innovation, while protecting privacy and competition.

Responses to Questions for the Record
U.S. Senate Committee on the Judiciary
Subcommittee on Competition Policy, Antitrust, and Consumer Rights
"Big Data, Big Questions: Implications for Competition and Consumers"
September 21, 2021

Markham Erickson
Vice President Of Government Affairs And Public Policy, Google, Inc.

Written Questions Submitted by Sen. Grassley to Markham Erickson:

Question 1. Google monetizes user's data by selling targeted advertisements. In the second quarter of 2021 Google had advertising revenues of $50.44 billion. How much is the average American's data worth to Google?

Google does not sell users' personal information. That is not our business model, and we have always made this policy a touchstone of Google's relationship with our users.

Google provides users with a range of controls over how their information is used, including for personalized ads. Users may opt to permit Google to personalize the ads they see using their activity and account data, but services like Search, Maps, Gmail, and Drive remain free for users who choose not to allow the use of their data for ad targeting. Indeed, ads on Google Search primarily rely on the context of the current search query to select ads, not user information. A user can see how ads are personalized to them and change their advertising settings at https://adssettings.google.com/. Users can also learn about Google's collection and use of data through our industry-leading, in-context notices, privacy reminders, and of course our Privacy Policy (available at https://policies.google.com/privacy).

Information regarding revenue generated by Google, by segment and source, is disclosed on a quarterly and annual basis in our Forms 10-K and 10-Q. Recent filings are available at https://abc.xyz/investor/.

Question 2. There is debate over whether Big Data should be regulated through the lens of consumer protection and privacy or whether antitrust laws should be used to address competition concerns with the collection of data. Do you have an opinion about the best approach to address this issue or should we be looking at a combination of different approaches?

We recognize policymakers and regulators are working to protect privacy while also considering whether making more data available among competitors would increase competition. These are complex issues, but we are encouraged to see some privacy and competition regulators working together to contribute their relevant expertise to the important questions being considered, including when a privacy-oriented practice is being evaluated in an antitrust context. We will continue to engage with policymakers and regulators, as well as other stakeholders, to support thoughtful regulation that encourages innovation and protects consumers. For example, we continue to publicly support federal privacy legislation in the United States (for more information, please see https://blog.google/outreach-initiatives/public-policy/the-urgent-necessity-of-enacting-a-national-privacy-law/).

Written Questions Submitted by Sen. Hawley to Markham Erickson:

Question 1. Please provide copies of all research findings or reports, whitepapers, slideshows, meeting recordings, or other documentation circulated within Google, over the past ten years, pertaining to each of the following topic areas:

- **a. Addiction or addictive behaviors associated with the use of Google's products and services;**
- **b. Depression and/or self-harm associated with the use of Google's products and services;**
- **c. Impact of Google's products and services on the mental health and wellness of users under age 18;**
- **d. Extent to which Google's products and services are accessed by users under age 13;**
- **e. Development of novel products or services targeted specifically to users under age 13.**

The relationship between technology use and physical and mental wellbeing is complex, especially for children and young people. Recent studies have highlighted that digital media use can help teens communicate with peers and family, seek helpful resources and support if they are experiencing distress, and find opportunities for learning and entertainment that can help combat isolation. We partner with expert organizations to inform our products and policies, and directly support and provide expertise to organizations that work directly with young people. Through Google.org, we have supported several organizations that support child and teen mental health, providing funding and technical expertise.

We take the health and well-being of all our creators and viewers seriously. Awareness and understanding of mental health is important and we support creators sharing their stories, such as posting content discussing their experiences with depression, self-harm, or other mental health issues. For much of this content, we show viewers viewers where they can find mental health support or suicide prevention resources, like referring them to the 24/7 Crisis Lifeline here in the US. However, we do not allow content that promotes self-harm or suicide.

Over the past several years, as part of our work to build a trusted environment for kids and families, we have worked with parents and experts across the globe in areas related to child safety, child development, digital literacy, and online safety. The advice from this group of trusted experts helps us build products that offer a positive experience for families, and was instrumental in the creation of the YouTube supervised experience, a solution for parents of teens and tweens launched in March 2021 on the main YouTube platform.

The YouTube supervised experience allows parents to choose among three different content choices: content generally suitable for viewers aged 9+; content generally suitable for viewers 13+; and the 'Most of YouTube' option, which excludes all age-restricted content (18+). To help parents understand more about the YouTube supervised experience, we have developed guides (such as those available at https://www.youtube.com/myfamily/), videos (such as https://www.youtube.com/watch?v=oVOa6nDU7HQ), and support pages (available at https://support.google.com/youtube/answer/10314940?hl=en), building on Google's successful Be Internet Awesome digital literacy resources, and in partnership with the National PTA, Parent Zone UK and other leading experts. We will continue to partner with these and other groups to provide easy to use resources specifically for parents to help them keep their kids safe online.

For our youngest users, we've also built a dedicated kids destination, the YouTube Kids app. We've invested heavily over the years to make YouTube Kids a safer, family-friendly place for kids to explore their imagination and curiosity. We have a higher bar for which videos can be a part of the app and also empower parents to control what content their child can and cannot see. If a channel has "Made for Kids" content, we use YouTube's quality principles for kids and family content to determine the monetization status of that content. We also have a made for kids ads policies to ensure we are providing protections and delivering age-appropriate experiences for ads on Google and we do not allow personalized targeting to kids under 13.

We care deeply about how families and children use technology and have engaged third parties to help us understand the challenges faced. For example, in 2019, we commissioned Fluent Research to conduct a study to examine the role digital technology plays in the wellbeing of families and to help us understand how we could better support healthy tech habits through our products (more information is available at https://services.google.com/fh/files/blogs/fluent_digital_wellbeing_report_global.pdf). This research, which included focus groups and/or survey respondents in eleven countries, has informed our approach to product and policy design, directly impacting our efforts to create experiences that help develop healthy tech habits, including the evolution of Family Link parental controls.

Question 2. Please provide the following information:

a. **How much revenue, in the aggregate, does Google estimate that it makes from users under 18?**

b. **How much revenue does Google estimate that it makes from *each individual* user under 18?**

c. **How much revenue, in the aggregate, does Google estimate that it makes from users under 13?**

d. How much revenue does Google estimate that it makes from *each individual* user under 13?

Google does not maintain, in the ordinary course of business, records of revenues at the user level. Our quarterly and yearly operating income numbers for all our business units are detailed in our public filings, available at https://abc.xyz/investor/.

Question 3. Has Google ever required a third party to alter search results, provide internal data, or make other nonmonetary contractual concessions in order to distribute or otherwise obtain access to Google's apps, including YouTube and YouTube TV?

Our agreements to distribute YouTube include a certification process in which new devices need to meet our technical requirements. This process exists to provide a consistent and high-quality YouTube experience for users across different devices.

For distribution partners whose devices provide users with a universal search experience that aggregates results across multiple content providers, YouTube requires that search results from YouTube are included among the results from other content providers. Partners have complete control on where to display the YouTube search results. Other content providers have similar requirements.

What is different about YouTube — in contrast to other content providers — is that we have an incredibly expansive content library with 500 hours uploaded every minute. YouTube makes a public Application Programming Interface (API) available so that all partners can query that API when a user issues a search query. If distribution partners do not have a universal search feature, we do not require them to display YouTube search results.

Written Questions Submitted by Sen. Tillis to Markham Erickson:

Question 1. The term "data" can have multiple meanings, which can sometimes generate confusion in policy discussions. For example you refer to the publicly available web as an important data set. How would you define "data" and "big data", as used in your written testimony?

- **a. How would you define consumer and user data, specifically what would be included and excluded from these definitions? For example, the section of data portability refers to the ability of users to export "their data".**
- **b. Would this include user uploaded videos, images, and text?**
- **c. Would such content be considered part of the "user" data, even if it includes content that originates from other sources?**
- **d. Does it include data in which intellectual property rights, including copyright, trade secret, trademark, or design rights, may subsist?**

Google's Privacy Policy (available at https://policies.google.com/privacy) explains what information Google collects, why Google collects it, and how users can update, manage, export, and delete their information. We are committed to giving users access and control over their data. We were one of the first companies to offer users a centralized portal to see and manage their data through easy-to-use tools with the launch of MyAccount in 2015 (now Google Account), and we encourage Google users to visit their Google Account (available at https://myaccount.google.com/) where they can review the data Google has collected and can choose to export or delete the data we store.

Our Privacy Policy describes in detail the categories of information we collect. The most common of these include:

- Identifiers such as name, phone number, and address, as well as unique identifiers tied to the browser, application, or device used.
- Demographic information, such as age, gender, and language.
- Commercial information such as payment information and a history of purchases made on Google's services.
- Internet, network, and other activity information such as search terms; views and interactions with content and ads; and activity on third-party sites and apps that use our services.
- Geolocation data, such as may be determined by GPS, IP address, and other data from sensors on or around a user's device, depending in part on the device and account settings.
- Other information created or provided by users, such as the content created, uploaded, or received (like photos, videos, emails, docs, or spreadsheets).

- Inferences drawn from the above, like ads interest categories, if permitted by the user's settings.

The types of data Google collects or stores may be different for users based on various settings the user has selected and what products they use. For example, if a user has signed in to their account and has "Web and App Activity" enabled, we may collect and store in the user's Account data about their activity on Google's services, like the user's search query and the URL they select on the Search results page. This can be helpful to users who wish to store this history; it also allows us to make better predictions about helpful results. If that user is not signed-in, however, we may still collect information about that query for use in some of our tools, like Google Trends (https://trends.google.com/), or to improve our products. We would not, however, associate that information with the user's Google account.

Additionally, Google has been a leader on data portability for over a decade, enabling our users to export their data and take it to another platform (for more information on this process and our recent improvements in this area, please see https://www.googblogs.com/author/markham-erickson/ and https://support.google.com/accounts/answer/3024190). Since 2011, Google has enabled users to easily move their content to competing services, with more than one billion gigabytes exported from Google products. This data download process, which we call Google Takeout, makes it possible for users to move their content to competing services, so no one feels they have to continue using Google if they prefer a service of another company (additional details are available at https://takeout.google.com/settings/takeout). This process can facilitate the export of data from more than 70 Google products, including Chrome, Gmail, Drive, Search, and YouTube. Users are able to export their data in a variety of industry standard formats that they can select based on product, type of data, and intended use. Users can also view a summary of the data saved in their Google accounts by following the instructions available at https://support.google.com/accounts/answer/162744. We know these features are being used - on average, we see 8.2 million exports per month with Google Takeout, and in 2021, more than 400 billion files were exported (a rate that has doubled since 2019).

Recognizing that data portability can be challenging for people who don't have high-speed internet, unlimited mobile data plans, or who don't have a personal device with extra storage, iIn 2018, we launched the Data Transfer Project (DTP), an open-source collaboration between Google, Apple, Meta, Microsoft, Twitter, and SmugMug to simplify data portability for people around the world. Unlike traditional methods of moving your files from one service to another, which require reliable broadband or drawing on mobile data plans, with DTP people can simply authorize a copy of the data to safely move to a new service without having to download it to a personal device first. (more information on this project is available at https://opensource.googleblog.com/2018/07/introducing-data-transfer-project.html and https://datatransferproject.dev/).

We recognize that privacy is not a one-size-fits-all proposition. Different users want to make different choices about how much information they share and how it is used. That is why we give our users control over their data privacy. To that end, we are continually focused on building tools that enable people to make the privacy choices that are right for them and their families.

Question 2. Ad-revenue used to support online piracy is a longstanding problem. Criminals profit by receiving advertising dollars in exchange for giving users free access to stolen movies, music, books, software, and other materials—stealing money from hardworking creators, including many small businesses and individual artists. A recent report found that over *a billion dollars a year* in advertising goes to supporting online pirated content.[1] Both the US and EU have been working on voluntary "follow the money" initiatives for several years with various actors, including Google, to stop funding theft. Yet the same report found that Google's advertising technologies provided 51 percent of ads to pirate apps.[2] This is particularly alarming given that other digital advertisers "almost never appear on piracy apps."[3]

a. **Why was Google identified as the top major brand involved in placing advertising on applications? What measures are you taking to change this?**

We share your interest in fighting online piracy and agree that one effective way to combat rogue sites that specialize in online piracy is to cut off their money supply. That is why we have worked diligently to block infringing sites and apps from using our services and work with other technology companies, publishers, and advertisers to develop and implement best practices for the advertising industry. These efforts have been successful. Around the world, online piracy has been decreasing, and spending on legitimate content is rising. Unfortunately, bad actors work hard to circumvent our systems and policies. While we recognize that we will never be able to fully eradicate piracy, we remain committed to these efforts and will continue to invest in our fight against piracy.

The report referenced in the question claims that advertisements of major brands are 24% of total ads on the reviewed applications. Of that 24%, advertisements for Google represented only 5% of those advertisements, which means that, according to the study, advertisements for Google were just 1.2% of the ads on the reviewed applications.

The report also notes that advertisements for major brands are 4% of total ads on the reviewed websites and that advertisements for Google were fewer than one percent of major

---

[1] Digital Citizens Alliance and White Bullet, Breaking (B)ads: How Advertiser-Supported Piracy Helps Fuel A Booming Multi-Billion Dollar Illegal Market (July 2021), https://www.digitalcitizensalliance.org/clientuploads/directory/Reports/Breaking-Bads-Report.pdf.
[2] *Id.*, pg. 34.
[3] *Id.*, pg. 17.

brand advertisements. This means advertisements for Google very rarely appeared on the reviewed websites.

It is also important to note that the methodology used in the report relies on a list of websites and apps that were identified by the author's own commercial machine-learning algorithm and includes data that is based on assumptions about ad revenue and traffic. Google is a leader in rooting out and ejecting rogue sites and apps from our publisher network. However, we acknowledge that no system is ever perfect and we remain committed to this work despite the challenges.

b. **Does Google receive money from placing advertising on websites that contain pirated content?**

We believe that one effective way to combat rogue sites that specialize in online piracy is to cut off their money supply. That is why we have been so committed to diligently blocking bad actors from using our services and helping set industry standards for safe online advertising. Our research has shown that AdSense ads, or ads that are matched with sites based on their content and visitors, appear on fewer than one-tenth of 1% of the pages that copyright owners identify in copyright removal notices for Search (more information on AdSense is available at https://support.google.com/adsense/answer/6242051).

c. **What steps does Google take, both in the United States and worldwide, to prohibit advertising on piracy websites and applications?**

We have always prohibited publishers from using our services to place ads on pages that contain pirated works, and we proactively monitor our network to root out bad publishers. In addition, when we receive a Digital Millennium Copyright Act (DMCA) notice for search, we take action to ensure that advertisements do not run on those same pages. Copyright holders can also notify us of pages or advertising that violates our policies through a webform.

We also work with other advertising leaders to craft best practices aimed at raising standards across the entire online advertising industry. Our efforts have been effective. In 2021, we blocked or removed 44.2 million advertisements that abused our policies related to copyright.

d. **Do you agree that supporting commercial-scale pirate websites and apps through advertising dollars is wrong?**

As noted above, we are and have been committed to diligently blocking bad actors from using our services and helping set industry standards for safe online advertising.

e. **Does Google, or its agents or subsidiaries, block payment for ad impressions on pirated content?**

We are always reviewing publisher pages for compliance with our policies. When we find ads running on pages that violate our policies, we remove the ads and stop the publisher from accruing further revenue on these pages.

f. **Does Google, or its agents or subsidiaries, conduct independent audits to ensure that any policies are being implemented effectively? How frequently are policies reviewed?**

We review our advertising policies and enforcement efforts regularly to ensure they remain up to date and effective. We have thousands of people globally working on policy development and enforcement. We actively track emerging trends and adversarial behavior and are quick to adapt our enforcement and policies accordingly. Additionally, in 2021, we added or updated over 30 policies for both advertisers and publishers.

We are active in industry associations that drive accountability through independent oversight on brand safety, operations, and reporting. YouTube was the first digital platform to ever receive accreditation from the Media Ratings Council's Enhanced Content Level Context and Brand Safety Guidelines, which are also sponsored by the American Association of Advertising Agencies, the Association of National Advertisers, and the Interactive Advertising Bureau. We also continue to work with the Global Alliance for Responsible Media on its strategic focus areas, such as exploring new reporting metrics on brand safety and improving brand safety tools across the industry to better manage advertising adjacency.

g. **Does Google collect data over its own ad placements that would allow it to prevent placement on websites or apps that pose a high risk for distributing illegal content, including pirated content?**

As detailed in our responses above, we currently use the most effective methods we can to prevent the placement of our own advertisements on websites and apps that contain potentially infringing content. We continue to examine ways that we can further improve.

h. **Google Ads is a tool offered to businesses and brands to place their ads in front of consumers. A brand chooses the type of audience it wants to reach and Google places the ad on the websites most likely to reach the target demographic. What steps are taken to ensure that ads are not placed on pirate websites?**

Please refer to our answer to Question 2c, above.

i. **What steps are taken to ensure that pirate publishers are prohibited from selling ad space through Google's advertising subsidiaries?**

Please refer to our answer to Question 2c, above.

j. **What steps is Google taking to enhance transparency of its activities on its advertising networks?**

We provide information about our policies and practices through our Google Transparency Report (available at https://transparencyreport.google.com/) and our Annual Ads Safety Report (available at https://blog.google/products/ads-commerce/ads-safety-report-2021/). We are committed to giving our users transparency, choice, and control when it comes to the ads they see on our platforms. We are working toward verification of all advertisers globally, and we recently announced that we are enhancing ad disclosures in the U.S. to link to advertiser pages that include an ad creative repository, the legal name, and country of origin for the advertiser.

Question 3. You stated in your testimony that Google does not sell data that it collects online.

a. **Does Google share data collected in one business unit with other business units?**

b. **Does it share data collected with any legal entities outside of Google?**

c. **Does it share any of this data in connection with a legal business transaction?**

At Google, we believe that data should be used to make consumers' lives better by improving the quality and diversity of products and services available, while protecting users' privacy and giving them control. Our business relies on earning our users' trust, specifically in how we use and protect their data. We work to maintain that trust by offering industry-leading controls to manage privacy. Three billion users visit their Google accounts every year, where they can review and change their privacy settings and delete data stored with their account.

Google does not sell users' personal information to anyone. That is not our business model, and we have always made this a touchstone of Google's relationship with our users. Google shares personal information with partners in the specific circumstances described in our Privacy Policy section on Google partners at https://policies.google.com/privacy/google-partners, including:

- With user consent: For example, if users use Google Home to make a reservation through a booking service, we will get their permission before sharing their name or phone number with the restaurant.
- For external processing: We provide personal information to our affiliates and other trusted businesses or persons to process it for us, based on our instructions and in compliance with our Privacy Policy and any other appropriate confidentiality and security measures. For example, we use service providers to help us with customer support.

- For legal reasons, such as to meet any applicable law, regulation, legal process, or enforceable governmental request.

In addition, our Privacy Policy (available at https://policies.google.com/privacy?hl=en-US) describes for users how we may use or combine data across our products, as well as the controls they have over their information. For example, depending on their settings, if a user watches videos of guitar players on YouTube, they might see an ad for guitar lessons on a site that uses our ad products. Some other examples of how we combine the information we collect include:

- When users are signed in to their Google Account and search on Google, they can see search results from the public web, along with relevant information from the content they have in other Google products, like Gmail or Google Calendar. This can include things like the status of an upcoming flight, restaurant, and hotel reservations, or their photos.
- If users have communicated with someone via Gmail and want to add them to a Google Doc or an event in Google Calendar, Google makes it easy to do so by autocompleting their email address when our users start to type in their name. This feature makes it easier to share things with people they know.

Question 4. Ms. Slaiman advocates for "a digital regulator to comprehensively the policy questions surrounding digital platforms."

a. **Do you agree that this is necessary?**

b. **Given the many issues beyond privacy and competition that address and implicate digital policy—including cybersecurity, national security, consumer rights, free speech, and intellectual property concerns—what existing agency would be the best situated, in your view, to carry out this role?**

c. **Is it important to you that the regulator should be politically accountable?**

We recognize policymakers and regulators are working to protect privacy while also considering whether making more data available among competitors would increase competition. We are encouraged to see some privacy and competition regulators conferring more formally to contribute their relevant expertise to the important questions being considered, for example when a privacy-oriented practice is being evaluated in an antitrust context. We will continue to engage with policymakers and regulators, as well as other stakeholders, to support thoughtful regulation that encourages innovation and protects consumers. For example, we continue to publicly support federal privacy legislation in the United States (more information is available at https://blog.google/outreach-initiatives/public-policy/the-urgent-necessity-of-enacting-a-national-privacy-law/).

Senator Tillis

Questions for the Record

Big Data, Big Questions: Implications for Competition and Consumers
Mr. John Robb, Global Guerillas Report

Q: The term "data" can have multiple meanings, which can sometimes generate confusion in policy discussions. How would you define "data" and "big data", as used in your written testimony?

A: The difference between data and "big data" is scale.

Big data has far more volume, variety, and velocity than traditional data. This complexity changes the way insight is generated from it. Instead of seeking definitive answers (customers are buying x more than y), analysts look for patterns. Patterns that can be useful in spotting opportunities, detecting problems, and shaping solutions. Finding these patterns through intentional analysis, particularly patterns that aren't ephemeral, is very difficult.

Big data is particularly useful for training AIs (machine learning). There's a high correlation between the amount of data used to train an AI and the quality of the AI. AIs trained using big data naturally find unexpected patterns and contextual cues that are useful in solving the problem they are trying to solve.

Q: How would you define consumer and user data, specifically what would be included and excluded from these definitions?

A: Traditional consumer data is mostly static demographic data. How much do you make, where do you live, and what is your education level?

That's radically changed with the arrival of networked user data. This new user data includes;

- Tracking data. Mouse and keyboard clicks. Page and site visits (on a single site and across sites). Physical location. Tracking over time and space. This is now expanding into detecting focus (eyeball tracking), physical measurement (health monitoring to hand movement), sensor data (pictures, videos, and other data collected by sensors in the environment, from a Tesla car to CCTV), etc.

- User-produced data. What people upload (both intentionally and unintentionally). Textual content (texting, blog posts, essays), voice content (podcasts to audio capture from Alexa or an iPhone), images (smartphone pictures to YouTube uploads). This data set is expanding.
- AI-training data (user-produced + tracking data at scale). User data is being used to actively train AIs. For example; Tesla uses user feedback and experiences to improve their self-driving system. Enlisting customers to actively train AIs is something we will see much more of in the future.
- Other firms strip mine the open Web (without consent) to build AIs (GPT-4 (text), Stable Diffusion (images), Google translate (text), etc.).

Q: Would this include user-uploaded videos, images, and text? A: Yes, see above.

Q: Would such content be considered part of the "user" data, even if it includes content that originates from other sources?

A: Tracking data and uploaded data are both "user data." Data brokers aggregate this data for sale to marketing departments/firms and firms building AIs.

Sometimes it is anonymized; sometimes, it isn't. Sometimes firms with access to user-tracking data sell it to generate extra revenue.

If the text or image being uploaded is from another source (somebody else took the picture or wrote the text), then it isn't user data, but the tracking data on the upload is. This is why the best approach to compensating people for data use is made in aggregate, at the population scale.

For example, a data ownership bill for the people of North Carolina would aggregate the data provided by people in the state. Data brokers, with a fiduciary duty to the people contributing to the data set, would compete to sign up people attached to this pool.

Data brokers representing individuals would solve the privacy problem in a way that doesn't destroy data (like in Europe). Data brokers, fueled by industry revenue, would have the lawyers and technologists needed to protect data and find new data sources collected by advancing technology. In contrast, privacy-based regulations rely on getting the attention of overwhelmed bureaucrats.

Q: Does it include data in which intellectual property rights, including copyright, trade secret, trademark, or design rights, may subsist?

A: No. There is already an industry that protects that data. However, firms that claim (like many social networks) all of the user-uploaded data and data collected about them, would not be allowed to claim ownership over it. That data would be owned by the individuals in question.

Q: How would you differentiate your proposal for people to own data from existing intellectual property rights-based approaches?

A: Technology has outpaced our laws. The data being generated by individuals isn't adequately protected by existing legal frameworks. Providing a mechanism for protecting the ownership rights of individuals in aggregate is critical to safeguarding against abuse (by corporations and the government) as well as providing a mechanism for participating in the AI-driven economy of the future.

To be precise: the data being strip-mined right now is being used to create the most valuable technological artifacts that have ever existed, without compensation to the people it is coming from. Making it possible for people to participate in the upside potential of this development will be as important as land ownership was to the development of capitalism (one of the most revolutionary aspects of the American Revolution, and why it was so important to early capitalism, was the ability of individuals without a hereditary title to own land).

Q: You advocate for a new form of digital identity. Could you please explain further what you mean by this, and how you envision it working in the current environment? Are there particular technologies that would need to be developed for this to be implemented?

A: Digital identity is necessary for the assignment of rights (of speech, ownership, etc.). It simply connects an online identity (collection of accounts, activities, etc.) to a living, breathing person in the physical world. Typically, this is done using the same approaches used for registering a financial account (government ID, etc.). It can become more sophisticated through the application of AI (as we are about to see with Twitter).

Q: Ms. Slaiman advocates for "a digital regulator to comprehensively the policy questions surrounding digital platforms." Do you agree that this is necessary?

A: If the digital regulator is overseeing the launch and establishment of a new industry (data brokers, etc.) and the technology standards that support it, then yes. If its intent is to build a regulatory enforcement body that is focused on privacy regulations and increasingly restrictive content moderation (as we see in the EU), then no. That would be a disaster (for example: China would win the AI race and the US and EU would suffer economic impoverishment due to it).

Q: Given the many issues beyond privacy and competition that address and implicate digital policy—including cybersecurity, national security, consumer rights, free speech, and intellectual property concerns—what existing agency would be the best situated, in your view, to carry out this role?

A: Something that looks like a cross between the SEC and Consumer protection. It would need to be focused on the individual, and their rights, while being able to manage the needs of growing a new industry (data brokers that represent the data pools that individuals join). This industry has the potential to rival finance in size over time (percentage ownership or royalty rights from big AIs could be worth tens of trillions in the not-too-distant future).

Q: Is it important to you that the regulator should be politically accountable?

A: Of course. However, if the political focus is on the micromanagement of user data collection to shape society, then no. The goal of political discussions on this issue should be focused on creating the minimum viable rule set for a prosperous and successful society.

Senator Blackburn

Questions for the Record to John Robb

The Global Guerrillas Report

Q: It's imperative for the U.S. to get a national consumer privacy law in place—the EU and China have already done so. Given consumer concerns about how their data is being used online, what should that regime look like? What are the obstacles the United States faces in getting to that point?

A: There are three systems in place:

1) EU privacy laws use aggressive regulatory oversight to limit and destroy data.
2) China assigns ownership of data rights to the government and assigns loyal corporations the right to fully gather and exploit it.
3) US doesn't have a centralized approach. With few exceptions, it lets corporations do whatever they want in regard to data collection and exploitation.

Here's how this will play out:

- The EU approach is that it will prevent the development of the AIs and products/services that will drive economic growth in the future. Their approach to data is likely to result in economic impoverishment long term.
- The Chinese approach will generate economic growth and success. However, it will also be used for networked authoritarianism by the Chinese government. It will provide the government with complete control over the entire population in real time. From behavior to perception (through control of augmented reality).
- The US approach will yield some economic success, but it will be a system completely controlled by big corporations and a few wealthy individuals. Almost all of the economic success generated by this approach will concentrate in the hands of the corporations. Furthermore, the control corporations have over data will allow them

to dominate politics (in short, corporate-run network authoritarianism).

The solution?

The solution that allows the US the ability to succeed economically and avoid authoritarianism is to provide people with digital rights and data ownership. That approach would create an industry response to user data (an industry of data brokers/banks, much like the financial industry, which has a fiduciary responsibility to protect this data and maximize its returns). It ensures that the data needed to fuel development is available to corporations while allowing the people who provide this data a means of participating in the great wealth created by it.

Senator Chuck E. Grassley

Questions for Mr. John Robb

Q: How important is the amount of data that a company has to their ability to effectively monetize that information?

A: A few thoughts on this:

- Data is key to success in a networked economy.
- The more you have and the better its quality, the more success you will have. NOTE: there is a high correlation between the amount of data you have available for an AI to train with and the quality of the AI.
- At the level of the economy, if corporations don't have access to data, they won't be able to match the products available from China that do have access.

Q: How difficult can it be for a startup or small business to collect enough data to be able to compete with companies that have large amounts of data?

A: It's hard, but it becomes impossible if the big companies control the small company's access to data. Big companies are using access to data as a weapon against the competition and as a means of extracting monopoly rents from their platforms. Apple and Google are good examples of this. This is already bad in the smartphone industry, it is going to become a catastrophe when augmented reality arrives (soon).

Q: Some commentators argue that the amount of data currently possessed by large incumbent companies forecloses the ability of new entrants to compete.

But, new data is being created every day and what data is important in the future may not be what is being collected today. If so, why isn't there an opportunity for additional companies to enter the market?

A: I agree. Data aggregation and privacy regulations (or "concerns') are being used by big companies to dominate marketplaces. New data is created, but these companies control the flow. For example, this control has allowed big companies in the smartphone market to charge a ~30% tax on transactions in the smartphone economy. It's extortionate.

Q: There is debate over whether Big Data should be regulated through the lens of consumer protection and privacy or whether antitrust laws should be used to address competition concerns with the collection of data. Do you have an opinion about the best approach to address this issue or should we be looking at a combination of different approaches?

Best approach: Data ownership for individuals. They contribute all of the data collected about them to big pools. These pools are managed by data brokers who have a fiduciary duty to protect this data and maximize the returns generated by it.

The data relationship between an app running on a smartphone or an augmented reality headset would be with the data brokers representing the individuals using the device. The device company wouldn't be able to use its control over data to extort monopoly rents. Instead, that benefit would flow to the individuals who contributed the data, providing them participation in the economy being built on this data.

A combo of SEC/banking (industry focus) and consumer protection agency would work best. The goal would be to set up a data brokerage/banking industry (with the individual as the client) that is so profitable that it could hire the people needed to enforce it.

February 21, 2023

The Honorable Richard J. Durbin Chairman
Committee on the Judiciary United States Senate
711 Hart Senate Building Washington, D.C. 20510

Dear Chairman Durbin:

Thank you for the questions for the record from the Senate Committee on the Judiciary, Subcommittee on Competition Policy, Antitrust, and Consumer Rights hearing entitled "Big Data, Big Questions: Implications for Competition and Consumers," held on September 21, 2021. Per your request, attached are answers for the record to your questions.

Sincerely,
Meta Platforms, Inc

Senator Marsha Blackburn
Questions for the Record to Steve Satterfield, Vice President of Privacy & Public Policy, Facebook

1) Please identify three distinct changes you have made to your platform to make it a safer and healthier experience for children.

At Instagram, we have been working for a long time to help provide age-appropriate experiences on our platform; as part of that work, we recently announced some new tools and features to support keeping young people even safer on Instagram. Although we have made a number of changes, here are three recent examples:

Parental Tools. We launched tools in March 2022 to help parents and guardians guide and support their teens on Instagram. They can ask teens to enable them to view how much time their teens spend on Instagram and set time limits. We've also given teens the option to notify their parents if they report someone, giving their parents the opportunity to talk about it with them. These tools are available in our new Family Center. We worked closely with experts, parents, guardians and teens to develop Family Center, a place for parents and teens to work together on their accounts within Meta technologies, set up and use supervision tools, and access resources on how to communicate with their teens about internet use. This is just one step on a longer path—our vision for Family Center is to eventually allow parents and guardians to help their teens manage experiences across Meta technologies, all from one central place.

Family Center includes an education hub where parents and guardians can access resources from experts and review helpful articles, videos and tips on topics like how to talk to teens about social media. Parents can also watch video tutorials on how to use the supervision tools available on Instagram today. We worked closely with groups like Connect Safely and Net Family News to develop these resources, and we'll continue to add new information to Family Center's education hub. These parental supervision tools on Instagram allow parents and guardians to send invitations to their teens to initiate supervision tools, which enable them to:

- View how much time their teens spend on Instagram and set time limits;
- Set specific times during the day or week to limit their teen's use of Instagram;
- View what accounts their teens follow and the accounts that follow them;
- See more information when their teen reports an account or post, including who was reported, and the type of report;
- See a list of the accounts their teen is currently blocking on Instagram. The block list is in order of recency and denotes any users that have been blocked in the last seven days by the teen;
- See the teen's account settings specific to: (1) account privacy (public / private); (2) who can send the teen message requests (anyone / followers / no one); (3) who can add theteen to a messaging group (everyone / only people they follow on Instagram); and (4) sensitive content controls (less / standard).

Additionally, in November 2022, we introduced updates on Facebook and Instagram to help further protect teens from online harm. For example, everyone who is under the age of 16 (or under 18 in certain countries) is now defaulted into more private settings when they join Facebook (a change we announced for Instagram in July 2021), and we encourage teens already on the app to choose these more private settings. We are also working with the National Center for Missing and Exploited Children to build a global platform for teens who are worried intimate images they created might be shared on public online platforms without their consent. This platform will be similar to work we have done to prevent the non-consensual sharing of intimate images for adults. It will allow us to help prevent a teen's intimate images from being posted online and can be used by other companies across the tech industry. In addition, we are working with Thorn and their NoFiltr brand to create educational materials that reduce the shame and stigma surrounding intimate images and empower teens to seek help and take back control if they've shared them or are experiencing sextortion.

Take A Break. We also launched "Take A Break" in certain countries to empower people to make informed decisions about how they're spending their time. If someone has been scrolling for a certain amount of time, we ask them to take a break from Instagram and suggest that they set reminders to take more breaks in the future. We show them expert-backed tips to help them reflect and reset. To make sure that teens are aware of this feature, we show them notifications suggesting they turn these reminders on.

Nudging Teens Towards Different Topics if They've Been Dwelling on One Topic for a While. Our research shows—and external experts agree—that if people are dwelling on one topic for a while, it could be helpful to nudge them towards other topics at the right moment. That's why we built an experience that will nudge people towards other topics if they've been dwelling on one topic for a while. This nudge is designed to encourage teens to discover something new and excludes certain topics that may be associated with appearance comparison.

We designed this feature because research suggests that nudges can be effective for helping people—especially teens — be more mindful of how they're using social media in the moment. In an external study on the effects of nudges on social media use, 58.2% of respondents agreed or strongly agreed that nudges made their social media experience better by helping them become more mindful of their time on-platform. Our own research shows they're working too: during a one-week testing period, one in five teens who saw our new nudges switched to a different topic.

In addition to this work, we continue to develop ways for people to verify their age on Instagram, allowing us to provide age-appropriate experiences. For example, in June 2022, we began testing new options for people on Instagram to verify their age, starting with people based in the US. If someone attempts to edit their date of birth on Instagram from under the age of 18 to 18 or over, we'll require them to verify their age using options such as uploading their ID or recording a video selfie. We're testing this so we can make sure teens and adults are in the right experience for their age group. We are also partnering with Yoti, a company that specializes in online age verification, to help ensure people's privacy.

Our age verification tests show that our tools are working to help keep people within age- appropriate experiences. Since we began these new tools on Instagram, we've found that approximately four times as many people were more likely to complete our age verification requirements (when attempting to edit their date of birth from under 18 to over 18), equating to hundreds of thousands of people being placed in experiences appropriate for their age. We also were able to stop 96% of the teens who attempted to edit their birthdays from under 18 to 18 or over on Instagram from doing so. And we have found that 81% of people presented with our menu of options chose to use Yoti's video selfie to verify their age.

Senator Chuck E. Grassley
Questions for the Record to Mr. Steve Satterfield, Vice President, Privacy & Public Policy, Facebook

1) Facebook monetize user's data by selling targeted advertisements. In the second quarter of 2021 Facebook had revenues of $29.08 billion. It has also been reported that the average American's data was worth $164 per year to Facebook. Is it accurate that the average America's data is worth $164 per year to Facebook?

We publicly report our Average Revenue per User ("ARPU") on Facebook, both for advertising and other revenue, broken out by geographic region. ARPU is a revenue-based metric and not a valuation of people's data. As stated in our public financial filings, we define ARPU as our total revenue in a given geography during a given quarter, divided by the average of the number of monthly active users in the geography at the beginning and end of the quarter. In the U.S. and Canada, Facebook's ARPU from advertising was $58.77 in the fourth quarter of 2022.

We also report the Average Revenue per Person ("ARPP") across Meta's family of apps, both foradvertising and other revenue. As with ARPU, ARPP is a revenue-based metric and not a valuationof people's data. As stated in our public financial filings, we define ARPP as our total revenue during a given quarter, divided by the average of the number of MAP at the beginning and end ofthe quarter. Meta's ARPP from advertising across its family of apps was $8.63 in the third quarterof 2022.

For more information, please see our latest earnings presentation (https://s21.q4cdn.com/399680738/files/doc_financials/2022/q4/Earnings-Presentation-Q4- 2022.pdf).

2) There is debate over whether Big Data should be regulated through the lens of consumer protection and privacy or whether antitrust laws should be used to address competition concerns with the collection of data. Do you have an opinion about the best approach to address this issue or should we be looking at a combination of different approaches?

Meta has long called for regulation in the digital space on issues like privacy and data security, combating foreign election interference, content moderation, and data portability. The issues facing the industry are complex, multi-faceted, and impact peoples' lives. Accordingly, Meta is committed to working with policymakers to craft the right regulations. Meta is amenable to reviewing proposed legislation and providing comments.

More information about our approach to regulation can be found here: https://about.meta.com/regulations/?utm_source=about.facebook.com&utm_medium=redirect.

Senator Josh Hawley
Questions for the Record to Steve Satterfield, Vice President of Privacy & Public Policy, Facebook

1) Please provide copies of all research findings or reports, whitepapers, slideshows, meeting recordings, or other documentation circulated within Facebook, over the past ten years, pertaining to each of the following topic areas:

   a) Addiction or addictive behaviors associated with the use of Facebook's products and services;
   b) Depression and/or self-harm associated with the use of Facebook's products and services;

c) Impact of Facebook's products and services on the mental health and wellness of users under age 18;
d) Extent to which Facebook's products and services are accessed by users under age 13
e) Development of novel products or services targeted specifically to users under age 13.

We want social media to be a positive force in teens' lives, so we're listening to feedback from experts and our community to build apps where teens can discover and create in an age-appropriateway; as part of that work, we have developed tools and features to support keeping young peopleeven safer on Instagram. For example:

Parental Tools. We are committed to working with parents and families, as well as experts inchild development, online safety, and children's health and media, to ensure we are building appropriate tools and features for families. That means building tools that promote meaningfulinteractions and helping people manage their time on our platform. It also means providing information, resources, and tools for parents and teens to work together to develop healthy andsafe online habits. And it means continued learning in this area.

We believe that parents and guardians know what is best for their teens, and we've developedmore than 30 tools to support teens and families, including developing supervision tools that allow parents and guardians to ask teens to enable them to be more involved in their teens' experiences. In March 2022, we rolled out supervision tools that allow parents and guardians to: (1) view how much time their teens spend on Instagram and set time limits; (2) be notifiedwhen their teen shares they've reported someone; and (3) view and receive updates on what accounts their teens follow and the accounts that follow their teens. In June 2022, weintroduced additional features that allow parents and guardians to send invitations to their teensto initiate supervision tools, set specific times when they would like to limit their teen's use of Instagram, and see more information when their teen reports an account or post, including whowas reported, and the type of report. We make video tutorials on how to use these supervisiontools available for parents and guardians in the Family Center's education hub.

Additionally, in November 2022, we introduced updates on Facebook and Instagram to help further protect teens from online harm. For example, everyone who is under the age of 16 (or under 18 in certain countries) is now defaulted into more private settings when they join Facebook (a change we announced for Instagram in July 2021), and we encourage teens already on the app to choose these more private settings. We are also working with the National Center for Missing and Exploited Children to build a global platform for teens who are worriedintimate images they created might be shared on public online platforms without their consent.This platform will be similar to work we have done to prevent the non-consensual sharing of intimate images for adults. It will allow us to help prevent a teen's intimate images from beingposted online and can be used by other companies across the tech industry. In addition, we areworking with Thorn and their NoFiltr brand to create educational materials that reduce the shame and stigma surrounding intimate images, and empower teens to seek help and take back control if they've shared them or are experiencing sextortion.

Take A Break. We also launched "Take A Break" in certain countries to empower people to make informed decisions about how they're spending their time. If someone has been scrollingfor a certain amount of time, we ask them to take a break from Instagram and suggest that theyset reminders to take more breaks in the future. We also show them expert-backed tips to helpthem reflect and reset. To make sure that teens are aware of this feature, we show them notifications suggesting they turn these reminders on.

Nudging Teens Towards Different Topics if They've Been Dwelling on One Topic for a While. Our research shows—and external experts agree—that if people are dwelling on one topic for a while, it could be helpful to nudge them towards other topics at the right moment. That's why we built an experience that will nudge people towards other topics if they've beendwelling on one topic for a while. This nudge is designed to encourage teens to discover something new and excludes certain topics that may be associated with appearance comparison.

We designed this feature because research suggests that nudges can be effective for helping people — especially teens — be more mindful of how they're using social media in the moment. In an external study on the effects of nudges on social media use, 58.2% ofrespondents agreed or strongly agreed that nudges made their social media experience better by helping them become more mindful of their time on-platform. Our own research shows they're working too: during a one-week testing period, one in five teens who saw our new nudges switched to a different topic.

In addition to this work, we prohibit people under the age of 13 from using Facebook and Instagram, and when we learn that someone under 13 years old is on our platform, we remove them. We also continue to develop ways for people to verify their age on Instagram, allowing us to provide age-appropriate experiences. For example, in June 2022, we began testing new optionsfor people on Instagram to verify their age, starting with people based in the US. If someone attempts to edit their date of birth on Instagram from under the age of 18 to 18 or over, we'll require them to verify their age using options such as uploading their ID or recording a video selfie.We're testing this so we can make sure teens and adults are in the right experience for their age group. We are also partnering with Yoti, a company that specializes in online age verification, to help ensure people's privacy.

Our age verification tests show that our tools are working to help keep people within age-appropriate experiences. Since we began these new tools on Instagram, we've found that approximately four times as many people were more likely to complete our age verification requirements (when attempting to edit their date of birth from under 18 to over 18), equating to hundreds of thousands of people being placed in experiences appropriate for their age. We also were able to stop 96% of the teens who attempted to edit their birthdays from under 18 to 18 or over on Instagram from doing so. And we have found that 81% of people presented with our menu of options chose to use Yoti's video selfie to verify their age.

Meta conducts research on these important issues to understand how people experience its apps. We use our research to inform changes to our apps and provide resources for the people who use them. We are committed to learning even more about issues related to well-being, and we welcome the opportunity to work with Congress and others in the industry on this important topic.

We offer researchers a number of privacy-protective methods to collect and analyze data. We welcome research that challenges us to innovate and that doesn't compromise the security of our platform or the privacy of the people who use it. Meta researchers have also published and shared hundreds of papers, and we will continue to work to publish research externally and to engage and collaborate with experts, including in data-sharing with researchers on issues related to young people. For more information about research we make available, please visit https://research.facebook.com/.

Finally, in December 2022, we held our first Meta Summit focused on Youth Safety and Well- Being to discuss this work. Safety advocates, mental health experts, educators, think tank researchers, policy writers and parents—many of whom helped inform the development of these tools—gathered in Washington, D.C. to discuss challenges families face in the digital age and explore opportunities to better serve teens and families. At the Summit, Nick Clegg, Meta's President of Global Affairs, called for global policymakers and regulators to work together on clear, consistent regulation when it comes to providing safe, age-appropriate experiences for young people online. We support regulators across the globe working together to establish clear, consistent laws that adapt to ever-evolving technologies, so they can be implemented successfully by companies across our industry. We're hopeful that continued regulation in this area will seek to preserve teens' rights to be online, while creating safe, supportive environments for them to express themselves.

2) Please provide the following information:

   a) How much revenue, in the aggregate, does Facebook estimate that it makes from users under 18?
   b) How much revenue does Facebook estimate that it makes from each individual
   c) user under 18?
   d) How much revenue, in the aggregate, does Facebook estimate that it makes from users under 13?
   e) How much revenue does Facebook estimate that it makes from each individual user under 13?

We publicly report our Average Revenue per User ("ARPU") on Facebook, both for advertising and other revenue, broken out by geographic region. In the US and Canada, Facebook's ARPU from advertising was $58.77 in the fourth quarter of 2022. We also report the Average Revenue per Person ("ARPP") across Meta's family of apps, both for advertising and other revenue. Meta's ARPP from advertising across its family of apps was $8.63 in the fourth quarter of 2022. For more information, please see our latest earningspresentation (https://s21.q4cdn.com/399680738/files/doc_financials/2022/q4/Earnings-Presentation-Q4- 2022.pdf). We do not break out this information publicly by age. We prohibit people under the age of 13 from using Facebook and Instagram, and when we learn that someone under 13 years old is on our platform, we remove them.

3) On September 27, Instagram head Adam Mosseri announced that the company was pausing efforts "to build an Instagram experience for people under the age of 13, often referred to as 'Instagram Kids,'" but "[stood] by the need to develop this experience" and intended "to work with parents, experts, policymakers and regulators, to listen to

their concerns, and to demonstrate the value and importance of this project for younger teens online today."

a) When, if at all, does Facebook project that it will resume development on "an Instagram experience for people under the age of 13"?

b) On the basis of what considerations did Facebook conclude that it was more important to develop a designated digital space for users under 13 than, conversely, to ramp up efforts to prevent use of the platform by these users altogether?

We started work to build an Instagram experience for tweens (aged 10-12) to address an issue seen across our industry: tweens are getting phones younger and younger, misrepresenting their age, and downloading apps that are meant for those 13 or older. This is an industry-wide concern, and other tech companies have built experiences for tweens. For example, YouTube and TikTok both have versions of their apps built specifically for those under 13. Additionally, we launched Messenger Kids in 2017 after meeting with thousands of parents, parenting organizations, child safety advocates and child development experts about the need for a messaging app that lets kids have fun connecting with friends and family while giving parents control over the experience.

The Instagram experience for tweens was intended to focus on delivering age-appropriate experiences and provide parents and guardians visibility and control over what their tweens are doing online. While we stand by the need to develop this Instagram experience, in September 2021, we announced that we were pausing this work. To be clear, our intention was not for this version to be the same as Instagram today. It was never meant for younger kids, but for tweens (aged 10-12). It would have required parental permission to join, we would not have shown ads, and it would have had age-appropriate content and features. Parents would have been able to supervise the time their tweens spent on the app and oversee who could message them, who could follow them, and whom they could follow.

We also continue to build technology to find and remove Instagram accounts belonging to people under the age of 13. We have tools and processes to identify and remove people who falsely state they are 13 years old or older. For example, anyone can report an underage account to us. Our content reviewers are also trained to flag reported accounts that appear to be used by people who are underage. If these people are unable to prove they meet our minimum age requirements, we delete their accounts. In the last two quarters of 2021, Meta removed more than 4.8 million accounts on Facebook and 1.7

million accounts on Instagram because they were unable to meet our minimum age requirement.

Senator Thom Tillis
Questions for the Record to Steve Satterfield, Vice President of Privacy & Public Policy, Facebook

1) The term "data" can have multiple meanings, which can sometimes generate confusion in policy discussions. How would you define "data" and "big data", as used in your written testimony?

   a) How would you define consumer and user data, specifically what would be included and excluded from these definitions?
   b) Would this include user uploaded videos, images, and text?
   c) Would such content be considered part of the "user" data, even if it includes content that originates from other sources?
   d) Does it include data in which intellectual property rights, including copyright, trade secret, trademark, or design rights, may subsist?

As explained in our Privacy Policy, we collect four basic categories of data about people: (1) data about their activity and information they provide; (2) data about their friends, followers, and other connections; (3) data about their app, browser and devices; and (4) data we receive from partners, vendors and third parties, including the websites and apps that use our business tools. Our Privacy Policy provides more detail about each of the four categories.

People retain ownership of the intellectual property rights (things like copyright or trademarks) in any such content that they create and share on our platforms. Nothing in our Terms of Service takes away the rights people have to their own content, and they are free to share their content with anyone else, wherever they want.

As far as the amount of data we collect about people, the answer depends on the person. People who have only recently signed up for Facebook have usually shared only a few things—such as name, contact information, age, and gender. Over time, as people use our products and interact with our services, we receive more data from them, and this data helps us provide more relevant content and services. That data will fall into the categories noted above, but the specific data we receive will, in large part, depend on how the person chooses to use Facebook. For example, some people use Facebook to share photos, so we receive and store photos for those people. Some people enjoy watching videos on Facebook; when they do, we receive information about the video they watched, and we can use that information to help show other videos in their Feeds. Other people seldom or never watch videos, so we do not receive the same kind of information from them, and their Feeds are likely to feature fewer videos.

The data we have about people also depends on how they have used our controls. For example, people who share photos can easily delete those photos. The same is true of any other kind of content that people post on our services. Through Facebook's Activity Log tool, people can also control information about their engagement—i.e., their likes, shares, and comments— with other people's posts. The use of these controls affects the data we have about people.

We also offer a variety of tools to help users understand the data Facebook has about them. These include the Access Your Information and Download Your Information tools available to people who use Facebook in their account settings. And to provide more transparency and control around these practices, Off-Facebook Activity lets people see a summary of apps and websites that send us information about their activity and allows them to disconnect this information from their account if they choose. For more information about this tool, please see our Help Center.

1) Ad-revenue used to support online piracy is a longstanding problem. Criminals profit by receiving advertising dollars in exchange for giving users free access to stolen movies, music, books, software, and other materials—stealing money from hardworking creators, including many small businesses and individual artists. A recent report found that over *a billion dollars a year* in advertising goes to supportingonline pirated content.[76] Both the US and EU have been working on voluntary "followthe money" initiatives for several years with various actors, including Facebook, to stop funding theft. Yet the same report found that Facebook was a top ad spender, accounting for 27% of major brand advertising appearing on piracy apps.[77] This is

[76] Digital Citizens Alliance and White Bullet, *Breaking (B)ads: How Advertiser-Supported Piracy Helps Fuel A Booming Multi-Billion Dollar Illegal Market* (July 2021), https://www.digitalcitizensalliance.org/clientuploads/directory/Reports/Breaking-Bads-Report.pdf.

[77] *Id.*, pg. 17.

particularly alarming given that other digital advertisers "almost never appear on piracy apps."[78]

a) What steps does Facebook take, both in the United States and worldwide, to prohibit advertising on piracy websites and applications?
b) Why was Facebook identified as the top major brands involved in placing advertising on applications? What measures is Facebook taking to change this?
c) Does Facebook agree that supporting commercial-scale pirate websites and apps through advertising dollars is wrong?
d) Does Facebook, or its agents or subsidiaries, identify websites or apps that posea risk of distributing or displaying copyright protected content without authorization?
e) Does Facebook, or its agents or subsidiaries, restrict the display of its advertisements on websites that infringe copyright, or pose a high risk of engaging in copyright infringement?
f) Does Facebook, or its agents or subsidiaries, block payment for ad impressionson pirated content?
g) Does Facebook, or its agents or subsidiaries, conduct independent audits to ensure that any policies are being implemented effectively? How frequently are policies reviewed?
h) Does Facebook collect data over its own ad placements that would allow it to prevent placement on websites or apps that pose a high risk for distributing illegal content, including pirated content?
i) What steps is Facebook taking to enhance transparency of its activities on its advertising networks?

Facebook takes creativity, copyright, and protection of intellectual property rights seriously. We strongly oppose the placement of our advertisements on websites and apps that either infringe or pose a high risk of infringing copyright (including on commercial-scale pirate websites and apps). We maintain a robust framework to combat misplacement of Facebook ads on third-party websites and apps. Part of that work involves taking proactive steps to protect IP and combat piracy and the sale and promotion of counterfeit goods.

[78] *Id.*, pg. 17.

Advertisement Fraud Management Framework. The goal of our advertisement fraud management framework is two-fold: (i) to prevent fraudulent traffic sources from bidding on or serving Facebook ads; and (ii) to prevent payments for identified fraud traffic. To accomplish these goals, our general practice is to request third-party agencies with whom we contract to proactively identify and protect against fraudulent traffic.

Our current ad fraud management framework is divided into three activities: (1) prevention; (2) detection; and (3) mitigation:

1) Prevention: Fraud prevention begins during advertisement network selection. From this selection process, Facebook contracts with industry-leading third-party digital media agencies to place ads for our platforms and services on external websites and apps. Our general practice is to request direct, transparent placements, and request that fraud terms be included in our agreements. In negotiating these agreements, we generally request that vendors agree to actively monitor ad campaigns for signs of fraudulent activity, and agree to alert us in the event that any such activity is detected or suspected. Our general practice also includes that vendors agree to ensure that our ads do not appear adjacent to any content promoting subjects such as pornography, non-gaming violence, or infringement of intellectual property rights (including music and video piracy) or on websites that promote those activities. While each agreement is unique, the foregoing reflects some of the terms that we strive to obtain in our agreements with vendors.
2) Detection: We utilize tools and fraud suites from third-party agencies, such as the Kochava Fraud Console and tools from Forensiq and DoubleVerify, to try to detect fraudulent placements (including advertisements on websites that either infringe or pose a high risk of infringing copyright). We monitor these placements and try to identify any anomalies that may signal fraudulent or suspicious activity. We, in close collaboration with these third- party agencies, also develop custom, threshold-based signals to detect app and web traffic that leads to suspicious activity.
3) Mitigation: We maintain global blocklists intended to prevent our ads from appearing on apps and websites associated with fraud, fake actors, or sensitive content. Our partnership with third-party agencies allows us to permanently block identified fraudulent ad sources, such as websites and apps, and to identify potentially problematic traffic,

which is flagged for investigation in partnership with the ad network/publisher. Since our November 2021 response to you on this topic, we have doubled down on the breadth of these efforts. We are now also working with industry stakeholders across the world to identify websites that may be dedicated to piracy or to facilitating copyright infringement. Once identified via our trusted sources, we use internal criteria to identify which URLs should be added to our blocklists. Meta ads will not appear on any external URL that has been added to the blocklist—thereby significantly reducing any risk of funding or facilitating piracy on the Facebook platform. Further, our mitigation framework consists of utilizing automatic and manual blocking technology to investigate problematic traffic with ad networks. Finally, if any fraud or violations of the underlying agreement with the ad placement agency are identified, our practice is to request refunds for the ad impression. We recognize that no matter our preventative measures, there must always be ongoing manual traffic reviews to spot and investigate suspicious signals. As such, we regularly assess and continue to make improvements to our detection and protection framework, to improve our detection of ads that appear on or are attributed to fraud traffic sources.

Through partnership with third-party agencies, we strive to update our blocklists weekly. Additionally, these third-party agencies have advised us that they conduct regular audits (on the weekly and monthly level) to evaluate fraud safety measures. Managing our ad placements globally can be challenging and is an iterative process. For example, for one of the ads referenced in the Breaking (B)ads report, our teams determined that ten versions or variations of the piracy app already appeared on our permanent blocklist. Further, as a result of the information provided in the report, our teams added an additional four variations of the app to our permanent blocklist. As detailed above, we, in close partnership with third-party vendors, continue to proactively identify how we can improve in this area, and take steps to help protect current and non-users from seeing ads on inappropriate websites and apps, including on those that either infringe or pose a high risk of infringing copyright advertisements.

3) Your written testimony states that there are "always risks when people transfer data online." Please elaborate on the nature and scope

of these risks, and the people and entities who are implicated by these risks.

a) What steps does Facebook take to inform others of these risks?

Last year, we rewrote and re-designed our Privacy Policy to make it easier to understand and clearer about how we use people's information, and we updated our Terms of Service to better explain what is expected from us and those who use our platforms. The updates to our Privacy Policy include detailed explanations about how we use and share information with third parties. Also, our Help Center contains information and answers to frequently asked questions. When a user decides to login with Facebook or connect their account, we provide information about where they are sending the data, what that destination will receive, and access to that destination's privacy policy.

b) How does the Data Transfer Project address these risks?

The open source Data Transfer Project is a collaborative effort by a group of companies, includingMeta, to build a common framework with open-source code that can connect any two online services, enabling a seamless user-initiated portability of data between platforms. The Data Transfer Project's open-source framework powers our Transfer Your Information tool, which enables people to transfer their Facebook photos and videos, notes, posts, and events directly to destinations including BackBlaze, Dropbox, Koofr, Google Photos, Photobucket, Google Calendar, Google Docs, Blogger, and WordPress.

In 2018, the Data Transfer Project published a white paper describing the fundamentals of the project and its principles on a range of topics including privacy and security.

Neither the Data Transfer Project, nor any one company acting alone can resolve the challenging tradeoffs involving data portability like those we identified in our own 2019 white paper on data portability.

4) Ms. Slaiman advocates for "a digital regulator to comprehensively the policy questions surrounding digital platforms."

a) Do you agree that this is necessary?
b) Given the many issues beyond privacy and competition that address and implicate digital policy—including cybersecurity, national

security, consumer rights, free speech, and intellectual property concerns—what existing agency would be the best situated, in your view, to carry out this role?

c) Is it important to you that the regulator should be politically accountable?

We support updated regulations in the digital space on issues like privacy and data security, combating foreign election interference, content moderation, and data portability, and we have called for the US to create a new digital regulator. The issues facing the industry are complex, multi-faceted, and impact peoples' lives. Accordingly, Meta is committed to working with policymakers to craft the right regulations, and is amenable to reviewing proposed legislation and providing comments.

We have been open about our support for updated regulations on key issues. More information about our approach to regulation can be found here: https://about.meta.com/regulations/?utm_source=about.facebook.com&utm_medium=redirect.

Big Data, Big Questions: Implications for Competition and Consumers
September 21, 2021 Response to Questions for the Record Charlotte Slaiman Competition Policy Director Public Knowledge Washington, D.C.

Responses to Senator Grassley

1) How important is the amount of data that a company has to their ability to effectively monetize that information?

One of the important features of data as an economic good is that it exhibits increasing returns to both scope and scale. That means that more data is exponentially more valuable, particularly when it comes from different sources. This makes it incredibly difficult for a startup company with only one source of data to properly compete against Big Tech's massive data collection operation.

2) How difficult can it be for a startup or small business to collect enough data to be able to compete with companies that have large amounts of data?

It can be very difficult. Consumers might have less trust in a name or brand they do not recognize. An already established Big Tech titan can use their other sources of data on you to "fill in the gaps" in a way that a smaller business with just one or two products cannot, unless they purchase that data from an external source. This allows for a greater degree of targeting and other data exploitation by Big Tech firms.

3) Some commentators argue that the amount of data currently possessed by large incumbent companies forecloses the ability of new entrants to compete. But, new data is being created every day and what data is important in the future may not be what is being collected today. If so, why isn't there an opportunity for additional companies to enter the market?

There is still not a fair opportunity for additional companies to enter the market because of the powerful market position of the largest platforms, together with the lack of fair competition rules such as interoperability and non-discrimination requirements. This allows the largest platforms to continue their control of new data points and makes it much harder for competitors to enter.

I addressed this question further in my written testimony on page 7:

> "The dominant platforms sometimes argue that data ages rapidly, so a new competitor could quickly amass the data needed to compete. This is theoretically true, but it is not just old data that today's dominant digital platforms control. Users are still today locked in to these platforms through their gatekeeper power, so the platforms continue to have access to ongoing data streams. These data streams can be used to continuously update algorithms to stay on top. They can also keep platforms updated about the users so as notto rely on just static or past data about them. This allows platforms to not just 'know' their users, but see how their users change over time—often in response to the algorithmsthat platforms created using older user data. This cycle of collection, use, and iteration gives platforms significant power over their users."

4) There is debate over whether Big Data should be regulated through the lens of consumer protection and privacy or whether antitrust laws should be used to address competition concerns with the collection of data. Do you have an opinion about the best approach to address this issue or should we be looking at a combination of different approaches?

I certainly believe that a combination of approaches is superior. Technology platforms present a myriad of issues for our society, and our solutions need to account for the interactions at play. Antitrust alone is not enough. There is a needed role for privacy, consumer protection, and civil rights. A privacy regime focused on data minimization and a more restrictive environment for the collection, spread, and use of consumer data would certainly help control for some of the advantages dominant platforms receive from their unchecked and pervasive collection of consumer data. Public Knowledge is supportive, for example, of bipartisan comprehensive privacy legislation that Congress is considering that would limit data collection practices of online platforms, data brokers, and others.

Consumers should not have to choose between competitive markets and their privacy. Congress must act to safeguard user privacy and to promote fair competition on and against the largest firms.

Responses to Senator Tillis

1) The term "data" can have multiple meanings, which can sometimes generate confusion in policy discussions. How would you define "data" and "big data", as used in your written testimony?

Your question gets at the complexity of the "data" definition in policy discussions. This can be a difficult question to answer and is perhaps why recent legislation (S. 2992, The American Innovation and Choice Online Act) calls for a Federal Trade Commission rulemaking to define "data." I would define "data" as anything a platform collects and uses to either monetize or improve its services. However, the term certainly can have multiple meanings, so it's important that we continue to define what we mean by "data" in different contexts. "Big data" refers to data sets large enough to be useful for training machine learning algorithms and similar purposes. Big Tech platforms have a built-in advantage in collecting big data sets.

a) How would you define consumer and user data, specifically what would be included and excluded from these definitions? For example, the section of data portability refers to "your data" – what would this include?

When it comes to protecting user privacy, consumer and user data can be defined as information that identifies or is linked or reasonably linkable, alone or in combination with other information, to an individual or a device that identifies or is linked or reasonably linkable to an individual and may include derived data and unique identifiers. This could be things like your IP address, your mobile phone's device identifier, location data, or anything collected about your personal behavior online or when combined with information collected online is reasonably likely to identify an individual. In the context of data portability, the definition of "your data" would be different for different product categories based on what is needed to promote a competitive marketplace. Ongoing communication across social media networks requires interoperability of different categories of data than porting a customer over to a rival phone carrier, for example. Of course, since portability or interoperability should only be happening at the user's request, the user would also decide which data categories they actually want to transfer.

b) Would this include user uploaded videos, images, and text?

Yes, in general I would expect effective data portability requirements to include these items. This means companies would need to offer this option to consumers, and consumers could choose which of their videos, images, or text communications—if any—to transfer.

c) Would such content be considered part of the "user" data, even if it includes content that originates from other sources?

Yes. A user should be able to download material they have uploaded, even when that content originates from other sources. Uploaded material (for example, in the form of memes, reaction images, or even emoji) is as much a part of how many people communicate online as their own words. Failing to allow this material to be exported would hamper the goals of competition and interoperability.

d) Does it include data in which intellectual property rights, including copyright, trade secret, trademark, or design rights, may subsist?

Not necessarily. I would think that the important part of most user's data is their relationship to a copyrighted work, not necessarily the work itself. For example, my user data might include positive interactions with the movie "Mad Max: Fury Road"—posts I've liked about it, me posting about it, etc. However, that data would not implicate any sort of IP rights in the actual movie. In some cases, users may upload content (e.g., memes or snippets of text) that are fair uses of copyrighted material. In any event, data portability requirements do not provide new grounds for the infringement of IP rights.

2) Your testimony advocates for "a digital regulator to comprehensively the policy questions surrounding digital platforms."

a) Given the many issues beyond privacy and competition that address and implicate digital policy—including cybersecurity, national security, consumer rights, free speech, and intellectual property concerns—what existing agency would be the best situated, in your view, to carry out this role?

There is no one agency today that is best suited to properly deal with the cross-cutting issues presented by technology platforms that your question identifies. That is why Public Knowledge advocates for a completely new agency. Both the Federal Trade Commission and the Federal Communications Commission have some tools and expertise in common with what a digital regulator would need—but either one would need additional authority, staffing, and budget to achieve the goals of a digital regulator.

b) Is it important to you that the regulator should be politically accountable?

Political accountability is important and can foster trust in an agency's decisions. Public Knowledge has advocated for a bipartisan commission-like structure (similar to the Federal Trade Commission or the Federal Communications Commission) as the structure that strikes the right balance between political insulation and accountability.

3) Your testimony refers to data portability as an important tool "to neutralize the power that Big Data confers upon dominant digital platforms."

   a) In your view, is the Data Transfer Project, described in Google's testimony as a partnership among Google, Apple, Facebook, Microsoft, and Smugmug, an acceptable way to address data portability?

While projects like the Data Transfer Project are laudable, I believe they are insufficient to solve data portability and interoperability problems. Company commitments without agency enforcement only get you so far. Firms might not make some key data available and can cut off portability to rivals that pose a competitive threat. This is a key component of the ongoing Facebook FTC litigation. Facebook offered access to its network to companies that would increase engagement with the core Facebook product but cut off would-be rivals like Vine. I strongly believe we need federal legislation in this area in the vein of the bipartisan ACCESS Act.

Chapter 2

Big Data: Privacy Risks and Needed Reforms in the Public and Private Sectors*

Committee on House Administration

House of Representatives,
Committee on House Administration,
Washington, DC.

The Committee met, pursuant to call, at 2:03 p.m., via Webex, Hon. Zoe Lofgren [Chairperson of the Committee] presiding.

Present: Representatives Lofgren, Raskin, Aguilar, Scanlon, Leger Ferna´ndez, Davis, Loudermilk, and Steil.

Staff Present: Sean Jones, Legislative Clerk; Jamie Fleet, Staff Director; Eddie Flaherty, Chief Clerk; Khalil Abboud, Deputy Staff Director; Tim Monahan, Republican Staff Director; Caleb Hays, Republican General Counsel and Deputy Staff Director; Nick Crocker, Republican Deputy Staff Director; Gineen Bresso, Republican Special Counsel.

The CHAIRPERSON. So the Committee on House Administration will come to order.

I note that a quorum is present. As we begin, I would note that we are holding this hearing in compliance with the regulations for Remote Committee Proceedings pursuant to House Resolution 8.

Generally, we ask Committee Members and witnesses to keep their microphones muted when not speaking to limit background noise, and all of us will need to unmute ourselves when seeking recognition or when

---

* This is an edited, reformatted and augmented version of Hearing Before the Committee on House Administration House of Representatives, Publication No. 49–431, dated February 16, 2022.

In: Big Data, Big Impact: Navigating Competition, Privacy, and Reform
Editor: Jessica Andrews
ISBN: 979-8-89530-538-6

recognized to speak. Witnesses will also need to unmute themselves when recognized for their testimony or when answering a question.

Members and witnesses, the rules require that we keep our cameras on at all times. Even if you need to step away for a moment, please do not leave the meeting or turn your camera off. I would also like to remind Members that the regulations governing remote proceedings require that Members cannot participate in more than one committee proceeding at the same time.

At this time, I ask unanimous consent that all Members have five legislative days in which to revise and extend their remarks and have any written statements be made part of the record.

And, hearing no objections, that is ordered.

I also ask unanimous consent that the chair be authorized to declare a recess of the Committee at any point.

And, without objection, that is also so ordered.

We are here today to confront one of the central challenges of our digital age. As nearly every facet of our society and economy has moved online, ever greater amounts of digital data are collected about each of us, spanning everything from who we are, to what we like, to who we are—who we communicate with, to what we do, often in minute detail.

While this mass data collection has some productive and valuable applications, it comes with profound risks that we are only beginning to truly understand, let alone to regulate effectively.

Privacy, as it is conventionally understood, means control over one's own personal information and the freedom to decide what to share, with whom, and how. We are all familiar with the classic privacy harms, whether it is government surveillance, identity theft and other economic crimes, or the social and economic harm that can befall us when some intimate details of our life become public against our will.

All these risks are still very much at play today with the rise of the internet and data-centric business models of many online firms. However, in some ways, privacy has become a catchall term for a larger and even more profound set of potential risks, some of which are truly novel or at least fundamentally different in the digital age.

What does it mean for our basic autonomy as individuals when both the government and private companies can amass large profiles about each of us and use them to predict and even potentially manipulate our behavior? What does it mean for our economy when some of the most popular online products and services revolve around opaque data collection and personalization? And what does it mean for our democracy when these data practices shape the public discourse and the flow of news and information? And what does it mean that, as individuals and internet users, we have little or no meaningful ability or visibility into how any of this really works, let alone genuine control over it?

The American public has long been deeply concerned about these questions. For example, in 2020, the Pew Research Center found that half of Americans had limited specific online activities out of privacy fears. The same year, another poll found that 88 percent are frustrated that they don't have more control over their personal information online.

I will note that these fears kind of cross many divisions in our society: economic, racial, geographic, and partisan. For all these reasons, the time for a comprehensive Federal policy framework is long overdue. There have been many proposals and lots of talk, but little or no action or clear progress.

I will note that Representatives Anna Eshoo and I have introduced the Online Privacy Act in several Congresses, including this one. This legislation sets forth the most thorough and aggressive set of privacy rights among the major proposals with the clearest restrictions on a wide variety of abusive and troubling data practices, and the strongest mechanisms to enforce the law and make digital privacy rights more than just an abstraction.

The Online Privacy Act also contains a set of privacy obligations on Legislative Branch agencies that this Committee oversees, requiring the Government Publishing Office, the Library of Congress, the Smithsonian, and the Chief Administrative Officer of the House to each identify concrete privacy risks in their operations and to take appropriate remedial steps.

Many of the risks and policy questions around data cut across both public and private sectors. We can take lessons from both in determining the best ways to address them. I am hopeful that today's hearing will not only advance this conversation, but also reinvigorate congressional attention on digital privacy toward the ultimate enactment of major reforms.

With that, I am now pleased to recognize our Ranking Member, Congressman Rodney Davis, for any comments that he would like to make.

Welcome, Rodney.

[The statement of The Chairperson follows:]

ZOE LOFGREN, CALIFORNIA
CHAIRPERSON

JAMIE RASKIN, MARYLAND
G.K. BUTTERFIELD, NORTH CAROLINA
PETE AGUILAR, CALIFORNIA
MARY GAY SCANLON, PENNSYLVANIA
VICE CHAIRPERSON
TERESA LEGER FERNANDEZ, NEW MEXICO

JAMIE FLEET
STAFF DIRECTOR

One Hundred Seventeenth
Congress of the United States
House of Representatives

COMMITTEE ON HOUSE ADMINISTRATION
1309 LONGWORTH HOUSE OFFICE BUILDING
WASHINGTON, DC 20515-6157
202-225-2061 | CHA.HOUSE.GOV

RODNEY DAVIS, ILLINOIS
RANKING MINORITY MEMBER

BARRY LOUDERMILK, GEORGIA
BRYAN STEIL, WISCONSIN

TIM MONAHAN
MINORITY STAFF DIRECTOR

Chairperson Zoe Lofgren
February 16, 2022
Big Data: Privacy Risks and Needed Reforms in the Public and Private Sectors
Opening Statement

We are here today to confront one of the central challenges of our digital age. As nearly every facet of our society and economy has moved online, ever greater amounts of digital data are collected about each of us, spanning everything from who we are, to what we like, to who we are, who we communicate and to what we do often in minute detail.

While this mass data collection has some productive and valuable applications, it comes with profound risks that we are only beginning to truly understand, let alone to regulate effectively. Privacy, as it is conventionally understood, means control over one's own personal information and the freedom to decide what to share, with whom, and how. We are all familiar with the classic privacy harms, whether it is government surveillance, identity theft and other economic crimes, or the social and economic harm that can befall us when some intimate details of our life become public against our will.

All of these risks are still very much at play today with the rise of the Internet and data-centric business models of many online firms. However, in some ways, privacy has become a catchall term for a larger and even more profound set of potential risks, some of which are truly novel or at least fundamentally different in the digital age.

What does it mean for our basic autonomy as individuals when both the government and private companies can amass large profiles about each of us and use them to predict and even potentially manipulate our behavior? What does it mean for our economy when some of the most popular online products and services revolve around opaque data collection and personalization? And what does it mean for our democracy when these data practices shape the public discourse and the flow of news and information? And what does it mean that, as individuals and internet users, we have little or no meaningful ability or visibility into how any of this really works, let alone guide genuine control over it?

The American public has long been deeply concerned about these questions. For example, in 2020, the Pew Research Center found that half of Americans had limited specific online activities out of privacy fears. The same year, another poll found that 88 percent are frustrated that they don't have more control over their personal information online. And I will note that these fears kind of cross many divisions in our society: economic, racial, geographic, and partisan. For all these reasons, the time for a comprehensive Federal policy framework is long overdue. There have been many proposals and lots of talk, but little or no action or clear progress.

I will note that Representatives Anna Eshoo and I have introduced the Online Privacy Act in several Congresses, including this one. This legislation sets forth the most thorough and aggressive set of privacy rights among the major proposals with the clearest restrictions on a wide variety of abusive and troubling data practices, and the strongest mechanisms to enforce the law and make digital privacy rights more than just an abstraction.

The Online Privacy Act also contains a set of privacy obligations on Legislative Branch agencies that this Committee oversees, requiring the Government Publishing Office, the Library of Congress, the Smithsonian, and the Chief Administrative Officer of the House to each identify concrete privacy risks in their operations and to take appropriate remedial steps.

Many of the risks and policy questions around data cut across both public and private sectors. We can take lessons from both in determining the best ways to address them. And I am hopeful that today's hearing will not only advance this conversation, but also reinvigorate congressional attention on digital privacy toward the ultimate enactment of major reforms.

Mr. DAVIS. Well, thank you, Madam Chairperson.

And thanks to our witnesses for joining us for today's hearing. It is a hearing on a rare topic for this Committee, but no doubt an important one: online data privacy. Yet policy discussions on creating nationwide privacy standards and a framework for enforcement need to take place in the primary committees of jurisdiction: Energy and Commerce and the Judiciary. It is clear to me that this discussion should be led by those primary committees and jurisdiction, and we should let them work out the underlying policy details before we consider application to the Legislative Branch.

304 bills have been referred to this Committee by the House, yet we are devoting our time today to this topic. It is rare we are even meeting on potential legislation this Congress. We have had exactly one other hearing on the policy underlying a bill and exactly zero markups.

Further, this Committee has not held comprehensive standard oversight hearings with our entities in nearly three years. For us not even to discuss FEC or EAC oversight hearings in an election year is shocking to me.

Eight months ago, I sent a letter to the Chairperson asking for this Committee to fulfill its duty and conduct oversight hearings with each of our Legislative Branch entities. Eight months later, I still have not received a response from the Chairperson, and the Committee continues to shirk its duties.

I look forward to this Committee having more oversight hearings soon to address the concerns that fall more directly within this Committee's jurisdiction.

Regarding the topic at issue today, the call for a workable national framework, increased transparency, and overall accountability in the technology industry, is all but universal at this point. Data privacy is at the forefront because it affects everyone. We all see the need. As a parent of three young adults, I believe this issue deserves not only Congress' attention, but it also demands it.

All anyone has to do is watch the news to see how data privacy affects everyone. Last week, filings by Special Counsel John Durham alleged that, in 2016, Democratic operatives, perhaps including Marc Elias, who multiple members of this Committee are familiar with, in his attempts to—in his attempts to challenge the legitimacy of elections, sought to exploit their access to non-public and/ or proprietary internet data to create a narrative tying President Trump to Russia, in the words of one outlet, to infiltrate Trump Tower and White House servers to link Trump to Russia. Talk about an election subversion. Unbelievable.

So, a responsible and workable nationwide solution for data privacy that can protect Americans' privacy and also curb bad political actors from attempting to subvert our political discourse is necessary. I know that our Chairperson has a special interest in this topic, and I imagine that her desire to raise the profile of her legislation is why we are here today. So, let's discuss it.

I spoke with my good friend, Energy and Commerce Ranking Member Cathy McMorris Rodgers, since her committee would be primary, and she offered me a lot of good thoughts, things I assume she would say if this hearing were before her committee, where it belongs first.

First, we share more personal information online now than ever before. As the internet has grown, so has the opportunity for our personal information to be used by people or businesses that we never intended.

Second, privacy does not end at State lines. This is a nationwide Commerce Clause issue that requires a congressional response. Americans cannot rely on conflicting State laws to keep their information safe. A patchwork solution is not viable for a concern that affects all of us. The only way to provide transparency in how Americans' information is collected, used, and shared is with a uniform approach.

We must also ensure that any congressional response is forward thinking and comprehensive while still being workable for compliance. Solutions that do not account for burdens placed on small businesses and innovators, such as the GDPR in the EU or the CCPA in California, are doomed to fail.

Finally, those who misuse personal information must be held accountable. There have been proposals that call for the creation of a new Federal agency to enforce its provisions. The Federal Trade Commission already has jurisdiction over these matters, as well as a longstanding relationship with the States' AGs. Creating a new agency to do the FTC's job is bureaucratic waste at the highest level.

Americans' call for a comprehensive solution to Big Data privacy issues is loud and clear, and they deserve an answer, an answer that is built with bipartisan buy-in, transparency, and accountability.

Even though this Committee isn't where we should be hosting this portion of this discussion, I am looking forward to today's panels, and I yield back.

[The statement of Mr. Davis follows:]

ZOE LOFGREN, CALIFORNIA
CHAIRPERSON

JAMIE RASKIN, MARYLAND
G.K. BUTTERFIELD, NORTH CAROLINA
PETE AGUILAR, CALIFORNIA
MARY GAY SCANLON, PENNSYLVANIA
VICE CHAIRPERSON
TERESA LEGER FERNANDEZ, NEW MEXICO

JAMIE FLEET
STAFF DIRECTOR

One Hundred Seventeenth
Congress of the United States
House of Representatives

COMMITTEE ON HOUSE ADMINISTRATION
1309 LONGWORTH HOUSE OFFICE BUILDING
WASHINGTON, DC 20515-6157
202-225-2061 | CHA.HOUSE.GOV

RODNEY DAVIS, ILLINOIS
RANKING MINORITY MEMBER

BARRY LOUDERMILK, GEORGIA
BRYAN STEIL, WISCONSIN

TIM MONAHAN
MINORITY STAFF DIRECTOR

Ranking Member Rodney Davis
February 16, 2022
Big Data: Privacy Risks and Needed Reforms in the Public and Private Sectors
Opening Statement

Thank you, Madam Chairperson. And thanks to our witnesses for joining us for today's hearing. It is a hearing on a rare topic for this Committee, but no doubt an important one: online data privacy. Yet policy discussions on creating nationwide privacy standards and a framework for enforcement need to take place in the primary committees of jurisdiction: Energy and Commerce and the Judiciary. It is clear to me that this discussion should be led by those primary committees of jurisdiction and we should let them work out the underlying policy details before we consider application to the Legislative Branch.

304 bills have been referred to this Committee by the House, yet we are devoting our time today to this topic. And it is rare we are even meeting on potential legislation this Congress. We have had exactly one other hearing on the policy underlying a bill and exactly zero markups. Further, this Committee has not held comprehensive standard oversight hearings with our entities in nearly three years. For us not even to have a discussion about FEC or EAC oversight hearings in an election year is shocking to me.

Eight months ago, I sent a letter to the chair asking for this Committee to fulfill its duty and conduct oversight hearings with each of our Legislative Branch entities. Eight months later, I still have not received a response from the chair, and the Committee continues to shirk its duties.

I look forward to this Committee having more oversight hearings soon to address the concerns that fall more directly within this Committee's jurisdiction. Regarding the topic at issue today, the call for a workable national framework, increased transparency, and overall accountability in the technology industry, is all but universal at this point. Data privacy is at the forefront because it affects everyone. We all see the need. And, as a parent of three young adults, I believe this issue deserves not only Congress' attention, it demands it.

All anyone has to do is watch the news to see how data privacy affects everyone. Last week, filings by Special Counsel John Durham alleged that, in 2016, Democratic operatives, perhaps including Marc Elias, who multiple Members of this

Committee are familiar with, in his attempts to challenges the legitimacy of elections, sought to exploit their access to non-public and/or proprietary Internet data to create a narrative tying President Trump to Russia, in the words of one outlet, to infiltrate Trump Tower and White House servers to link Trump to Russia. Talk about an election subversion. Unbelievable.

So a responsible and workable nationwide solution for data privacy that can protect Americans' privacy and also curb bad political actors from attempting to subvert our political discourse is necessary. I know that our chair has a special interest in this topic, and I imagine that her desire to raise the profile of her legislation is why we are here today. So let's discuss it. I spoke with my good friend, E&C ranking Member Cathy McMorris Rodgers, since her committee would be primary, and she offered me a lot of good thoughts, things I assume she would say if this hearing were before her committee, where it belongs first.

First, we share more personal information online now than ever before. As the Internet has grown, so has the opportunity our personal information to be used by people or businesses that we never intended. Second, privacy does not end at States lines. This is a nationwide Commerce Clause issue that requires a Congressional response. Americans cannot rely on conflicting State laws to keep their information safe. A patchwork solution is not viable for a concern that affects all of us. The only way to provide transparency in how Americans' information is collected, used, and shared is with a uniform approach.

We must also ensure that any congressional response is forward thinking and comprehensive while still being workable for compliance. Solutions that do not account for burdens placed on small businesses and innovators, such as the GDPR in the EU or the CCPA in California, are doomed to fail. Finally, those who misuse personal information must be held accountable. There have been proposals that call for the creation of a new Federal agency to enforce its provisions. The Federal Trade Commission already has jurisdiction over these matters, as well as a longstanding relationship with the States' AGs. Creating a new agency to do the FTC's job is bureaucratic waste at the highest level.

Americans' call for a comprehensive solution to Big Data privacy issues is loud and clear, and they deserve an answer, an answer that is built with bipartisan buy-in, transparency, and accountability. Even though this Committee isn't where we should be hosting this portion of this discussion, I am actually looking forward to today's panels, and I yield back the balance of my time. Thank you, Madam Chairperson.

The CHAIRPERSON. The gentleman yields back.

I just would note for the record that the Committee's jurisdiction is generally determined by House Rules specifically, House Rule X—and this Committee has been, along with other committees, assigned jurisdiction.

I want to thank the Ranking Member for his comments.

I would also like to recognize our first witness, who is someone who has led the U.S. Government Publishing Office with great distinction of late.

He is the 28th person to lead the GPO since it opened its doors in 1861 and has served in this role in 2019. Hugh Nathaniel Halpern was selected this month—the GPO was selected as one of the best employers in the country, ranking first on Forbes' list of midsize agencies in government services.

I really do think, Hugh, that it is a reflection on your leadership as well as your fine staff at the GPO.

As you know—this is not your first time to be a witness—your entire written statement will be made part of the record, and we would ask that you summarize your testimony in about five minutes.

So, Mr. Halpern, you are now recognized for five minutes.

Statement of Hugh Halpern, Director, Government Publishing Office, Washington, D.C.

Mr. HALPERN. Thank you so much and thank you for acknowledging the achievement of making that Forbes list. I will take some credit if it is assigned, but it really belongs to the men and women here at GPO. So, thank you so much for having me today, both to the Chairperson and to the Ranking Member, and all the Members of the Committee.

I appreciate the opportunity to testify about GPO's approach to handling personally identifiable information, commonly known as PII. On behalf of GPO's more than 1,500 craftspeople and professionals, know that we take our responsibility seriously to protect PII every day.

GPO operates as a hybrid. It is a government agency that operates as a business, complete with customers, products, and profit and loss. Thus, we face many of the same kinds of problems facing private-sector firms when it comes to the handling of PII.

GPO is entrusted with PII belonging to our teammates, customers, and, by nature of our business, the general public. Robust protection of PII is critical to building trust with our customers and stakeholders. Without that trust, we can never achieve our vision of an America informed.

GPO operates a Privacy Program overseen by our privacy officer in our information technology business unit. This program establishes a framework for the protection of PII itself, regardless of how it is stored, as well as the protection of related information systems.

The program has several fundamental principles. First, access to PII is limited to only those agency teammates and contractors with a specific need.

Second, each business unit has someone who is responsible for the privacy function and answers to that business unit's leadership.

Third, any GPO teammate or contractor that suspects a breach in PII security is obligated to report the problem as soon as possible.

Fourth, violations will be addressed by appropriate corrective action, including termination for our teammates, debarment for contractors, and criminal prosecution if appropriate.

While my written testimony goes into more detail as to how this program works, today I would like to talk about three separate examples of privacy issues at GPO and how we deal with them.

First, GPO and its print procurement contractors produce materials that require the use of PII. For instance, GPO's Security and Intelligent Documents Unit manufactures and personalizes trusted traveler smart cards, such as the global entry card used to at border crossings for identification and for expedited processing.

By the very nature of these products, GPO must handle vast amounts of highly sensitive PII within our systems. GPO works closely with its customers to maintain a series of firewalls that ensure that GPO only receives encrypted PII that is only decrypted when it is needed to produce and distribute those cards. When GPO finishes production of the product, that PII is scrubbed from our systems. You can't leak information you don't have.

Second, there are vast amounts of PII included in some of our regular publications, such as the Congressional Record and Federal Register. The good news, particularly with the Federal Register, is that most of that PII is contained in historic volumes, and very little is being published currently. Where it is, we have both automated and manual systems to redact that information from our digital collections when we find it.

The bigger challenge is with historic information, particularly as we work to digitize older collections. For instance, at one time, it was common for the Department of Defense to include military officers' Social Security numbers on promotion lists later printed in the Congressional Record.

As we digitize volumes that contained that information, we scan for it and redact that PII in preparation before posting it on Govinfo.gov, our ISO-certified, trusted digital repository. And, while we alert our partners when we find PII in tangible collections that we don't possess ourselves, we do not have the resources to visit every collection across the country and manually redact that information.

The third and final category are instances where the information is not quite PII but is information that people don't want easily accessible on the internet. This comes up most often with our collection of U.S. court opinions on Govinfo.gov, and that is the repository's single largest collection of data. It is understandable that some parties of Federal court cases may not want that information to be easily accessible, and they often come to GPO asking us to remove that opinion from our collection.

However, it is important to remember that GPO is only making that data accessible, and it is not our data. Our Library Services Division refers individuals to petition the owner of the data, the Administrative Office of the U.S. Courts, to have the opinion sealed and removed from our systems if the judge determines that public disclosure is problematic.

I hope that this overview of our operations was helpful in your exploration of this critical issue. I look forward to answering any questions you may have and assisting the Committee with its inquiry.

Thank you so much.

[The statement of Mr. Halpern follows:]

THE HONORABLE HUGH NATHANIAL HALPERN

Director

United States Government Publishing Office

Testimony of Government Publishing Office Director Hugh N. Halpern before the Committee on House Administration Hearing on "Big Data: Privacy Risks and Needed Reforms in the Public and Private Sectors"

February 16, 2022
2:00 P.M.

Thank you, Chairperson Lofgren and Ranking Member Davis, for inviting me to testify today on behalf of the more than 1,500 craftspeople and professionals who make up the Government Publishing Office to discuss our approach to the critically important issue of protecting personally identifiable information (PII) and safeguarding individual privacy. GPO is entrusted with PII belonging to our teammates, customers, and, by nature of our business, the general public. We devote considerable time, attention, and resources to securing and protecting that information, and we are always interested to share our experiences and learn from the experience of others.

Robust protection of PII is critical to building trust with our customers and stakeholders. Without that trust, we can never achieve our vision of an America Informed.

GPO's Approach to PII Protection

GPO's approach to protecting PII is laid out in our Privacy Program, which is overseen by our Privacy Officer, who reports to our Chief Information Officer. The Privacy Program establishes a framework for the protection of PII from unauthorized use, access, disclosure, or sharing as well as the protection of related information systems from unauthorized access, modification, disruption, or destruction.

Originally established in 2010, the Privacy Program was most recently updated in 2021 through GPO Directive 825.41B. GPO's privacy program applies to our teammates and contractors alike. It rests on a few fundamental principles:

- First, the only people who may access PII held by GPO are authorized Agency staff and contractors trained in the protocols required to protect that information;
- Second, each business unit within GPO must have a designated privacy point of contact that reports directly to the business unit leadership;
- Third, it is the affirmative obligation of any GPO employee or contractor who suspects a breach of PII security to promptly report the concern; and
- Fourth and finally, the directive provides that failure to comply with agency PII protection standards and procedures is grounds for corrective actions up to and including termination for employees, debarment for contractors, or even criminal prosecution if appropriate.

As part of his duties in administering the Privacy Program, GPO's Privacy Officer coordinates two significant processes —GPO's ongoing PII management and protection and responding appropriately to a possible PII security breach.

GPO's Privacy Officer proactively requires the periodic performance of Privacy Threshold Assessments (PTA) and Privacy Impact Assessments (PIA) by GPO business units. These assessments evaluate how those business units maintain, secure, and utilize PII in their daily operations.

The second process relates to how GPO responds to a potential breach of systems containing PII, and is referred to as the Privacy Incident Response Team (PIRT) Framework. Whenever a GPO employee or contractor suspects a breach in PII security has occurred that individual is required to report it through a Privacy Incident Report shared with his or her supervisor. The Business Unit Manager and Privacy Point of Contact are then responsible for notifying GPO's Privacy Officer, who convenes the Privacy Incident Response Team to assess the scope of the breach and determine the scope of the Agency's response, up to and including the possibility of alerting the United States Computer Emergency Readiness Team (US-CERT) within the Department of Homeland Security.

In developing and executing these policies and procedures that guide its Privacy Program, GPO has sought to follow the recommendations laid out by the National Institute of Standards and Technology (NIST) in their "Guide to Protecting the Confidentiality of Personally Identifiable Information (Special Publication 800-22)," which identifies six imperatives for Federal agencies:

- Identifying all the PII residing in their environment;
- Minimizing the use, collection, and retention of PII to what is strictly necessary to accomplish their business purpose and mission;
- Categorizing PII by confidentiality impact level;
- Applying the appropriate safeguards for PII based on the confidentiality impact levels;
- Developing an incident response plan to handle breaches involving PII; and
- Encouraging close coordination among their chief privacy officers, chief information officers, chief information security officers, and legal counsel when addressing issues related to PII.

I believe GPO's Privacy Program is responsive to each of them, and today I want to highlight two of them that have particular salience to GPO's administration of its govinfo trusted digital repository and GPO's overall system of providing online access to Government information.

Those recommendations relate to the categorization of PII by confidentiality impact levels and the application of safeguards based on those confidentiality impact levels.

Changes in technology have driven everyone's concern about the ease with which personal information is available. On the one hand, there is a lower concern about a stray piece of PII in a printed document in a library because it is comparatively more difficult to access. Similarly, using that information in a nefarious way is also more difficult without our modern technology infrastructure. On the other, because we have made this information more accessible, the threat from the use of that information has also exponentially increased.

For example, in preparation for this hearing one of my colleagues remarked how as late as the 1990s his college used students' social security numbers as identifiers on their student ID cards, something that was completely unremarkable at the time. Another colleague remarked how a relative found her social security number because it appeared on a digitized Department of Defense document. Things that were at one time innocent practices with little impact are today serious breaches of protocol with potential wide-ranging impacts.

For GPO this amounts to a dual challenge — keeping current with the most effective strategies to protect PII in our current operations while also devising flexible solutions to PII disclosure challenges caused by the fact sensitive PII simply wasn't protected during the initial publication of tens of thousands of Government publications already in circulation.

To do this effectively without compromising the American people's access to important Government information, GPO differentiates among the various types of PII potentially housed in the collections that we either provide access to or host.

Using the NIST report and related OMB guidance to inform our approach to PII categorization, GPO considered the potential harm of disclosure to determine which forms of PII should be considered high-impact PII versus those that should be categorized as low-impact PII.

By differentiating between these two categories of PII, GPO believes it improves its ability to restrict or suppress that identifying information which is most likely to cause specific individuals harm upon disclosure without compromising the utility of the underlying public documents. GPO's definition of high-impact PII includes personal identification numbers issued by government or financial institutions printed in conjunction with an individual's name, such as full or partial social security numbers, taxpayer identification numbers, patient identification numbers, financial account numbers, or credit card numbers. In our view the unauthorized disclosure of these types of information are likely to pose the greatest risk to any individual.

Low-impact PII in our view would include a person's name, their street address, phone number, names of family members, and photographic images. Attempting to redact every such instance in which low-impact PII could be found in Government publications we believe would present a far greater challenge, with less obvious benefit, and considerably greater impact on the usability of the affected publications.

Protecting PII in GPO's Daily Operations

GPO's operations consist of two basic activities: producing Government information and identification documents and making Government information widely available. The Agency needs to protect any PII in both of those modes.

On the production side, there is no better example than what we do with PII than our work on secure identification documents. GPO's Security and Intelligent Documents operations involve significant amounts of PII and we take extraordinary steps to protect it every day. The PII data that comes into GPO is encrypted and once it is in our servers it is then decrypted and sent to the production machines. For instance, GPO manufactures and personalizes several varieties of identification cards. Specifically, the trusted traveler "smart" cards are used at both the Northern and Southern border crossings for identification and for expedited processing. By the very nature of these products, GPO must handle vast amounts of highly sensitive PII within our systems. GPO works closely with its customers and their contractors to maintain a series of firewalls that ensure that GPO only receives encrypted PII that is only decrypted when it is needed to produce and distribute those cards. When GPO finishes production of the product, that PII is scrubbed from our systems.

Much of our work to protect PII occurs as we work to make Government information more available. Since the passage of the GPO Electronic Information Access Enhancement Act of 1993, GPO has been working to broaden the availability of Government information on the Internet. What began nearly 30 years ago with the GPO Access website posting the daily Congressional Record and little more has now grown into the world's only ISO-certified trusted digital repository giving people worldwide free public online access to authenticated Government content. The volume of documents available online has grown to nearly 2.2 million packages, with over 320,000 packages added in FY 2021 alone. Last month we celebrated the 9 billionth retrieval of content through GPO's system of online access since the original GPO Access site first went live in 1994.

Today, 97 percent of all Federal Government publications are "born" digital and the growth in the electronic accessibility of Government information is significant enough that I recently established the Task Force on a Digital Federal Depository Library Program, comprised of 23 members representing the Depository Library Council, the Depository Library Community, Federal Agency partners, and library associations, to study what until recently might have been unthinkable: the feasibility and advisability of moving toward an all-digital Federal Depository Library Program.

Recognizing the importance of protecting PII that may have inadvertently found its way into our publicly accessible systems, the Superintendent of Documents adopted a policy requiring the redaction of high-impact PII whenever it is discovered within the publicly accessible files in GPO's system of online access, or within content being prepared for ingest into that system. To fulfill legal requirements of GPO's affiliate agreement with the National Archives and Records Administration, we must maintain unredacted preservation copies of those materials, but the PII can be redacted from the versions we put online.

In addition, because GPO's Partnership program provides a guide to materials that are beyond GPO's direct custodial control, GPO also takes proactive steps to alert those entities with which GPO has partnership agreements whenever GPO learns that materials in those partner's collections might reveal high-impact PII. This enables GPO's content partners to take appropriate action to redact or obscure PII that they may not have been aware existed.

In 2008, the Joint Committee on Printing authorized GPO to redact PII in the electronic access copies of congressional publications. For congressional publications published today, GPO can act immediately to suppress protected information in access copies of those publications without altering the underlying content. Where GPO's task becomes more challenging is when we are engaged in efforts to digitize historical collections of documents.

The most prominent example of this may be GPO's efforts in partnership with the Library of Congress to digitize every volume of the Congressional Record back to its inception in 1873 and make them available through govinfo, a project that GPO completed in 2019. The Library of Congress digitized millions of pages that contained thousands of instances of PII — particularly the entire or partial social security numbers of thousands of individuals. Many of these occurrences were related to the promotion of career staff, particularly in the Armed Forces.

While we haven't caught every single instance of PII appearing in the electronic copies of congressional publications prior to making them available to the public in electronic form, we have the infrastructure in place to systematically discover and remediate PII on an ongoing basis.

GPO maintains a contract with a vendor to provide high-impact PII redaction services that covers both historic, digitally-imaged content, as well as content already within the govinfo system on an as-discovered basis. Specifically, this contract covers both historic and contemporary congressional publications including the Serial Set, Digitized Hearings, the Daily Congressional Record, Bound Congressional Record, and any future digitization work that has the potential to contain PII. We also have access to software that enables us to manually redact such high-impact PII whenever we encounter it.

To date, our PII redaction contract has allowed us to find and redact 1,598 documents containing instances of PII both in publications currently found on govinfo as well as those we are in the process of digitizing. With significant anticipated digitization efforts planned in the future — for example the ongoing multi-year collaborative project with the Law Library of Congress to digitize the U.S. Congressional Serial Set and the possible digitization of thousands of congressionally mandated reports identified in the Congressionally Mandated Reports Act currently being considered in Congress — we expect to make considerable additional PII redaction investments in the years ahead.

Congress should be aware, however, that even if we are immensely successful in redacting such high-impact PII from those Government information collections we are digitizing ourselves, those we make available directly via govinfo, and those we provide access to via partnership agreements with other institutions, it is unlikely that such sensitive PII information will vanish completely from the Internet. This is because other well-intentioned institutions have undertaken efforts to make digitized copies of such Government publications electronically available in the past, and still others may choose to do so in the future.

To date, a few of the institutions who have done some of this work have demonstrated a willingness to remove high-impact PII from their digitized collections when we have made them aware of the issue, and Google Books and HathiTrust are worthy of recognition on that front. Still others lack either the resources to find and redact PII in their collections or the interest in doing so, and there's no legal authority for GPO to compel those third parties to take that action.

Additionally, it is important to remember that much of this digitization is based on existing tangible documents and those documents are distributed across the Nation, even if they aren't always easy to locate. By way of illustration, through the early 1990s GPO produced and disseminated nearly 20,000 copies of the Congressional Record each day — more than 10 times our current production level — so we are certain that there will always be some tangible copies of Government documents that contain PII that we will be unable to locate. The sheer number of tangible copies of older Government publications that contain sensitive, high-impact PII is going to continue to pose challenges for all of us for years to come.

Beyond the issue of the exposure of high-impact PII, there's the more general issue of potentially embarrassing personal information about specific individuals becoming easier to find because of the increasing electronic accessibility of Government publications. It has been my experience that people often try to conflate information which is merely unflattering with PII in order to hide that information from public view. It's important that we maintain the distinction between the two.

We can all agree that it is in the public interest to ensure that U.S. Federal Court opinions are accessible via the United States Courts Opinions (USCOURTS) collection on govinfo. This is a collaborative effort between GPO and the Administrative Office of the United States Courts to provide public access to opinions from select United States appellate, district, and bankruptcy courts, consistent with the E-Government Act's requirement for the substance of all written opinions, issued after April 16, 2005, to be made available in a text searchable format [Section 205 of Pub. L. No. 107-347].

However, on occasion individuals referenced in those opinions prefer that their involvement with those proceedings remain unknown and demand that GPO remove the relevant opinion from the collection. It is critical to understand that this data belongs to our customers and GPO has no independent authority to redact or remove an opinion, and per the Superintendent's policy with regard to online redactions or removal from collections, GPO will only take action in response to a request from the originating agency, the courts that issued the opinions.

When these inquiries arise, GPO refers individuals to the Administrative Office of the U.S. Courts for information about applying to the court that issued the opinion, which may decide to seal the opinion if the judge determines it warrants withdrawal from public access.

That concludes my testimony. I hope that this discussion of our practices, procedures, and capabilities was helpful to the Committee and I welcome your questions.

Hugh Nathanial Halpern,
GPO Director

Hugh Nathanial Halpern is the U.S. Government Publishing Office (GPO) Director, the agency's chief executive officer. The agency is responsible for publishing and printing information for the three branches of the Federal Government. Halpern is the 28th person to lead GPO since the agency opened its doors for business on March 4, 1861, the same day Abraham Lincoln was inaugurated as the 16th President of the United States.

President Donald Trump nominated Halpern to be GPO Director on October 17, 2019, and the U.S. Senate confirmed him on December 4, 2019.

Biography

Prior to coming to GPO, Halpern held a succession of leadership positions during his 30 years on Capitol Hill. He served as the Director of Floor

Operations for the Speaker of the U.S. House of Representatives. In that role, Halpern was the highest-ranking floor staffer in the House and served as Speaker Paul Ryan's Chief Advisor on all procedural matters. He managed the daily floor operations of the House, served as the liaison to all leadership offices, and oversaw legislative interactions between The White House, House and Senate. In 2018, he received the John W. McCormack Award of Excellence, the highest award given to a staff member in the House. The award recognizes a lifetime of bipartisan service to the House.

In addition to his position in the Speaker's Office, Halpern has more than a decade of experience serving on the senior leadership staff. He has a proven track record of successfully leading teams to achieve results.

During his career, he served half a dozen different committees in both policy development and procedural roles. During his 11 years on the House Committee on Rules, Halpern served as Staff Director leading the management and terms of debate on the House floor. In 2001, he was named General Counsel by Chairman Mike Oxley for the newly established House Committee on Financial Services. During his tenure, the committee provided legislation addressing terrorist financing and money laundering, improving investor confidence in the wake of the Enron and WorldCom scandals and granting consumers important new tools to fight identity theft. During the 1990s, Halpern served on the House Committee on Energy and Commerce, where he handled a variety of legislative issues, including automobile safety, insurance, FTC consumer protection and tobacco regulation.

Halpern began his career in Congress as an intern for Rep. E.G. "Bud" Shuster in 1987.

Halpern served a number of temporary positions during his time on Capitol Hill. He was the Parliamentarian to the First Select Committee on Homeland Security, which created the Department of Homeland Security, General Counsel to the Select Committee to investigate the voting irregularities of August 2, 2007, and Assistant Parliamentarian to the 2008, 2012, and 2016 Republican National Conventions.

A native of Hollidaysburg, PA, Halpern received bachelor's and master's degrees in Political Science from American University in 1991 and 1992, respectively. He also received a law degree from George Mason University in 1997. Halpern has been included in Roll Call's list of 50 most powerful Congressional staffers 14 times and featured in a National Journal profile as one of "The New Power Players" on Capitol Hill.

The CHAIRPERSON. Thank you so much, Director Halpern. It is great to hear this testimony.

Now is the time when Members can ask questions, and we will turn first to the Ranking Member, Mr. Davis, for five minutes of his questions.

Mr. DAVIS. You would think I would know how to work the mute button right now, Madam Chairperson. I apologize for the delay.

Hugh, great to see you, man.

Mr. HALPERN. You, too.

Mr. DAVIS. I looked. The last time you were called to testify before this Committee was on March 30—March 3rd of 2020——

Mr. HALPERN. Yes.

Mr. DAVIS [continuing]. Nearly two full years ago. It is nice to finally have you back, but I wish it was to get a comprehensive update on GPO's operations and the initiatives you have launched and successes you have had as well as the agency's health post pandemic.

Unfortunately, we are here to talk about a much narrower topic, but one that GPO clearly excels at, and that is protecting the PII, the personally identifiable information you spoke about, and its work to print passports, create global entry cards, and other sensitive projects.

In your testimony, you shared the impressive work GPO has undertaken to follow the recommendations laid out by the National Institute of Standards and Technology and their guide to protecting the confidentiality of PII.

Do you currently believe that you, as the Director of GPO, have all the necessary authority to continue a high level of excellence in protecting PII?

Mr. HALPERN. Thanks so much for the question.

The short answer is, at the moment, I think we do. We have got the authority we need to work with our customers, to design systems that protect the PII that they give us, and in our relationship with our own vendors, whether that is a contractor that we hire on behalf of the executive branch for work that they are doing for the IRS or other government agencies. That—we are able to construct systems that protect that level of PII.

Now, one of the things that we must remain vigilant about is the PII of our own teammates. And frankly, if there was a large body of PII that the agency maintains, that is it. It is our payroll information. It is our time and attendance information. It is our personnel files.

We work both with folks here in the building and with our vendors over at the Department of Agriculture, who handle our payroll and other systems, to make sure that that information is protected. We are doing our level best to protect the nearly 1,600 people who work here at GPO from running into any problems, as well as the information of anybody who is working with GPO or working with our customers.

Mr. DAVIS. Great. How often is GPO's privacy program reassessed or updated to remain at this high level of effectiveness?

Mr. HALPERN. So, it is constantly undergoing assessment. Our— the directive that governs our privacy program is supposed to be reviewed, I believe, every three years. We are constantly going through our policies, our procedures, and our actual practices to make sure that we are doing our level best. And that is both on the digital side, where we have an extremely competent team on our information technology team, but also just with our safety and security team.

Now, I get an update three, four times a year as our safety and security team walks the building to make sure that things are shipshape. I can tell you they have flagged folks who have inadvertently left PII sitting on their desk, not having it stored properly. So, it is a good reminder to all of us that we need to be proactive in protecting this information, whether it is digitally or tangibly here in the real world.

Mr. DAVIS. I couldn't agree more.

One last question. What has GPO learned from the OPM breach that happened several years ago?

Mr. HALPERN. I think it is very similar to the lessons that a lot of government agencies are learning. We have got to secure our systems, and we spend a lot of resources. We have a dedicated appropriation for that purpose. And it requires a lot of vigilance on our part.

And, you know, knock on wood, thank God, certainly during my tenure here, we have not had anything that even indicated that folks were close to a breach of those kinds of systems, and it is something we dedicate a lot of resources to every single day.

And, you know, the one thing that the OPM breach, I think, taught all of us is you can't rest on your laurels. Security needs to be everybody's job every single day.

Mr. DAVIS. Well, thanks, Hugh.

Thank you, Madam Chairperson. I yield back.

The CHAIRPERSON. Thank you.

I now recognize Mr. Raskin for his questions for five minutes.

Mr. RASKIN. Thank you, Madam Chairperson, and thanks for calling this important hearing.

Ms. Fitzgerald, discrete bits of personal information can seem relatively harmless or trivial, but, when they are all combined together with other data, they can have a far more sweeping impact and create special dangers.

What lessons does this point contain for privacy regulation? What are the biggest risks that Congress should be considering in terms of the large-scale aggregation of data?

The CHAIRPERSON. I would note that Ms. Fitzgerald is on our second panel, so——

Mr. RASKIN. Oh, I am sorry. I thought I saw her there. Forgive me. Then I will come, then, to Mr. Halpern.

So, what are the greatest privacy risks that GPO faces in its operations? What are the specific harms in this area that you are most focused on right now?

Mr. HALPERN. Well, as I was saying, I think the largest single trove that we maintain over a long—over a longer period is our employees' own data. And that is something that we are focused very, very closely on protecting.

Most of the other places where we have PII and we need to focus on that, we have developed systems to make sure that we are holding onto that PII for the minimum amount of time possible.

So, for instance, in the example I used with the global entry card, we literally have a contractor sitting on the other side of the wall from our smart card manufacturing facility who will send the encrypted data that we will need to produce those cards into the smart card room, we will utilize that information to produce those cards, and then scrub that from our systems, send it back to the customer once we are done with it, so that we are not holding on to any more data than we need.

Our biggest problem in terms of other folks' data is historical data. And, as we fulfill, I think, the greater public good of working backwards and trying to digitize old records, we are going to find more PII because, frankly, twenty or thirty years ago, folks were a lot less conscious about what they were putting in a congressional hearing or the Congressional Record or the Federal Register. Because those were all tangible documents, it was a lot harder for somebody to get that information and then to do something with it, because the internet just wasn't developed as it is now.

We have got a program in place to scan for PII in those older documents. And, as we digitize them, we are working to redact that from our digital collections.

Mr. RASKIN. Thank you for that. I know that GPO routinely publishes documents and information that originate elsewhere in the Federal

Government, so you are not the original custodian and source of all the information you publish. And so how does this affect your privacy policies and practices?

Mr. HALPERN. We are often the middle person in this transaction. The good example is the one I gave in my testimony about U.S. courts—court opinions. As you can well imagine, there are a lot of opinions that folks may not be happy are out there in the world or easily searchable. And, while as a general matter, that serves a greater public good, there is that problem with, you know, maybe having an opinion where there is information in there that somebody is uncomfortable with having out in the public.

So, what we have done is we have a number of different places. If you go to gpo.gov/privacy, it talks about our entire privacy program, including who you need to talk to over at the Administrative Office of the U.S. Courts to deal with a court document that may have issues.

Similarly, just a few years ago, we revamped our Ask GPO system, which is now powered by a modern contact management system. And there, we have also got links so that, if folks find an opinion or something like that that raises an issue, they can ask about it, we can root that to the proper person and make sure they get the information to talk to the Administrative Office of the U.S. Courts to get that particular record sealed if that is appropriate.

In terms of——

Mr. RASKIN. Thank you so much. I yield back, Madam Chairperson.

Mr. HALPERN. Thanks.

The CHAIRPERSON. Thanks so much, and I will recognize the gentleman from Georgia now for his questions for five minutes, Mr. Loudermilk.

Mr. LOUDERMILK. Well, thank you, Madam Chairperson. And, Hugh, it is good to see you again.

Mr. HALPERN. Likewise.

Mr. LOUDERMILK. I appreciate all the work that you are doing over at GPO. And you said something a few minutes ago that was music to my ears, and I have been saying this ever since I have been in Congress. It is a lesson I learned working in intelligence on the IT side when I was in the Air Force. One of the primary principles that was just engraved into our every policy we have is you don't have to secure what you don't have. If you don't need it, then discard it.

We had procedures built around that to analyze data, whether we needed it or not. You had to justify keeping it. And then it was destroyed.

The problem we have—I have been saying this ever since I have been in Congress, and especially on Financial Services Committee, as we are dealing with these same issues—is there is many in Congress and in the Federal Government that aren't applying that principle, and so much legislation is being passed that is getting the Federal Government to grab more data or forcing businesses to acquire more data of individuals, and somebody is keeping that and storing it as data that does not need to be kept.

I appreciate hearing you say that because there is very few government officials or, quite frankly, people in Congress that you ever hear say that: If you don't need it then don't keep it.

So, has GPO experienced any data breaches or identified attempted attacks in recent years?

Mr. HALPERN. So yes, on the attack side. No on the breach side. The good news is my IT security folks were doing their job, and to the best of our knowledge, we have not had a breach, certainly during my tenure or even in the years leading up to it.

Shortly after I became the Director of GPO—I still remember it— I was at an event on Saturday night at my synagogue when I suddenly learned that somebody that we believe affiliated with the Iranians had defaced the front of one of our sites. The good news is that is all the farther they got. We were able to restore that site. We are in the process—we are in the process of moving that over to a more secure infrastructure.

And, the good news is that my team has a really good process in place to make sure that our systems are secure. As updates come out, they are tested thoroughly before we do those upgrades. So we don't necessarily have—we don't necessarily have the exposures you might have from unknown vulnerabilities. So we really work hard to try and get that right.

Mr. LOUDERMILK. Well, it sounds like you are doing a good job at that, because, if you would have answered my question then, "Well, we haven't had any data breaches and no attempted attacks," I would have said, "Then you are not doing your job," because I guarantee you, you are being attacked. And, if you don't know it, then there is something wrong.

Also, the updates, they are crucial. That is what caused the Equifax data breach, was simply a failure in the IT department to not do a firmware update that was needed to be done.

So, I am comfortable with the answers you have given. And that is why we haven't seen any data breaches. In the thirty years I spent in IT and data security, I could tell you the question isn't if you are going to be hacked; it is when. It is going to happen at some point, and it is a race to stay just ahead of the bad guy.

I use the analogy of when I used to hunt in Alaska, and we would go bear hunting. Somebody inevitably would put on a pair of tennis shoes and say: What that is for? So, well, if we see a grizzly, I want to have my tennis shoes on.

They say: Well, you can't outrun a grizzly. They would say: No, I just have to outrun you.

All right? So, it is the same thing, is you have got to stay ahead of the bad guy and stay one step above someone else because, if they can't get into you, they will go on to somebody else.

So, it sounds like I have already heard the answer to this question, but do you have all the tools you need to keep carrying out this level of privacy and security, or is there additional things that we can do in Congress to help?

Mr. HALPERN. At the moment, I think we are in pretty good shape. The things are—we have the flexibility. We have the tools that we need. Obviously, it is always a question of resources, but, as we start automating processes here at GPO, we are really focused on figuring out how we make our dollars go farther. And that has really been one of the hallmarks of GPO all through history. So, we are putting that emphasis on security and trying to do it with tools we have got. And, where we don't have tools, we make the investments we need. That is—you know, to some extent, that is one of our advantages. Only about twelve percent of our total revenue comes from appropriations. The rest is what we charge our customers.

So, the State Department expects us to keep their passports fully secure, and we spend a lot of money doing that. But the State Department reimburses us for those investments. And the same with our other customers. We are pretty comfortable with where we are, but we are always happy to talk about things and figure out how we can do better.

Mr. LOUDERMILK. Well, this is an ever-changing environment, and it is a job that is never done, because once you think that you are secure and you are not staying on top of it, the bad guys are going to beat us. Thank you for all you are doing.

Madam Chairperson, I yield back.

The CHAIRPERSON. The gentleman yields back. Mr. Aguilar is recognized for five minutes.

Mr. AGUILAR. Thank you, Madam Chairperson.

And thanks, Director Halpern, for the update and the information. A lot to review here, and I appreciate your commitment to safeguarding that PII.

What I was kind of interested in is—and you talked about some of the digital versus the historical documents that you are in charge to protect. Your testimony kind of speaks to that and said that 97 percent of the Federal documents now are born digital.

So, what distinctions does GPO make between the digital versus paper documents in terms of privacy risks and how they can be addressed by your team and by the contractors, and how has that transition been to the Digital Age and the privacy risks that are associated with that on your operational side?

Mr. HALPERN. Thanks so much, sir, for that.

The short answer is that, for new documents that we produce, we have an airtight system for trying to scan those documents as we are producing them, looking for PII. As I mentioned, with the Federal Register, they are under the OPM policies regarding PII, so there is not a lot that is coming in.

We do need to check the Congressional Record, and we work very hard to redact any PII that might appear there. But I think even Congress is being more circumspect about that stuff going forward.

Our biggest problem is stuff that exists in the tangible form, so a printed paper that was printed historically twenty or thirty years ago, or even a lot longer. And what we are running into are two issues there. One is, as we are trying to digitize that information. We are taking committee hearings from the 1970s or the 1980s and trying to digitize those and put them on Govinfo.gov.

There, both our contractor and our library team are looking at those documents. Where they see and where they catch PII, we are redacting that from the digital copies that go online.

When it comes to those paper documents, we simply don't have the capacity to literally travel the world to find every copy of the Congressional Record from the late 1800s forward, check those volumes for PII, and redact them. So we are, in some respects, reliant on our partners, the Federal depository libraries and our other libraries across the world, where a lot of this information goes.

But, that said, as I mentioned before, I think, because that information is comparatively hard to access—you need to go to a physical place, and you need to open a physical volume to find that— because it is harder to access, that is a little bit lower of a threat than what is going out in the digital domain.

It is not a zero threat, but—and, where we find PII, we try to try and redact it. We just don't have the resources in terms of people, money, and all those kinds of things to do a full scrub for every place where one of these paper documents might exist in the world.

Mr. AGUILAR. Understood. And how do you kind of keep—what is the digital, you know, kind of hygiene? How do you stay ahead of the evolving threats and the digital privacy landscape piece of it? Is it through the OPM guidance? Is it through, you know, contractors, or how do you kind of stay ahead of the risks that are in front of you?

Mr. HALPERN. So, one of the great things about being a legislative branch agency is we can take the best practices all across the government. We are not necessarily confined by what OPM provides.

I know that our IT security team both works with the other CISOs here in the Legislative Branch as well as broader across the government. As we do work for our other Federal customers, we are obviously talking to them, figuring out what their requirements are, and how we can meet those. So, there is a lot of variety of avenues for us to be exposed to the sort of changing landscape and what folks' requirements are, and we are always going to make sure that our systems are designed in such a way as to protect the security of those documents.

Whether it is producing smart cards, whether it is the U.S. passport, one of the reasons that they come to GPO is because we can produce those documents securely in government facilities with the highest quality you are going to find any place in the world and do it at a reasonable price and in a reasonable timeframe.

So——

Mr. AGUILAR. Thanks.

Mr. HALPERN [continuing]. We think we have got some advantages there.

Mr. AGUILAR. Thank you so much. Appreciate it. I yield back, Madam Chairperson.

The CHAIRPERSON. Thank you. Mr. Steil is now recognized for five minutes.

Mr. STEIL. Thank you very much, Madam Chairperson. Mr. Halpern, appreciate you being here today.

Long day on Zoom staring at screens for all of us, and I think we are all looking forward to getting back in person before too long. But I appreciate you being here, and I think maybe in a future Committee hearing, we will get an opportunity to talk to some of your Legislative Branch colleagues, what is just a critical issue.

I can't tell you how often I hear from folks across Wisconsin about the importance of data privacy. They are thinking about it. They are thinking about being hacked. There is really a timely Politico article that came out just a little bit ago talking about our reporters being hacked through apps. It is nonstop that this is something that we are talking about, and I think important that we are talking about it here.

The proposed piece of legislation that would mandate GPO action in the data privacy space, the Online Privacy Act of 2021 that we are talking about, were you consulted in the drafting of the legislation, specifically Section 5?

Mr. HALPERN. We were not consulted on the front end, although we did have subsequent discussions with the Committee. From our reading, it is a flexible standard in the proposed legislation, and it is something that we think we can meet with the program that we are running today, and it will give us an opportunity to take a look at and make sure that there is—if there are any places where we need to tighten things up, we definitely can do that.

Mr. STEIL. Understood. Appreciate your commentary on that. That is helpful.

Under national data privacy laws, there is really—it is really kind of a balance in ways to minimize compliance costs for small businesses while still providing appropriate levels of protection to individuals. Can you kind of comment on how you try to strike that balance?

Mr. HALPERN. So, for most of our interactions with small businesses, that is through our print procurement program. And the requirements there are largely driven by our customers.

Now, that said, there are any number of small and medium size businesses that can participate in our print production or print procurement program. To give you an idea, I was just up in Pennsylvania—I think it was a few months ago—and we visited with one of our contractors that does a lot of work with GPO. And we use that contractor specifically because they have a great system for keeping track of information and keeping track of documents with sensitive information in it and give us a great paper trail. They do a fantastic job of handling those types of jobs for us and doing it in a way where we are confident that that information is safe and secure.

I think there are some other companies across the country that can do that work for us. There aren't a ton, to be a hundred percent honest with you. And, when we have run into problems where, say, one contractor has experienced labor shortages, which isn't something that is uncommon these days, there aren't a lot of other places to go. But some of the small and medium size businesses that we work with have gotten really good at having internal systems that can protect that information. And, frankly, sometimes they do a better job of it than some of our larger contractors.

Mr. STEIL. Great. I appreciate that feedback, Mr. Halpern. Madam Chairperson, I will yield back.

The CHAIRPERSON. The gentleman yields back. Ms. Scanlon is recognized for five minutes.

Ms. SCANLON. Thank you, Madam Chairperson.

Mr. Halpern, what remedial measures do the GPO have in place if one of its publications contains nonpublic personal information about a private individual, especially if it is sensitive or otherwise potentially harmful in nature?

Mr. HALPERN. Absolutely. As I mentioned, we have both automated and manual systems to redact information that is found in our digital collection.

So, for instance, let's just say for the sake of argument something slipped through tonight's edition of the Congressional Record. There was something that had some PII in it and all our checks failed. The good news is, when that is brought to our attention, our team can go in, change the record in Govinfo.gov, our trusted digital repository, and redact that information out of the digital record.

We can't really fix the printed copies, but the volume of those copies for something, say, like the Congressional Record is much smaller than it was even a decade and a half ago.

So, to give you an idea, in the 1990s, the daily circulation of the Congressional Record was north of 20,000 copies a day. Today, we are only producing about 1,500 copies a day. So, it is a much smaller universe in the printed world, and we have tools in place to fix any problems that might occur on the back end through our digital systems.

Ms. SCANLON. I mean, when you were talking about the court systems, that kind of caught my attention, because that is where I spent my pre-congressional career, and certainly judges will talk about a lot of facts as they are ruling on a case. So, you know, would an affected individual have the right or the ability to get personally identifiable information deleted, redacted, or otherwise remediated?

Mr. HALPERN. So, the way that works right now, it is not our process; it is the court's process. So, they can petition the Administrative Office of the U.S. Courts, and it is up to the judge to decide whether or not to seal those particular records or parts of a record. And, depending on that decision, we will either pull the record out of Govinfo.gov, or put in a redacted version depending on what the constraints are of the judge's order.

As I mentioned in my testimony, this is sort of that gray area. It doesn't necessarily fall into the category of the standard PII, people's Social Security numbers, their other key identifiers. But it may describe facts that somebody is uncomfortable with. And, in those kinds of cases, we are not going to be the best folks to make a decision as to whether that needs to stay in the public domain or it needs to be removed. The judge who was involved in that case or another judge really needs to be the person who makes that decision. And, depending on what that decision is, we will act accordingly.

Ms. SCANLON. Well, if it was something within your domain, is there currently a right of an individual to be able to get personally identifiable information redacted? If, for example, a Social Security number or a—I don't know—a credit card number or something somehow had slipped through, is there a right to have it removed?

Mr. HALPERN. I can get back to you on what the statutory background is on that. I can tell you, for GPO's policies and directives, if we come across that information and can redact it from our—primarily from our digital collection, we are going to do so. And, if somebody brings that to our attention, it may not be the person whose information that is. It could be a third party.

But, if we become aware of that and we—you know, we agree that that is PII, we will make the effort to redact that from the digital side.

Ms. SCANLON. Okay. Thank you. Madam Chairperson, I yield back.

The CHAIRPERSON. Thank you.

I now recognize the gentlelady from New Mexico for five minutes.

Ms. LEGER FERNA´NDEZ. Thank you so very much, Chairperson Lofgren. And thank you for holding this hearing, because I can tell you that this issue comes up a lot as I talk to my constituents.

They are concerned, and we are concerned with regards to the manner in which our data is protected.

Director Halpern, I truly appreciated your comments about how protection of our personal data held by the government is linked to people's trust in our government, and I think you would agree that this link will only grow stronger as more of our lives move into the digital space.

I also appreciated your comments about how GPO and other Federal agencies are discussing best practices with each other. Do you believe that—can you elaborate a bit more on what we are doing here at the Legislative Branch that we might strengthen based on the information you are hearing and sharing with the other Federal agencies so that we can make sure that we have those protections against the cyber-attacks, as well as protecting individuals' personal information as you described it?

Mr. HALPERN. Sure. I will do my best.

Then—it happens on a number of different axes is probably the best way to think of it. As I mentioned before, our computer information security folks have a lot of back and forth, and there is a lot of discussion about what are those best practices, how do we secure our systems?

And, frankly, particularly with GPO and the Congress, there is a lot of interchange that occurs on a daily basis. You are sending us information. We are sending it back to you. And we are working with the Library to make things available via Congress.gov.

So, there is a lot of discussion about those particular flows, and, frankly, what our CISOs are experiencing day to day: Where are these attacks coming from? How do you secure against them? And what are the appropriate countermeasures?

The other area that we are working on is our obligation as an employer. So, I just got the update this morning. Right now, we are at 1,547 people working directly for GPO, plus, you know, a few hundred contractors. We have an obligation to secure that information—payroll information, health information, all sorts of things.

The Chief Administrative Officer of the House has a similar obligation. So our officials are talking all the time about how we—how we maintain our systems both from the cyber standpoint and from the more mundane operational standpoint.

And as I mentioned before, my safety and security team literally walk our building. We have a million square feet under roof, and we walk every inch of that building. And one of the things that they look for is, is there PII not being stored properly?

That is a little bit harder to do in the congressional space. You know, I spent thirty years working in the House, so it is a little bit different there. But, some of those same practices, whether it is the Chief Administrative Officer or the Secretary of the Senate or House Sergeant at Arms, all of us are talking all the time to try and figure out what is the best way forward? And there is a lot of information sharing that goes on.

Ms. LEGER FERNA´NDEZ. Thank you so much. And I take it that you have no control over, you know, the fact that—and I think we will hear testimony that every search is saved and mined, right? So, as individuals might be searching within the Congressional Record for information, that—tell me, do we—do you have any way of protecting any of those searches, or is that something that is left to the individual with regards to his or her computer use and privacy settings?

Mr. HALPERN. So, it is a great question, and I will get you a more detailed answer as to the information we retain and don't retain. The short answer is, is we try to retain the minimum amount of information we possibly can about searches in Govinfo.gov or any of our other systems.

So, for instance, in the case of Govinfo.gov, we use the smallest, most mundane kinds of cookies we possibly can. We don't track people across the internet. And, frankly, unlike Congress.gov, we don't have logins, we don't persistently save those searches for folks.

That said——

Ms. LEGER FERNA´NDEZ. I see my time has expired. I do thank you and your organization for respecting, as is proper, the privacy of the users in the documents and in the searches.

I yield back, Madam Chairperson.

The CHAIRPERSON. Thank you.

Just a couple of further questions.

First, Director Halpern, I just want to commend you and your staff for your proactive work protecting privacy. It is admirable.

And in your statement, you said you can't, if you don't save the material, it can't be abused.

And that is the principle of the Online Privacy Act, to really prevent the unnecessary retention of information, because if you don't have it, you can't data mine it, you can't abuse it.

And that is what you are doing in your agency and something that I think we want to look at. Because if you are using a search engine to search something in the Congressional Record, the search engine retains it, even though you don't.

And so, government—you are doing the right thing, but people's searches or inquiries can still be abused and manipulated.

Just two quick questions.

First, really you are doing everything with NIST and OMB guidance and your directives. You are doing that because you want to do the right thing. But it is not—your policies are not required by law at this time, are they?

Mr. HALPERN. No. The short answer is, it is one of the blessings and curses of being in the Legislative Branch.

I actually, am a big Article I guy, so I like the flexibility that this gives us to survey the landscape and pick the policies that meet our values.

Our values are we are going to protect our customer. We are going to be transparent with folks. And we are going to do everything we do, whether it is with our folks here in the building or our customers, in a respectful way. And part of being respectful is protecting that data.

The good news is, while there may not be pure statutory requirements that say you have to do this, one, we believe that our oversight committees expect us to do this, and it is the right thing to expect. And two, our customers expect us to do it.

And both of those are driving imperatives for us here at GPO, and it helps us get into the position where it is easier for us to do the right thing that we were planning to do anyway.

The CHAIRPERSON. All right.

Just one final question. In your written testimony, you mention that GPO distinguishes between high impact and low impact personally identifiable information. I am interested in how or whether you reevaluate the level of risk for different types of PII that may change over time.

And as you classify that, do you consider the potential impact when information is aggregated by third parties in combination with other personally identifiable information, for example, using machine learning or other data processing techniques that are outside of your agency?

Mr. HALPERN. We are always trying to learn. And there are a lot of very clever folks across the country who are coming up with new ways to use that sort of ubiquitous data that is out there. But we do draw a distinction between certain kinds of PIIs.

So, for instance, those unique identifiers, your Social Security number, the card numbers, or passport numbers that the Department of State or Department of Homeland Security use, those are key pieces of information that have the potential to unlock so much else, including biometrics and a whole slew of other things. We are going to work much harder to protect that information.

Lower impact data are things like addresses, photos, names, and that stuff is really kind of ubiquitous. So, for instance, when you do a special order and you are congratulating the coach of your high school football team, you are going to call that person by that name, and that is PII. But we are not going to redact that from the Congressional Record, because that, one, isn't a huge security risk, and two, if we did, it totally eviscerates the point of that special order.

The CHAIRPERSON. Exactly.

I want to thank you, Director Halpern, for your great testimony today. And as you know from your years here on the Hill, we do keep the record open if we have additional questions. So, if that occurs, we will send them right on to you and I know you will get back to us.

I just want to thank you for being here with us today. It has been very informative. And please let your team know how much we think of them and how proud we are of them.

Mr. HALPERN. Thank you very much, ma'am. I really appreciate it.

The CHAIRPERSON. Thank you.

We will now go to our second panel of witnesses and let me brief ly introduce them.

First, we have Shoshana Zuboff, who is the Charles Edward Wilson Professor Emerita at Harvard Business School.

Professor Zuboff is an internationally recognized expert and the author of several major works on digital privacy issues, such as "In the Age of the Smart Machine: The Future of Work and Power" and "The Support Economy: Why Corporations Are Failing Individuals and the Next Episode of Capitalism."

Her most recent book, "The Age of Surveillance Capitalism: The Fight for a Human Future at the New Frontier of Power," investigates the new surveillance economy, which is driven by consumer data.

Our next witness is Caitriona Fitzgerald, who is the Deputy Director at the Electronic Privacy Information Center, or EPIC. She leads EPIC's policy work, working to advance strong privacy, open government, and algorithmic fairness and accountability laws. She recently authored, "Grading on a Curve: Privacy Legislation in the 116th Congress," which sets out the key elements of modern privacy law, including the creation of a U.S. data protection agency. The next witness is Marshall Erwin, who is the Chief Security Officer of Mozilla, where he focuses on data security, privacy, and surveillance.

He has previously worked as a counterterrorism and cybersecurity analyst and has served as the counterterrorism and intelligence adviser to Senator Susan Collins on the Senate Homeland Security and Government Affairs Committee and was the intelligence specialist at the Congressional Research Service.

And finally, we have Daniel Castro, Vice President of the Information Technology and Innovation Foundation, or ITIF, and the Director of the Center for Data Innovation, an ITIF-affiliated research institute focusing on the intersection of data technology and public policy.

I will remind the witnesses that your entire written statements— which, by the way, are excellent—will be included and made part of our permanent record, and that that record will remain open for at least five days for additional material to be submitted.

We ask that you summarize your testimony in five minutes so that the Members of the Committee will have time to pose questions to you.

So, first, Professor Zuboff, we would love to hear from you for five minutes.

Statements of Ms. Shoshana Zuboff, Charles Edward Wilson Professor Emerita, Harvard Business School; Ms. Caitriona Fitzgerald, Deputy Director, Electronic Privacy Information Center; Mr. Marshall Erwin, Chief Security Officer, Mozilla Corporation; and Mr. Daniel Castro, Vice President, Information Technology and Innovation Foundation

Statement of Shoshana Zuboff

Ms. ZUBOFF. Chairperson Lofgren, Ranking Member Davis, and Members of the Committee, thank you so much for this opportunity to discuss the challenges of privacy, privacy law, in a world without privacy.

I have spent the last 43 years of my life studying the rise of the digital as an economic force that is driving our transformation into an information civilization. Over these last two decades, I have observed as the fledgling internet companies morphed into a sweeping surveillance-based economic order founded on the premise that privacy must fall, empowered by economic operations that I have called surveillance capitalism.

Surveillance capitalism maintains core elements of traditional capitalism—private property, commodification, market exchange, growth, and profit—but these cannot be realized without the technologies and social relations of surveillance.

Hidden methods of observation secretly extract human experience, until recently considered private, and translate it into behavioral data. These methods operate outside of human awareness, engineered to do so, robbing actors of the right to know and with it the right to combat.

Ill-gotten human data are then immediately claimed as corporate property, private property, available for aggregation, computation, prediction, targeting, modification, and sales.

The theory of surveillance capitalism challenges this property claim and redefines it as theft. Surveillance capitalism was invented at Google during the financial emergency of the dot-com bust. It migrated to Facebook, became the default model of the tech sector, and is now reordering diverse industries, from insurance, retail, banking, and finance, to agriculture, automobiles, education, healthcare, and much, much more.

As one tech executive recently described it to me, all software design assumes that all data should be collected, and most of this occurs without the user's knowledge.

All roads to economic and social participation now lead through surveillance capitalism's institutional terrain, a condition that has only intensified during these two years of global plague.

The abdication of these spaces to surveillance capitalism has become the meta crisis of every republic because it obstructs solution to all the other crises for which we require information integrity and the sanctity of communications.

The world's liberal democracies now confront a tragedy of the "unommons" as mission critical information in communication spaces, that most people have assumed to be public, are now owned, operated, and mediated by private commercial interests for profit maximization, while almost entirely unconstrained by public law. No democracy can survive these conditions.

The deficit I describe here reflects a larger pattern. The United States and the world's liberal democracies have thus far failed to construct a coherent political vision of a digital century that advances democratic values, principles, and government, while the Chinese, for example, in contrast, have focused on designing and deploying digital technologies in ways that advance their system of authoritarian rule.

This failure left a void where democracy should be, leaving our citizens now to march naked into the third decade of surveillance capitalism without the rights, laws, and institutions necessary for a democratic digital future.

Instead, we have stumbled into an accidental dystopia, a future that we did not and would not choose. In my view, we must not and cannot allow this to be our legacy.

Survey evidence, some of which has already been referred to here, now shows that Americans are moving ahead of their lawmakers in a massive rupture of faith with these companies.

We see extraordinary majorities calling for action to curb the unaccountable social power of these firms, a realization that the emperor of surveillance capitalism not only has no clothes, but is dangerous, and a clear sense that human rights, the durability of society, and democracy itself are on the line. What was undiscussable has become discussable. What was settled is now being questioned. To end, we are still in the very early days of our information civilization. This third decade is a crucial opportunity to build the foundations for a democratic digital century. Democracy may be under siege, but it is, however paradoxically, the kind of siege that only democracy can end.

Thank you so much for your attention. [The statement of Ms. Zuboff follows:]

HARVARD UNIVERSITY
GRADUATE SCHOOL OF BUSINESS ADMINISTRATION
GEORGE F. BAKER FOUNDATION

Privacy Must Fall
Surveillance Capitalism and the Meaning of Privacy Law After Privacy

Written testimony of
Professor Shoshana Zuboff

Before the
Committee on House Administration
U.S. House of Representatives

For the hearing on
Big Data: Privacy Risks and Needed Reforms in the Public and Private Sectors February 16, 2022

Chair Lofgren, Ranking Member Davis, and members of the Committee, thank you for this opportunity to discuss the challenges of privacy law in a world without privacy.

I have spent forty-three years studying the rise of the digital as an economic force driving our transformation into an information civilization. Over these last two decades, I've observed the consequences as fledgling internet companies morphed into surveillance empires founded on the premise that privacy must fall and powered by global operations of behavioral monitoring, analysis, targeting, modification, and prediction that I have called 'surveillance capitalism'.[1]

I. A Tragedy of the Uncommons

In this written testimony, I pose the following questions to the Committee on House Administration: What kind of legislative action is required to protect privacy in the aftermath ofits wholesale destruction? What is the nature and purpose of privacy law after privacy? While these questions and their answers beg explanation, I confine myself here to the essential pointsnecessary for meaningful deliberation.

In an information civilization, societies are defined by questions of knowledge — how it is distributed, the authority that governs its distribution, and the power that protects that authority. *Who knows? Who decides who knows? Who decides who decides who knows?* Surveillance capitalists now hold the answers to each question, though we never elected them to govern. Theyclaim the authority to decide 'who knows' by asserting ownership rights over human-generated information, and they defend that authority with the power to control critical information spaces, systems, and infrastructures.[2] On the strength of their surveillance capabilities and for the sake of their surveillance profits, the new empires engineered an anti-democratic *epistemic coup* — a takeover of knowledge and knowing — marked by unprecedented concentrations of knowledge about individual and collective behavior along with the unaccountable power that accrues to suchknowledge.

---

[1] Shoshana Zuboff, "Big Other: Surveillance Capitalism and the Prospects of an Information Civilization," *Journal of Information Technology* 30, no. 1 (March 1, 2015): 75–89, https://doi.org/10.1057/jit.2015.5; Shoshana Zuboff, *The Age of Surveillance Capitalism: TheFight for a Human Future at the New Frontier of Power* (New York: PublicAffairs, 2019).

[2] Pascale Davies, "Meta Warns It May Shut down Facebook and Instagram in Europe," *Euronews*, February 7, 2022, https://www.euronews.com/next/2022/02/07/meta-threatens-to-shut-down-facebook-and-instagram-in-europe-over-data-transfer-issues.

The world's liberal democracies now confront a tragedy of the 'un-commons,' as mission-critical information and communication spaces and functions have been ceded to surveillance capital.

Digital territories that most people have assumed to be public are now owned, operated, and mediated by private commercial interests for maximum profit while almost entirely unconstrained by public law. All roads to economic and social participation now lead through surveillance capitalism's institutional terrain, a condition that has intensified during nearly two years of global plague. The abdication of these spaces to surveillance capitalism has become themeta-crisis of every republic because it obstructs solutions to all other crises. No democracy cansurvive these conditions.

This third decade demands a reckoning with the most basic questions of the digital century: howdo we reinvent the operations and governance of information and communication in ways that sustain and advance democratic values, principles, and aspirations? The liberal democracies skipped this most crucial step at the dawn of the information age, leaving a void that was filled by surveillance capital.

The result is the feeling that we've stumbled into a future that we did not and would not choose,one that is increasingly ruled by the antidemocratic and unaccountable power of surveillance capitalism. A sure test of this statement is that when our young people and our artists contemplate the future, they invariably assume the overriding presence of omniscient dystopianpower. This must not be our legacy.

I begin this discussion by defining surveillance capitalism as an economic logic that depends upon the destruction of privacy as a condition of its success. I then briefly discuss the historical conditions that enabled this surprising economics to root and flourish. Next, I examine the stagesof surveillance capitalism's development from its origins in the destruction of individual privacyto its current status as a sweeping institutional order vying with democracy over the principles and laws that will govern society. With these elements identified, I consider the legislative and institutional challenges of this third decade and their bearing upon the renewal of privacy as a necessary condition of a democratic digital century.

II. What is Surveillance Capitalism?

Surveillance capitalism maintains core elements of traditional capitalism: private property, market exchange, growth and profit, but these cannot be realized without the technologies and social relations of surveillance. So, here is the startling new economics of surveillance capitalism: Hidden methods of observation secretly extract human experience once considered private and translate it into behavioral data. These methods operate outside of human awareness, robbing actors of the right to know and, with it, the right to combat. In an extraordinary development, these ill-gotten human data are then immediately claimed as corporate property available for manufacture and sales. The theory of surveillance capitalism challenges this property claim and redefines it as theft.

Human data thus extracted join complex supply chains and travel to computational factories, known as "machine learning" or "artificial intelligence," where they are computed into behavioral predictions and targeting algorithms. Predictions are ultimately sold to business customers in a new kind of market that trades in predictive knowledge of human behavior. These are commodity markets in human futures akin to markets in pork belly futures, or wheat, or oil. Surveillance capitalists sell certainty, which demands data extraction at a massive scale that is impossible to grasp. A leaked 2018 Facebook document provides a glimpse.[3] The company describes its "prediction engine" that "ingests trillions of data points every day," to produce thousands of "models," and its "prediction service" that churns out "more than 6 million predictions per second."

Surveillance capitalism developed into a global institutional order in only two decades, in part because of the many ways in which it learned to persuade America and the world of its inevitability. Nevertheless, this institution was and is anything but inevitable. Its success is owed to action and choice. People made it. Chance made it. Ideology, economics, and politics made it.

The year was 2000, when a mere 25% of the world's information was stored digitally, and a tiny but brilliant Silicon Valley internet startup called Google faced ruin from the financial crisis known as the dotcom bust. Even as Google's search engine was considered the best, founders Larry Page and Sergey Brin faced extreme pressure from their powerful venture capitalist investors. The company had not yet found a way to turn search into money, and their backers insisted on a fast track to monetization.

Between 2000 and 2001, the Google team stumbled into a series of discoveries that revealed the rich predictive signals embedded in the "data exhaust" left over from users' search and browsing activities, signals that

---

[3] Sam Biddle, "Facebook Uses Artificial Intelligence to Predict Your Future Actions for Advertisers, Says Confidential Document," *The Intercept*, April 13, 2018, https://theintercept.com/2018/04/13/facebook-advertising-data-artificial-intelligence-ai/.

could be aggregated and analyzed to predict user behavior. This leftover behavioral data was a surplus, more than what was required for product improvement. The founders had argued that advertising would corrupt the search experience, but financial emergency created a state of exception, and they suspended their principles.[4] Advertising became their lifeboat as they learned how to analyze behavioral surplus to predict click-through rates, the solid gold that launched their vast and lucrative online ad markets.

Surveillance is the keystone of this economic foundation. From the start, data scientists and engineers understood that these operations would have to be hidden, lest they risk user rebellion or lawmakers' anger. Soon, its scientists were inventing ways to surveil and capture behavioral surplus across the internet without leaving a trace, proud of their ability to construct, infer, and deduce user profiles with insights that individuals never chose to disclose — personality, sexual orientation, political leanings … and much more. Later, the mobile revolution would move these secret extraction activities into the real worlds of everyday life. Such hidden-taking-without- asking is normally characterized as theft, and it is on the strength of this secret theft that 'users' once private lives are transformed into others' proprietary assets.

The discovery of behavioral surplus and the related sciences of inference, computation, modeling, algorithms, prediction and targeting known loosely as 'artificial intelligence' undermine the validity of rational choice theory or the contractual integrity of notice and consent. One may exercise rational choice in the decision to share specific information with a platform, but that information is an insignificant drop in the ocean of surplus that is hunted and captured and delivered to sophisticated machine procedures to produce more surplus. I cannot make a rational choice about what is concealed from me – the known unknown.

Google had been a technology company. Its business plan called for selling search engine licenses to large internet companies and other corporate clients. It even produced a device, the "Google Search Appliance," to help companies locate information in their own databases.[5] All of that was swept away.

---

[4] Sergey Brin and Lawrence Page, "The Anatomy of a Large-Scale Hypertextual Web Search Engine," *Computer Networks and ISDN Systems*, Proceedings of the Seventh International World Wide Web Conference, 30, no. 1 (April 1, 1998): 107–17, https://doi.org/10.1016/S0169-7552(98)00110-X.

[5] Andrew Zipern, "Technology Briefing | Internet: Google Enters Corporate World," *The New York Times*, February 12, 2002, sec. Business, https://www.nytimes.com/2002/02/12/business/technology-briefing-internet-google-enters- corporate-world.html.

Founder Larry Page laid it out in 2001, shortly after the breakthrough that would change everything. "If we did have a category," Page ruminated, "it would be personal information … The places you've seen. Communications … Sensors are really cheap … Storage is cheap.

Cameras are cheap. People will generate enormous amounts of data … Everything you've ever heard or seen or experienced will become searchable. Your whole life will be searchable."[6]

Instead of selling search to users, Google would achieve revenue growth by searching its users and seizing whatever it found. Escape from financial ruin, it was decided, depended upon turning Google's search engine into a sophisticated surveillance medium for the massive-scale seizure of human-generated data.

Privacy did not disappear, exactly. Instead, it was expropriated from people and concentrated in the corporate domain. Google used its capabilities in surveillance to keep the new economic operations secret. Founders and executives were determined to hide their breakthrough from competitors, but they also feared that users would rebel against corporate mass surveillance.

Worst of all was the anxiety that lawmakers might be stirred to action. According to the company's first brand manager, Douglas Edwards, Page opposed anything that might "stir the privacy pot and endanger our ability to gather data." He even questioned the prudence of the legendary electronic ticker display in the company's Mountain View lobby, and its continuous stream of search queries.[7]

Page also wanted to hide the astonishing financial implications of Google's invention. Between 2001, when the new economics of surveillance advertising were first applied, and 2004, when Google went public, its revenues increased by 3,590 percent. This 'surveillance dividend' established the secret massive-scale extraction of human-generated data as the foundation of a new economic order.

Facebook was Google's first follower. Like Google a few years earlier, its founder Mark Zuckerberg had not found a way to turn popularity into profit. He changed his destiny in 2008 by hiring Sheryl Sandberg as his second in command. Sandberg had joined Google in the breakthrough year of 2001 and became a key leader of the surveillance capitalism advertising revolution. She led the build-out of Google's advertising engine, AdWords, and its AdSense

---

[6] Douglas Edwards, *I'm Feeling Lucky: The Confessions of Google Employee Number 59* (New York: Houghton Mifflin Harcourt, 2011), 291.

[7] Edwards, 340–45.

program, which together accounted for most of the company's $16.6 billion revenues in 2007.[8]

By the mid-2010s, surveillance economics had become the default economic model in the tech sector. Success drew surveillance economics inexorably into the 'normal' economy, where it has continued to migrate and reorder diverse sectors from insurance, retail, banking and finance to agriculture, automobiles, education, healthcare and more. Every product called "smart," and every service called "personalized" are loss leaders for the human data that flow through them. Today every 'app,' no matter how apparently benign, is designed as a data mule, shuttling personal information from devices to the servers at Google, Facebook, and ad tech companies.

As one Silicon Valley executive recently described it to me, "The underlying norm of virtually all software and apps design now is data collection. All software design assumes that all data should be collected, and most of this occurs without the user's knowledge." Extraction operations and their supply chains range far beyond their original settings on computers, laptops, and smartphones to cities and villages, buildings and roads, homes and cars — every form of activity in every domain of daily life.

Among the five leading surveillance capitalist corporations — Google, Facebook, Amazon, Apple, and Microsoft — each participates in surveillance advertising and surveillance economics, though the specifics of their business models vary. Google and Facebook are data companies and surveillance-advertising "pure plays" whose revenues derive almost entirely from surveillance advertising markets.[9] The others have multiple lines of business that include varying configurations of data, services, software, and-or physical products. Despite these distinctions, all five contribute to, benefit from, and build upon surveillance capitalism's institutional strategies, operations, and revenues in conjunction with their complex ecosystems, the ad tech behemoths, the telcos, the internet service providers, and a growing majority of market-based organizations across the commercial universe. It is therefore not surprising that in 2021 the five giants were also five of the six largest publicly traded companies by market capitalization in the world.[10]

---

[8] Jessi Hempel, "Sheryl Sandberg: Facebook's New Number Two," *CNN Money*, April 11, 2008, https://money.cnn.com/2008/04/11/technology/facebook_sandberg.fortune/.

[9] "Google: Ad Revenue 2001-2020," Statista, n.d., https://www.statista.com/statistics/266249/advertising-revenue-of-google/; "Facebook: Annual Segment Revenue 2020," Statista, n.d., https://www.statista.com/statistics/267031/facebooks- annual-revenue-by-segment/.

[10] Jenna Ross, "The Biggest Companies in the World in 2021," Visual Capitalist, June 10, 2021, https://www.visualcapitalist.com/the-biggest-companies-in-the-world-in-2021/.

III. Windfall

Nothing was inevitable. Ours is an accidental dystopia.

Surveillance capitalism is neither a technology nor a corporation nor an executive. It is a political-economic institution that owes its existence to a windfall of unique economic, political, ideological, and material conditions that permitted this extractive economic logic to root and flourish. I have documented these conditions in detail in other work, and here I shall mention only a few highlights.[11]

In 1970, three years before Larry Page's birth, the New York Times Magazine lent its prestigious pages to "A Friedman Doctrine," the libertarian call to arms giving popular voice to a radical free market world view that would be essential to Page's, and surveillance capitalism's, astounding success.[12] "There is one and only one social responsibility of business," the University of Chicago economist thundered, "to use its resources and engage in activities designed to increase its profits …"

Friedman was a self-described "extremist" partial to sharp dualisms, absolutes, and unequivocal policy positions that frequently triggered public controversy.[13] His ideology was forged in the aftermath of World War II as a response to the collectivist nightmares of German and Soviet totalitarianism. As the old central planning enemies receded, new ones took their place: the regulatory powers of the democratic state, its social legislation and welfare policies, labor unions and the institutions of collective bargaining, and principles of equality and justice. These were replaced by the market's version of truth. Growth would be accelerated by unimpeded market competition sustained by supply-side reforms, including comprehensive deregulation, privatization, and lower taxes.

By mid-decade, as the Nixon and then the Ford White House searched for a way out of the stagflation crisis, Professor Friedman advised both Presidents. By 1979 he was economic advisor to Presidential candidate Ronald Reagan, a relationship that endured throughout Regan's presidency. President Reagan and British Prime Minister Margaret Thatcher famously established

---

[11] Zuboff, The Age of Surveillance Capitalism.

[12] Milton Friedman, "A Friedman Doctrine-- The Social Responsibility Of Business Is to Increase Its Profits," The New York Times, September 13, 1970, sec. Archives, https://www.nytimes.com/1970/09/13/archives/a-friedman-doctrine-the-social-responsibility-of- business-is-to.html.

[13] Angus Burgin, The Great Persuasion: Reinventing Free Markets since the Depression (Cambridge, MA: Harvard University Press, 2012), chap. 5.

Friedman's radical free market doctrine as governmental policy. The market must rule. Democratic institutions must recede.

From the start, the internet and its commerce were claimed for Friedman's radical freedom, and the overarching theme of internet-related governmental policy was "self-regulation" for the sake of Friedman-style profit maximization. This ideological zeitgeist dominated those crucial post- World Wide Web years of the mid to late 1990s finding iconic expression in a 1997 Clinton- Gore whitepaper.[14] The Administration's policy vision for "Global Electronic Commerce" begins with its primary principle: "The private sector should lead." The Google founders became the unwitting heirs apparent of the Friedman Doctrine.

The report denigrated to the point of caricature government's role and capabilities in the governance of digital information and communication spaces, insisting on "minimal government involvement or intervention … Existing laws and regulations that may hinder electronic commerce should be reviewed and revised or eliminated ..." The Administration's approach was not only to get out of the way, but to proactively cede whole governance functions to the internet companies. When it came to privacy protections, the whitepaper's prescriptions rested on formulations that even in 1997 were not easily defensible. This shortfall became more dangerous once the science of behavioral surplus extraction, inference, and computation was invented. The Clinton-Gore framework left 'users' naked at the altar of the rational choice theory assumed in the whitepaper's advocacy of privacy protections such as, "market resolution of privacy concerns by empowering individuals to obtain relevant knowledge," "self-regulatory privacy regimes," "industry-developed solutions to privacy problems," and "market driven mechanisms to assure customer satisfaction about how private data is handled."

By 2000, however, a majority of FTC commissioners, including Chair Robert Pitofsky, concluded that self-regulatory initiatives "cannot ensure that the online marketplace as a whole will follow the standards adopted by industry leaders ... notwithstanding several years of industry and governmental effort." In their report to Congress, the Commissioners cited the explosion of secret online tracking and monitoring for chasing eyeballs with new hidden

---

[14] President William J. Clinton and Vice President Albert Gore, Jr., "A Framework For Global Electronic Commerce" (The White House, n.d.), https://clintonwhitehouse4.archives.gov/WH/New/Commerce/read.html.

methods like "cookies" and "web bugs."[15] They noted that a mere 8 percent of popular websites featured a seal of approval from one of the internet industry's privacy watchdogs, intended as an important mechanism for self-regulation.

The report argued that only federal law could protect online consumers. Proposed stipulations included clear and conspicuous notice of information practices; consumer choice over how personal information is used; individuals' access to all personal information including rights to correct or delete; and enhanced security of personal information.[16] Even these basic privacy protections would have set America and the world on a different path to the digital century, but history, contingency, and chance had other plans: September 11, 2001.

According to Peter Swire, chief counselor for Privacy in the Clinton Administration and later a member of President Barack Obama's Review Group on Intelligence and Communication Technologies, "With the attacks of September 11, 2001, everything changed. The new focus was overwhelmingly on security rather than privacy."[17] The legal provisions debated just months

---

[15] Robert Pitofsky et al., "Privacy Online: Fair Information Practices in the Electronic Marketplace: A Federal Trade Commission Report to Congress," *Federal Trade Commission*,May 1, 2000, 35.

[16] Pitofsky et al. The report's legislative proposals set forth a basic level of privacy protection forall visits to consumer-oriented commercial websites to the extent not already provided by the Children's Online Privacy Protection Act (COPPA). Such legislation would set out the basic standards of practice governing the collection of information online and provide an implementing agency with the authority to promulgate more-detailed standards pursuant to the Administrative Procedure Act, including authority to enforce those standards. All consumer- oriented commercial websites that collect personal identifying information from or about consumers online, to the extent not covered by the COPPA, would be required to comply with the four widely accepted fair information practices: (1) Notice. Websites would be required to provide consumers clear and conspicuous notice of their information practices, including what information they collect, how they collect it (e.g., directly or through nonobvious means such as cookies), how they use it, how they provide Choice, Access, and Security to consumers, whether they disclose the information collected to other entities, and whether other entities are collecting information through the site. (2) Choice. Websites would be required to offer consumers choices as to how their personal identifying information is used beyond the use for which the informationwas provided (e.g., to consummate a transaction). Such choice would encompass both internal secondary uses (such as marketing back to consumers) and external secondary uses (such as disclosing data to other entities). (3) Access. Websites would be required to offer consumers reasonable access to the information a website has collected about them, including a reasonable opportunity to review the information and to correct inaccuracies or delete information. (4) Security. Websites would be required to take reasonable steps to protect the security of the information they collect from consumers.

[17] Peter Swire, "The Second Wave of Global Privacy Protection: Symposium Introduction," *Ohio State Law Journal* 74, no. 6 (2013): 845, https://kb.osu.edu/handle/1811/71601.

earlier vanished from the conversation more or less overnight, giving way to a new preoccupation with "Total Information Awareness."

Friedman's ideology of radical market freedom took care of the supply side, shielding the nascent surveillance capitalist firms from laws that would have curbed the destruction of privacy and all that followed from it. Then, 9/11 thrust the intelligence community, the US government, and, indeed, governments around the world into an unfamiliar demand curve, mobilized by outrage and anxiety. In America, a 'state of exception' was invoked to unleash a new human data imperative: velocity and volume at any price. In this new environment "Congress lost interest in regulating information usage in the private sector," Swire recalls. "Without the threat of legislation, the energy went out of many of the self-regulatory efforts that industry had created."[18]

In the US and across the EU, legislation was quickly put in place that decisively expanded surveillance activities.[19] Instead of federal legislation to outlaw the novel surveillance practices, the new aim was to enrich the conditions for their expansion and application outside constitutional, legal, and regulatory constraints. Yale legal scholar Jack Balkin explained that while the US Constitution inhibits surveillance by government actors, privacy protections for information held in private servers is "limited if not nonexistent." If the intelligence community was to indulge its obsession to ascertain the future, then it would have to "rely on private enterprise to collect and generate information for it."[20]

Google took the lead and in the process surveillance capital was given a free pass to invent, own, and operate the twenty-first century production,

---

[18] Swire, 846.

[19] Paul M. Schwartz, "Systematic Government Access to Private-Sector Data in Germany," *International Data Privacy Law* 2, no. 4 (November 1, 2012): 230, 235, https://doi.org/10.1093/idpl/ips026; W. Gregory Voss, "After Google Spain and Charlie Hebdo: The Continuing Evolution of European Union Data Privacy Law in a Time of Change," *Business Lawyer* 71, no. 1 (January 6, 2016), https://papers.ssrn.com/abstract=2711996; Mark Scott, "Europe, Shaken by Paris Attacks, Weighs Security With Privacy Rights - The New York Times," *New York Times - Bits Blog*, November 18, 2015, https://web.archive.org/web/20151119015821/https://bits.blogs.nytimes.com/2015/11/18/europe- shaken-by-paris-attacks-weighs-security-with-privacy-rights/; Frank A. Pasquale, "Privacy, Antitrust, and Power," *George Mason Law Review* 20, no. 4 (2013): 1009–24; Pasquale, 1009– 24; Alissa J. Rubin, "Lawmakers in France Move to Vastly Expand Surveillance," *The New YorkTimes*, May 5, 2015, sec. World, https:// www.nytimes.com/2015/05/06/world/europe/french-legislators-approve-sweeping-intelligence-bill.html; Georgina Prodhan and Michael Nienaber, "Merkel Urges Germans to Put aside Fear of Big Data," *Reuters*, June 9, 2015, sec. Technology News, https://www.reuters.com/article/us-germany-technology-merkel- idUSKBN0OP2EM20150609.

[20] Jack Balkin, "The Constitution in the National Surveillance State," *Minnesota Law Review* 93, no. 1 (2008), https://openyls.law.yale.edu/handle/20.500.13051/1545.

concentration, and use of human-generated data. By 2010, former NSA director Mike McConnell publicly acknowledged that collaboration was inevitable noting, "With more than 90 percent" of the physical infrastructure of the web "owned by private industry … the challenge is to shape an effective partnership with the private sector so information can move quickly back and forth from public to private …"[21]

IV. Our Accidental Dystopia: Surveillance Capitalism's Stages of Development

Most of us are whipsawed by each day's headlines bleating the latest atrocity: the loss of privacy, the spread of disinformation, collective-scale behavioral modification. The issues are siloed, fragmented. We are forever trying to grasp the elephant while fixating on its parts, leaving us in a tangle of disorientation and confusion with little grasp of economic cause and social harm effect. If we have learned anything from this state of affairs, it's that we cannot fix what we do not understand.

The value of reinterpreting surveillance capitalism as a developing institutional order is that this tower of Babel finally resolves into a coherent picture – linked effects of a unitary process evolving in time. Each stage is defined by more complex economic operations that cause new social harm effects and enable the absorption of new governance functions. Each stage creates the conditions for the next. Each builds on what went before. Seemingly disparate social harms are organically related in time – the effects of economic operations also related in time. This picture alerts us to the ways in which effective remedies for later stage social harms depend upon changing early-stage operational causes. In other words, the durable solutions lie upstream, where this river originates.

Four stages of surveillance capitalism's institutionalization are visible thus far: Extraction, Expropriation, Exploitation, and Enforcement. I'll describe them briefly.

---

[21] Mike McConnell, "Mike McConnell on How to Win the Cyber-War We're Losing," *The Washington Post*, February 28, 2010, http://www.washingtonpost.com/wp- dyn/content/article/2010/02/25/AR2010022502493.html.

Stage One: Extraction

The first stage introduces the secret massive-scale extraction of human generated data, the formative achievement that lays the economic foundation for all that follows. Human-generated data are concentrated in the surveillance capitalist order.

And there is no law to stop it.

Stage Two: Expropriation

In his 1967 dissenting opinion in the Fourth Amendment case of Warden v. Hayden, Justice William O. Douglas wrote, "Privacy involves the choice of the individual to disclose or to revealwhat he believes, what he thinks, what he possesses ... Those who wrote the Bill of Rights believed that every individual needs both to communicate with others and to keep his affairs to himself. That dual aspect of privacy means that the individual should have the freedom to select for himself the time and circumstances when he will share his secrets with others and decide the extent of that sharing."[22]

Douglas's "freedom to select" alerts us to a class of rights that precede privacy, and the enactment of such rights are the proximate cause of privacy. These rights to know are 'epistemic rights,' which in modern democratic societies have been considered inalienable and elemental rights of individuals. With the secret seizure of human data from domains of experience that have long been considered private, the epistemic rights embedded in Douglas's "freedom to select" are expropriated and accumulated as corporate rights. Because privacy is an effect of this "freedom to select," the expropriation of epistemic rights eliminates the privacy choice. This dynamic clarifies the advancement of stage two from concentrations of human data, to concentrations of epistemic rights, to concentrations of privacy, to concentrations of recently private knowledge about people as corporate property.

These concentrations are not metaphorical. They reflect elaborate infrastructures of material and people. For example, a comprehensive review of AI's global institutional structure concludes that the artificial intelligence

---

[22] "WARDEN, MARYLAND PENITENTIARY, Petitioner, v. Bennie Joe HAYDEN.," Cornell Law School - Legal Information Institute, n.d., https://www.law.cornell.edu/supremecourt/text/387/294.

landscape is almost entirely controlled by "big tech." These firms evangelize AI because they stand to benefit from improvements in their own businesses. Some of the vertical ecosystems have gone global as "scale begets learning through the accumulation of data and increases competitive advantage". The surveillance capitalist giants control the capital, the data, the technologies, the scientists, and the science. They acquire most AI firms and poach most AI talent. Consistent with the structure of concentration in these corporations, the report observes that "Secrecy rather than patenting remains the preferred strategy to protect their research findings."[23]

The social harm effects are the wholesale destruction of privacy and the construction of a new axis of inequality defined by the growing gap between 'what I can know and what can be known about me.' At this stage of development, surveillance capitalism governs the production of and access to knowledge about people and society for its own advantage, which establishes its dominance over and information society.

And there is no law to stop it.

Stage Three: Exploitation

Now, growing concentrations of knowledge are transformed into power. "Targeting" is the preferred euphemism as the scale and scope of data feed a range of digital cueing mechanismsengineered to tune, herd, constrain, direct, and condition individual and collective behavior tomaximize engagement for maximum predictability and extraction. Operations engineered for profit maximization are systemically biased toward more corrupt and inflammatory content, which is proven to yield higher levels of "engagement."[24]

These economic operations cause social harm effects across multiple vectors as they produce epistemic chaos. Such chaos begins with the degradation of information integrity, as defactualized content is artificially driven to the center of social discourse by algorithmic targeting engineered for

---

[23] Michael G. Jacobides, Stefano Brusoni, and Francois Candelon, "The Evolutionary Dynamics of the Artificial Intelligence Ecosystem," *Strategy Science* 6, no. 4 (December 2021): 412–35, https://doi.org/10.1287/stsc.2021.0148.

[24] For example, Soroush Vosoughi, Deb Roy, and Sinan Aral, "The Spread of True and False News Online," *Science* 359, no. 6380 (March 9, 2018): 1146–51, https://doi.org/10.1126/science.aap9559; Laura Edelson et al., "Understanding Engagement with U.S. (Mis)Information News Sources on Facebook," in Proceedings of the 21st ACM Internet Measurement Conference (New York, NY, USA: Association for Computing Machinery, 2021), 444–63, https://doi.org/10.1145/3487552.3487859.

engagement. Such targeting aims to shape behavior through a variety of mechanisms including subliminal cues, engineered social comparisons, psychological microtargeting, rewards and punishments, and more. These mechanisms further intensify inequality as expressed in the growing gap between 'what I can do and what can be done to me,' degrading the integrity of individual and collective behavior. And as targeting operationsmediate information and communication, they erode common sense and produce a more splintered and polarized society.[25]

The governance functions associated with these harms are illustrated in the *Wall Street Journal's*"Facebook Files," which showed Mr. Zuckerberg's power to play his celestial keyboard, reinforcing or extinguishing the behavior of billions of people. Anger is rewarded or ignored.

News stories become more trustworthy or unhinged. Publishers prosper or wither. Politicaldiscourse turns uglier or more moderate. People live or die.[26]

And there is no law to stop it.

Stage Four: Enforcement

At this stage firms begin to enforce governance prerogatives by leveraging their ownership and control of information and communication spaces, systems, and infrastructures. By now the institutional order is sufficiently entrenched to openly vie for governance of mission-critical spheres of democratic capabilities (such as healthcare), but also to openly contest democratic institutions and their elected and appointed officials. The aim now is to absorb political governance functions in an increasingly open showdown over governance.

There have been more frequent sightings of this stage four behavior – Facebook's current threats to withdraw from Europe, Facebook's Oversight Board, the Google-Facebook contest with the Australian parliament. April 2020 brought a showdown between the European Commission and its member

---

[25] For example, Fernando P. Santos, Yphtach Lelkes, and Simon A. Levin, "Link Recommendation Algorithms and Dynamics of Polarization in Online Social Networks," *Proceedings of the National Academy of Sciences* 118, no. 50 (December 14, 2021), https://doi.org/10.1073/pnas.2102141118; Ro'ee Levy, "Social Media, News Consumption, and Polarization: Evidence from a Field Experiment," *American Economic Review* 111, no. 3 (March2021): 831–70, https://doi.org/10.1257/aer.20191777.

[26] "The Facebook Files," *Wall Street Journal*, October 1, 2021, sec. Tech,https://www.wsj.com/articles/the-facebook-files-11631713039.

governments on the one hand, and Apple and Google on the other. The companies had abruptly introduced a COVID-19 exposure notification protocol for Androids and iPhones that was incompatible with government-supported exposure notification and contract tracing applications already in development. Tense negotiations followed, as democratically elected leaders and government officials tried unsuccessfully to persuade Apple's CEO Tim Cook, Google's Sundar Pichai, and assorted corporate executives to adapt their operating system for the use of European public health authorities and urgent epidemiological research.

And there is no law to stop it.

Surveillance capitalism's whirlwind two-decade developmental journey now reveals itself as one vector of a larger contest between institutional orders. At each developmental stage we see a zero-sum dynamic in which the deepening institutional order of surveillance economics propagates democratic disorder.

This clash of institutional orders clarifies the reason for Congressional action. We have drifted into an accidental dystopia. The only countervailing institutional order capable of obstructing surveillance capitalism's path to dominance is the liberal democratic state. Surveillance capitalism is the younger challenger, but it embodies many unprecedented strengths. And while it is true that democracy is the old and slow incumbent, it brings powerful advantages that are difficult to rival. Chief among these is the legitimate authority and requisite power to make, impose, and enforce the rule of law. What laws must be devised if there is to be any hope of rescuing the digital century for democracy?

V. A Democratic Resurgence

A century ago, the corporate concentration of power was understood as economic power, and owners had all the authority on the strength of their property rights. The harms of concentration fell on people in their economic roles as workers, consumers, and competitors. Decades of contest and collective action eventually produced antitrust laws, but also new charters of rights for workers and consumers, the laws to protect them, and the public institutions charged with their enforcement and governance.

As important as those creations remain today, they do not protect us from the new harms we face. Ours is an accidental dystopia for the many reasons we have reviewed, including these: neither lawmakers nor citizens anticipated the harms that follow when the dominant economic institutional order is founded on the secret extraction of personal human experience once assumed to be private and now transformed into raw material for commercial operations. Nor did we grasp the harms that follow when revenues depend upon making all human behavior more predictable across all domains of everyday life. Nor did we imagine the social degradation unleashed when information and communication spaces are owned, operated, and mediated by an economic system in which information integrity is negatively correlated with revenues.

These conditions illuminate the changing nature of corporate concentration. In the age of surveillance capitalism, corporate power is not only economic but social. Its social harms are not confined to individuals in their roles as workers and consumers. They fall upon 'users': a new category of humanity that means all of us, all the time, everywhere. Ours is a young information civilization that has not yet found its footing in democracy because the social harms we face cannot be shoehorned into Cinderella's 20th century legal slipper. So, now it is we who march naked, without the rights, laws, and institutions purpose-built to govern our digital century in the name of democracy.

The tech giants and their fellow travelers have been willing to treat their destructive effects on people and society as collateral damage — the unfortunate but inevitable byproduct of digital technologies employed in perfectly legal economic operations. In April 2020 as the world tried to come to grips with Covid-19, former Google CEO Eric Schmidt, boasted that the pandemic would teach Americans to be "a little bit grateful" for powerful tech companies.[27] Other tech executives welcomed what they believed would be the inevitable end of 'techlash' thanks to widespread pandemic-induced dependency.

But as we enter the third decade of the digital century, something extraordinary is occurring: the aura of inevitability is giving way to the realization that the emperor is not only naked but dangerous. The data from prominent US attitude surveys suggests a public rupture of faith with surveillance capitalism and the power of its dominant corporations. Instead of a little gratitude there is a lot of anger and dismay.

I will tailor my remarks to just a few of the most recent surveys and the extraordinary majorities that voice dissent over surveillance capitalism's

---

[27] Theodore Schleifer, "Google's Former CEO Hopes the Coronavirus Makes People More 'Grateful' for Big Tech," *Vox*, April 14, 2020, https://www.vox.com/recode/2020/4/14/21221141/coronavirus-eric-schmidt-google-big-tech- grateful.

social harms. As evidenced in the following surveys, the American population is overwhelmingly calling for action to curb the unaccountable power of surveillance capitalism and its giant protagonists. Americans want an end to the social harms that spin from these corporate orbits with increasing velocity and destructive force. There is a clear sense that human rights, the durability of society, and democracy itself are on the line.

A Knight Foundation/Gallup survey in July 2020 found that 77 percent of adult Americans believe Big Tech companies have too much power.[28] Ninety-four percent of respondents were concerned about privacy and 92 percent were concerned about the spread of disinformation and its effects on society. Only 30 percent were concerned about innovation. An Accountable Tech survey in January 2021 found 71 percent of respondents favoring regulatory intervention.[29] Eighty-one percent preferred privacy over the benefits of targeted advertising, and 73 percent were opposed to behavioral tracking and personal data collection for the sake of targeted ads.

Finally, in significant majorities, respondents were in favor of banning social media companies from boosting extreme content (84 percent) as well as banning the collection of personal data for targeting (81 percent). Another 86 percent favored holding companies legally accountable for boosting violent content on their platforms.

Data published six months later in July 2021 further suggest that the American public no longer accepts the secret massive-scale extraction of human data as either inevitable or desirable. In an extensive US survey commissioned by the Future of Technology Commission, 93 percent of respondents agreed with the following statement: "It should be illegal for private companies to collect information about people without their permission."[30] It was the largest majority in agreement with any statement in this lengthy section of the study.

In 2022, the American public finally may be ready to shout that the emperor has no clothes, redefining illicit data extraction as theft and thus

---

[28] American Views 2020: Trust, Media and Democracy" (Gallup and Knight Foundation, August 4, 2020), https://knightfoundation.org/reports/american-views-2020-trust-media-and-democracy/.

[29] "America's Views on Surveillance Advertising" (Accountable Tech, n.d.), https://accountabletech.org/research/surveillance-advertising/.

[30] "Poll: Nine out of Ten Voters Support Strong Online Privacy Protections While Eight Out of Ten Strongly Support Holding Social Media Companies More Accountable for 'Illegal and Harmful Content' Posted on Their Sites," *Future of Tech Commission*, September 23, 2021, https://www.futureoftechcommission.org/press-release-launch-poll.

dismantling the keystone of surveillance capitalism's profits and power: the secret massive-scale extraction of human generated data.

An early vanguard of privacy-oriented scholars feared the internet companies' concentrated power and corrosive effect on democracy.[31] It is useful to note that these pioneers now have been joined by a new wave of scholarship mobilized by concerns over the startling concentrations of power in the giant tech firms and their implications for the democratic social order.[32]

Where does the widespread rupture of public faith leave us? Democracy is the only countervailing institutional order with the legitimate authority and power to change our course. If the ideal of human self-governance is to survive the digital century, then all solutions point to one solution: a democratic resurgence. But instead of the usual laundry lists of remedies, lawmakers need to proceed with a clear grasp of the adversary: a single hierarchy of economic causes and their social harm effects.

While liberal democracies have begun to engage with the challenges of regulating today's privately owned information spaces, the sober truth is that we need lawmakers ready to engage in a once-a-century exploration of far more basic questions. How should we structure and govern information, connection, and communication in a democratic digital century? What new charters of rights, legislative frameworks and institutions are required to ensure that data collection and use serve the genuine needs of individuals and society? What measures will protect citizens from unaccountable power over information, whether it is wielded by private companies or governments?

Privacy law after privacy looks like this:

1) Interrupt supply by outlawing secret massive-scale extraction of human-generated data.

We can't rid ourselves of later-stage social harms unless we interrupt and outlaw their foundational economic causes. This means we move beyond the

---

[31] Paul M. Schwartz, "Privacy and Democracy in Cyberspace," *Vanderbilt Law Review* 52, no. 6 (1999): 1607, https://doi.org/10.2139/ssrn.205449; Peter Swire, "Markets, Self-Regulation, and Government Enforcement in the Protection of Personal Information, in Privacy and Self- Regulation in the Information Age by the U.S. Department of Commerce.," *Department of Commerce*, 1997, https://doi.org/10.2139/ssrn.11472; Dennis D. Hirsch, "The Law and Policy ofOnline Privacy: Regulation, Self-Regulation, or Co-Regulation?," *Seattle University Law Review* 34, no. 2 (February 8, 2011): 439, https://papers.ssrn.com/abstract=1758078.

[32] See for example Dina Srinivasan, ed., "The Antitrust Case Against Facebook: A Monopolist's Journey Towards Pervasive Surveillance in Spite of Consumers' Preference for Privacy," *Berkeley Business Law Journal* 16, no. 1 (2019): 39–101.

current focus on downstream issues where we argue about content moderation, illegal content, and 'filter bubbles,' as lawmakers and citizens stamp their feet at recalcitrant executives who have already claimed these unceasing data flows as their property. Downstream is where the companies want us to be, so consumed in the details of the property contract that we forget the real issue, which is that their property claim itself is illegitimate. The edifice of surveillance economics is built on this foundation of sand. Every argument that begins with 'data' is an argument that we have already lost. Like a magician's rabbit, the endless, and often pointless, downstream discussions direct our attention away from the mechanics of the trick. It's like arguing over the details of a seven-year old's factory contract instead of outlawing child labor. Similarly, structural solutions like "breaking up" the tech giants may be valuable in some cases, but they will not affect the underlying economic operations of surveillance capitalism.

Instead, we need to focus laser-like on the bedrock of surveillance economics, which is the secret extraction of human data from realms of life until recently assumed as "private." Remedies that focus on regulating and eliminating extraction are content neutral. They do not threaten freedom of expression. Instead, they liberate social discourse and information flows from the "artificial selection" of profit-maximizing commercial operations that allow for misinformation with no regard for integrity. They restore the sanctity of social communications and individual expression.

No secret extraction means no illegitimate concentrations of knowledge about people. No concentrations of knowledge mean no targeting algorithms. No targeting means that corporations can no longer control and curate information flows and social speech or shape human behavior to favor their interests. Regulating and outlawing extraction would eliminate the surveillance dividend and with it the financial incentives for surveillance, opening the competitive landscape to new forms of information capitalism that reunite the digital technologies with the real needs of people and society, as data collection is tied to fundamental rights and data use is tied to the public good.

2) New conditions summon new rights.

A democratic information civilization cannot progress without new charters of epistemic rights. Citizens of democratic societies have regarded personal experience as inseparable from the individual: inalienable. It follows that the right to know about one's own personal experience has been considered elemental — bonded to each of us like a shadow. My epistemic rights are the cause of which my privacy is the effect. We each decide if and how our experience is shared, with whom, and for what purpose.

Justice Douglas's "freedom to select" is the elemental epistemic right to decide who knows us, how, when, and to what purpose. It is the right from which cause from which all privacy flows.

For example, as the natural bearer of such rights, I do not give Amazon's facial recognition system the right to know if I am afraid or happy. I do not give the corporation the right to exploit my fear for targeting and behavioral prediction that benefit others' commercial objectives. It's not simply that my feelings are not for sale, it's that my feelings are unsale-able because they are inalienable. Though I do not give Amazon my fear, they take it from me anyway, just another data point in the trillions gathered that day.

New legal rights are crystalized in response to the changing conditions of life. Justice Brandeis' commitment to privacy rights, for example, was stimulated by the spread of photography and its ability to invade and steal what was regarded as private. In 1890 he wrote, "Political, social, and economic changes entail the recognition of new rights, and the common law, in its eternal youth, grows to meet the demands of society."

Our elemental epistemic rights are not codified in law because until now they have not come under systematic threat, any more than we have laws to protect our rights to stand up or sit down or yawn. But the surveillance capitalists have declared their "right to know" our lives, mobilizing pervasive surveillance at a scale and depth of intimacy that beggar imagination, while claiming the right to own and profit from that knowledge. Thus dawns a new age, founded on and shielded by the false inevitability of surveillance capitalism. Now the once taken-for-granted right to know and to decide who knows 'about me' must be codified in law and protected by democratic institutions, if it is to exist at all.

3) Unprecedented harms demand unprecedented solutions.

Just as new conditions of life reveal the need for new rights, the unprecedented harms of the epistemic coup require purpose- built solutions. This is how law evolves, growing and adapting from one era to the next — Brandeis's "eternal youth."

A mature democratic information society will require independent trustworthy public oversight institutions that hold the market and the state to account in the knowledge that the solution to surveillance capitalism is not a

Big Brother state. These institutions are dedicated to a democratic digital future: transparent, governed by the rule of law, immune to political interference, and empowered with the budgetary, technological, and human resources necessary to oversee and enforce the availability and integrity of information for people and democracy.

4) Interrupt and outlaw demand for illicit data collection.

Solutions that interrupt illicit data supply are complimented by solutions that interrupt demand by disrupting the financial incentives that reward surveillance economics. We can outlaw markets that trade in human futures because we have seen their antihuman, antisocial, and antidemocratic harms. This is not a radical prospect. Democratic societies have outlawed other markets that produce reliably dangerous consequences: Markets that trade in human beings were outlawed, even when they supported whole economies. We outlaw markets that trade in human organs and babies because they inflict damage on people and society.

****

When it comes to privacy law after privacy, the digital century forces us to choose: *We may be asurveillance society, or we may be a democracy, but we cannot be both.* The liberal democraciesmust take the lead because they have the power and legitimacy to do so. But they should know that their allies and collaborators include the people of every society struggling against the double insult of an accidental dystopian future. We have a democratic digital century to build, and there is no time to waste.

The CHAIRPERSON. Thank you very much, Professor.

Let me call now on Ms. Fitzgerald for her testimony for five minutes.

Statement of Caitriona Fitzgerald

Ms. FITZGERALD. Thank you, Chairperson Lofgren, Ranking Member Davis, and Members of the Committee. Thank you for holding this important hearing and the opportunity to testify today. I am Caitriona Fitzgerald, Deputy Director at the Electronic Privacy Information Center, or EPIC.

EPIC is an independent, nonprofit research organization in Washington, D.C., established in 1994 to protect privacy, freedom of expression, and democratic values in the Information Age. For over 25 years, EPIC has been a leading advocate for privacy in both the public and private sectors.

The United States faces a data privacy crisis. Large and powerful technology companies invade our private lives, spy on our families, and gather the most intimate details about us for profit. These companies have more economic and political power than many countries and States.

Through a vast, opaque system of databases and algorithms we are profiled and sorted into winners and losers based on data about our health, finances, location, race, and other personal information. Private companies are not the only problem. Government agencies have also dramatically increased the collection and use of personal data, often purchased, or obtained from those same private companies, while failing to address the significant risks to privacy and cybersecurity.

The impact of this uncontrolled data collection and use by both private companies and the government is especially harmful for marginalized communities, fostering systemic inequities.

These industries and systems have gone unregulated for more than two decades, and this is where it has left us. The system is broken. Technology companies have too much power and individuals have too little.

To restore the balance, we need comprehensive baseline privacy protections for every person in the United States, changes to the business models that have led to today's commercial surveillance systems, and limits on government access to personal data. Most crucially, we need strong enforcement of privacy protections.

In my written statement I go into detail about the crisis we face and the elements of a strong privacy law, but I want to focus here on the importance of enforcement.

Without strong enforcement, many businesses will simply ignore privacy laws and accept the small risk of an enforcement action as a cost of business, as we have seen with privacy laws enacted in Europe and in several States.

Strong enforcement must include a private right of action. This is not new. Congress included private rights of action in the Cable Communications Privacy Act, the Video Privacy Protection Act, FCRA, TCPA, and the Driver's Privacy Protection Act. The statutory damages set in those privacy laws are not large in individual cases, but they really provide powerful incentives for companies to comply with privacy laws.

Strong enforcement also requires Congress to establish an independent data protection agency, or a DPA. The United States is one of the few democracies in the world that does not have a data protection agency. U.S. companies are leaders in technology, and the U.S. Government should be a leader in technology policy.

When you think about the omnipresence of technology in our lives and our economy, it seems obvious that we should have Federal agencies dedicated to overseeing and regulating it.

A data protection agency could promote innovation and competition while protecting privacy by setting rules that help level the playing field for smaller technology companies who currently struggle to compete with tech giants.

A DPA could also be a central authority within the Federal Government on privacy issues. We saw a glaring example of agency failure to properly consider privacy risks of data collection just this month. The IRS sparked outrage after a report surfaced that it had contracted with third-party vendor ID.me to require taxpayers to submit to facial recognition to access tax records online.

Thankfully, following pressure from advocates and Members of Congress, the IRS backtracked, but this contract should have never been signed in the first place. A DPA could ensure that privacy is carefully considered when agencies are weighing contracts like this. There is broad support for this idea. A recent Data for Progress poll showed that 78 percent of Americans across the political spectrum support establishing a data protection agency.

The good news is that Congress, and indeed this Committee, has a strong bill before it that would restore privacy online for Americans.

The Online Privacy Act, filed by Chairperson Lofgren and Representative Eshoo, is a comprehensive framework that would place strict limits on the collection and use of personal data, extend civil rights protections online, and establish strong enforcement mechanisms via a private right of action and the creation of a U.S. data privacy agency.

EPIC recommends swift action on the Online Privacy Act. There is widespread bipartisan agreement that we need a Federal privacy law. It is time for Congress to act.

Thank you for the opportunity to testify today. [The statement of Ms. Fitzgerald follows:]

Statement of Caitriona Fitzgerald Deputy Director, Electronic Privacy Information Center (EPIC) Hearing on "Big Data: Privacy Risks and Needed Reforms in the Public and Private Sectors" Before the House Committee on House Administration United States House of Representatives

February 16, 2022

Chair Lofgren, Ranking Member Davis, and members of the Committee, thank you for the opportunity to testify today concerning the privacy risks from Big Data and the need for reform in both the public and private sectors. My name is Caitriona Fitzgerald, Deputy Director at the Electronic Privacy Information Center, or EPIC. EPIC is an independent nonprofit research organization in Washington, DC, established in 1994 to protect privacy, freedom of expression, and democratic values in the information age. For over 25 years, EPIC has been a leading advocate for privacy in both the public and private sectors. In 2020, EPIC released Grading on a Curve: Privacy Legislation in the 116th Congress,[33] setting out the key elements of a privacy law.

The United States faces a data privacy crisis. Large and powerful technology companies invade our private lives, spy on our families, and gather the most intimate details about us for profit. These companies have more economic and political power than many countries and states. Through a vast, opaque system of databases and algorithms, we are profiled and sorted into winners and losers based on data about our health, finances, location, gender, race, and other personal information. The impacts of these commercial surveillance systems are especially harmful for marginalized and multi-marginalized communities, fostering discrimination and inequities in employment, government services, health and healthcare, education, and other life necessities.

These industries and systems have gone unregulated for more than two decades. And the result has been uncontrolled data collection, large scale data breaches, and an ecosystem dependent on a few large commercial surveillance platforms. And the enormity of the challenge we face is only going to grow. Americans have no meaningful choice in limiting the collection and use of

---

[33] EPIC, *Grading on a Curve*, https://epic.org/documents/grading-on-a-curve/.

their personal data online; and they can't simply "log off" services that have become central to our modern society. The more we depend on online platforms to carry out our most basic and essential activities, the more important it is to ensure that those systems are secure and do not undermine our rights to privacy, autonomy, and equity. We need comprehensive, baseline privacy protections for every person in the United States, changes to the business models that have led to today's commercial surveillance systems, limits on government access to personal data, and strong enforcement of privacy protections.

In my testimony today I will discuss (1) the problems we face today due to the failure of policymakers in the United States to create adequate data protection standards; (2) the current state of privacy law in the U.S.; and (3) what a comprehensive approach to data protection and privacy in the United States should look like. EPIC recommends that Congress enact a privacy law that: (1) limits the collection and use of personal data; (2) prohibits discriminatory uses of data; (3) requires algorithmic fairness and accountability; (4) bans manipulative design and unfair marketing practices; (5) limits government access to personal data; (6) provides for a private right of action; (6) preserves states' rights to enact stronger provisions; and (7) establishes a federal data protection agency to enforce these new rules.[34]

I. The United States' Data Privacy Crisis

A. Unfettered Data Collection and Exploitation Harms Autonomy and Democracy

The lack of a comprehensive U.S. privacy law threatens individual autonomy and undermines our democratic institutions and national security. Without clear and enforceable data protection rules, there has been widespread overcollection, abusive data practices, and targeting that threatens our rights and institutions. Robust data privacy standards are essential to ensure the protection of human rights, human dignity, and the healthy functioning of our democracy.

Due to the failure of policymakers in the United States to create adequate data protection standards, rather than innovating around privacy-protective

---

[34] Privacy and Digital Rights for All, *The Time is Now: A Framework for Comprehensive Privacy Protection and Digital Justice in the United States* (2021), https://epic.org/wp-content/uploads/2022/01/Privacy-and-Digital-Rights-For-All-Framework.pdf.

ways to advertise, the business models of advertising firms were permitted to grow unencumbered into corporate surveillance systems driven by collecting and commodifying every tiny bit of personal data about us.[35] These firms track us across our devices and all over the internet, building detailed profiles about us simply so they can target us with more ads, at the cost of exposing us to ever-increasing risks of breaches, data misuse, manipulation, and discrimination.[36]

Cross-site and cross-device tracking is one reason why the notice-and-consent approach does not work when it comes to privacy. The intricacies and breadth of the commercial surveillance industry are impossible for the vast majority of Internet users to fully grasp. In 2020, The Markup found that one-third of websites they surveyed contained Facebook's tracking pixel, which allows Facebook to identify users (whether or not they are logged into Facebook) and connect those website visits to their Facebook profile.[37] The Markup also scanned hundreds of websites on sensitive topics and discovered an alarming amount of tracking, including:

- a state agency page on how to report child abuse sending data about its visitors to sixad tech companies;
- WebMD and Everyday Health sending visitor data to dozens of marketingcompanies; and
- Eighty U.S. abortion providers whose sites included third-party trackers, some ofwhich sent data to Facebook to be connected to user profiles.[38]

These trackers collect millions of data points each day that are then sold or transferred todata brokers, who combine them with other data sources linked to us to build invasive profiles. Sometimes these profiles are used to target people with "personalized" advertisements that stalkthem across the web, and in other instances the data profiles are fed into secret algorithms used

---

[35] See generally Shoshana Zuboff, The Age of Surveillance Capitalism, Profile Books (2019).

[36] See Consumer Federation of America, Factsheet: Surveillance Advertising: How Does the Tracking Work? (Aug. 26, 2021), https://consumerfed.org/consumer_info/factsheet-surveillance-advertising-how-tracking-works/.

[37] Julia Angwin, What They Know… Now, The Markup (Sept. 22, 2020),https://themarkup.org/blacklight/2020/09/22/what-they-know-now.

[38] Aaron Sankin and Surya Mattu, The High Privacy Cost of a "Free" Website, The Markup (Sept. 22, 2020), https://themarkup.org/blacklight/2020/09/22/blacklight-tracking-advertisers-digital-privacy-sensitive-websites.

to determine the interest rates on mortgages and credit cards, raise consumers' interest rates, or deny people jobs.[39]

This expansive network of surveillance, profiling, and data extraction is creepy and exploitative, but it has also been weaponized in ways that undermine our political systems and public discourse. The Cambridge Analytica case[40] provided a clear illustration of the ways that limitless data collection and retention threatens election integrity and our democratic institutions.[41] When personal data is collected and used to refine, propagate, and amplify hate, extremism, and disinformation, that threatens our self-determination, our elections, and our democracy. Just as advertising companies use profiles about us to manipulate us into purchases, so too can they manipulate our views by filtering the content we see.[42]

When Congress was considering consumer privacy legislation in the 1990s, the problem was new and emerging.[43] But since then, data collection has grown unchecked for over two decades and it is now beyond a crisis. In poll after poll, Americans say they want privacy. In a survey recently conducted by the Future of Technology Commission, a staggering 86% of Americans agreed that "it should be illegal for private companies to sell or share information about people no matter what" and only 46% agreed that it would be okay for companies to "sell consumers' data as long as they are

---

[39] *See* EPIC, *Data Brokers*, https://epic.org/issues/consumer-privacy/data-brokers/.

[40] Robinson Meyer, *The Cambridge Analytica Scandal, in Three Paragraphs*, The Atlantic (Mar. 20, 2018), https://www.theatlantic.com/technology/archive/2018/03/the-cambridge-analytica-scandal-in-three- paragraphs/556046/.

[41] *See e.g.* Corin Faife and Alfred Ng, *After Repeatedly Promising Not to, Facebook Keeps Recommending PoliticalGroups to Its Users*, The Markup (June 24, 2021), https://themarkup.org/citizen-browser/2021/06/24/after-repeatedly-promising-not-to-facebook-keeps-recommending-political-groups-to-its-users; Heidi Schlumpf, *Pro- Trump group targets Catholic voters using cellphone technology*, Nat'l Catholic Reporter (Jan. 2, 2020), https://www.ncronline.org/news/parish/pro-trump-group-targets-catholic-voters-using-cell-phone-technology; Sam Schechner, Emily Glazer, and Patience Haggin, *Political Campaigns Know Where You've Been. They're Tracking Your Phone*, Wall Street Journal (Oct. 10, 2019), https://www.wsj.com/articles/political-campaigns-track- cellphones-to-identify-and-target-individual-voters-11570718889;

[42] Colin Lecher and Leon Yin, *One Year After the Capitol Riot, Americans Still See Two Very Different Facebooks*, The Markup (Jan. 6, 2022), https://themarkup.org/citizen-browser/2022/01/06/one-year-after-the-capitol-riot-americans-still-see-two-very-different-facebooks.

[43] *See Hearing on S. 809: The Online Privacy Protection Act of 1999*, S. Comm. on Commerce, Sci, and Trans., Subcomm. on Communications (July 27, 1999) (testimony of Marc Rotenberg, Exec. Dir., EPIC), https://archive.epic.org/privacy/internet/EPIC_testimony_799.pdf ("For those who are willing to look closely, thereis little indication that self-regulation is working. Privacy policies read more like warning notices and disclaimers.")

transparent about how the data is used and make it clear to consumers."[44] In a Morning Consult poll last year, more than 4 in 5 voters said Congress should prioritize privacy legislation.[45] Congress needs to address this crisis now.

B. Government Use of Personal Data

The commercial exploitation of personal data is not the only threat to privacy.

Government agencies have also dramatically increased their collection and use of personal data while failing to address the significant risks to privacy and cybersecurity posed by modern data systems. Agencies are far behind where they need to be in terms of securing, protecting, and properly minimizing data. The lack of up-to-date rules has led to a default presumption of broad collection and use without necessary protections. The two principal statutes that regulate the federal government's use of personal data, discussed below, were passed twenty and forty-eight years ago.

We saw a glaring example of agency failure to properly consider privacy risks of data collection just this month. Reports that the Internal Revenue Service had contracted with third- party vendor ID.me for identity verification, requiring taxpayers to submit to facial recognition identification in order to access tax records online, sparked immediate controversy.[46] The plan would have forced individuals to submit biometric data to ID.me, who would have held on to that data for a minimum of seven years. Following pressure from advocates and members of Congress, the IRS announced last week that it was reversing course and will not go through with the plan to require individuals to use the privacy identity verification service ID.me to access the IRS website.[47]

And government agencies are especially vulnerable to data breaches. A recent Department of Homeland Security Inspector General report found that Customs and Border Protection (CBP) failed to safeguard pictures of travelers

---

[44] Benson Strategy Group, Future of Tech Commission: Tech Attitudes Survey (July 20, 2021 - July 29, 2021), https://d2e111jq13me73.cloudfront.net/sites/default/files/uploads/pdfs/bsg_future_of_technology_topline_c1-1.pdf.

[45] Sam Sabin, States Are Moving on Privacy Bills. Over 4 in 5 Voters Want Congress to Prioritize Protection of Online Data (Apr. 27, 2021), https://morningconsult.com/2021/04/27/state-privacy-congress-priority-poll/.

[46] Drew Harwell, *IRS plan to scan your face prompts anger in Congress, confusion among taxpayers*, Wash. Post (Jan. 28, 2022), https://www.washingtonpost.com/technology/2022/01/27/irs-face-scans/.

[47] Alan Rappeport and Kashmir Hill, *I.R.S. to End Use of Facial Recognition for Identity Verification*, N.Y. Times (Feb. 7, 2022), https://www.nytimes.com/2022/02/07/us/politics/irs-idme-facial-recognition.html.

obtained for a facial recognition pilot program.[48] 184,000 facial images were exposed in a data breach of a CBP subcontractor, Perceptics, LLC. The Inspector General found that the CBP failed to undertake sufficient information security practices to prevent Perceptics from obtaining the data.

Rashida Richardson has outlined best practices for government procurement of data- driven technologies.[49] Many of these solutions could be implemented without legislative or regulatory action.

C. Self-Regulatory Approaches Have Failed Time and Again to Protect Privacy

Congress should not need further evidence to prove that industry self-regulation does not work when it comes to personal data – it has had nearly three decades to succeed, but instead hadled us to the crisis we face today.[50]

In November 1999, the FTC and Department of Commerce announced the formation of the Network Advertising Initiative (NAI), shortly after DoubleClick, an online target advertising company, was the subject of an FTC investigation. Less than a year later and with little involvement from consumer and privacy groups, the self-regulatory NAI principles were publicized.[51] The NAI standards were unsurprisingly weak. NAI members could transfer information between themselves to an unlimited degree, so long as it is used for advertising. No meaningful enforcement mechanism was incorporated.

Around the same time, the World Wide Web Consortium (W3C) released the Platform for Privacy Preferences (P3P) protocol.[52] P3P was a complex and confusing protocol made it more difficult for Internet users to protect their privacy.

---

[48] Joseph Cuffari, Review of CBP's Major Cybersecurity Incident during a 2019 Biometric Pilot, Dep't ofHomeland Sec. Off. of Inspector Gen. (Sept. 21, 2020).

[49] Richardson, Rashida, *Best Practices for Government Procurement of Data-Driven Technologies* (May 2021),available at https://ssrn.com/abstract=3855637.

[50] *See* Robert Gellman & Pam Dixon, Many Failures: A Brief History of Privacy Self-Regulation in the United States (Oct. 2011), http://www.worldprivacyforum.org/wp-content/uploads/2011/10/WPFselfregulationhistory.pdf;*see also* Center for Digital Democracy and U.S. PIRG, *Cookie Wars, Real-Time Targeting, and Proprietary Self Learning Algorithms: Why the FTC Must Act Swiftly to Protect Consumer Privacy*, FTC Privacy Roundtables – Comment, Project No. P095416 (Nov. 4, 2009), https://www.ftc.gov/sites/default/files/documents/public_comments/privacy-roundtables-comment-project-no.p095416-544506-00013/544506-00013.pdf.

[51] *See* Letter from EPIC to S. Comm. on Commerce (July 28, 2000),https://archive.epic.org/privacy/internet/NAI_letter.html.

[52] EPIC, *Pretty Poor Privacy: An Assessment of P3P and Internet Privacy* (June 2000), https://archive.epic.org/reports/prettypoorprivacy.html.

Despite stating in a report to Congress in May 2000 that self-regulatory programs fell "well short" of expectations,[53] the Federal Trade Commission itself released self-regulatory principles in 2009 and again in 2012.[54] The 2009 principles sparked the creation of the Digital Advertising Alliance (DAA), which was comprised of industry associations. The DAA promoted weak privacy standards with little enforcement, rubber stamping existing business practices.

Most recently, the Digital Advertising Alliance has promoted its self-regulatory principles,[55] which involve "opt-out" models that are inscrutable and hard for average users to navigate. These systems are designed in every way possible to push people away from privacy protections, to give the appearance of user "control," but in fact to prevent individuals from exercising any agency over what is done with their data.

None of these self-regulatory systems have worked. They simply cement the existing harmful business practices that form surveillance capitalism. It is past time to move away from self-regulation.

D. Corporate Surveillance is Especially Harmful to Marginalized Communities

The monetization of Americans' personal data has an acute impact on marginalized communities.[56] Invasions of privacy deprive people of opportunities and they perpetuate systemic inequities in our society. We have all had the experience of being creeped out by an ad targeted at us – many people assume that companies like Facebook must be using the microphones on our phones to listen to us because the ads are so often related to something we just had a conversation about. They are not really listening to us, but the reality is even creepier - they do not need to hear us to know what we are

---

53 Fed. Trade Comm'n, *Privacy Online: Fair Information Practices in the Electronic Marketplace, A Report To Congress* 35 (2000), https://www.ftc.gov/sites/default/files/documents/reports/privacy-online-fair-information-practices-electronic-marketplace-federal-trade-commission-report/privacy2000text.pdf.

54 Fed. Trade Comm'n, FTC Staff Report: *Self-regulatory Principles For Online Behavioral Advertising: Tracking Targeting, And Technology* (Feb. 2009); Fed. Trade Comm'n, *Protecting Consumer Privacy In An Era Of Rapid Change: Recommendations For Businesses And Policymakers* (Mar. 2012).

55 Digital Advertising Alliance, DAA Self-Regulatory Principles, https://digitaladvertisingalliance.org/principles.

56 *See Protecting Consumer Privacy in the Age of Big Data*, 116th Cong. (2019), H. Comm. on the Energy & Comm., Subcomm. on Consumer Protection and Comm. (Feb. 26, 2019) (testimony of Brandi Collins-Dexter, Colorof Change), https://energycommerce.house.gov/sites/democrats.energycommerce.house.gov/files/documents/Brandi%20Collins%20Dexter%2002.26.2019.pdf.

saying or thinking because that is how much data they are collecting about us – the websites we visit, where we are going, who our friends are, and what those friends are reading and doing.[57] They are tracking so many data points about us that it really seems like they are listening to us.

For some people, that means being creeped out by an ad. But for marginalized communities, it can often mean not being shown ads for housing or job openings, depriving individuals of life opportunities, and perpetuating systemic inequities in our society.

These data practices threaten individual privacy and autonomy, and companies have proven time and again that they cannot police themselves. Rather than continuing to tweak a system that demonstrably does not work, this problem requires a legislative and regulatory solution.

II. Current Law is Inadequate to Protect Individual Privacy and our Democracy

A. Federal Agencies are Subject to the Privacy Act and E-Government Act

The Privacy Act of 1974[58] was created in response to concerns about how the creation and use of computerized databases might impact individuals' privacy rights. Executive departments, military departments, independent regulatory agencies, and government-controlled corporations are all covered by the Privacy Act. It safeguards privacy through creating four procedural and substantive rights in personal data. First, it requires government agencies to show an individual any records kept on him or her. Second, it requires agencies to follow certain principles, called "fair information practices," when gathering and handling personal data. Third, it places restrictions on how agencies can share an individual's data with other people and agencies. Fourth and finally, it includes a private right of action, allowing individuals to sue the government for violating the Privacy Act's provisions.

The important purposes of the Privacy Act have been undermined over the last three decades by the numerous and broad exceptions asserted by most agencies. These exceptions (as well as the practical difficulties involved with maintaining and regulating such a vast system of databases) mean that

[57] Elec. Frontier Foundation, *Behind the One-Way Mirror: A Deep Dive Into the Technology of CorporateSurveillance* (2019), https://www.eff.org/wp/behind-the-one-way-mirror.

[58] 5 U.S.C. § 552a.

individual privacy is not often as carefully protected as the drafters of the Privacy Act might have liked. Since "records," "systems of records" and "agencies" are narrowly defined, the Act may not cover many types of databases and data-gathering activities. Also, there are certain exceptions given for "law enforcement purposes." Finally, the "routine use" exception allows government agencies to disclose individually identifiable information simply by stating their plans to disclose that type of information when they create or alter the database.

The Privacy Act simply defines "routine use" as "the use of such record for a purpose which is compatible with the purpose for which it was collected."[59] Note that a routine use does not have to be a purpose identical to the purpose for which the record was collected, only a compatible purpose. This phrasing can often lead to mission creep for a system of records, in which the routine uses for a particular database gradually increase until its scope is far greater than its originally stated goals.[60]

The rights provided for under the Privacy Act have also been severely curtailed by a series of misguided court decisions. In 2004, the Supreme Court ruled that individuals whose data is misused by a federal agency are not entitled to the statutory damages that the Privacy Act is intended to provide, but must instead prove actual damages.[61] In 2012, the Court ruled that individuals cannot recover damages under the Privacy Act for mental and emotional distress, even when an agency wrongly discloses highly sensitive information like a person's HIV status.[62] These decisions have not only made it exceptionally difficult for individuals to obtain relief for the misuse of their personal information by federal agencies; they have also weakened a key incentive for agencies to comply with the Privacy Act in the first place.

The lesson from the Privacy Act when applied to comprehensive privacy legislation covering the private sector is that if legislation does not set strict purpose and use limitations, and establish robust mechanisms for enforcement of those limitations, there will always be an incentive for companies to retain and use data beyond its initial purpose—to the point where the restriction becomes no restriction at all.

The E-Government Act, enacted in 2002, was intended to make federal agencies more accessible to the public by electronic means. The Act created

---

[59] *Id.* at § 552a(a)(7).

[60] Gellman, Robert, *From the Filing Cabinet to the Cloud: Updating the Privacy Act of 1974*, 23-37 (May 12, 2021), *available at* https://ssrn.com/abstract=3844965.

[61] *Doe v. Chao*, 540 U.S. 614 (2004).

[62] *FAA v. Cooper*, 566 U.S. 284 (2012).

an Office of Electronic Government within the Office of Management and Budget and requires that regulatory proceedings and other material appear on agency web sites. Crucially, section 208 of the Act requires agencies to perform Privacy Impact Assessments (PIAs) before procuring an information system that will process personal data or initiating a new collection of personal information.

When implemented properly, PIAs force government agencies and other institutions to carefully evaluate and publicly disclose the privacy risks of a proposed action, system, or project. An impact assessment enables the entity to identify privacy risks, to determine how and if those risks can be mitigated, and to make an informed decision whether the proposed collection or system can be justified in light of its privacy impact. An impact assessment also serves to inform the public of a data collection or system that poses a threat to privacy.

Privacy impact assessments—or data protection impact assessments—are also required by the European Union's General Data Protection Regulation (GDPR) for all high-risk data processing activities. Article 35 of the GDPR states:

> Where a type of processing in particular using new technologies, and taking into account the nature, scope, context and purposes of the processing, is likely to result in a high risk to the rights and freedoms of natural persons, the controller shall, prior to the processing, carry out an assessment of the impact of the envisaged processing operations on the protection of personal data.[63]

However, the key to making impact assessments effective lies in enforcement. Without proper guidance and enforcement mechanisms, agencies and private companies will simply see PIAs as a box-checking exercise that must be completed for compliance rather than a substantive analysis of whether and how the entity should collect or use personal data.[64]

A recent example lies in the PIA conducted by the Internal Revenue Service prior to contracting with third-party vendor ID.me for identity verification.[65] The PIA lifts language directly from ID.me's corporate

---

[63] Regulation (EU) 2016/679 of the European Parliament, Article 35.

[64] *See* Ari Ezra Waldman, *Privacy, Practice, and Performance,* California Law Review, Vol. 110, 19-21 (2021).

[65] Internal Revenue Service, *Privacy Impact Assessment: SADI CSP – ID.me* (Nov. 2021), https://www.irs.gov/pub/irs-pia/id-me-pia.pdf (hereinafter "IRS PIA").

materials.[66] The PIA also doesn't make mention of the one-to- many facial recognition system that ID.me has admitted to using.[67] In fact, despite the massive and well-known privacy and bias issues with facial recognition technology, the only facial matching technology referenced in the PIA is "comparing still … or video ... selfies against the photo evidence uploaded by the user."[68]

As with the Privacy Act, courts have made it exceedingly difficult to enforce the personal data provisions of the E-Government Act through private action. In a pair of decisions from 2017 and 2019, the D.C. Circuit held that organizations and individuals cannot rely on an agency's failure and publish a PIA to stop the agency's unlawful processing of personal information.[69] As a result, there are few if any consequences for agencies that bypass the requirements of section 208.

This demonstrates just how critical it is that Congress establish a broad and express private right of action in privacy legislation. Rulings under the Privacy Act and E-Government Act have shown that without a robust private right of action, statutory rights will not be adequately enforced and privacy harms will continue undeterred. As I discuss later in my testimony, it also demonstrates the need for a federal Data Protection Agency that can serve as a central authority on privacy in the federal government, with the expertise necessary to guide agencies as they conduct PIAs.

B. Private Sector Data Collection and Use Governed by Sectoral Laws

There is no comprehensive law in the United States governing the collection and use of personal data. Instead, some types and uses of data are regulated by sector-specific laws such as the Health Insurance Portability and Accounting Act (HIPAA), the Fair Credit Reporting Act (FCRA), the Children's Online Privacy Protection Act (COPPA), the Family Educational Rights and Privacy Act (FERPA), and others, while many types of data are not protected at all.[70]

---

[66] *See Id.* at 10 and ID.me, Privacy Policy, 5, https://www.id.me/privacy.

[67] Tonya Riley, *ID.me CEO backtracks on claims company doesn't use powerful facial recognition tech*, Cyberscoop (Jan. 26, 2022), https://www.cyberscoop.com/id-me-ceo-backtracks-on-claims-company-doesnt-use- powerful-facial-recognition-tech/; Ina Fried, *ID.me CEO apologies for misstatements on IRS facial recognition*, Axios (Jan. 27, 2022), https://www.axios.com/idme-ceo-apologizes-misstatements-irs-facial-recognition-88ce2ee2-9ae9-426c-b69e-c0b42ad82f61.html.

[68] IRS PIA, *supra* note 8 at 8.

[69] *EPIC v. United States Dep't of Com.*, 928 F.3d 95 (D.C. Cir. 2019); EPIC *v. Presidential Advisory Comm'n onElection Integrity*, 878 F.3d 371 (D.C. Cir. 2017).

[70] *See* Cong. Research Service, R45631, *Data Protection Law: An Overview* (2019), *available at* https://crsreports.congress.gov/product/pdf/R/R45631.

In addition to leaving huge gaps in coverage that have allowed the expansion of data collection and abuse across many different sectors, most notably online services, this also leads to confusion by the public about what types of personal data are protected and how and increased compliance costs for businesses. The US needs a comprehensive, coherent approach to privacy and data protection.

C. Comprehensive State Privacy Laws

In recent years, largely in response to Congressional inaction, some states have enacted their own privacy laws. In 2018, the California State Legislature enacted the California Consumer Privacy Act of 2018 ("CCPA"), the first comprehensive consumer privacy law enacted in the United States. The CCPA established the right of residents of California to know what personal information about them is being collected; to know whether their information is sold or disclosed and to whom; to limit the sale of personal information to others; and to access their information held by others. The CCPA gives individuals a right to delete their data and prohibits businesses from selling the personal information of CA residents under the age of 16 without their opt-in consent. The CCPA was further updated by a ballot question approved by voters in 2021, creating the California Privacy Protection Agency.

In the past year, Virginia and Colorado have also passed broad consumer privacy laws, though of at varying levels of effectiveness when it comes to protecting privacy. And this year, state legislatures in Massachusetts, Washington, Alaska, Oklahoma, New York, Ohio, Indiana, Florida, and elsewhere are considering comprehensive privacy legislation.

III. Solutions: Congress Should Enact Comprehensive Privacy Legislation and Establish a Data Protection Agency

The basic structure of information privacy law is to place responsibilities on organizations that collect personal data and to give rights to the individuals whose data is collected. This is sensible for many reasons, including the fact that it is the entity in possession of the data that controls its subsequent use and is in the best position to limit access and protect against abuse or breach. Information privacy law also promotes transparency by making data practices more open to scrutiny and encourages the development of innovative technical approaches.

EPIC, joined by ten other privacy, consumer, and civil rights groups, has set forth a framework for Congress to use when developing a privacy law that:

(1) limits the collection and use of personal data; (2) prohibits discriminatory uses of data; (3) requires algorithmic fairness and accountability; (4) bans manipulative design and unfair marketing practices; (5) limits government access to personal data; (6) provides for a private right of action; (6) preserves states' rights to enact stronger provisions; and (7) establishes a federal data protection agency to enforce these new rules.[71] I detail each of these principles below.

A. Limit the Collection and Use of Personal Data

Federal legislation should not take a "notice and choice" approach or rely on industry self-regulation to protect data privacy. Instead, the law should place strict limits on the collection, use, storage, and transfer of personal data. Legislation should build on the U.S. Code of Fair Information Practices and OECD Privacy Guidelines, which are widely followed and form the basis of other data protection regimes. These frameworks create obligations for companies that collect personal data and establish individual data rights. Core principles include:

- Strict data collection and use limitations
- Data minimization and deletion requirements
- Transparency about business practices
- Purpose specification
- Access, correction, and deletion rights
- Data accuracy
- Confidentiality and security requirements
- Compliance and accountability

The adoption of "data minimization" techniques is essential to data protection across the board. A company implementing data minimization measures should collect only the data necessary to provide a good or service, and not more.[72] Companies complying with their data minimization

---

[71] Privacy and Digital Rights for All, *The Time is Now: A Framework for Comprehensive Privacy Protection and Digital Justice in the United States* (2021), https://epic.org/wp-content/uploads/2022/01/Privacy-and-Digital-Rights-For-All-Framework.pdf.

[72] *See* EPIC and Consumer Reports, *How the FTC Can Mandate Data Minimization Through a Section 5 Unfairness Rulemaking* (January 2022), https://epic.org/documents/how-the-ftc-can-mandate-data-minimization- through-a-section-5-unfairness-rulemaking/; *see also* Access Now, *Data minimization: Key to protecting privacyand reducing harm* (May 2021), https://www.accessnow.org/data-minimization-guide/.

requirements must also delete personal information when it is no longer needed.

The landmark privacy law passed by Congress, the Privacy Act of 1974, which applies to government agencies, requires data minimization. Each agency that collects personal data shall "maintain in its records only such information about an individual as is relevant and necessary to accomplish a purpose of the agency required to be accomplished by statute or by executive orderof the President."[73]

The recently passed update to the California Consumer Privacy Act also includes provisions requiring data minimization.[74] The European Union General Data Protection Regulation (GDPR) requires companies, among other things, to minimize collection of consumer data to what is "[a]dequate, relevant, and limited to what is necessary in relation to the purposes for which they are processed."[75]

Personal data that is not collected cannot be at risk of a data breach. Recognizing the need to limit private data collection, the National Telecommunications and Information Administration ("NTIA") has identified "reasonable minimization" as a "critical Privacy Outcome."[76]

Some types of data, and some uses of data, are especially sensitive and deserve even stricter regulation. For instance, biometric and genetic data are inherently sensitive, but even information about the products people buy and the services they search for can be used to make inferences about their health, religious beliefs, economic situations, and other characteristics that are sensitive in nature. In these situations, prohibiting certain data collection and use may be necessary.

B. Prohibit Discriminatory Uses of Data

Privacy legislation should protect against discriminatory uses of data and extend civil rights protections online.[77] Processing that leads to disparate treatment or adverse disparate impacts should be prohibited. The law should

---

[73] 5 U.S.C. § 552a (e)(1).

[74] Cal. Civ. Code § 1798.100(c).

[75] Regulation (EU) 2016/679 (General Data Protection Regulation) Art. 5 § 1(c).

[76] Nat'l Telecomms. & Info. Admin., U.S. Dep't. Commerce, *Developing the Administration's Approach to Consumer Privacy*, Request for Comments, Docket No. 180821780-8780-01 (Oct. 11, 2018), https://www.federalregister.gov/documents/2018/09/26/2018-20941/developing-the-administrationsapproach-to- consumer-privacy.

[77] *See* Kristen Clarke and David Brody, *It's time for an online Civil Rights Act*, The Hill (Aug. 3, 2018),https://thehill.com/opinion/civil-rights/400310-its-time-for-an-online-civil-rights-act.

also prohibit predatory data collection practices and uses that target economically disadvantaged or marginalized communities.[78]

C. Require Algorithmic Fairness and Accountability

Automated systems that use artificial intelligence or other big data tools to make decisions about individuals pose significant risks to fundamental rights. Public and private actors are increasingly using AI systems to make decisions about eligibility for jobs, education, housing, parole and bail, credit, insurance, healthcare, and government services.[79] The error, bias, and discrimination embedded in these systems perpetuate systemic inequities,[80] yet public agencies and private companies are not currently required to evaluate the potential impacts andbiases of these systems before they use them.

Indeed, many AI systems have been deployed by both government agencies and private companies with little to no oversight and with questions regarding their effectiveness.[81] A 2019 National Institute of Standards and Technology ("NIST") study of facial recognition tools— which are typically "AI-based"[82]—found that the systems were up to 100 times more likely to return a false positive for a non-white person than for a white person.[83] Specifically, NIST found that "for one-to-many matching, the team saw higher rates of false positives for African American females," a finding that is "particularly important because the consequences could include false accusations."[84] A separate study by Stanford University and MIT, which looked at three widely deployed commercial facial recognition tools, found an error rate of 34.7% for dark-skinned women compared to an error rate of 0.8%

---

[78] *See generally* Leadership Conf. on Civil and Human Rights, *Civil Rights Principles for the Era of Big Data*,https://civilrights.org/2014/02/27/civil-rights-principles-era-big-data/.

[79] Danielle Keats Citron & Frank Pasquale, *The Scored Society: Due Process for Automated Predictions*, 89 Wash.L. Rev. 1 (2014).

[80] *See* Richardson, Rashida, *Racial Segregation and the Data-Driven Society: How Our Failure to Reckon with RootCauses Perpetuates Separate and Unequal Realities*, 36 Berkeley Tech. L.J. 3 (2022).

[81] David Freeman Engstrom, Daniel E. Ho, Catherine M. Sharkey, & Mariano-Florentino Cuéllar, *Government by Algorithm: Artificial Intelligence in Federal Administrative Agencies* 6 (Feb. 2020) https://www-cdn.law.stanford.edu/wp-content/uploads/2020/02/ACUS-AI-Report.pdf.

[82] Nat'l Inst. Standards & Tech., *Face Recognition Vendor Test (FRVT) Part 3: Demographic Effects* 14 (Dec.2019), https://nvlpubs.nist.gov/nistpubs/ir/2019/NIST.IR.8280.pdf.

[83] Nat'l Inst. Standards & Tech., *NIST Study Evaluates Effects of Race, Age, Sex on Face Recognition Software* (Dec. 19, 2019), https://www.nist.gov/news-events/news/2019/12/nist-study-evaluates-effects-race-age-sex-face-recognition-software.

[84] *Id.*

for light-skinned men.[85] A review of Rekognition—an Amazon-owned facial recognition system marketed to law enforcement— revealed indications of racial bias and found that the system misidentified 28 members of U.S. Congress as convicted criminals.[86]

Legislation should require meaningful transparency, enable oversight of these AI systems by developing standards for and requiring independent assessments of algorithmic impact, conducting routine and randomized screening of new systems, and requiring publication of system details and audit results.[87] The law should also require a right to human review of automated decisions. Uses of AI that subvert human and civil rights should be prohibited, such as many uses in the criminal justice system, for mass surveillance, and emotion detection.

Unless express, binding limits on the use of AI are established *now*, the technology willquickly outpace our collective ability to regulate it. Congress should not make the same self- regulatory mistakes with AI that it made with data collection and use.

D. Ban Manipulative Design and Unfair Marketing Practices

Legislation should prohibit dark patterns designed to manipulate individuals into making choices that are in the businesses' interests rather than their own.[88] Pay-for-privacy provisions or take-it-or-leave-it terms of service, which discriminate against those with less means, should be illegal.

E. Limit Government Access to Personal Data

Privacy legislation frequently includes specific provisions that limit government access topersonal data held by companies. These provisions help ensure that the government collects only the data that is necessary and

---

[85] Joy Buolamwini and Timnit Gebru, *Gender Shades: Intersectional Accuracy Disparities in Commercial GenderClassification,* Proceedings of Machine Learning Research 81:1–15 (2018), https://www.media.mit.edu/publications/gender-shades-intersectional-accuracy-disparities-in-commercial-gender-classification/.

[86] Russell Brandom, *Amazon's facial recognition matched 28 members of Congress to criminal mugshots*, The Verge (July 26, 2018), https://www.theverge.com/2018/7/26/17615634/amazon-rekognition-aclu-mug-shot- congress-facial-recognition.

[87] *See e.g.* H.R.6580, 117th Cong. (2022) (Algorithmic Accountability Act requires transparency and accountabilityfor automated decision making systems).

[88] *See generally* Rohit Chopra, *Statement of Commissioner Rohit Chopra Regarding Dark Patterns in the Matter ofAge of Learning, Inc.*, FTC File No. 1723186 (Sep. 2, 2020), https://www.ftc.gov/system/files/documents/public_statements/1579927/172_3086_abcmouse_-_rchopra_statement.pdf; *See, e.g.*, Complaint of EPIC, *In re In the Matter of Amazon.com, Inc.* (Feb. 23, 2021), https://epic.org/wp-content/uploads/privacy/dccppa/amazon/EPIC-Complaint-In-Re-Amazon.pdf.

appropriate for a particular criminal investigation. Without these provisions, the government is able to collect personal data in bulk from companies, a form of "mass surveillance" enabled by new technologies. The Supreme Court also recently said in the *Carpenter* case that personal data held by private companies, in some circumstances, is entitled to Constitutional protection.[89]

Federal agencies are using data collected by private companies for law enforcement, immigration, and other purposes. This undermines legal mechanisms intended to limit such government access, such as the 4th Amendment. A detailed report in *The Wall Street Journal* in early 2020 revealed that federal agencies are accessing cell phone location data without warrantsor judicial oversight.[90] These agencies are engaging in warrantless location surveillance despite the Supreme Court's ruling in *Carpenter v. United States*[91] that officers must obtain a warrant inorder to collect cell phone location data. The sale of location data by data brokers, which made this warrantless tracking possible, is a threat to the privacy and security of all Americans.

Congress should close the loopholes that have allowed warrantless location tracking to takeplace.

Federal privacy legislation should require that any government collection of personal datashould have a lawful basis, be performed in accordance with applicable data protection laws, be limited in time and scope to the original purpose of collection, and be subject to independent oversight. With few exceptions, it should be conducted only with the consent of those whose personal data is collected. Personal data should not be collected in bulk, from third-party data brokers without a warrant, or through warrantless surveillance. Legislation should require agencies to appoint a Chief Privacy Officer at the leadership level with the authority to oversee and address privacy issues across the agency.

F. Provide for a Private Right of Action

Robust enforcement is critical to effective privacy protection. The inclusion of a private right of action with statutory damages is a crucial tool to supplement government enforcement, particularly for marginalized communities. If a company violates federal privacy law, individualsand groups

---

[89] *Carpenter v. United States*, 138 S. Ct. 2206, 2223 (2018).

[90] Byron Tau & Michelle Hackman, *Federal Agencies Use Cellphone Location Data for Immigration Enforcement*,Wall St. J. (Feb. 7, 2020), https://www.wsj.com/articles/federal-agencies-use-cellphone- location-data-for- immigration-enforcement-11581078600.

[91] 138 S. Ct. 2206 (2018).

of individuals, or their agents, should be able to pursue a private right of action that provides meaningful redress without a showing of additional harm. While government enforcement is essential, the scope of data collection online is simply too vast for one entity to regulate. Individuals and groups of individuals who use these online services are in a good position to identify privacy issues and bring actions to vindicate their interests.

The inclusion of a private right of action is the most important tool Congress can give toAmericans to protect their privacy.

Many privacy laws include a private right of action, and these provisions have historically made it possible to hold companies accountable for their privacy violations. In crafting liability provisions in privacy statutes, Congress has frequently included a liquidated damages provision to avoid protracted disputes over quantifying privacy damages. This is necessary because it is often difficult to assign a specific economic value to the harm caused by a privacy violation.

For example, when Congress passed the Cable Communications Policy Act in 1984, theyestablished privacy rights for cable subscribers and created a private right of action for recovery of actual damages not less than liquidated damages of $100 per for violation or $1,000, whichever is higher.[92] The Video Privacy Protection Act specifies liquidated damages of $2,500.[93] The Fair Credit Reporting Act affords individuals a private right of action that can be pursued in federal or state court against credit reporting agencies, users of credit reports, and furnishers.[94] In certain circumstances, individuals can also recover attorney's fees, court costs, and punitive damages. The Drivers Privacy Protection Act similarly includes a private right of action.[95] The Telephone Consumer Protection Act allows individuals who receive unsolicited telemarketing calls to recover actual monetary loss or up to $500 in damages per violation.[96]

The statutory damages set in privacy laws are not large in an individual case, but they canprovide a powerful incentive in large cases and are necessary to ensure that privacy rights will betaken seriously and violations not tolerated. In the absence of a private right of action, there is a very real risk that companies will not comply with the law because they think it is unlikely that they would get caught or fined. Private enforcement ensures that data

---

[92] 47 USC § 551(f).
[93] 18 USC § 2710(c)(2).
[94] 15 U.S.C. §§ 1681n-1681o.
[95] 18 U.S.C. § 2724.
[96] 47 USC § 227(c)(5).

collectors have strong financial incentives to meet their data protection obligations.

G. Preserve States' Rights to Enact Stronger Protections

A well-established principle in the United States is that federal privacy law should operate as a floor and not a ceiling. That means that Congress often passes privacy legislation that sets a minimum standard, or "baseline," for the country and allows individual states to develop new and innovative approaches to privacy protection. Historically, federal privacy laws have not preempted stronger state protections or enforcement efforts. Federal consumer protection and privacy laws, as a general matter, operate as regulatory baselines and do not prevent states from enacting and enforcing stronger state statutes.

The Fair Credit Reporting Act, The Electronic Communications Privacy Act, the Right to Financial Privacy Act, the Cable Communications Privacy Act, the Video Privacy Protection Act, the Employee Polygraph Protection Act, the Telephone Consumer Protection Act, the Driver's Privacy Protection Act, and the Gramm-Leach-Bliley Act are just a few of the laws which allow states to craft protections that exceed federal law.

The consequences of federal preemption are potentially severe and could include both a reduction in privacy protection for many consumers, particularly as states continue to enact their own privacy laws, and also a prohibition on state legislatures addressing new challenges as they emerge. That could leave consumers and businesses exposed to increasing levels of data breach and identity theft from criminal hackers and foreign adversaries.

Today the states are on the front lines of consumer protection in the United States. They are updating privacy laws to address new challenges. They are bringing enforcement actions to safeguard American consumers. They are establishing the data protection standards that are safeguarding the personal data of Americans from attack by foreign adversaries.

It is absolutely essential to the development of privacy safeguards that Congress establish baseline standards that all states must follow, but leave states with the freedom to update their privacy laws as new technologies and business practices emerge. As Justice Brandeis famously explained, the states are the laboratories of democracy.[97] And these laboratories are all the more

---

[97] "It is one of the happy incidents of the federal system that a single courageous state may, if its citizens choose,serve as a laboratory[.]" *New State Ice Co. v. Liebmann*, 285 U.S. 262, 311 (Brandeis, J. dissenting).

crucial in the area of technology policy, which is defined by persistent and rapid change.

H. Establish a U.S. Data Protection Agency

For more than two decades, EPIC has worked to support the Federal Trade Commission in its efforts to safeguard the privacy of American consumers. But it is our view that the consumer-centric, industry-by-industry approach to privacy regulation is unworkable. Congress should establish an independent Data Protection Agency in the United States to regulate, enforce, and coordinate data protection policies across all industries and governmental entities.

The United States has historically approached privacy with a consumer lens, but that view is outdated. The commercial surveillance systems that profile us and sort us into groups through a vast, opaque system of algorithms are perpetuating systemic inequities in our society.

The harms to individuals, groups of individuals, and society at large are real, and they requirereal solutions that do not fit neatly into the "consumer" box.

In order to move away from the commercial approach and tackle the very real threats Big Tech poses to civil rights, individual autonomy, and democracy, the United States must create a dedicated data protection agency ("DPA"). The United States is one of the few democracies in the world that does not have a federal data protection agency, even though the original proposal for such an institution emerged from the U.S. in the 1970s. The United States was once a global leader on privacy. The Fair Credit Reporting Act, passed in 1970, was viewed at the time as the first modern privacy law—a response to the growing automation of personal data in the United States. There is an urgent need for leadership from the United States on data protection. Virtuallyevery other advanced economy has recognized the need for an independent agency to address thechallenges of the digital age. Current law and regulatory oversight in the United States is woefully inadequate to meet the challenges. We also now face threats from foreign adversaries that target the personal data stored in U.S. companies and U.S. government agencies. The U.S. urgently needs a Data Protection Agency.

The DPA should be dedicated to privacy and data protection, oversight, and enforcement,with the authority and resources to address emerging privacy challenges. The DPA should examine the social, ethical, and economic impacts of data processing and oversee compliance and impact-assessment obligations. The DPA should work with the FTC and Department of Justice to address competition and growing concentration in the technology sector by reviewing and issuing guidance on the privacy and data protection implications of proposed mergers.

Congress should empower a DPA with adequate resources, rulemaking authority, and effectiveinvestigatory and enforcement powers.[98]

Ideally, a DPA would be given the proper oversight and enforcement tools to ensure that companies innovate around and improve privacy, rather than simply pursuing penalties for privacy violations.[99] One mechanism for this has been proposed in Senator Gillibrand's Data Protection Act[100] – the DPA could require and oversee impact assessments of high-risk data practices, such as consumer scoring or the use of or AI or biometric data. As opposed to the FTC's unfair and deceptive acts and practices authority, which is backward looking and attempts to remedy harms that already occurred, the DPA's ability to regulate high-risk data practices could stop privacy harms before they happen and help technology companies innovate around privacy.

There is broad public support for the creating of a Data Protection Agency. A recent Data for Progress poll showed that 78% of Americans across the political spectrum support establishing a federal agency "specifically dedicated to creating and standardizing a regulatory framework aimed at protecting Americans' data privacy."[101]

The U.S. is one of the few advanced economies in the world without a data protection agency. The consequence is that the U.S consumers experience the highest levels of data breach, financial fraud, and identity theft in the world. And U.S. businesses, with their vast collections of personal data, remain the target of cyber-attack by criminals and foreign adversaries. Meanwhile companies collect vast amounts of personal data about Americans without their knowledge and without any meaningful data protection standards. The longer the U.S. continues on this course, the greater will be the threats to consumer privacy, democratic institutions, and national security. The need for an effective, independent data protection agency has never been greater.

---

[98] See EPIC, The U.S. Urgently Needs a Data Protection Agency, https://epic.org/dpa.

[99] See Julie Cohen, How (Not) to Write a Privacy Law, Knight First Amendment Institute (Mar. 2021), https://knightcolumbia.org/content/how-not-to-write-a-privacy-law ("An essential strategy for scaling enforcementauthority involves leveraging gatekeeper power to demand and guarantee adherence to the design, operational, andmonitoring requirements that public oversight processes have defined.")

[100] S. 2134, 117th Cong. § 3 (2021).

[101] Data for Progress, Poll, 10 (July 2021), https://www.filesforprogress.org/datasets/2021/7/dfp_DPA_202107_toplines.pdf.

IV. Congress Should Enact the Online Privacy Act

Congress can address these issues and strengthen data privacy protections in the United States by taking up a bill that incorporates many, if not all, of the suggestions outlined above. The Online Privacy Act filed by Chairwoman Lofgren and Representative Eshoo is comprehensive framework that would place strict limits on the collection and use of personal data, extend civil rights protections online, and establish strong enforcement mechanisms via a private right of action and the creation of a U.S. Data Protection Agency.[102]

The Online Privacy Act would also make important updates to require the House of Representatives, Government Publishing Office, Library of Congress, and Smithsonian Institution to implement measures to prevent the disclosure of personal information by those entities and to minimize the risk of privacy harms in their operations.

One of the Online Privacy Act's strengths lies in its enforcement mechanisms. Without strong enforcement, many businesses will simply ignore privacy laws and accept the small risk of an enforcement action as a cost of business, as we have seen in Europe and in several states. Without independent oversight, privacy law simply becomes, as Professor Ari Ezra Waldman says, "compliance, rather than a substantive, task," or "privacy theater."[103] The inclusion of a private right of action and establishment of a Data Protection Agency avoid this fate by ensuring that the incentives to comply with privacy statutes are in place.

The Illinois Biometric Information Privacy Act (BIPA) has proven to be the most effective privacy law in the nation due to the inclusion of a private right of action.[104] Last November, Facebook announced that it was shutting down its face recognition system and deleting more than a billion people's facial recognition templates.[105] Many advocates believe pending BIPA lawsuits against the use of facial recognition were a major factor in Facebook's decision. In 2020, Clearview AI ended all contracts with private companies

---

[102] H.R.6027, 117th Cong. (2021).

[103] Ari Ezra Waldman, *Privacy Law's False Promise*, 97 Wash. U. L. Rev. 0773, 776 (2020); Ari Ezra Waldman,How Big Tech Turns Privacy Laws Into Privacy Theater, Forbes Future Tense (Dec. 2, 2021), https://slate.com/technology/2021/12/facebook-twitter-big-tech-privacy-sham.html.

[104] Woodrow Hartzog, *BIPA: The Most Important Biometric Privacy Law in the US?*, AI Now Institute (2020),https://ainowinstitute.org/regulatingbiometrics-hartzog.pdf.

[105] Facebook, *An Update On Our Use of Face Recognition* (Nov 2. 2021), https://about.fb.com/news/2021/11/update-on-use-of-face-recognition/.

and non-law enforcement entities nationwide and canceled all accounts belonging to any entity in Illinois in response to a BIPA suit it was facing.[106]

In addition to its strong enforcement mechanisms, the Online Privacy Act would also add prohibitions for discriminatory processing of data, mandate data minimization, require opt-in consent for the sale of personal information, ban dark patterns, grant data subject rights to users, and impose data security requirements on covered entities. Enactment of the Online Privacy Act would help restore the current power imbalance between the companies who collect data and individuals. EPIC recommends that Congress enact the Online Privacy Act this session.

V. Conclusion

The lack of a U.S. privacy law places not only our individual autonomy, but our democracy at risk. We have seen an increased interest among federal policymakers in recent years, but now we need action. We need comprehensive privacy legislation, robust enforcement, and resources and attention dedicated to making our online world more secure and preserving the privacy and fairness of new data systems.

Thank you for the opportunity to testify today.

The CHAIRPERSON. Thank you very much, Ms. Fitzgerald.

We will turn now to you, Mr. Erwin, for your testimony for five minutes.

Statement of Marshall Erwin

Mr. ERWIN. Thank you, Chairperson Lofgren, Ranking Member Davis, and Members of the Committee. Thank you for offering me the opportunity to testify today.

My name is Marshall Erwin. I am the Chief Security Officer at Mozilla.

Mozilla is a nonprofit organization and open-source community. Our products, including the Firefox browser, are used by hundreds of millions of

---

[106] Nick Statt, *Clearview AI to stop selling controversial facial recognition app to private companies*, The Verge (May 2020), https://www.theverge.com/2020/5/7/21251387/clearview-ai-law-enforcement-police-facial- recognition-illinois-privacy-law.

people around the world. Mozilla is constantly investing in security and privacy and advancing movements to build a healthier internet.

Now, in our view, privacy online is a mess today. Consumers are constantly under attack. They are stuck in a vicious cycle in which their data is collected without their knowledge or understanding, then shared to build profiles about them. That data is then used to target and manipulate them in ways that can be actively harmful.

Today I am going to talk about what Mozilla is doing to address this problem and then what we think Congress needs to do.

In the Firefox browser there have been two focus areas for us. The first is that we have been driving major initiatives, such as the standardization of TLS 1.3 or founding Let's Encrypt, a free nonprofit certificate authority. This has resulted in an increase in encrypted web traffic up to almost 85 or 95 percent from below fifty percent a few years ago.

What this is doing is protecting your browsing activity and your information from attackers in the middle of a network who would otherwise collect that information to use it to build a profile about you.

The second big area of focus for us has been on eliminating what we call cross-site tracking. These are parties following you around from the website to website that you visit, again collecting your information about your browsing activity and then building that profile about you.

In 2019, we turned on what we called Enhanced Tracking Protection in the browser, turned that on by default because we believe the onus shouldn't be on consumers to protect themselves from opaque risks they can't see or understand.

So that is just a little bit of what we have been doing to try to address this problem. I want to talk a little bit about what we think Congress needs to do, first focusing on baseline Federal privacy legislation, and then talk a little bit about transparency into online harms.

First, in our view, technical privacy protections from companies and baseline regulations are complementary and necessary. Neither alone are sufficient. The internet was not designed with privacy and security in mind, which is why technical solutions like the ones that we offer are necessary to create a less permissive environment overall.

At the same time, we can't solve every privacy problem with a technical fix. There is an essential role for regulation here as well. To give you just one example, we know that dark patterns are pervasive across the software and applications that people use. Unfortunately, there is little that a browser can do when a person visits a website directly and then is deceived into handing over their information without proper consent or understanding.

And this is where law plus a robust enforcement regime must step in. That is why provisions like the one in the Online Privacy Act, which would prohibit dark patterns, are so critical.

More generally, Mozilla supports privacy and data protection laws around the world, including in the United States. The U.S. must enact baseline privacy protections to ensure that the public and private actors treat consumers fairly. We need clear rules of the road for entities using personal data, strong privacy rights for people who are interacting with those entities, and effective authorities, agencies with the authority to take enforcement action.

Second, it is important to complement Federal privacy legislation with solutions that provide direct transparency and accountability into online harms.

Many of the harms that we see today are a direct result of the pervasive data collection happening. We know from recent whistleblower disclosures things like recommendation systems and targeting systems can have pernicious effects if abused.

These systems are really powered by people's data. It is easier to discriminate against people, manipulate people, or deceive people if you know more about them. Therefore, privacy and some of these online harms are really inherently linked.

The problem is that this harm is mostly hidden from the public and from regulators. That is why we have called for things like an establishment of a safe harbor to protect researchers doing investigations into the activities of major online platforms.

This would protect research into the public interest and help us better understand the harm happening on these platforms. There is a real public benefit that can be had here by such a safe harbor. Similarly, we have advocated for more robust disclosure regimes governing online ads. We have been leading the push for full ad disclosure in the European Union. We are encouraged by recent proposals in Congress that would require disclosure of ads for public benefit and understanding.

These approaches would provide transparency into the opaque world of online advertising. It is necessary, and we think it could be done without creating privacy risks.

In conclusion, at Mozilla we seek to advance privacy technology and to ensure that privacy considerations are at the forefront of policymakers' minds in considering how to protect consumers and grow the economy.

We appreciate the Committee's focus on these issues and look forward to the discussion.

[The statement of Mr. Erwin follows:]

Written Statement of Marshall Erwin, Chief Security Officer Mozilla Before the Committee on House Administration United States House of Representatives
"Big Data: Privacy Risks and Needed Reforms in the Public and Private Sectors" February 16, 2022

Chairperson Lofgren, Ranking Member Davis, and Members of the Committee, thank you for holding this hearing today on such an important issue, and for the opportunity to testify.

I'm Marshall Erwin, Chief Security Officer at Mozilla.

Our Public Mission and Incentives

Mozilla is a unique public benefit organization and open source community formed as a non-profit foundation. We build the open-source Firefox web browser, Mozilla VPN, and the Pocket "read-it-later" application. These products are used by hundreds of millions of individuals around the world. As a mission-driven technology company and a non-profit foundation, we are dedicated to putting people in control of their online experience, and creating an internet that is open and accessible to all.

To fulfill this mission, we are constantly investing in the security of our products, the privacy of our users and in advancing the movement to build a healthier internet. Mozilla has influenced major companies to adopt better privacy practices such as browser anti-tracking measures and empowered people directly with tools to better understand and block third party data collection. For Mozilla, privacy is not optional. It is an integral aspect of our founding principles, which state that individuals' security and privacy on the internet are fundamental and must not be treated as optional.

Mozilla's Meaningful Protections by Default and Design

We have worked hard to make Mozilla's vision for privacy and security a reality in the products we build and the technologies we develop. We do this by leading and participating in the creation of web standards that make the internet more secure and more protective of privacy, and by pioneering the product-level implementation of privacy and security-enhancing browser technologies through Firefox. These open innovations are available to the wider internet: other organizations, internet applications, and consumers.

For example, we have made online commerce and navigation safe through protocols and initiatives like TLS 1.3 and Let's Encrypt. TLS 1.3 is the protocol that powers every secure transaction on the internet. Let's Encrypt is a major internet security success story; because of its creation, 85% of online traffic is now encrypted with HTTPS (signaled by a green padlock on many web browsers), compared to less than 30% in 2014.

We have always put privacy first in our own products and features.

- In 2019 we enabled Enhanced Tracking Protection[107] by default in Firefox, protecting our people from cross-site tracking. While anti-tracking features had been available for many years in Firefox, we turned this feature on by default because we believe[108] that the onus should not be on consumers to protect themselves from sophisticated privacy risks they do not understand.
- Last year, we introduced one of our strongest privacy protections to date, Total Cookie Protection,[109] to provide additional protections from cross-site tracking.
- Mozilla has also been instrumental in the technological development and product roll-out of technologies to encrypt web traffic. This

---

[107] Dave Camp, "Firefox Now Available with Enhanced Tracking Protection by Default Plus Updates to Facebook Container, Firefox Monitor and Lockwise," Mozilla dist://ed (June 4, 2019), *at* https://blog.mozilla.org/en/products/firefox/firefox-now-available-with-enhanced-tracking-protection-by-default/.

[108] Steven Englehardt, "Why we need better tracking protection," Mozilla Security Blog (Sept. 5, 2018), *at* https://blog.mozilla.org/security/2018/09/05/why-we-need-better-tracking-protection/.

[109] Selena Deckelmann, "Latest Firefox release includes Multiple Picture-in-Picture and Total Cookie Protection," Mozilla dist://ed (Feb. 23, 2021), *at* https://blog.mozilla.org/en/products/firefox/latest-firefox-release-includes-multiple-picture-in-picture-and-total-cookie-protection/.

includes most recently our work on DNS over HTTPs[110] - or DoH - the protocol that encrypts domain name look-ups and closes one of the last great security vulnerabilities in the internet architecture.

- Our VPN (Virtual Private Network)[111] helps people create a secure, private connection to the internet.
- And our end-to-end encrypted Firefox Sync[112] service by default protects all your synced data so Mozilla can't read it.

We also support practical solutions to help companies have a healthier relationship with data, through our Lean Data Practices (LDP) framework and trainings.[113] LDP helps other organizations to reduce the amount of user data that is initially collected and focuses on only collecting essential data to lower risk and promote trust with users. We have published this framework under an open license, and have worked with organizations around the world to educate other businesses on the benefits of such an approach. We have learned through LDP workshops with public sector participants that the absence of a uniform data protection law causes challenges to minimize, delete, and limit the sharing of data today. Especially at the local level, there may also be a lack of resources to better secure data or explain to constituents how it is used and shared.

Addressing the Systemic Privacy Problem Through Legislation

While we play an important role in keeping people secure and protecting privacy on the internet, we nonetheless recognize that the lack of privacy online today is a systemic problem. We need structural change to protect data and empower people. We therefore believe that law and regulation have an essential role to play in creating a healthier internet. Relying on the voluntary adoption of protocols and practices like the ones we have designed is an incomplete solution.

In our view, technical privacy protections by companies and privacy regulation are complementary and necessary. Neither alone is sufficient. The internet was not originally designed with privacy and security in mind, which

---

[110] Patrick McManus, "Improving DNS Privacy in Firefox," Firefox Nightly News (June 1, 2018), *at* https://blog.nightly.mozilla.org/2018/06/01/improving-dns-privacy-in-firefox/.

[111] Mozilla VPN, *at* https://www.mozilla.org/en-US/products/vpn/more/what-is-a-vpn/.

[112] Firefox Sync, *at* https://www.mozilla.org/en-US/firefox/sync/.

[113] Mozilla Lean Data Practices, *at* https://www.mozilla.org/en-US/about/policy/lean-data/.

is why technical solutions are necessary to create a less permissive environment that is more protective of people. But we cannot solve every privacy problem with a technical fix.

For example, we know that dark patterns are pervasive across the online applications that people engage with daily. Unfortunately, there is little any browser can do when a person visits a website directly and is deceived by the website into handing over and sharing their data without meaningful consent. This is where law, plus a robust enforcement regime, must step in. That is why provisions such as the one in the Online Privacy Act that prohibit dark patterns are so critical.

Another example is what we call browser fingerprinting, which is a technique used to track consumers by constructing an identifier from the characteristics of their browser. Fingerprinting is opaque to users and would fail to satisfy many user privacy rights regimes. Mozilla attempts to block fingerprinting in Firefox, but we recognize that we will not be able to defeat all fingerprinting activities, no matter how we change our browser. In areas like these, technical solutions will not be enough.

This is why Mozilla strongly supports privacy and data protection laws around the world, including in the US. The US should enact baseline federal privacy protections, to ensure public and private actors treat consumers fairly. We need clear rules of the road for entities using personal data, strong rights for people who interact with those entities, and effective authority for the Federal Trade Commission (FTC) to make and enforce these rules as technologies evolve. Ultimately, privacy, security, and consumer data protection are best-served when policy is based upon a comprehensive framework of protections.

Greater Transparency into Hidden Harms

Many of the harms we see on the internet today are in part a result of pervasive data collection and underlying privacy risk. Targeting and personalization systems generate real value for consumers. But, as we have learned from recent whistleblower disclosures, these systems also can be abused, resulting in real world harm to individuals and communities. They are powered by people's data. Indeed, the more you know about someone, the easier it will be to deceive, or peddle disinformation, or discriminate against them.

The world has now had a few years of experience with global and state laws covering baseline data and security requirements. Unfortunately, there remains a looming gap, which is that we lack sufficient insights into how people experience online discrimination and harm when their data is collected, used and shared without meaningful awareness or consent. This includes what ads are presented to you and why, and what content is recommended to you and why. To address this, we need complementary regulatory solutions to federal privacy legislation that would provide greater levels of transparency into the ecosystem impact of our online data.

At Mozilla, we support solutions that will provide greater transparency into online discrimination and harms that today are hidden from the public and from regulators. Accordingly, we have called for establishing a safe harbor allowing researchers, journalists, and others to access relevant datasets, free from threats of legal action. Such a safe harbor should protect research in the public interest as long as researchers handle data responsibly and adhere to professional and ethical standards. We know there is enormous value this can provide to the public. Mozilla has one of the earliest Bug Bounty programs in software. We make clear that we will not threaten or bring any legal action against anyone who makes a good faith effort to comply with our vulnerability notification policy because this encourages security researchers to investigate and disclose security issues. Their research helps make the internet a safer place.

Similarly, we advocate for a more robust disclosure regime governing the ads people see online. We have been leading the push for full ad disclosure in the European Union's Digital Services Act and we are encouraged by recent proposals in Congress that would require disclosure of ads for public benefit and understanding. These approaches would bring transparency into the opaque world of online advertising and can be done in ways that do not pose privacy risk to users.

Structural Solutions Should Be Used to Limit First Party Data Use

Federal privacy law, while essential, should also be bolstered by regulation and enforcement to foster stronger consumer protection and competition. The most dominant technology companies today are the largest third-party trackers on the internet. At the same time, the same companies also have extensive first party relationships with consumers and have benefited the most from the absence of oversight to protect consumers.

We support efforts by regulators to tackle this problem through interventions governing how data can be shared and used within the holding structures of large platforms. For example, we strongly support Google's recent commitments to UK regulators to foreclose the use of data from Android, Chrome browsing history and sync data, Google Analytics, and Customer Matching for targeting after implementation of Chrome Privacy Sandbox proposals. This is a positive direction for the evolution of a more private and secure internet that will benefit consumers around the world. Indeed, all dominant platforms should embrace commitments like this and start practicing them immediately, beyond just advertising or browser technologies, to ensure a fairer and more interoperable internet for everyone.

At the same time, it is important that competition concerns not be a pretext to prevent better privacy for everyone. Many parties, large and small, have built their business models to depend on extensive user tracking. Many third-party advertising companies that depend on ubiquitous user tracking seek to prevent privacy innovation. Closing privacy gaps necessarily means denying data to these parties. That is a good thing. Consumer welfare is at the heart of both competition and privacy enforcement. Focusing on consumers and their needs will ensure regulation doesn't inadvertently freeze the evolution of internet technologies that can offer consumers advances in privacy and security.

Conclusion

At Mozilla, we seek to advance a favorable environment for privacy-enhancing technologies, and to ensure that privacy considerations are front and center of policymakers' minds when considering how to protect consumers and grow our economy.

We believe through our product and policy work we can help address the data privacy gaps that exist today, impacting consumers, companies, and the public sector alike. Despite being a powerhouse of technology innovation for years, the United States is behind globally when it comes to recognizing consumer privacy and protecting people from indiscriminate data collection and use. We appreciate the Committee's focus on this vital issue and look forward to further discussions with Congress. Thank you.

The CHAIRPERSON. Thank you, Mr. Erwin.

And now we turn to our last but certainly not our least witness, Mr. Castro, for your testimony for five minutes.

Statement of Daniel Castro

Mr. CASTRO. Thank you. Chairperson Lofgren, Ranking Member Davis, and Members of the Committee, I appreciate the invitation to speak with you today.

U.S. data privacy is at a crossroads. Many consumers are justifiably frustrated by the frequency with which they learn about new data breaches and the seeming lack of accountability for those who misuse their personal information.

At the same time, many firms are overwhelmed by a tsunami of new data-protection obligations and growing restrictions on how they can use personal information for legitimate business purposes. All are often confused by the multitude of ever-changing laws and regulations.

Three States, California, Virginia, and Colorado have passed comprehensive data privacy legislation, and many other States are considering it. Over the past three years, 34 State legislatures have introduced a total of 72 bills and more are coming.

These new State privacy laws can impose significant costs on businesses, both direct compliance costs and decreases in productivity, and undermine their ability to responsibly use data to innovate and deliver value to consumers.

Moreover, these laws create high costs, not just for in-State businesses, but also for out-of-State businesses that can find themselves subject to multiple and duplicative laws. For example, California's recently enacted privacy law will likely cost $78 billion annually, with California's economy bearing $46 billion and the rest of the U.S. economy bearing the other $32 billion.

In the absence of Federal data privacy legislation, the growing patchwork of State privacy laws could impose out-of-State costs between $98 billion and $112 billion annually. Over a ten-year period, the costs would exceed $1 trillion. The burden on small businesses would be substantial, with U.S. small businesses bearing $20 billion to $23 billion annually.

The United States needs a new Federal data privacy law, but it should not back away from the light-touch approach it has historically taken to regulating the digital economy. Instead, it should focus on the following goals.

First, data privacy legislation should establish basic consumer date rights. For example, Congress should give individuals the right to know how organizations collect and use their personal data or when their information has been part of a data breach.

Congress should also give consumers the right to access, port, delete, and rectify their sensitive data in certain contexts. For example, consumers should have a right to obtain a copy of their health or financial data and move it to a competing service.

Second, lawmakers should establish uniform privacy rules for the entire Nation by preempting State and local privacy laws. Consumers should have the same protections regardless of where they live, and companies should not be faced with 50 different sets of laws and regulations.

A patchwork of State laws, with varying definitions and standards, creates a complex regulatory minefield for businesses to navigate, especially if potential violations risk costly litigation.

Third, Congress should ensure there is robust and reliable enforcement of Federal privacy law. Congress should not create a private right of action, and instead rely on Federal and State regulators to hold organizations accountable.

Illinois, which has a private right of action for its biometrics law, has seen hundreds of lawsuits in the past two years even when there has been no consumer harm.

And, to avoid unnecessary litigation, businesses should have a reasonable period to address a violation without penalty in cases with no demonstrable consumer harm, such as a sixty-day notice- and-cure period.

Fourth, Congress should set a goal of repealing and replacing potentially duplicative or contradictory Federal privacy laws. The U.S. Code right now is littered with privacy statutes, from major sections on health and financial data to narrow ones on video rental histories, and each one has its own set of definitions and rules to comply with.

Finally, Federal data privacy legislation should minimize the impact on innovation. To that end, Congress should not include data-minimization, purpose-specification, or privacy-by-design requirements because these provisions can reduce access to data, limit data sharing, and constrain its use, thereby limiting beneficial innovation.

Congress has the benefit of hindsight to avoid some of the problems found in other data privacy laws, particularly Europe's GDPR, or General Data Protection Regulation. The GDPR has imposed massive compliance costs on businesses, not only in the EU, but around the world. For example, Fortune 500 companies have spent nearly $8 billion to comply with the GDPR.

Unfortunately, the GDPR has not delivered on many of its goals. For example, the EU's own surveys show that the law has had virtually no impact on consumer trust in the internet. A majority of companies also report that some of the most expensive requirements, like appointing a data protection officer, serve no valuable business function.

Policymakers should also be aware of the unintended consequences of poorly crafted legislation, such as not considering the implications of a law on emerging technologies like artificial intelligence and blockchain.

Finally, Congress should note that the primary purpose of the GDPR was to harmonize data protection laws across EU member states. Ironically, as States pursue their own laws, they are creating the exact type of fragmentation in the U.S. that the EU created the GDPR to solve.

So, therefore, it is essential for Congress to act swiftly to pass comprehensive privacy legislation that preempts State laws, streamlines regulation, establishes basic consumer data rights, and minimizes the impact on innovation.

Again, thank you for the opportunity to be here today. I look forward to any questions.

[The statement of Mr. Castro follows:]

Testimony of Daniel Castro Vice President Information Technology and Innovation Foundation Before the Committee on House Administration

Hearing on "Big Data: Privacy Risks and Needed Reforms in the Public and Private Sectors"

February 16, 2022
1310 Longworth House Office Building Washington, DC

Chairperson Lofgren, Ranking Member Davis, and members of the committee, thank you for the opportunity to appear before you to discuss privacy risks and potential reforms.

I am the vice president of the Information Technology and Innovation Foundation (ITIF). ITIF is a nonprofit, nonpartisan think tank whose mission is to formulate and promote public policies to advance technological innovation and productivity. I am also the director of the Center for Data Innovation, a research institute at ITIF focusing on the intersection of data, technology, and public policy.

In my testimony today, I would like to provide an overview of why Congress should pass data-privacy legislation, what that legislation should look like, and how the United States can avoid the mistakes made in the EU's General Data Protection Regulation (GDPR) and other data-privacy laws.

Why Congress Should Pass Data-Privacy Legislation

U.S. data privacy is at a crossroads. Many consumers are justifiably frustrated by the frequency with which they learn about new data breaches and the seeming lack of accountability for those who misuse personal information. At the same time, many businesses are overwhelmed by the tsunami of new data-protection obligations they face and the growing restrictions on how they can use personal information. And all are confused by the multitude of ever-changing laws and regulations.

These conditions have created a groundswell of support for new data-protection laws. Over the past few years, federal and state lawmakers have proposed various privacy laws to regulate the collection and use of personal data. Three states—California, Virginia, and Colorado—have passed comprehensive data-privacy legislation that gives consumers in those states new rights regarding the collection of their personal information and imposes new obligations on businesses. Many other states have considered enacting similar privacy laws.

Between 2018 and 2021, 34 state legislatures have introduced a total of 72 bills, which have advanced to various stages of the legislative process.

These new state privacy laws can create confusion for consumers and impose significant costs on businesses— both direct compliance costs and decreases in productivity—and undermine their ability to responsibly use data to innovate and deliver value to consumers. Moreover, these laws create high costs not just for in-state businesses, but also for out-of-state businesses that can find themselves subject to multiple and duplicative rules. For example, California's recently enacted privacy law will likely cost $78 billion annually, with California's economy bearing $46 billion and the rest of the U.S. economy bearing the other $32 billion.

California small businesses will bear $9 billion of in-state costs, while out-of-state small businesses face $6 billion of costs.[114]

---

[114] Daniel Castro, Luke Dascoli, and Gillian Diebold, "The Looming Cost of a Patchwork of State Privacy Laws," (Information Technology and Innovation Foundation, January 2022), https://itif.org/publications/2022/01/24/looming-cost-patchwork-state-privacy-laws.

In the absence of federal data-privacy legislation, the growing patchwork of state privacy laws could impose out-of-state costs between $98 billion and $112 billion annually.[115] Over a 10-year period, these costs would exceed $1 trillion. The burden on small businesses would be substantial, with U.S. small businesses bearing $20 billion to $23 billion annually.[116]

What Federal Data-Privacy Legislation Should Accomplish

Although the United States needs a federal data privacy law, it should not back away from the light-touch approach it has historically taken to regulating the digital economy. Instead of pursuing a broad, European- style data-privacy law that would impose significant costs on the U.S. economy, Congress should craft targeted legislation that creates a national privacy framework that establishes basic consumer data rights, preempts state laws, ensures reliable enforcement, streamlines regulation, and minimizes the impact on innovation. Such legislation should address concrete privacy harms, not hypothetical ones, and improve transparency so consumers better understand how businesses use their data. It should strengthen oversight and enforcement through the FTC and avoid unnecessary litigation costs by not including a private right of action. It should also protect and promote innovation by minimizing compliance costs and restrictions on data use, such as by avoiding data minimization and purpose specification requirements.

First, federal data privacy legislation should establish basic consumer data rights. Lawmakers should not treat all data the same, but instead create rules that are tailored for different types of data and the contexts in which they are collected. To that end, privacy legislation should make a distinction between sensitive and non-sensitive personal data, because sensitive personal data— such as medical or location information— presents higher risk to people if it is made public.

The idea is to create a sliding scale where the most sensitive personal data collected in the most sensitive contexts (e.g., a doctor's office collecting a patient's health data) is subject to the strictest rules and penalties to prevent misuse, and non-sensitive data collected in a non-sensitive context (e.g., a grocery store tracking what kind of cereal shoppers buy) would be subject to the fewest requirements. With a tiered set of rules like this, consumers would

[115] Ibid.
[116] Ibid.

receive stronger privacy protections where it matters most, and businesses could avoid undue compliance burdens.

Congress should give individuals the right to know how organizations collect and use any of their personal data or when their information has been part of a data breach, but consider limiting other rights, such as the right to access, port, delete, or rectify their data, to only sensitive data in certain contexts. For example, consumers should have a right to obtain a copy of their health or financial data and move it to a competing service.[117] Similarly, Congress should establish user consent requirements for data collection, sharing, and use based on a similar sliding scale. For example, health apps should need to obtain permission from consumers before sharing their sensitive health information with third-party researchers, but florists should be able to send their loyal customers a coupon unless they opt out.

Second, lawmakers should establish uniform privacy rules for the entire nation by preempting state and local privacy laws. Consumers should have the same protections regardless of where they live, and companies should not be faced with 50 different sets of laws and regulations. A patchwork of state laws with varying definitions and standards creates a complex regulatory minefield for businesses to navigate, especially if potential violations risk costly litigation. The goal of Congress should be to minimize unnecessary compliance costs for businesses so that they can concentrate their resources not on hiring more privacy lawyers to protect them from potential fines for non-compliance but on investments that will lead to more secure and privacy-preserving products and services.

Third, Congress should ensure there is robust and reliable enforcement of federal privacy law. Congress should give the Federal Trade Commission (FTC) sufficient resources and authority to fine organizations that impose actual harms on individuals through data misuse. Congress should also give the FTC authority to conduct limited rulemakings for data privacy for issues like deciding the right way for companies to disclose their data handling practices. However, the legislation should be very specific in how the FTC can exercise its authority to ensure regulators do not impose heavy-handed rules about the design of user experiences for websites and mobile apps (i.e., "dark patterns").

Enforcement is important because it enables regulators to have oversight over organizations while ensuring they are held accountable when they do not

[117] Daniel Castro, "Improving Consumer Welfare with Data Portability," (Center for Data Innovation, November 2021), https://www2.datainnovation.org/2021-data-portability.pdf.

follow the rules. However, Congress should be careful not to create duplicative or inconsistent enforcement mechanisms that would impose high costs for organizations. Indeed, if both regulators and private parties can pursue cases for identical reasons, firms can be tied up in lawsuits for years and pay hefty fees for each incident. To that end, Congress should not allow a private right of action, and instead rely on federal and state regulators to hold organizations accountable. In addition, organizations should only be subject to significant fines if they have caused actual economic harm. And to avoid unnecessary litigation, federal privacy legislation should allow for a reasonable period of time for organizations to address a violation without penalty in cases with no demonstrable consumer harm (e.g., establish a 60-day notice and cure period).

Fourth, Congress should set a goal of repealing and replacing potentially duplicative or contradictory federal privacy laws. The U.S. code is littered with privacy statutes—from major sections on health and financial data to narrow ones on video rental histories—and each one has its own set of definitions and rules to comply with.[118] Congress should create a roadmap to repeal and replace all of them with a single, comprehensive data privacy law. Such a major overhaul may sound daunting, but the alternative—adding another layer to the pile—will undermine the purpose of new legislation.

Finally, federal data privacy legislation should minimize the impact on innovation. To that end, Congress should not include data-minimization requirements, purpose-specification requirements, or privacy-by-design requirements because these provisions can reduce access to data, limit data sharing, and constrain its use, thereby limiting innovation. For example, purpose-specification requirements obligate organizations to disclose to users the purposes for which they are collecting information and then not use this collected data for any other reasons. This requirement limits organizations from reusing data for new purposes, which limits innovation. Purpose-specification requirements also limit organizations that may already be collecting useful data from extracting value from that information, such as by applying data analytics. Neither should Congress impose limitations on data retention or automated decision-making, as these provisions would similarly restrict organizations from efficiently using data.

---

[118] For example, the Health Insurance Portability and Accountability Act (HIPAA), the Gramm-Leach-Bliley Act (GLBA), and the Family Educational Rights and Privacy Act (FERPA) apply to data in the health, financial, and educational sectors, respectively.

How to Avoid the Mistakes of the GDPR and Other Privacy Laws

Consumers and businesses would clearly benefit from a federal data-privacy law, but imposing a European- style law on American businesses recovering from a global pandemic would slow economic recovery by saddling companies with unnecessary red tape while limiting beneficial uses of data. Indeed, Congress can benefit from hindsight by looking back at some of the negative consequences of GDPR, which went into effect in May 2018, and other privacy laws.

Avoid Excessive Compliance Costs

Congress should avoid enacting a privacy law that imposes excessive compliance costs. The GDPR has imposed massive compliance costs on businesses, not only in the EU but around the world. The Global Fortune 500 has spent an estimated €7 billion in compliance costs for GDPR.[119] In one survey, over 40 percent of companies, including U.S. firms with a data presence in the EU, had spent $10.1 million in compliance efforts.[120] In another, companies reported spending an average of $1.3 million in 2017 on GDPR compliance and were expected to spend an additional $1.8 million in 2018.[121]

Understand That More Regulation Does Not Always Benefit Consumers

Although some tout the GDPR as the gold standard for consumer protection, it has not always lived up to its reputation. For example, the law has had virtually no impact on consumer trust in the digital economy: Six months after it went into effect, consumer trust in the Internet was at its lowest in a decade

---

[119] Forbes, "The GDPR Racket: Who's Making Money From This $9bn Business Shakedown" (May 2, 2018), https://www.forbes.com/sites/oliversmith/2018/05/02/the-gdpr-racket-whos-making-money-from-this-9bn-business- shakedown/#38765ac234a2.

[120] PriceWaterhouseCoopers, "Pulse Survey: GDPR budgets top $10 million for 40% of surveyed companies" (December 9, 2017), https://www.pwc.com/us/en/services/consulting/library/general-data-protection-regulation-gdpr-budgets.html.

[121] IAPP and Ernst & Young, "Annual Governance Report 2018" (IAPP and Ernst & Young, 2018), https://iapp.org/resources/article/iapp-ey-annual-governance-report-2018/.

in the EU.[122] A year after the law went into effect, nearly two-thirds of Europeans (63 percent) had never heard of the GDPR (31 percent) or did not know exactly what it is (32 percent).[123] The European Commission has found that "at a country level there is no consistent relationship between awareness of GDPR and the level of control respondents feel they have over the personal information they post online."[124] Moreover, many of these costs appear to do nothing to enhance consumer privacy. According to an October 2018 survey, a majority of companies that have appointed a data protection officer (52 percent) say they established one for compliance reasons only, and that the role does not serve a valuable business function.[125]

Ensure Sufficient Resources for Regulators

Congress should ensure regulators have sufficient resources to handle any new obligations. The GDPR caught many regulators flat-footed. For example, the UK's Information Commissioner's Office (ICO) said its staff and services were overwhelmed by companies "over-reporting" potential data breaches because of concerns over high penalties if they failed to notify the data protection authority (DPA) within the GDPR's tight 72- hour reporting deadlines.[126] Similarly, a spokesman of CNIL, the French DPA, declared that "the resources of the CNIL are insufficient" to enforce the GDPR.[127]

---

[122] Daniel Castro and Eline Chivot, "The GDPR Was Supposed to Boost Consumer Trust. Has it Succeeded?" European Views, June 6, 2019, https://www.european-views.com/2019/06/the-gdpr-was-supposed-to-boost-consumer-trust-has-it- succeeded/.

[123] European Commission, "Special Eurobarometer 487a, The General Data Protection Regulation" (June 2019), http://ec.europa.eu/commfrontoffice/publicopinion/index.cfm/survey/getsurveydetail/instruments/special/surveyky/2222.

[124] Ibid.

[125] IAPP and Ernst & Young, "Annual Governance Report 2018" (IAPP and Ernst & Young, 2018), https://iapp.org/resources/article/iapp-ey-annual-governance-report-2018/.

[126] Information Commissioner's Office, "CBI Cyber Security: Business Insight Conference. ICO Deputy Commissioner (Operations) James Dipple-Johnstone – speech to the CBI Cyber Security: Business Insight Conference" (ICO, September 12, 2018), https://ico.org.uk/about-the-ico/news-and-events/news-and-blogs/2018/09/cbi-cyber-security-business-insight-conference/.

[127] Wall Street Journal, "European Privacy Regulators Find Their Workload Expands Along With Authority" (April 12, 2019), https://www.wsj.com/articles/european-privacy-regulators-find-their-workload-expands-along-with-authority-11555061402.

Beware of Unintended Consequences

Perhaps the most important lesson for policymakers from the GDPR is to beware of the unintended consequences of poorly crafted data-privacy legislation. For example, because the drafters of the GDPR never fully considered the implications of the law on emerging technologies like artificial intelligence and blockchain, they included a number of provisions that make it difficult, and sometimes virtually impossible, for businesses to use them.[128]

Some of the most significant unintended consequences are economic. For example, the GDPR has negatively impacted venture funding for EU tech firms. Between May 2018 and April 2019, the overall venture funding for EU tech firms decreased by $14.1 million per month per member state.[129] The decrease in investments for young ventures caused by the GDPR could result in a yearly loss of up to approximately 30,000 jobs in the EU.[130] Or consider that 55 percent of the 539 mergers and acquisitions (M&A) professionals from Europe, Africa, and the Middle East surveyed in July 2018 declared having worked on transactions that did not go through due to concerns about companies' compliance with the GDPR.[131]

Some of these unintended consequences are also felt directly by consumers. Two months after the GDPR went into effect, a third of the largest U.S. news websites had to block access to the EU as they had not yet managed to comply.[132] Almost a year later, in March 2019, 1,129 U.S. news websites still remain blocked, including Pulitzer prize-winning publishers like the Chicago Tribune.[133] Companies have also interrupted some of their online services in the EU because of concerns over complying with the GDPR,

---

[128] Eline Chivot and Daniel Castro, "The EU Needs to Reform the GDPR To Remain Competitive in the Algorithmic Economy," Center for Data Innovation, May 13, 2019, https://datainnovation.org/2019/05/the-eu-needs-to-reform-the-gdpr-to-remain-compe titive-in-the-algorithmic-economy/.

[129] Jian Jia, Ginger Zhe Jin, and Liad Wagman, "The Short-Run Effects of GDPR on Technology Venture Investment" (May 31, 2019), http://dx.doi.org/10.2139/ssrn.3278912.

[130] Jian Jia, Ginger Zhe Jin, and Liad Wagman, "The short-run effects of GDPR on technology venture investment" (VOX CEPR Policy Portal, January 7, 2019), https://voxeu.org/article/ short-run-effects-gdpr-technology-venture- investment.

[131] Merrill Corporation, "GDPR Burdens Hinder M&A Transactions in the EMEA Region, According to Merrill Corporation Survey" (Merrill Corporation, November 13, 2018), https://www.merrillcorp.com/us/en/company/news/press-releases/gdpr-burdens-hinder-m-a-transactions-in-the-emea- region.html.

[132] NiemanLab, "More than 1,000 U.S. news sites are still unavailable in Europe, two months after GDPR took effect" (August 7, 2018), https://www.niemanlab.org/2018/08/more-than-1000-u-s-news-sites-are-still-unavailable-in-europe- two-months-after-gdpr-took-effect/.

[133] Joseph O'Connor, "Websites not available in the European Union after GDPR" (March 20, 2019), https://data.verifiedjoseph.com/dataset/websites-not-available-eu-gdpr.

including Czech platform Seznam, which had to shut down its student social network, and online gaming company Gravity Interactive, which blocked European users from accessing its games and services.[134]

Policymakers should also consider how individuals might misuse new privacy laws. For example, one of Finland's highest courts ruled in August 2018 that the GDPR's "right to be forgotten" could give a convicted murderer the right to have publicly available information about his crime removed from Google search listings, superseding the country's and the EU's own laws protecting freedom of speech and the right to access information.[135] Online tools have also been created to weaponize the GDPR against companies, such as overloading businesses with GDPR-authorized data requests that must be addressed within 30 days with the stated purpose to "waste their time."[136]

The COVID-19 pandemic also offered a lesson on the unintended consequences of the GDPR. At the beginning of the pandemic, Italy, one of the countries in Europe hit hardest by COVID-19, found that the GDPR prevented businesses from taking basic steps to track and trace potential infections, such as employers recording body temperatures to ensure compliance with safety protocols for essential workers. Similarly, the French data regulators noted that the GDPR prevented employers from using thermal cameras to automatically check temperatures of their workers.[137]

As the pandemic progressed, it became clear that the GDPR had also become a barrier to biomedical research—the very research necessary to save lives and reopen the economy. The GDPR creates significant challenges for research organizations in the EU sharing data with researchers located in most countries outside the EU. Indeed, a team of researchers from the United States, Canada, and the EU published an article in Science arguing that "the GDPR's limitation on data transfers will hamper science globally in general and biomedical science in particular."[138]

---

[134] CNN Business, "These companies are getting killed by GDPR" (May 11, 2018), https://money.cnn.com/2018/05/11/technology/gdpr-tech-companies-losers/index.html.

[135] Center for Data Innovation, "The EU's Right to Be Forgotten Is Now Being Used to Protect Murderers" (September 21, 2018), https://www.datainnovation.org/2018/09/the-eus-right-to-be-forgotten-is-now-being-used-to-protect- murderers/.

[136] Ship Your Enemies GDPR, "Ship Your Enemies GDPR," (n.d.) https://shipyourenemies gdpr.com/.

[137] Daniel Castro, "The Pandemic Reveals Some of the Noxious Side Effects of the GDPR," April 14, 2021, Center for Data Innovation, https://datainnovation.org/2021/04/the-pandemic-reveals-some-of-the-noxious-side-effects-of-the- gdpr/.

[138] Jasper Bovenberg et al., "How to Fix the GDPR's Frustration of Global Biomedical Research," *Science*, October 2, 2020, Vol. 370, No. 6512, pp. 40-42, https://www.science.org/doi/abs/10.1126/science.abd2499.

Prevent Costly Lawsuits

In addition to the GDPR, Congress can learn from some of the state privacy laws. In particular, the Illinois Biometric Information Privacy Act (BIPA) demonstrates the risk of costly litigation when privacy laws create a privacy right of action. BIPA was designed to regulate the collection of biometric data by companies operating in Illinois or whose products reached consumers in that state. Although BIPA passed into law in 2008, it was not until 2019 that the Illinois Supreme Court held that individuals are not required to show actual harm to bring consumer class action lawsuits and employer lawsuits. This ruling means that individuals can file lawsuits even when there has only been a technical violation of the law.[139] Since then, the number of BIPA lawsuits has skyrocketed—In 2019, there were around 300 lawsuits, and the number of cases referencing BIPA doubled in 2020.

California offers another example of this dynamic. The California Consumer Privacy Act of 2018 (CCPA) applies to firms that do business in California, including those without a physical presence. The law allows consumers to seek damages when their personal information is inappropriately accessed or disclosed because a business failed to maintain reasonable security procedures. Since California enacted the law in 2020, plaintiffs have filed approximately 195 lawsuits against businesses in many different industries.[140]

Lawsuits can lead to major settlements, thereby threatening the viability of smaller businesses and imposing steep costs on larger ones. Even if a business can prevail in a lawsuit, the costs of the lawsuit are often significant, especially in state courts that are often more favorable for plaintiffs in class action litigation compared with federal courts and allow for expensive discovery processes, such as requesting documents and witness interviews, that can drive up the costs of litigation very quickly.

Conclusion

It is essential for Congress to craft well-designed federal data privacy legislation. Poorly designed data privacy laws can impose a substantial toll on the economy through both direct compliance costs and indirect costs from

---

[139] "The BIPA Litigation Landscape and What Lies Ahead," Woodruff Sawyer, April 1, 2021, https://woodruffsawyer.com/cyber-liability/bipa-litigation-landscape/.

[140] "CCPA Litigation Tracker, Updated as of December 2021," Perkin Coie, n.d., https://www.perkinscoie.com/en/ccpa-litigation-tracker.html (access February 14, 2022).

lower productivity and constraints on innovation. Unnecessarily restrictive rules for the digital economy reduce innovation in ways that harm both businesses and consumers. By raising compliance costs, increasing legal risks, and reducing the effectiveness of online business models, poorly drafted rules can lead to a reduction in the supply of, and demand for, digital services.

It is equally important for Congress to proceed swiftly with new data privacy legislation. In the absence of a new law, states will continue to enact their own competing, and potentially contradictory, data privacy laws. One of the primary purposes of the GDPR was to harmonize data protection laws across EU member states, and ironically, by pushing for new laws modeled after the GDPR, state legislatures are creating the exact type of fragmentation in the United States that the EU created the GDPR to solve.

To avoid conflicting laws and unnecessary costs, Congress should act swiftly to pass comprehensive privacy legislation that preempts state laws, streamlines regulation, establishes basic consumer data rights, and minimizes the impact on innovation (e.g., by avoiding requirements for data minimization, universal opt-in, purpose specification, limitations on data retention, or privacy-by-design). This legislation should not include a private right of action and instead rely on federal and state regulators for enforcement. Establishing a comprehensive federal privacy law would also simplify compliance for businesses, especially small businesses working across multiple U.S. jurisdictions, as well as help consumers better understand their privacy rights and avoid the confusion resulting from a patchwork of state laws.

Thank you again for this opportunity to appear before you today.

The CHAIRPERSON. Thank you very much, Mr. Castro, and to all our witnesses.

We will go now to Members of the Committee who may have questions, and I will turn first now to our Ranking Member, Mr. Davis.

Mr. DAVIS. Thank you, Madam Chairperson.

And thanks again to our witnesses. Enjoyed your testimony. Mr. Castro, let me start with you.

There have been proposals introduced in Congress that if implemented would create a private right of action for individuals and a collective right of action for certain nonprofits to sue on behalf of individuals. Is this the best approach to ensure protection and accountability for a Federal data privacy framework?

Mr. CASTRO. No, I don't think it is. Right now, we have a very effective regulator in the FTC and we have State attorney generals that can obviously also take up that slack.

What we have seen in States that have implemented these private rights of action, like with the Biometrics Information Privacy Act, once a court ruled that you could bring lawsuits under this for cases where there is no actual harm to consumers, we saw a flood of lawsuits. And these lawsuits are being driven by class action lawsuits where they are just going after the attorney fees, and this has led to very significant fines without any real payoff for consumers.

So, in the past year we have seen over $100 million in settlements for companies like Facebook, ADP, Walmart, Six Flags, Wendy's, TikTok, and the list goes on. And these aren't instances, again, where we have seen any consumer harm. It was pure technical violations.

That is not an effective use of dollars that could be going back into investing in technology and processes that would protect consumers' privacy, make it more secure, and protect them from harm.

So, a private right of action, to me, is just taking money out that could be used on actual protections for consumers.

Mr. DAVIS. Well, thank you, Mr. Castro.

Hey, I am sure you have read the media reports about Special Counsel John Durham's allegations that Democrat political attorneys perhaps, Marc Elias specifically, infiltrated servers at The Trump Organization and at the White House.

Would nationwide data privacy legislation have protected President Trump from these data espionage attempts?

Mr. CASTRO. Well, it depends. Certainly, privacy legislation would restrict what companies might be able to keep on hand and what they might share.

But at the end of day, what you really want to see if you want better security is better transparency, so consumers know what they are getting. In this case, The Trump Organization, the Trump campaign, would know what kind of security and privacy controls they are getting when they purchase a service, and they will know how their data could be shared.

And so, getting more transparency is really what we should be looking for in the future.

Mr. DAVIS. Well, I agree, transparency matters. But so do penalties for bad actors if these allegations are borne out.

Do you know if the FTC would have any enforcement penalties if these allegations were borne out?

Mr. CASTRO. The FTC can impose penalties on companies for violations. Particularly the way this works right now is most companies have statements in their privacy policies, their terms of service, that say, we respect your privacy, and we are going to secure your data. And when they do not do that, that is a misrepresentation, and the FTC can and has gone after companies for that.

We can certainly consider giving the FTC more authority. Certainly, if we are increasing their budget, I think we should be saying exactly what we want them to be doing with that additional money. I think that is the best way to go forward.

What we don't want to do, I think, is give the FTC too much latitude, though, to start doing its own rulemaking that goes outside of congressional intent, because it becomes very risky, that the FTC might decide that they want to start deciding how companies should design their websites or how they should be designing their mobile apps, all under the name of maybe ensuring consumers aren't being manipulated. But on the other hand, the FTC is not made up of engineers and user experience designers.

Mr. DAVIS. Very good points. But this agency does exist to address concerns already.

The Online Privacy Act of 2021, a bill referred secondarily to this Committee, calls for the creation of a new Federal agency called the Digital Privacy Agency.

Not only is this a clear example of Congress shifting its legislative authority to the executive branch, but it also seems like an extreme waste of resources given the existing structure already established in the Federal Trade Commission and with the States' attorneys general.

Mr. Castro, do you believe that a new Federal agency is necessary to accomplish the goal of data privacy?

Mr. CASTRO. I think the FTC has the authority it needs and the reputation and experience to do this job. I don't think we need a new agency to solve that problem.

I would also mention that when we think about protecting consumer privacy, this overlaps with fraud and security, and that is something the FTC is also focused on or should be focused on. And I think if we split up that mission, we weaken protection for consumers.

Mr. DAVIS. Well, Mr. Castro, thanks for joining us, and to all the witnesses.

I yield back the balance of my time, Madam Chairperson.

The CHAIRPERSON. Thank you.

Mr. Raskin, you are now recognized five minutes.

Mr. RASKIN. Thank you, Madam Chairperson.

Ms. Fitzgerald, I was eager to ask you the question about the aggregation of data, about how the aggregation and processing of data in large quantities can pose risks that might not be apparent when we are just talking about a single piece of discrete information. I am wondering what can be done about that.

Ms. FITZGERALD. Thank you, Representative Raskin.

I think the lesson we can take from all these data points being combined about us is, one, it shows how important it is to have a comprehensive privacy law that covers personal data generally rather than the sectoral laws—HIPPA, FCRA, COPPA, FERPA, the acronyms go on and on—that leave huge gaps in protection for personal data not covered by those laws.

And these flows of personal data also show why notice and consent doesn't work. The breadth of the commercial surveillance industry is just impossible for the vast majority of internet users to fully grasp. A user may consent to have the website they are visiting use their data, but does that mean they are consenting to that data being passed on to hundreds of data brokers they have never heard of?

We saw an example of this last summer when a Catholic priest was outed by a news outlet who obtained supposedly anonymized location data from the dating app Grindr. I know that following that revelation you and Rep. Porter sent a letter to the FTC and FCC, signed by a few members of this Committee, asking them to conduct a rulemaking to strengthen privacy protections for location data. And that is something that could also be integrated into privacy legislation.

Mr. RASKIN. Thank you much.

Ms. Zuboff, I have read your book about surveillance capitalism. I know it is hard to synthesize an entire book, but who is Big Brother today? Is Big Brother the state as we have traditionally conceived it, or is Big Brother corporate—the corporate sector, or is it some combination thereof?

Ms. ZUBOFF. Well, thank you so much, Representative Raskin. I am flattered and thrilled to hear that you have read my book. So, thank you for that as well.

As you know, because you have read the book, I develop a concept that I call Big Other. So Big Brother was a notion of a totalitarian state, which had a very specific ideology and wanted people to believe certain things and talk in certain ways and act in certain ways.

We have surveillance capitalism, not a totalitarian state. Surveillance capitalism really doesn't care what you think. It doesn't care what you believe. It doesn't care how you act.

What it does care about is that you think and believe and act in ways that it can capture the data to do the aggregation that you are asking about, because with that aggregation is the possibility of computation, applying artificial intelligence, coming up with predictive algorithms, targeting methodologies.

With those targeting methodologies, various functions are achieved, including increasing engagement, which is a euphemism for increasing the footprint for greater data extraction.

And also, as we increase engagement, using our knowledge from this deep computation, AI, using our knowledge about you for things like subliminal cues, psychological microtargeting, engineered social comparison dynamics, so we really, really know a lot about you.

And that way we can use messaging and different—not only the content of messaging, but the forms of messaging, to actually begin to modify your behavior, and to do that in a way that is consistent with the commercial objectives of the company and its business customers.

So, at the end of the day, this Big Other is a—sorry. I will just wrap it up with the notion that this Big Other is ubiquitous, is pervasive, it is not totalitarian, but it is full-on control, and full-on opacity, full-on power.

Mr. RASKIN. We haven't yet enacted a comprehensive Federal privacy statute to address the rise of the Big Other. But a lot of States and some other countries have attempted to do so.

I wonder if you can just tell us what you think have been the best lessons and the best efforts at a comprehensive privacy framework to protect us individually, but also to protect the people's possession of interest and ownership of their own characteristics and their own behavior.

Ms. ZUBOFF. Well, the gold standard right now, and we couldn't have said this a few weeks ago, but the Digital Services Act and the Digital Markets Act in the EU. These are not the total solution. We have very specific things to accomplish ahead of us.

As far as setting a new standard, defining a new frontier for the kinds of rights—when I use the word "users," I try to do it with air quotes, because users is all of us. Users is kind of the synonym for humanity at this point.

And these pieces of legislation, they are ambitious, they are comprehensive, they have the buy-in of the European Parliament now and the member states. A few details left to be worked out in the spring.

But these set a new standard for rights of users, the enforcement powers of a government to really for the first time put democratic governance back in control of our information and communication spaces, to work with the private sector, rather than have the private sector as what it has been for the past two decades, a completely autonomous force, essentially unimpeded by relevant law.

And all the social harms that we have been describing this afternoon are the result of that situation.

The CHAIRPERSON. Thank you so much. And the gentleman's time has expired.

We will turn now to the gentleman from Georgia, Mr. Loudermilk for five minutes.

Mr. LOUDERMILK. Well, thank you, Madam Chairperson.

And it is a very interesting topic that we are talking about, I have been dealing with for quite some time.

Mr. Castro, one of the issues that I have seen from a financial services perspective, and I assume it is going to be the same here, is the multitude of data privacy standards and laws we have across the country in the different States.

You mentioned in your testimony that there were 34 State legislatures that introduced bills in the space from 2018 to 2021. I want to get your thoughts on the importance of having a uniform Federal standard for data privacy that would go across the board.

Mr. CASTRO. Yes. I really appreciate that question. Thank you so much, Representative Loudermilk.

For I think so many companies, especially the smaller companies, when you think about data privacy, we are often—I think the first thing people think about are Facebook and Google.

But these laws impact everyone. They impact the local florist, the barber shop, the grocery stores. And complying with those laws can be very expensive and very difficult, because even though at the end of the day most of these laws are basically saying the same thing, they say it all a little differently.

And actually, complying with those laws so that you are not held in violation, so that, especially if there is a private right of action, so that you are not sued for making technical violation if you have not, for example, put a certain term up on your privacy policy on your website, you might be in violation of California's law.

All these obligations add costs for businesses. And these businesses, instead of hiring another engineer or giving a raise to their workers, they must go out and hire a privacy lawyer. A lot of the privacy lawyers really like privacy laws because it is good business for them.

And the issue here is we don't need more laws, we need one good law. I am glad to see we are having this conversation, because I think we can get to that one good law. Hopefully we can get there sooner rather than later, because the more we wait the higher those costs get.

Mr. LOUDERMILK. So, what kind of effect does this have on American competitiveness in the international marketplace?

Mr. CASTRO. It is very significant right now. When we think about—a lot of U.S. companies are doing a very good job with protecting privacy better than, for example, companies in China. But because the U.S. does not have a Federal law and we have taken a sectoral approach and other countries have not taken that sectoral approach, a lot of countries will say the U.S. doesn't care about privacy.

I don't think that is true. I don't think that is true in terms of when I hear the FTC defending the work that they are doing. I think they are doing very respectable work. I think the State attorney generals are doing great work. I think some of the State laws can even be effective.

And so, I don't think it is fair to say the U.S. isn't doing good work on privacy. But we don't have a national privacy law. And so, so often that fact is used to say a U.S. company should not get a particular contract.

We are seeing that used right now. That is hurting transatlantic data flows in part because European lawmakers are saying the U.S. isn't doing enough to protect consumer privacy.

So, I think one of the best ways we can promote U.S. competitiveness, again not just from the tech sector but across the board, is to create this Federal law so that we can show the U.S. is taking this seriously.

Mr. LOUDERMILK. I think everybody on this Committee is committed to and I think most individuals recognize the importance of protecting personal data and an individual's privacy. Definitely, I do as well, and I know you do.

But with that being said, you mentioned in your testimony a concern that I share as well, which is the compliance cost to small businesses due to State privacy laws.

Is there a State that you can point to that has successfully executed a data privacy law that balances those concerns?

Mr. CASTRO. I think Virginia is probably the closest we have gotten so far. They are trying to strike the right balance.

Again, the biggest problem is that when you see these State laws, the State legislatures are not thinking about the costs that would be borne by States outside their borders.

And so, again and again, as we see each new State go down this path, they are putting up laws that force companies to go rehire lawyers, to ask them to reevaluate their privacy policies, make technical changes to their systems, all the same compliance, again, without any discernible improvement in actual consumer privacy. And so, if the goal is consumer privacy, let's address this top down rather than have fifty different rules for how to do it and have so much more consumer confusion about what is going on and who is protecting your data.

Mr. LOUDERMILK. All right. I agree wholly.

I see my time is quickly running out. So, thank you for that. And, Madam Chairperson, I yield back.

The CHAIRPERSON. The gentleman yields back. Mr. Aguilar is recognized for five minutes.

Mr. AGUILAR. Thank you, Madam Chairperson.

Mr. Erwin, I wanted to talk with you a little bit about the lessons that Mozilla has learned from its own experience in building privacy-protective tools. That may be relevant to us here in the public sector and for government agencies that we have oversight over to consider how they are going to handle personal information and to minimize risk for their own operations.

What are your thoughts on what you have learned and what is applicable to the public space?

Mr. ERWIN. Yes. So, I think there are two important ways that we approach this question.

The first is to think about, like, our core privacy practices and the data that we are going to collect from our consumers and how we are going to be really transparent and provide them with control of that.

We really work hard to sort of follow these what typically is referred to as data-minimization practices where we are really only collecting what we need to run our business and optimize and build a great product for our users.

And that is a practice that, frankly, isn't followed very expansively across our industry with the underlying problems that I think that we see and really think needs to be fixed.

And then once we have that data, we will work to protect it aggressively, which is I think basic applicability of this idea of data minimization, and plus sort of a strong set of security controls on the back end is one that really needs to apply both to the public and the private sector.

We also work hard to build kind of what I mentioned earlier, these privacy features into the browser that protect our users from web encryption, blocking, tracking in the browser.

The interesting thing that—experience we have there is, like, that can be a little bit disruptive for the industry in a way that, like, right now we have a permissive internet, many parties that depend on that permissiveness to build their data practices and build their business.

That is fundamentally actually a problem. And so, some amount of disruption is healthy. We don't always get a positive response when we roll out privacy features. I think that is a positive signal that we are going in the right direction. But it certainly creates a little bit of headwind for us when we try to roll out privacy features.

Mr. AGUILAR. Understood. Sometimes being at the forefront means that you take on a lot of folks with differing viewpoints as well.

Ms. Fitzgerald, what are some of the best ways that we can limit the risks and harms of the aggregations of personal information over time from multiple different sources that we know exist?

Ms. FITZGERALD. Thank you, Representative Aguilar.

I think this process of data minimization that has been talked about a few times, especially in the first panel, I was thinking if private companies treated our data like the GPO did, we would be in much better shape. The point was made, if you don't have it, you don't have to protect it.

So, the obligation should be on the companies to minimize the amount of data they are collecting, delete it when they don't need it anymore. That protects users from having their information passed on and it protects them in the case of a data breach.

Mr. AGUILAR. Thanks. I appreciate that.

Mr. Erwin, back again, what are some of the privacy risks and harms that we have that may not have a primarily technological solution? I guess what I am trying to ask is issues that instead require changes to business practices or laws. We are trying to balance the regulatory side here, and I wanted your thoughts on how we balance those pieces.

Mr. ERWIN. Yes. So, we bump up against this problem all the time in our work in the browser where, for example, the challenges that we can solve, a user visits a website, for example, and there is a hidden third party on that website that the user doesn't know about and is collecting data about them.

That is a third-party relationship. We can do something about that in the browser, because typically there is, like, a network request, to get a little bit technical, that calls out to that third party. So we can actually just block that.

So that is typically the role of, like, the browser, or the operating system can jump in and say, we are going to prevent these third parties from sort of tracking your behavior.

What we can't do as much of is when the user has a direct, first-party, what we refer to as a first-party relationship with a website or business. And that comes down to a question of business practices, not technical problems. And there is little we can do to sort of adjudicate the relationship between a user who has decided to engage directly with a first-party business, but that business isn't upstanding, and the user might not know about it.

And that is where I think law and regulation really needs to step in where the technical fixes ultimately aren't going to get us what we need.

Mr. AGUILAR. I appreciate that. Thanks so much. I yield back.

The CHAIRPERSON. The gentleman yields back. Mr. Steil is recognized for five minutes.

Mr. STEIL. Thank you very much, Madam Chairperson.

I want to pick up where my colleague Mr. Aguilar left off a little bit. But I want to shift over to you if I can, Ms. Fitzgerald, on the topic.

I was reading some of your testimony, and you referenced that the biometric and genetic data is especially sensitive, it deserves stricter regulation. Is that correct?

Ms. FITZGERALD. Yes, absolutely.

Mr. STEIL. And you raised some concerns about how healthcare data is used. Is that correct?

Ms. FITZGERALD. Yes. Health data is particularly sensitive.

Mr. STEIL. And so, I think a lot of people think that HIPPA is protecting their healthcare data, as it extends to big tech or health apps, but that is not correct. Would you agree?

Ms. FITZGERALD. Right. HIPPA only applies to the relationship with your doctor and with your health insurance company and with certain health exchanges, it doesn't cover health data that is in apps.

Mr. STEIL. Yes, I think that is a really interesting distinction that I think a lot of Americans might find interesting, and building on what was previously being discussed with Mr. Erwin on these kind of third-party apps, third-party relationships that exist on certain websites and the impact that this could have.

And so Congress recently passed the 21st Century Cures Act to protect patient data, in particular to require patient data to move from the doctor's office to healthcare apps of the patient's choosing. There are a lot of reasons that is a good thing. There are some things that we want to make sure we get right.

Because you want to be able to make sure patients can control their data. But I also want to ensure that they don't lose control of their data by sending it in a third party that they might not be aware of would find interest in their healthcare data, their biometric data, or others.

Do you think the risk is bigger in some of these apps that might send—that individuals, that the risk might be greater if they are sending information to some of these types of apps kind of under the rules and regulations of the 21st Century Cures Act?

Ms. FITZGERALD. The reason biometric data is so sensitive is because we can't change it. We can't change our face print, we can't change our fingerprints.

Mr. STEIL. So, let's shift off for a second. I totally agree. I think that is a great topic.

Let's shift and talk about medical data. Does that give you unique concern?

Ms. FITZGERALD. Yes, sure, because of the ways it can be used against us. You think about the insurance companies using it to determine our rates or even an employer possibly not wanting to hire someone with a health condition if they are going to be paying their health insurance premiums.

Mr. STEIL. I appreciate your commentary. I think it is an area that we need to just really keep an eye on. I think there is a lot of real positive things. We want to make sure innovation is here in the United States. We want patients to control their data.

But at the same time, we want to make sure that patients are protected, and where there might be a third-party player involved where the patient might not fully appreciate the risk that they are engaging in, in sharing their data. I just think it is something that we really should spend time and think about.

Let me shift gears if I can. Thank you very much, Ms. Fitzgerald. Let me shift gears to you, Mr. Castro.

There is a lot of laws that govern privacy for different types of institutions. The Gramm-Leach-Bliley Act Federal law required financial companies to explain their information-sharing practices to their customers and to safeguard some of their data.

And before creating new laws, I think there is a real opportunity for Congress to look at how current privacy laws are working and how they interact with each other so that we are not duplicative of regulations.

And so, could you shine some light, since the passage of GDPR in the EU, what have we seen in that sweeping legislation? Has it stifled innovation? Has it grown innovation? What big takeaway should we take from that, from the EU's work?

Mr. CASTRO. In many areas it certainly has stifled innovation. When you look at the cost of compliance, when you look at the impact it has had on startups in the European tech economy, there are many areas where just the data points again and again show that European businesses are suffering.

The one area——

Mr. STEIL. So let me, Mr. Castro, only because we have got limited time, if we shift gears slightly and we say let's jump over to California.

California Consumer Privacy Act, what lessons can we take away from the State of California if we were to take that and run that out nationally.

Mr. CASTRO. One of the biggest problems with California is we have seen hundreds of lawsuits related to enforcement. That has been a problem.

One of the biggest positives of it is the idea of a thirty-day cure, which I think could be extended nationally, where the goal is not to penalize companies for mistakes, but to get them to take corrective action. That has been——

Mr. STEIL. Thank you very much. Only cognizant of time. I appreciate everybody's time here.

I think what is really important is we have got a lot of laws already on the books, State laws, we can look at the EU, we can look at what financial services committees are doing, we can look at the 21st Century Cures Act. I think it is critical that we are looking at all of these legislations, learning lessons from them, so we can help consumers protect their data, but also maintain innovation here in the United States of America.

I appreciate you holding today's hearing, Madam Chairperson and I will yield back.

The CHAIRPERSON. The gentleman yields back. Ms. Scanlon is recognized for five minutes.

Ms. SCANLON. Thank you, Madam Chairperson.

I guess I would like to pull on this thread a little bit more since we certainly do hear quite a bit about this on the company side and the agency side: How do they navigate all these different laws that are being promulgated between

States, but also between countries, because, as we are aware, the internet does not have national boundaries in the same way?

So, Ms. Fitzgerald, could you talk about that? What are the most important privacy rights that you have seen that have been proposed that you think Congress should work on adopting?

Ms. FITZGERALD. Well, the most important thing, I think, when you are thinking about privacy legislation is we can't just be telling people what companies are collecting about them. That is not enough. We need to put obligations on the companies that are collecting data to limit that collection, limit what they are doing with it after they collect it and have them delete it when they are done using it.

Ms. SCANLON. Okay. In terms—do you have any suggestions about which are the best models for us to look at, whether there is State models, or the EU has been mentioned?

Ms. FITZGERALD. Sure. So, I think State models, you know, California has the strongest right now in the United States. The CCPA in California is the strongest model we have seen. But, that still is even limited, only allows users to opt out of the sale of their personal data. It doesn't as much put obligations on companies to minimize the data they are collecting.

The Online Privacy Act by Chairperson Lofgren is a great model. That includes data minimization. It also includes provisions protecting against discriminatory uses of data. That is really important.

You also want to make sure you are requiring algorithmic fairness and accountability. We don't want to make the same mistakes with AI that we have made with data collection. This is the next wave of technology. Let's get ahead of it, set the rules now, encourage companies to innovate around privacy and autonomy.

Ms. SCANLON. Okay. I mean, one of the typical—I don't know— tools that people talk about with the privacy laws is the notion of consent. I gather that you are a little bit skeptical about the usefulness of consent as a focus of privacy protections.

Can you talk about that a little bit?

Ms. FITZGERALD. Yes. Absolutely. There is just no way for an individual to understand kind of the web that their data gets passed through if they are consenting. You know, if you are just hitting that consent button to make the banner go away on a website——

Ms. SCANLON. Yes.

Ms. FITZGERALD [continuing]. You don't realize that what you are saying is: Sure, take my personal data and do whatever you please with it. There are no rules.

Ms. SCANLON. Right. Well, and certainly we have seen that proliferate recently with—to get access to almost anything, you either decide to click, or you decide not to——

Ms. FITZGERALD. Exactly.

Ms. Scanlon [continuing]. Protect it.

So, with respect to discriminatory data uses, how do we address that? What are your top-line recommendations there?

Ms. FITZGERALD. Well, groups such as Color of Change, Lawyers' Committee for Civil Rights, Leadership Conference have great proposals on what we need to do to make sure that civil rights are protected online, you know, making sure that—I don't know—publicaccommodations are protected; you know, that extends to online spaces.

You need to make sure that the algorithms that companies are using are not being used in ways that deprive people of life opportunities like, you know, ads for housing and ads for jobs, that those are data—our personal data isn't being used to show those in discriminatory ways.

Ms. SCANLON. That is interesting.

Okay. Thank you, Madam Chairperson. I yield back.

The CHAIRPERSON. The gentlelady yields back.

The gentlelady from New Mexico is now recognized for five minutes.

Ms. LEGER FERNA´NDEZ. Thank you so much, Madam Chairperson.

As we have heard today, our personal data is extremely valuable. You know, we take a question, a quiz on Facebook, look up directions. The companies collect our information. They then sell our information, often without our consent, to a third party. And then they use our information—our information—for a range of activities, from showing an ad for clothing, to sometimes more dangerous, like targeting disinformation to manipulate our behaviors or beliefs.

And it is all invisible to the true owners of the data. Me, my neighbors, our fellow Americans, I want to focus a bit on how data privacy or the lack thereof impacts our elections and our democracy. The Elections Subcommittee of this Committee recently held a roundtable in Miami on the creation and dissemination of disinformation about our elections and the pandemic, and this disinformation targets Spanish-speaking communities.

We learned how the disinformation is then exported to other States, including New Mexico, and then amplified based on this data harvesting that we have heard about today and read in this testimony.

Ms. Fitzgerald, you noted that actors can weaponize our data to undermine our election integrity and democratic institutions. In practice, what does this weaponization look like?

Ms. FITZGERALD. Sure. Thank you, Representative Leger Ferna´ndez.

You know, just as advertising companies use profiles about us to manipulate us into purchases, you know, so too can they manipulate our views by filtering the content we see. So, the ways they can do that are—you know, The Markup did a great investigation right after January 6th showing the two different Facebooks that Republicans and Democrats were seeing. And it is just a stark view of kind of the different information that both sides are seeing and how that shapes your views.

Even if someone doesn't click through to an article, just seeing that headline, having it in the back of their head as they are voting, it is—these companies are able to kind of manipulate our political views by determining what we see.

Ms. LEGER FERNA´NDEZ. Professor Zuboff, I really appreciated your poignant written remarks about how democracy is simultaneously the only legitimate authority capable of helping the surveillance capitalism but also a prime target. So, I appreciate that and would welcome you expanding on that, but the question I want to get to first is Mr. Castro suggested that a private right of action is unnecessary and that we should focus solely on transparency.

Do you agree, and, if not, why?

The CHAIRPERSON. You need to unmute, Professor Zuboff.

Ms. ZUBOFF. Sorry.

I don't agree with that. I think the private right of action is very important. When we pass a law, whether it is the California law or any other law, that is only the beginning. What must happen is these laws are tested, and they evolve, and they develop. As a society, we learn what they can mean, what they can mean for us, and how they are going to protect us in society.

So, what the private right of action does is it creates the opportunity not only for individuals, but for groups of people, for collectives to really bring issues into the judicial system, to have those issues explored, and to create precedence.

And this is—you know, this is what is called the life of a law, how the law evolves and how we can move forward into this century, not just with statutes that are frozen in time, but with laws that are evolving according to what Justice Brandeis once called the eternal youth——

Ms. LEGER FERNA´NDEZ. Right.

Ms. ZUBOFF [continuing]. Of the law, because we have these kinds of international processes. So this really is——

Ms. LEGER FERNA´NDEZ. Yes, and I wanted to completely agree.

Our civil rights laws would have had no effect if we hadn't had the right of private action.

I did want to ask you, though, to elaborate in the few seconds left with regards to what you believe is most important to protect our democracy in an Online Privacy Act?

Ms. ZUBOFF. Well, the first thing is you notice so much of our discussion has been we minimize data or how is the data used and things like that. Once we start a discussion talking about data, we have already lost primary ground.

The key thing is now that we are all targets for massive scale secret data collection, much of which should not be collected in the first place. The decision should lie—the decision rights should lie with the individual: Do I want to share this information about the cancer that runs in my family, and do I want to share that with a research operation or a federation of researchers that are going to make progress on this disease and help the world? Maybe so.

But do I want Google or Facebook or any other company to just be inferring information about my cancer from my searching and my browsing? Absolutely not.

So we need to reestablish decision rights, as Justice Douglas offered in 1967, the idea that every individual should have the freedom to select what about their experience is shared and what remains private. These decision rights are the cause of which privacy is the effect.

We need to establish now finally in law juridical rights that give us the choice of what is shared and what remains private. Then we have got a whole new ball game where all kinds of innovations like Mozilla and all of the Mozillas that are waiting to come on stream, not just obviously in search and browse, but in all kinds of businesses, in every sector.

Ms. LEGER FERNA´NDEZ. Thank you.

Ms. ZUBOFF. We are all waiting to get in the game.

Ms. LEGER FERNA´NDEZ. Thank you. I know we have overgone our time limit.

Thank you, Madam Chairperson ——

Ms. ZUBOFF. Thank you.

Ms. LEGER FERNA´NDEZ [continuing]. And I yield back.

The CHAIRPERSON. The gentlelady yields back. I just have a few final questions.

First, thanks to all of the witnesses for really very excellent, interesting, and enlightening testimony.

I wonder, Mr. Erwin, in your testimony, you refer to dark patterns as one of several privacy abuses that demand regulation, that technology alone couldn't adequately address them.

Can you explain in further detail for the Committee and for those watching this hearing what dark patterns are, what are some of the most troubling examples of dark patterns, and what is the best legal approach to reining them in?

Mr. ERWIN. Yes. A dark pattern is a sort of broad umbrella term used to refer to what is typically sort of user experiences that can deceive a user into opting into data collection or consenting to data collection without being explicit about what is really happening under the hood. And that can be—a dark pattern could be sort of text that is intended to deceive the user, or it might be sort of if you have got to click through five things to opt out of the data collection. All of those, I think, are typically—are sometimes referred to as dark patterns.

We see those everywhere across the web. And, as I mentioned, that is the type of area where the browser can't really do much when the user is actively engaging with the first party. It is an area where I think we really do need to see some regulatory engagement.

Obviously, like, we don't want a regulator designing a user experience in the browser. Sort of our user experience team doesn't want me designing the experience in the browser, so we definitely don't want a regulator doing that. But actually, acting to say here is what the standard should be, and here is what looks like a deceptive practice, and here is what is a sound practice; that is where I think we really do need to see a regulatory voice.

The CHAIRPERSON. Standards instead of design?

Mr. ERWIN. Yes.

The CHAIRPERSON. You know, we have talked a lot about the rights of individuals for privacy and, you know, some of the disinformation, digital addiction, harmful impacts on children on certain internet platforms. But I think whether there should be a private right of action.

I think the core issue really, as Mr. Halpern said, if you don't have the data, you can't use it to manipulate. And I think—it is my view that the victims of manipulation, whether it is for political, societal, cultural, or commercial purposes, it is not just the individuals being manipulated but the public at large.

If you are manipulating for a commercial purpose, you are a Big Tech company and you have got all this data, you know, you are at an unfair advantage to smaller companies that have not acquired all that data. If you are manipulating for a cultural or societal purpose to move society in one direction or another, the public is also a victim of that. Individuals have been removed from their agency and have been — and are less free because a private corporation is manipulating them through their own data.

So, let me ask you, Ms. Fitzgerald, isn't really the crux of this to restrain the collection and retention of data?

Ms. FITZGERALD. Yes, absolutely. It is not enough to—for users to just know what companies are collecting about us. It has to be restrained. The obligations have to be on the data collectors to limit what they are collecting.

The CHAIRPERSON. I just want to mention briefly—and maybe any of the witnesses can talk. Ms. Fitzgerald, you may have studied this in your nonprofit. You know, I am a fan of the FTC, but I have been advised by many who served there that the sheer number of individuals who are really technologically savvy is fairly minimal compared to the actual army of digital, you know, engineers, software-savvy people in these large companies, and that, frankly, they are no match for the gigantic companies with the computer and digital expertise that those companies have, which is why we are looking at how do we better arm a regulatory agency to actually be successful in facing off with these gigantic corporations?

Is that capacity of the FTC off base, Ms. Fitzgerald, in your view?

Ms. FITZGERALD. Absolutely. I mean, look, we are encouraged by recent actions at the FTC on privacy, but the FTC has limited resources and an incredibly broad mandate that covers everything from antitrust to horse racing safety, tractor parts, and laundry tags. The task of data protection is best done by a specialized, independent regulator. When you think about the outsized presence of technology in our lives and our economy, I just think this is something where, twemty years down the line, no one will question why we have a data protection agency just as now we don't question why we have an FAA or an EPA.

The CHAIRPERSON. Let me just ask a question of you, Mr. Erwin. In your written testimony, you state, quote, "it is important that competition concerns not be a pretext to prevent better privacy for everyone."

Can you explain that tension and how Congress might strive to strike the right balance on that?

Mr. ERWIN. Yes. I mean, this is something we see often. Again, like the basic challenge we have here right now is the internet was designed in a very permissive way, and that allows for a large diversity of parties to collect data.

In some cases, those are the largest parties, but also the smaller ones. And closing down some of these privacy gaps necessarily means denying data to both the big parties and the small ones. And sometimes we will hear this argument that we shouldn't close the privacy gap because that will have certain competition implications.

We really sort of reject that stream of thinking, the basic idea being that, like, we should leave the internet being more permissive in order to protect some set of business models.

You know, what we want to see is an overall but more protective platform that has an even playing field that all big and small companies can compete on. That is the approach that we, I think, are in favor of. We are going to push back aggressively on any suggestion that we should leave privacy holes in the browser or in your operating systems in order to protect some certain business model that might be competing against Big Tech.

The CHAIRPERSON. Right. I will just close with this.

I live in California. The California law has not really stopped the kind of collection that I think its authors intended.

I will say, however, that, despite some decrying the regulation, the formation of businesses in the tech sector is at an all-time high. Business is good. Actually, job creation in Silicon Valley is carrying the entire State. So, it has not had these horrible impacts in the tech sector.

I am mindful that, if we constrain the collection and retention of data by internet companies, especially in the internet space, it will require a change in their business models. I think that is necessary because, right now, the propensity and the capacity to manipulate every person in America is unacceptably high.

So, I am wondering, Professor Zuboff, you talked about, in your New York Times essay recently, about how democracies are confronting the tragedy of the uncommons and how we need to get back to protect our society, for lack of a refined thing.

Can you expand what is the most important thing to accomplish that goal in your judgment?

Ms. ZUBOFF. Well, you know, the digital century opened with great promise. It was supposed to be the democratization of knowledge. I am not ready to let that dream die.

The problem is we have gone on this kind of accidental path. In my written testimony, I gave a lot of background as to how that happened. A certain market ideology, certain national security concerns, the accidents of financial emergency in Silicon Valley, and how surveillance capitalism was invented in order to get tiny little Google in the year 2000, you know, over the hurdle when its investors threatened to pull out in the dot-com bust—a bunch of accidents, and that is why I call where we are an accidental utopia. But what we really have is an opportunity for the digital century to be a century where data is being used to further the needs of society, to solve our core, most important problems. And data collection is being used in ways that are aligned with what we consider in the digital century to be necessary fundamental rights.

This is work that we have not yet undertaken. We have got to figure it out. It would be like having lived through the 20th century without ever having tackled workers' rights or consumers' rights and the laws to oversee those rights and the institutions to oversee all of that. We created all that in the 20th century.

We are in a new century, new material conditions, new kind of capitalism. We have got to do that fundamental creative work all over again. And that, finally brings us to a point where right now, there is this very in-depth census of how artificial intelligence is developing around the world, the ecosystem of artificial intelligence, and what it shows very plainly is that the five Big Tech companies own almost all of the artificial intelligence scientists, the science, the data, the machinery, the computers, everything pertaining to artificial intelligence is concentrated in a small handful of companies.

All of that knowledge and capability and material is going to work to solve the commercial problems of these companies and their business customers—surveillance capitalism. It is not being used for society.

So, the public is being—not only is agency being subtracted from individual life, but the benefits of the digital are being sequestered from the life of our publics, our societies, our democracies. We have the opportunity to get that back and get us back on track to a digital century that actually fulfills its promise of knowledge, democratization, and really solving the problems that face us. That is what it is all about.

The CHAIRPERSON. Thank you so much, Professor. And thanks to all of our witnesses.

As I mentioned, the record of this Committee will be held open for at least five days. The Committee may have additional questions for you, and, if so, we will send them to you and humbly request that you answer them. I think that we have advanced our knowledge of this situation substantially today, and it is due to the very helpful and thoughtful testimony provided by these excellent witnesses.

At this point, our hearing will be adjourned, and we will see the Members of the Committee tomorrow for our oversight hearing of the Capitol Police.

So, with that, without objection, this hearing is adjourned with thanks.

[Whereupon, at 4:22 p.m., the Committee was adjourned.]

Questions for the Record

COMMITTEE ON HOUSE ADMINISTRATION
FEBRUARY 16, 2022, HEARING: "BIG DATA: PRIVACY RISKS AND NEEDED REFORMS IN THE PUBLIC AND PRIVATE SECTORS"
MAJORITY QUESTIONS FOR THE RECORD

Hugh Halpern:

1. How, if at all, has the Government Publishing Office considered potential interactions between the materials it publishes and artificial intelligence technologies -- for example, third parties using AI to mine or process government documents for some purpose? Have possible applications of AI informed GPO's privacy policies or practices in any way?

Yes, because GPO houses govinfo.gov, which receives more than 70 million document retrieval requests each month; maintains the online Catalog of Government Publications; and administers the Federal Depository Library Program (FDLP), we have a good deal of experience with data mining technologies and approaches. AI can make data mining more efficient and increase the likelihood that someone can find the information they're looking for. Conversely, it also increases the likelihood that any Personally Identifiable Information (PII) available online can be found.

Fundamentally, what GPO seeks to do is to redact and suppress Personally Identifiable Information (PII) that may appear in our collections and those other collections that can be accessed through GPO's overall system of online access. With respect to "born digital" content, we aim to do this contemporaneously with the posting of publications that may contain some incidental PII, but when we look at historical content that may already be online we recognize that we have to be vigilant in finding instances in which PII may be in existing collections. GPO employs contractors to help with this work and our own LSCM staff are adept at finding and remediating such PII. We also collaborate closely with our FDLP partners to make sure they are aware when we locate PII in their collections.

In September of 2019, GPO's Superintendent of Documents issued a policy statement on the redaction of Personally Identifiable Information. That extensive policy can be found here and it aims to proactively redact personally identifiable information (PII) from content discovered in, or being readied for ingest into, the Government Publishing Office's (GPO) system of online access.

Additionally, some of these same AI and machine learning tools could assist with work to identify and redact PII currently performed by contractors. GPO constantly assesses new technology to protect policy.

2. What are the main ways that GPO coordinates its privacy policies and practices with those of other federal agencies? In your view, is there sufficient coordination on digital privacy issues between agencies -- including those in both the executive and legislative branches?

Government Publishing Office (GPO) takes privacy of its employees, contractors, and customers seriously and in that regard, GPO has established its Privacy Program (GPO Directive 825.41B) that promulgates policies, processes, best practices, and training required to guide GPO employees and contractors to protect the Personally Identifiable Information (PII) and Protected Health Information (PHI) (collectively referred to as PII) during all stages of the information lifecycle — when collecting, storing, using, disseminating, or disposing of PII. The goal is to protect the PII because the loss, compromise, or unauthorized disclosure of PII may potentially lead to identity theft or other fraudulent uses that could result in substantial harm, embarrassment, or inconvenience to the affected individuals and tarnish the Agency's reputation.

GPO researched and reviewed the Federal privacy laws, regulations, and standards and studied how such guidance is being practiced at Federal agencies. This process provided the basis for GPO's Privacy Program that is also driven by the same Federal PII guidelines, memorandums, and publications referencing the Privacy Act of 1974 (as amended), the Office of Management and Budget (OMB) memorandums, and the National Institute of Standards and Technology (NIST) standards. GPO Privacy Program specifically promulgates provisions and best practices published under the following laws, regulations, and memorandums:

- *The Privacy Act of 1974*, as amended, section 552a of title 5, United States Code (Privacy Act). The guidelines and practices published under this Act are helping GPO to promote the following four basic policy objectives:
    - Restrict disclosure of personally identifiable records maintained by GPO.
    - Grant employees & contractors increased rights of access to PII maintained on themselves.
    - Grant employees & contractors the right to seek amendment of the PII maintained on themselves upon a showing that the records are not accurate, relevant, timely, or complete.

- Establish a code of "practices" that requires GPO to comply with statutory norms for the collection, maintenance, and dissemination of records.

- *E-Government Act of 2002.* The GPO Privacy Program utilizes the guidance provided in the E-Government Act of 2002. This law was enacted to improve the use of information technology (IT) and also introduced privacy protections for Federal IT systems. Section 208 of the E-Gov Act has two privacy centric provisions, sections 208(b) and 208(c). The first provision requires the completion of a privacy impact assessment (PIA) for all new IT systems, or when major changes are made to existing systems. PIAs identify and mitigate privacy risks of the information system, more fully described below. The second provision requires agencies to maintain privacy policies on their websites and in machine readable format. GPO practices E-Government Act of 2002 by developing PIAs for all systems handling PII.

- Office of Management and Budget (OMB) Memorandum M-16-14, *Category Management Policy 16-2: Providing Comprehensive Identity Protection Services, Identity Monitoring, and Data Breach Response*, July 1, 2016

- OMB Memorandum M-17-06, *Policies for Federal Agency Public Websites and Digital Services*, November 8, 2016

- OMB Memorandum M-17-12, *Preparing for and Responding to a Breach of Personally Identifiable Information*, January 3, 2017

- National Institute of Standards and Technology (NIST) Special Publication 800-84, *Guide to Test, Training, and Exercise Programs for IT Plans and Capabilities*, September 2006

- NIST Special Publication 800-122, *Guide to Protecting the Confidentiality of Personally Identifiable Information (PII)*, April 2010

With regard to the second part of this question, GPO coordinates extensively with our Executive, Legislative, and Judicial Branch counterparts on a wide range of IT, cybersecurity, and privacy issues, and always welcomes opportunities for enhanced collaboration. From our perspective, the level of engagement on these issues is and has been robust in recent years, and we don't have anything additional to recommend at this time. At the same time, we will be happy to pursue any recommendations for expanded engagement if proposed by Congress or the Administration.

epic.org ELECTRONIC PRIVACY INFORMATION CENTER

Majority Questions for the Record

Caitriona Fitzgerald

Deputy Director, Electronic Privacy Information Center (EPIC)

Hearing on "Big Data: Privacy Risks and Needed Reforms in the Public and Private Sectors"

Before the

House Committee on House Administration
United States House of Representatives

September 29, 2022

Thank you for the opportunity to respond to your questions for the record concerning the privacy risks from Big Data and the need for reform in both the public and private sectors. My name is Caitriona Fitzgerald, Deputy Director at the Electronic Privacy Information Center, or EPIC. EPIC is an independent nonprofit research organization in Washington, DC, established in 1994 to protect privacy, freedom of expression, and democratic values in the information age. For over 25 years, EPIC has been a leading advocate for privacy in both the public and private sectors.

1. **Major digital privacy bills have been introduced in successive Congresses for more than a decade, but they have seen little-to-no progress despite nearly every stakeholder and advocate calling for at least some form of legislative action. In your view, what are the main substantive stumbling blocks to the enactment of a comprehensive federal framework, and how might those be resolved?**

At the time of this Committee's hearing in February, the most recent legislative negotiations had broken down over two stumbling blocks: preemption and private right of action. But in June, leaders of the House Energy & Commerce Committee and Senate Commerce Committee introduced the American Data Privacy and Protection Act ("ADPPA"),[1] a bipartisan bill that would establish important protections for all individuals in the U.S. and strikes a compromise on these issues: it includes a private right of action with certain restrictions, as well as a ceiling preemption provision with certain carveouts.

As with most political compromises, these measures have been criticized by many stakeholders. But the political reality is that more than ten years of concerted effort to reach a deal for comprehensive privacy legislation had failed until this compromise was struck in the ADPPA.

EPIC has long argued that federal privacy laws should set a floor, allowing states to enact stronger protections. We still believe this is the best approach and would prefer that the ADPPA took that approach, but we recognize that compromise is necessary to enact a national standard that would protect the privacy and civil rights of all Americans.[2]

---

[1] H.R. 8152, 117th Cong. (2022).
[2] *See* Alan Butler and Caitriona Fitzgerald, *Evaluating the American Data Privacy and Protection Act*, Tech Policy Press (Aug. 8, 2022), https://techpolicy.press/evaluating-the-american-data-privacy-and-protection-act/.

2. **While Congress has deliberated on digital privacy, many other jurisdictions have enacted their own privacy laws, both in U.S. states and other countries around the world. What are the main lessons that we should take from these other efforts? What successes should be duplicated in U.S. federal legislation? What should be done differently?**

Despite having a strong rights-based approach and broad geographic impact, Europe's General Data Protection Regulation has faced criticism for its indeterminacy and a lack of strong enforcement.[3] That is why it the primary lesson Congress should take from the EU's experience with the GDPR is that a U.S. privacy law must establish clear and comprehensive rules backed by robust enforcement. Congress should establish an independent Data Protection Agency ("DPA") in the United States to regulate, enforce, and coordinate data protection policies across all industries and governmental entities. The DPA must be adequately funded and have strong rulemaking authority. The DPA should have the authority to:

- Investigate violations of the law, audit business practices, obtain preliminary and permanent injunctions, issue cease-and-desist orders, impose civil penalties, and secure equitable monetary relief.
- Require changes to harmful business practices, including banning serious or repeat offenders from engaging in certain lines of business.
- Conduct ongoing oversight over companies who have violated data privacy laws, including by conducting random audits.
- Regulate high-risk data practices, ensuring data processing and algorithms are fair, just, transparent, and non-discriminatory;
- Conduct investigations and adjudicate or otherwise act on complaints from consumers;
- Impose data protection standards and promulgate guidelines and policies for use by the private sector;
- Order disgorgement of data & algorithms; and
- Impose personal liability for executives for deliberate violations.

The California Consumer Privacy Agency is a good model for what a U.S. DPA could look like. State attorney general and private enforcement via a private right of action with stipulated damages should serve as complementary enforcement tools.

---

[3] *See, e.g.*, Ilse Heine, Ctr. for Nat'l Sec. Studies, *3 Years Later: An Analysis of GDPR Enforcement* (2021), https://www.csis.org/blogs/strategic-technologies-blog/3-years-later-analysis-gdpr-enforcement.

State laws in the U.S. have also provided some lessons learned. Laws in California, Colorado, Connecticut, Utah, and Virginia have generally applied either "opt-in" or "opt-out" frameworks — a requirement that companies must either ask for affirmative permission for secondary processing, or that they must give consumers the ability to turn off secondary processing. Both models can be flawed in practice: opt-in models can overwhelm consumers with constant requests for permission and are often manipulative.[4] Meanwhile opt-out regimes are both difficult to use and wildly impractical if one is to protect oneself in any meaningful way, if consumers have to manually opt out of secondary use for every website, app, or business they interact with, which can amount to thousands of organizations.[5] As a result of both approaches, consumers are forced to take too many steps to safeguard their data. A better model would be to require businesses to minimize the collection, use, and transfer of personal data to that which is reasonably necessary and proportionate the provide or maintain a specific product or service requested by the individual to whom the information pertains.

3. **In recent years, both the legislative and executive branches have devoted increasing attention to fostering competition in online apps, services, and platforms. How does this goal interact with the protection of digital privacy? Can privacy and competition efforts conflict with one another -- for example, in requiring that a platform provide third parties with access to user data -- and if so, how might Congress balance these goals?**

A handful of technology companies now assert unprecedented control over the digital economy. Google and Facebook achieved their dominance through unrivaled access to consumer data. While these two companies may be known for offering search and social media services to Internet users, their real customers are advertisers, and the products they offer are the users. Over 80 percent of Google's revenue comes from advertising,[6] while advertising accounts for nearly all of Facebook's revenue.

---

[4] *Most cookie banners are annoying and deceptive. This is not consent.*, Privacy International (May 21, 2019), https://privacyinternational.org/explainer/2975/most-cookie-banners-are-annoying-and-deceptive-not-consent.
[5] *Consumer Reports Study Finds Significant Obstacles to Exercising California Privacy Rights*, Consumer Reports (Oct. 1, 2020), https://advocacy.consumerreports.org/press_release/consumer-reports-study-finds-significant-obstacles-to-exercising-california-privacy-rights/.

[6] Paresh Dave and Nivedita Balu, *Google search ads beat targets despite global 'uncertainty'*, Reuters (July 26, 2022), https://www.reuters.com/technology/google-parent-alphabet-posts-higher-quarterly-revenue-2022-07-26/.

The more dominant these companies become, in turn, the greater their ability to collect consumer data and increase their share of the market. The consolidation of user private data into the hands of a small group of firms is not good for individual privacy or for privacy innovation. Therefore we need new rules that counter this anticompetitive trend while ensuring that the disclosure of personal data for purposes of interoperability is limited by setting strong data minimization rules. Privacy must be a central consideration when developing interoperability rules.[7]

[7] Bennet Cyphers and Cory Doctorow, *Privacy Without Monopoly: Data Protection and Interoperability* (Feb. 12, 2021), https://www.eff.org/wp/interoperability-and-privacy.

moz://a

27 May 2022

Marshall Erwin, Chief Security Officer
Mozilla Corporation

Committee on House Administration
United States House of Representatives

"Big Data: Privacy Risks and Needed Reforms in the Public and Private Sectors"
Questions for the Record.

1. How has Mozilla's experience designing privacy-enhancing products for consumers informed its views of user consent and user decision-making in privacy law? In crafting a comprehensive federal framework, how should Congress balance user choice and flexibility to share data with third parties against the practical risks that consent will be manipulated, uninformed, etc.?

    Consent should remain *a part* of the solution to protect people's privacy. However, unlike existing privacy laws which merely require some form of consent, we believe that the bar for consent must be raised, such that consumers have clear and simple choices, presented in a manner that enables them to make meaningful decisions about personal data. We know, for example, that consumers are not given meaningful opportunities to understand how their data is used or what their choices are when they are overloaded with technical information buried in lengthy privacy policies. And yet this is the industry norm today in which consumers are required to "agree to" companies using their data in multiple ways prior to using any new service and again on new product updates. Privacy policies serve important functions as disclosure documents. More importantly, however, we believe it is better to engage people so they are informed at the time that it is relevant, of data collection and sharing that would be privacy invasive or risky.

    At the same time, consumers cannot reasonably be expected to make informed decisions based on complicated technical information about data collection, usage and sharing; especially when these decisions must be made continuously and daily with every consumer interaction with a company or product. This places the burden of privacy on consumers. It is much better, we believe, for federal law to *protect* consumers by requiring companies to offer privacy, security, and transparency by default. This should be complemented by strong consumer rights and clear rules for companies to limit and disclose how data is collected and used.

Our experience within Firefox has shown us that leaning too heavily only on consent will often leave consumers at risk. We know that privacy risks are often opaque and silent and the technology underpinning those risks is often too complex for even subject matter experts to understand. These challenges are compounded by the fact that consent flows are riddled with dark patterns that trick people into data collection and/or push them to use affiliated services over competitors. Recent research shows both the form these design practices can take, and also the direct harm suffered by consumers. In the case of a web browser, consumers cannot be expected to make separate choices about third-party trackers on each website that they visit. They have neither the time nor the knowledge to do so.

2. Some have called for a right of personal data ownership in privacy legislation, drawing on concepts from intellectual property law. What view, if any, does Mozilla have of such proposals?

Privacy legislation must include strong baseline rights for consumers that place people in control of their data and privacy. This should include the right to access, rectify and delete data, along with data portability rights that allow consumers to export their data and potentially move it to another platform.

However, we are more skeptical of some privacy proposals that would hue too closely to intellectual property law and that would create a right of personal data ownership. While interesting in concept, such proposals run the risk of making problems within the data economy worse, encouraging people to own and then license their data to third parties that might not have the operational skill or interests sufficient to really protect people's privacy. We believe these ideas, along with concepts like data trusts and data fiduciaries that would serve as holding entities for the data people own, require more examination and exploration before they are incorporated into privacy legislation.

COMMITTEE ON HOUSE ADMINISTRATION
FEBRUARY 16, 2022, HEARING: "BIG DATA: PRIVACY RISKS AND NEEDED REFORMS IN THE PUBLIC AND PRIVATE SECTORS"
MAJORITY QUESTIONS FOR THE RECORD

Daniel Castro:

1. Your testimony calls for federal privacy legislation that would establish "basic consumer data rights." Would you support minimization in the collection, retention, sharing, and/or use of personal data as one of these rights? If so, how should Congress craft a minimization right?

Establishing basic consumer data rights in federal privacy legislation empowers consumers to manage how others collect, use, and share their personal information. These data rights should include: the **right to be informed** about how organizations collection and use their personal data; the **right to be notified** about data breaches involving their personal data; the **right to consent** about the use of their personal data (opt-in consent for sensitive personal information in certain contexts; opt-out consent for most others); the **right to access** a copy of their personal information; the **right to delete** their personal information; the **right to rectify** incorrect their personal information; and the **right to port** a copy of their personal information. Creating these basic consumer data rights obligates organizations that collect and process personal data to respond to consumer requests.

Data minimization is the principle that organizations should collect and store the least amount of data possible about individuals to fulfill a specific purpose. If Congress establishes basic consumer data rights, then it would be unnecessary to create data minimization requirements because consumers already could learn how organizations use their personal information, opt out of data collection they do not support, and require that organizations that have collected their personal data delete it.

And data minimization does not come without cost. First, data minimization creates legal uncertainty for businesses because determining what data is "reasonably necessary" for a given purpose is subjective. This legal uncertainty discourages firms from investing in innovative uses of data because of increased regulatory risk. Second, minimizing the data organizations collect and store artificially limits how organizations can innovate with data. Consider a company that provides direct-to-consumer genetic testing like 23andMe or Helix. Data minimization would say that these companies should throw out consumer genetic data after they run a test and only keep the results. But keeping the data allows them to do more analysis. For example, the company might discover later that there are additional genetic markers that they can test to give their customers more accurate results or new insights. Collecting data is expensive. Throwing data away, rather than reusing it, is unnecessarily wasteful—it's the data equivalent of drinking from single-use plastic bottles.

2. Your testimony calls for "preempting state and local privacy laws" in federal legislation. As you know, this has been a major topic of disagreement among stakeholders and advocates, which could be an obstacle to legislative progress. In your view, are there any possible middle grounds on the question of preemption? For example, might Congress leave more room for state and local laws on certain topics while leaving less room on other topics?

All Americans should have the same data privacy protections regardless of where they live, and companies should not be faced with 50 different sets of data privacy laws and regulations. A patchwork of state data privacy laws with varying definitions and requirements would create a complex regulatory minefield for businesses to navigate, especially if potential violations risk costly litigation. The goal of Congress should be to minimize unnecessary compliance costs for businesses so that they can concentrate their resources not on hiring more privacy lawyers to protect them from potential fines for non-compliance but on investments that will lead to more secure and privacy-preserving products and services.

Some stakeholders and advocates oppose state preemption because they want to ensure that if they do not get certain measures in a federal law, there is still a door open for them to pass those provisions in some states. For example, some stakeholders and advocates want to create a private right of action that would greatly benefit trial lawyers but do little for consumers. Others would tack on additional regulations for specific types of data, such as biometric data or children's personal data. Indeed, there are 50 state data breach laws, each slightly different, although they all share the same purpose. But these types of carve-out and variations raise costs for compliance, confuse consumers, and erode the benefits of creating a uniform federal law.

One way to achieve a middle ground on state preemption is to give state attorneys general more authority in enforcing future federal data privacy rules. While there should be one set of national rules, and one set of interpretation of those rules, state attorneys general should be allowed to bring cases against firms that break these rules and involve a substantial number of that state's residents. Allowing for broad enforcement capabilities will ensure that states can remain responsive to local needs. This type of enforcement would be especially beneficial if a federal data privacy law includes a 60 or 90-day cure period, wherein firms have a designated period to fix any alleged violation before further enforcement action occurs, because it would expedite oversight and compliance.

3. In recent years, both the legislative and executive branches have devoted increasing attention to fostering competition in online apps, services, and platforms. How does this goal interact with the protection of digital privacy? Can privacy and competition efforts conflict with one another -- for example, in requiring that a platform provide third parties with access to user data -- and if so, how might Congress balance these goals?

As Justice Louis Brandeis once wrote, privacy is the right to be left alone. Unfortunately, many of the proposed remedies to foster competition online involve requiring interoperability between various platforms that would undermine this notion of privacy. For example, interoperability requirements between competing social networks could make it harder, if not outright impossible, for these platforms to prevent harassment, spam, phishing attempts, and other unsolicited (and often unwelcome) messages—in essence making it harder for individuals to be left alone. The result of imposing interoperability requirements could be social networks where users are bombarded with robocalls and spam texts, much like many consumers experience on their mobile phone today, and platforms struggle to keep out malicious actors.

Moreover, interoperability requirements could force apps, services, and platforms to expose personal information they collect about their users to competitors. These competitors may not have sufficient safeguards to protect personal data. Moreover, there would likely be no restrictions to prevent these apps, services, and platforms from sharing data with a foreign competitor that may present an economic or national security threat to the United States.

Some stakeholders and advocates say that the presence or absence of data privacy measures in online apps and services reflects product quality. Moreover, they argue that online apps and services that collect and use data, such as for targeted advertising, are necessarily indicative of poor quality and therefore the presence of these types of products is a sign of insufficient competition. But this critique ignores that consumers have different privacy preference and disregards the fact that consumers can often choose alternatives, including paying for online apps and services that offer additional privacy protections.

If Congress is concerned about privacy as a non-price factor in competition among online apps, services, and platforms it should address this concern by passing federal data privacy legislation. Congress should not use competition policy to address privacy concerns (or vice versa). While there may be important pro-competitive effects from some data privacy proposals, such as establishing a right to data portability, the primary rationale for those proposals is to maximize the value of personal data for consumers.

Submissions for the Record

National Association of Assistant United States Attorneys

Safeguarding Justice for All Americans

February 25, 2022

Chairperson Zoe Lofgren
House Committee on
House Administration
1309 Longworth House Office Bldg
Washington, DC 20515

Ranking Member Rodney Davis
House Committee on
House Administration
1309 Longworth House Office Bldg
Washington, DC 20515

RE: NAAUSA Testimony for the House Administration Hearing on Big Data: Privacy Risks and Needed Reforms in the Public and Private Sectors

Dear Chairperson Lofgren, Ranking Member Davis, and Members of the Committee:

On behalf of the National Association of Assistant United States Attorneys (NAAUSA), representing the interests of the 6,300 Assistant U.S. Attorneys (AUSAs) working in the 93 U.S. Attorney Offices, I write you to express our perspective on privacy security issues impacting federal law enforcement, and particularly AUSAs.

On July 19, 2020, a disgruntled attorney targeted the home of U.S. District Court Judge Esther Salas. The assailant opened fire on Judge Salas' 20-year-old son, Daniel, who tragically died in the attack. Judge Salas' husband, Mark, was critically injured. This devastating case shed light onto concerns regarding a potential criminal's access to personal, private information on members of the law enforcement community and their families.

Unfortunately, it is not an isolated incident. The judges, federal prosecutors, and law enforcement officers who represent the front line and front face of our federal law enforcement system are constantly under threat of attack.

Data from the Department of Justice indicates that nearly 500 threats or inappropriate communications were levied against AUSAs in the last three years. Of these, 129 were death threats against AUSAs or their families. While the risk of a vengeful criminal attack is one many AUSAs dutifully take on in pursuit of justice for victims, our families should not be subject to these harms and reasonable steps must be taken to prevent these threats from actualizing.

Like many of the privacy issues discussed during this hearing, these privacy concerns transcend state lines. So, while several states have laws protecting private personal information about law enforcement, the lack of such a law at the federal level leaves dangerous privacy gaps.

The Senate Judiciary Committee has considered Daniel Anderl Judicial Security and Privacy Act of 2021 (S. 2340). This legislation, named in honor of U.S. District Judge Esther Salas' son, is a bipartisan effort to protect federal judges from violent criminals seeking revenge for the judge's role in the criminal justice system. This is an important Act that will undoubtedly make judges safer by protecting their personally identifiable information in public records and providing judicial security training.

2800 West Higgins Road • Suite 440 • Hoffman Estates, IL 60169
Tel: 847-885-8796 • www.naausa.org

While NAAUSA supports the focus on protecting federal judges, Congress must recognize that many members of the federal community face similar threats and security risks as federal judges. **We have urged lawmakers to amend the Daniel Anderl Judicial Security and Privacy Act of 2021 to include federal prosecutors so to extend the protections afforded to federal judges to federal prosecutors and all federal employees.**

Doxing, as it has been called, is becoming an increasingly common tool for criminal actors seeking revenge against the U.S. justice system in the internet age. Congress, States, and the Department of Justice must work quickly to prevent this violent trend from endangering the lives of more government employees and their families.

We should not wait until another member of the law enforcement community is attacked to take action to protect their class of coworkers.

Last Congress, NAAUSA endorsed the Public Servant Protection Act introduced by Senator Tom Cotton. This bill would have given all government employees, elected officials, and appointees at all levels (Federal, State, Local, and Tribal) the right to have their home addresses and phone numbers—or the home addresses and phone numbers of their immediate family members—removed from any publicly-displayed website. The bill also made it a criminal offense to post a government official or their immediate family member's home address or phone number online with the intent to cause physical harm. NAAUSA supported this bill particularly because of its protection for *all* federal employees rather than some.

To further improve this legislation, NAAUSA recommended the civil action penalty be increased to create a greater incentive for information to be quickly removed from the internet. For example, under the civil provision of California Law 6254.21 the penalty includes a damages award to public official to a maximum of three times the actual damages but in no cases less than $4,000.

Given the increasing hostility toward members of the law enforcement profession and federal employees generally, NAAUSA feels it is critical that Congress work to deter violent acts against all federal employees and their families.

NAAUSA applauds this Committee's interest in privacy issues. The lack of data security and the ease at which criminal actors can access highly personal information about law enforcement presents real dangers to federal officials. As this Committee continues considers ways to improve privacy protections, we urge you to consider protecting the private personal information of federal officials. The Daniel Anderl Judicial Security and Privacy Act of 2021 and the Public Servant Protection Act are great places to start.

NAAUSA also has robust data on state level reforms that may aid this Committee in understanding present models for addressing this issue on the federal level. Please do not hesitate to reach out to Natalia Castro (ncastro@shawbransford.com) if we can be of further assistance on this matter.

Respectfully,

Steven B. Wasserman
President

ZOE LOFGREN, CALIFORNIA
CHAIRPERSON

MARY GAY SCANLON, PENNSYLVANIA
VICE CHAIRPERSON

JAMIE RASKIN, MARYLAND
G.K. BUTTERFIELD, NORTH CAROLINA
PETE AGUILAR, CALIFORNIA
TERESA LEGER FERNANDEZ, NEW MEXICO

JAMIE FLEET
STAFF DIRECTOR

One Hundred Seventeenth
Congress of the United States
House of Representatives

COMMITTEE ON HOUSE ADMINISTRATION

1309 LONGWORTH HOUSE OFFICE BUILDING
WASHINGTON, DC 20515-6157
202-225-2061 | CHA.HOUSE.GOV

RODNEY DAVIS, ILLINOIS
RANKING MINORITY MEMBER

BARRY LOUDERMILK, GEORGIA
BRYAN STEIL, WISCONSIN

TIM MONAHAN
MINORITY STAFF DIRECTOR

June 22, 2021

The Honorable Zoe Lofgren
Chairperson
Committee on House Administration
1309 Longworth House Office Building
Washington, DC 20009

Chairperson Lofgren:

I write today to request that the Committee on House Administration hold oversight hearings regarding the current operations of the Library of Congress (LOC) and Smithsonian Institution. In May of this year, I requested operational status updates from each legislative branch entity to inform our committee's understanding of reopening progress and, ultimately, the legislative branch's service to the American people.

The findings were concerning. We found that 410 professional staff from the LOC's Congressional Research Service remain in telework, and 77 additional LOC employees have been on administrative leave for thirty pay periods – in which they remain to this day. At the Smithsonian Institution, 4,500 employees remain in telework, and only 25 percent of their workforce is estimated to be vaccinated. Additionally, concerning conversations are occurring regarding permanent timed-ticket reservation systems across all Smithsonian museums, limiting the public's access to American treasures well beyond the timeline of the recent pandemic.

Our nation is celebrating its victory over COVID-19. The *New York Times* reports that infection rates continue to decrease throughout the Washington, DC-area with cases per 100,000 averaging in single digits.[1] More importantly, every adult in the Washington, DC-area has had free access to receive both doses of a vaccine for well over a month. Beyond the beltway, the Centers for Disease Control and Prevention (CDC) reports that at least 64.5 percent of adults, nationwide, have at least one vaccination.[2] Theaters, office buildings, sports arenas, restaurants, and more have reopened. People across the country are returning to work and the same goes for Congress. The halls of the House and Senate office buildings are active once again, and there is no excuse for legislative branch support offices to not be fully operational or to continue to have employees on COVID-related administrative leave. I believe the same holds true for America's premier network of museums and research centers that fall under the umbrella of the Smithsonian Institution.

---

[1] https://www.nytimes.com/interactive/2021/us/washington-district-of-columbia-covid-cases.html
[2] https://covid.cdc.gov/covid-data-tracker/#vaccinations

The lack of guidance provided for these entities has resulted in uneven policies, creating confusion and wasteful spending. For these reasons, I am requesting that our Committee begin conducting oversight hearings to fully grasp the operational status of the entities within our jurisdiction and, if needed, get their employees back to work.

I eagerly await your response as I am desperate to get this government and this country back to work.

Sincerely,

Rodney Davis
Ranking Member
Committee on House Administration

CATO

February 15, 2022

The Honorable Zoe Lofgren
Chair
Committee on House Administration
U.S. House of Representatives
Washington, D.C. 20515

The Honorable Rodney Davis
Ranking Member
Committee on House Administration
U.S. House of Representatives
Washington, D.C. 20515

Dear Chairperson Lofgren, Ranking Member Davis, and members of the committee,

My name is Matthew Feeney. I am the director of the Cato Institute's project on emerging technologies. Tomorrow's hearing, titled "Big Data: Privacy Risks and Needed Reforms in the Public and Private Sectors," is relevant to my research, which focuses on how new and emerging technologies affect our civil liberties. The private and public use of "Big Data" is a critical issue at a time when there is bipartisan concern about the role of prominent technology companies and their influence on our civic and family lives.

Today's most popular online services collect vast troves of information about their users. As former Google CEO Eric Schmidt once put it in 2010, "With your permission, you give us more information about you, about your friends, and we can improve the quality of our searches. We don't need you to type at all. We know where you are. We know where you've been. We can more or less know what you're thinking about."[1] While services such as Google and Facebook remain popular among Americans, their collection of personal information prompts an understandable sense of unease, not least because law enforcement agencies at the state, local, and federal level analyze "Big Data" while conducting surveillance. Unfortunately, the state of 4th Amendment jurisprudence leaves much to be desired.

Congress can make reforms to address "Big Data" concerns, but these reforms should be carefully tailored to ensure that Americans are protected from unreasonable searches and seizures by the government without hampering growth and innovation in America's technology sector.

Government Use of Big Data

In recent years, the most prominent examples of government use of Big Data for surveillance were those revealed by former National Security Agency contractor Edward Snowden.[2] Bookshelves worth of books and articles have been written about the revelations, and an extensive accounting of them would

---

[1] Nick Saint, "Google CEO: 'We Know Where You Are. We Know Where You've Been. We Can More Or LessKnow What You're Thinking About.'" *Business Insider*, October 4, 2010, https://www.businessinsider.com/eric-schmidt-we-know-where-you-are-we-know-where-youve-been-we-can-more-or-less-know-what-youre-thinking-about-2010-10.

[2] Lawfare, "Snowden Revelations," accessed February 14, 2022, https://www.lawfareblog.com/snowden-revelations.

require many more pages. For the purposes of this statement, it is enough to note that the Snowden revelations unveiled the vast scale of government access to personal information, which had previously been unknown to the public.

More recently, reporting suggests that the Central Intelligence Agency (CIA) has been conducting mass surveillance on Americans, a sad reflection on the state of reform many lawmakers and civil libertarians hoped for in the wake of the Snowden revelations.[3]

Government use of Big Data is not reserved to intelligence agencies that cite national security concerns as justification for surveillance. Domestic agencies have also engaged in surveillance fueled by Big Data. The Department of Homeland Security (DHS) has exploited the "border exception" to the Fourth Amendment, for example, allowing officers to conduct warrantless searches of electronic devices at international border crossings. In 2014, Palantir Technologies secured a contract to build a vast intelligence system capable of collecting data on a subject's "schooling, family relationships, employment information, phone records, immigration history, foreign exchange program status, personal connections, biometric traits, criminal records, and home and work addresses."[4]

State, local, and federal law enforcement agencies use surveillance tools to monitor Americans. Such tools include social media snooping software, cell site simulators, and facial recognition technology.[5]

Facial recognition is one of the most widely discussed surveillance technologies cited by civil libertarians. More than 2,200 law enforcement agencies and private companies in twenty-seven countries have used Clearview AI, a controversial facial image search engine.[6] Clearview AI

---

[3] Matthew Guariglia and Andrew Crocker, "We Need Answers About the CIA's Mass Surveillance," *Electronic Frontier Foundation*, February 11, 2022, https://www.eff.org/deeplinks/2022/02/we-need-answers-about-cias-mass-surveillance.

[4] Spencer Woodman, "Palantir Provides the Engine for Donald Trump's Deportation Machine," *The Intercept*, March 2, 2017, https://theintercept.com/2017/03/02/palantir-provides-the-engine-for-donald-trumps-deportation-machine/.

[5] Brennan Center for Justice, "Third-Party Vendors of Social Media Monitoring Tools for Law Enforcement Agencies," November 17, 2021, https://www.brennancenter.org/our-work/research-reports/third-party-vendors-social-media-monitoring-tools-law-enforcement; American Civil Liberties Union, "StingrayTracking Devices: Who's Got Them?" November 2018, https://www.aclu.org/issues/privacy- technology/surveillance-technologies/stingray-tracking-devices-whos-got-them.

[6] Ryan Mac, Caroline Haskins, and Logan McDonald, "Clearview's Facial Recognition App Has Been UsedBy The Justice Department, ICE, Macy's, Walmart, And The NBA," *BuzzFeed News*, February 27, 2020, https://www.buzzfeednews.com/article/ryanmac/clearview-ai-fbi-ice-global-law-enforcement.

scrapes billions of images from social media platforms such as Instagram, Facebook, and Twitter. Investigators can search this database, uploading photos of suspects in the hopes of confirming their identity.[7]

Government use of Big Data is not reserved to law enforcement and intelligence agencies. Local governments are increasingly looking to "Smart City" technology to improve infrastructure.[8] Smarter infrastructure could result in fewer car crashes, less congested traffic, and more efficient public transport. Although not ostensibly related to mass surveillance, these initiatives have the potential to unveil intimate details. One of the best examples of how collection of personal transport data can reveal intimate details of private lives is a blog post (which has since been deleted) published by Uber detailing one-night sexual encounters among users.[9]

The Privacy Paradox

Any attempts at Big Data regulation or legislation will have to tackle the privacy paradox at the heart of debates surrounding data and privacy. On the one hand, Americans claim to care about their privacy, yet their behavior suggests otherwise. Amid complaints about "surveillance capitalism" we should keep in mind that Americans are keen users of services that collect information about them. Fortunately for those Americans more privacy-focused there are many services available that allow them to communicate and browse the web without revealing personal information.[10]

The Institute for Progress' Alec Stapp summarized the Privacy Paradox well, writing:

> "There is a paradox at the heart of how people treat privacy. They say they value privacywhile their actions imply they don't. In other words, their stated preferences contradict their revealed preferences. Is this just another example of cheap talk? Research from behavioral economics and

---

[7] Kashmir Hill, "The Secretive Company That Might End Privacy as We Know It," *The New York Times*, November 2, 2021, https://www.nytimes.com/2020/01/18/technology/clearview-privacy-facial- recognition.html.

[8] Jonathan Woetzel et al., "Smart cities: Digital solutions for a more livable future," *McKinsey & Company*,June 5, 2018, https://www.mckinsey.com/business-functions/operations/our-insights/smart-cities- digital-solutions-for-a-more-livable-future.

[9] Bradley Voytek, "Rides of Glory," *#UberData* (blog), Uber, https://web.archive.org/web/20140827195715/http://blog.uber.com/ridesofglory.

[10] End-to-end encrypted chat service Signal and the web browser TOR being among perhaps the mostnotable.

related fields has shown that privacy valuations are highly context-dependent and subject to social-desirability bias and endowment effects."[11]

Stapp went on to provide examples from a number of surveys showing that although many people claim to value their privacy, they often value their personal information at a low cost.

That "privacy" is not an absolute value must be considered by those concerned about "Big Data." Privacy is a condition people enjoy when they control information about themselves.[12] The age of social media has shown us the wide variety of ways in which people control such information. Some people like to post photos of their meals, themselves, or their romantic partners. Others would never post such content, choosing instead to volunteer personal information in political forums or e-commerce platforms. Others enjoy Amazon and YouTube recommendations based on viewing and purchasing histories. There is no one-size-fits-all approach to privacy. Fortunately, the market currently provides Americans of all privacy views a variety of social media platforms and communications tools.

Lawmakers considering regulation or legislation related to Big Data ought to be reassured by the fact that most Americans are aware that popular online services analyze their personal data and that alternatives are available to Americans concerned about their privacy. Contrary to what many lawmakers have been saying over the last few years, popular online communication and web browsing services are not monopolies.

Reform

Those seeking to address concerns associated with Big Data should consider the following principles guiding reform:

1) Update legislation.

---

[11] Alec Stapp and Ryan Hagemann, "Regulatory Comment: Hearings on Competition and Consumer Protection in the 21st Century, The Intersection Between Privacy, Big Data, and Competition," *Niskanen Center*, August 20, 2018, https://www.ftc.gov/system/files/documents/public_comments/2018/08/ftc-2018-0051-d-0027-152798.pdf.

[12] Jan Holvast, "History of Privacy," (conference paper, IFIP Advances in Information and CommunicationTechnology, 2008), https://citeseerx.ist.psu.edu/viewdoc/down load?doi=10.1.1.1037.5642&rep=rep1&type=pdf.

The Electronic Communications Privacy Act (ECPA), passed in 1986, has yet to undergo a comprehensive revision accounting for more than thirty years of technological changes. The law allows law enforcement to access a wide range of intimate content such as emails, social media chats, and texts more than six months old without a warrant.[13] Congress should address the loopholes in ECPA that currently allow law enforcement to access troves of personal communications without a warrant.

Congress should also improve upon Supreme Court precedent and impose a warrant requirement for searches of electronic devices at the border.

Lawmakers from both parties have supported such legislation.[14]

2) Control, don't ban, facial recognition

More than half of American adults have images of their faces stored in databases that law enforcement officials can search while conducting facial recognition queries.[15] This is in large part thanks to the fact that many state departments of motor vehicles allow law enforcement to search their databases of driver's license photos.[16] The result is what Georgetown researchers have called the "Perpetual Lineup."[17] Concerns about facial recognition have promoted calls for a ban on the technology.[18] This is not the best approach.

Although facial recognition does pose a significant threat to civil liberties it is not without benefits. Facial recognition has the potential to ease queues at cinemas, grocery stores, and train stations. In addition, it can be used to enhance security and could be used to aid in searches for missing children or adults with dementia. Jettisoning these benefits is fortunately not necessary in order to protect civil liberties. As I have outlined before, there are policies that could ensure facial recognition is used by law enforcement in a narrow and transparent way that would not infringe on civil liberties.[19] These policies

---

[13] Electronic Privacy Information Center, "Electronic Communications Privacy Act (ECPA)," accessed February 15, 2022, https://epic.org/ecpa/.

[14] Protecting Data at the Border Act, S. 1606, 116th Cong. (2019).

[15] Clare Garvie, Alvaro Bedoya, and Jonathan Frankle, "The Perpetual Line-up: Unregulated Police FaceRecognition in America," *Georgetown Law Center on Privacy and Technology*, October 18, 2016, https://www.perpetuallineup.org.

[16] Ibid.

[17] Ibid.

[18] Fight for the Future, "Ban Facial Recognition," accessed February 14, 2021, https://www.banfacialrecognition.com.

[19] Matthew Feeney, "Should Police Facial Recognition Be Banned?" *Cato at Liberty* (blog), Cato Institute, May 13, 2019, https://www.cato.org/blog/should-police-facial-recognition-be-banned.

include a ban on real-time identification, removing data related to law-abiding Americans from databases, and open source, accuracy, and transparency requirements.[20]

3) Embrace transparency

A regrettable feature of modern American law enforcement is its lack of transparency. Too often, Americans learn about what surveillance devices their governments use from journalists rather than elected officials. Federal agencies should be required to regularly release information about 1) how often they ask technology firms for users' personal data, 2) what new surveillance tools its officers are using, and 3) how and when data related to closed cases are purged.

4) Resist calls for "data ownership"

It is not uncommon in discussion about "Big Data" to hear "data ownership" proposals that would grant a property right in personal data. Although perhaps at first glance attractive, such proposals are conceptually confused and are not necessary to protect privacy.

Data is very different from traditional property. A property right entails a "bundle" of other rights, such as the right to exclude and alter property. If you have a property right in a house you can exclude others from it and alter it. It is also clear who owns a home and other pieces of property. Data does not have these qualities. Data is not excludable in the same way as a house. My enjoyment of data is not affected if you use the same data or alter the data for yourself.

Similarly, it is not clear how such a property right would be allocated. Does my birthdate contain data about me, my mother, or my father? Should property rights in marriage data be assigned to one spouse or both?

Most importantly, allowing for a property right in data is not necessary for privacy, as Center for Growth and Opportunity scholar Will Rinehart has explained:

> "[A] property right in data isn't needed to establish consumer privacy rights. For evidence of this fact, one only needs only to consult the current laws in the United States. The Gramm-Leach-Bliley Act (GLBA), the

---

[20] Ibid.

> Fair Credit Reporting Act (FCRA), the Children's Online Privacy Protection Act (COPPA), and the California Consumer Privacy Act (CCPA), just to name a few, all protect privacy without creating property rights. As Stanford Law Professor Lothar Determann has said quite bluntly, 'no one owns data' because data are already 'subject to a complex landscape of access rights and restrictions.' Privacy regulation already defines certain kinds of entitlements to control and contract upon data. Adding a superordinate property right on top of these existing restrictions would make the entire enterprise all that more complicated and undermine current efforts togrant consumers control. If data property rights were implemented, for example,would an individual be able to limit critical information from being shared with credit rating agencies?"[21]

As lawmakers consider regulations and legislation they should be wary of the risks of regulatory capture. Market incumbent firms such as Microsoft, Google, and Facebook are well positioned to comply with whatever new regulations and legislation emerge from Congress. History teaches us that these firms will invest in preparing for new regulation, and competition may suffer if regulations and legislation results in costs for market entrants. One of the best examples of this dynamic can be found in Google's preparation for the European Union's General Data Protection Regulation (GDPR), its flagship set of privacy regulations. Google reportedly spent hundreds of years worth of human time preparing for GDPR, a set of regulations that has benefitted the Silicon Valley giant:

> "Google, for example, has seen some unique market benefits following the activation ofGDPR in May 2018. From April to July of last year, Google's market share increased by 0.93% while most other adtech vendors in North America and Europe lost ground. Thelowest rank of adtech companies — the top 150 to 100 — lost the most market share, a decline of 31.86% on average. Google was of course prepared for privacy

---

[21] *Hearing on Data Ownership: Exploring Implications for Data Privacy Rights and Data Valuation, Beforethe Committee on Banking, Housing, and Urban Affairs*, 116th Cong. (2019) (testimony of Will Rinehart, Director of Technology and Innovation Policy at the American Action Forum), https://www.banking.senate.gov/imo/media/doc/Rinehart%20Testimony10-24-19.pdf.

regulation ahead of time, having spent "hundreds of years of human time" and, ostensibly, billionsof dollars to shore up its defenses."[22]

Lawmakers on this side of the Atlantic should be wary of repeating Europe's experience.

Thank you for giving your attention to these important issues. I would welcome the opportunity to discuss my thoughts further with you or your staff.

Yours,

Matthew Feeney
Director, Project on Emerging Technologies Cato Institute

United States District Court for the District of Columbia

UNITED STATES OF AMERICA
v. Criminal Case No. 21-582 (CRC)
MICHAEL A. SUSSMANN,
Defendant.

Government's Motion to Inquire into Potential Conflicts of Interest

The United States of America, by and through its attorney, Special Counsel John H. Durham, respectfully moves this Court to inquire into potential conflicts of interest arising from the representation of the defendant by his current counsel, Latham & Watkins LLP ("Latham"). The Government has discussed these matters with the defense and believes that any potential conflicts likely could be addressed with a knowing and voluntary waiver by the defendant upon consultation with conflict-free counsel as appropriate. The Government believes that any such waiver should be put on the record prior to trial. As set forth in further detail below, it is possible that conflicts of interest could arise from the fact that Latham and/or its employees (i)

---

[22] Alex Moazed, "How GDPR is Helping Big Tech and Hurting Competition," *Applico*, accessed February 14, 2022, https://www.applicoinc.com/blog/how-gdpr-is-helping-big-tech-and-hurting-the-competition/.

previously represented others in the Special Counsel's investigation whose interests may conflict with those of the defendant, (ii) previously represented the defendant and his prior employer in connection with events that likely will be relevant at trial or at any sentencing, and (iii) maintained professional and/or personal relationships with individuals who could be witnesses in these proceedings. Accordingly, for the reasons set forth below, the government respectfully requests that the Court inquire into the potential conflicts of interest set forth herein. Defense counsel has advised that the defendant has been apprised of these issues, understands that he has the right to consult independent counsel, and presently intends to waive any potential conflict of interest. In support of this Motion, the government represents the following:

Factual Background

The defendant is charged in a one-count indictment with making a materially false statement to the FBI, in violation of Title 18, United States Code, Section 1001 (the "Indictment"). As set forth in the Indictment, on Sept. 19, 2016 – less than two months before the 2016 U.S. Presidential election – the defendant, a lawyer at a large international law firm ("Law Firm-1") that was then serving as counsel to the Clinton Campaign, met with the FBI General Counsel at FBI Headquarters in Washington, D.C. The defendant provided the FBI General Counsel with purported data and "white papers" that allegedly demonstrated a covert communications channel between the Trump Organization and a Russia-based bank ("Russian Bank-1"). The Indictment alleges that the defendant lied in that meeting, falsely stating to the General Counsel that he was not providing the allegations to the FBI on behalf of any client. In fact, the defendant had assembled and conveyed the allegations to the FBI on behalf of at least two specific clients, including (i) a technology executive ("Tech Executive-1") at a U.S.-based Internet company ("Internet Company- 1"), and (ii) the Clinton Campaign.

The defendant's billing records reflect that the defendant repeatedly billed the Clinton Campaign for his work on the Russian Bank-1 allegations. In compiling and disseminating these allegations, the defendant and Tech Executive-1 also had met and communicated with another law partner at Law Firm-1 who was then serving as General Counsel to the Clinton Campaign ("Campaign Lawyer-1").

The Indictment also alleges that, beginning in approximately July 2016, Tech Executive-1 had worked with the defendant, a U.S. investigative firm retained by Law Firm-1 on behalf of the Clinton Campaign, numerous cyber researchers, and employees at multiple Internet companies to assemble the purported data and white papers. In connection with these efforts, Tech Executive-1 exploited his access to non-public and/or proprietary Internet data. Tech Executive-1 also enlisted the assistance of researchers at a U.S.-based university who were receiving and analyzing large amounts of Internet data in connection with a pending federal government cybersecurity research contract. Tech Executive-1 tasked these researchers to mine Internet data to establish "an inference" and "narrative" tying then-candidate Trump to Russia. In doing so, Tech Executive-1 indicated that he was seeking to please certain "VIPs," referring to individuals at Law Firm-1 and the Clinton Campaign.

The Government's evidence at trial will also establish that among the Internet data Tech Executive-1 and his associates exploited was domain name system ("DNS") Internet traffic pertaining to (i) a particular healthcare provider, (ii) Trump Tower, (iii) Donald Trump's Central Park West apartment building, and (iv) the Executive Office of the President of the United States ("EOP"). (Tech Executive-1's employer, Internet Company-1, had come to access and maintain dedicated servers for the EOP as part of a sensitive arrangement whereby it provided DNS resolution services to the EOP. Tech Executive-1 and his associates exploited this arrangement by mining the EOP's DNS traffic and other data for the purpose of gathering derogatory information about Donald Trump.)

The Indictment further details that on February 9, 2017, the defendant provided an updated set of allegations – including the Russian Bank-1 data and additional allegations relating to Trump – to a second agency of the U.S. government ("Agency-2"). The Government's evidence at trial will establish that these additional allegations relied, in part, on the purported DNS traffic that Tech Executive-1 and others had assembled pertaining to Trump Tower, Donald Trump's New York City apartment building, the EOP, and the aforementioned healthcare provider. In his meeting with Agency-2, the defendant provided data which he claimed reflected purportedly suspicious DNS lookups by these entities of internet protocol ("IP") addresses affiliated with a Russian mobile phone provider ("Russian Phone Provider-1"). The defendant further claimed that these lookups demonstrated that Trump and/or his associates were using supposedly rare, Russian-made wireless phones in the vicinity of the White House and other locations. The Special Counsel's Office has identified no support for these allegations. Indeed, more complete DNS data that the Special Counsel's Office obtained from a company that assisted Tech Executive-1 in assembling these allegations reflects that such

DNS lookups were far from rare in the United States. For example, the more complete data that Tech Executive-1 and his associates gathered – but did not provide to Agency-2 – reflected that between approximately 2014 and 2017, there were a total of more than 3 million lookups of Russian Phone-Provider-1 IP addresses that originated with U.S.-based IP addresses. Fewer than 1,000 of these lookups originated with IP addresses affiliated with Trump Tower. In addition, the more complete data assembled by Tech Executive-1 and his associates reflected that DNS lookups involving the EOP and Russian Phone Provider-1 began at least as early 2014 (i.e., during the Obama administration and years before Trump took office) – another fact which the allegations omitted.

In his meeting with Agency-2 employees, the defendant also made a substantially similar false statement as he had made to the FBI General Counsel. In particular, the defendant asserted that he was not representing a particular client in conveying the above allegations. In truth and in fact, the defendant was representing Tech Executive-1 – a fact the defendant subsequently acknowledged under oath in December 2017 testimony before Congress (without identifying the client by name).

Applicable Law

The Sixth Amendment guarantees that "[i]n all criminal prosecutions, the accused shall ... have the Assistance of Counsel for his defense." U.S. Const. Amend. VI. A defendant's Sixth Amendment right includes the "right to representation that is free from conflicts of interest," Wood v. Georgia, 450 U.S. 261, 271 (1981), but also carries a "presumption in favor of counsel of choice," Wheat v. United States, 486 U.S. 153, 160 (1988). At the same time, a criminal defendant's right to retain counsel of his choice is not absolute. The "essential aim" of the Sixth Amendment "is to guarantee an effective advocate for each criminal defendant rather than to ensure that a defendant will inexorably be represented by the lawyer whom he prefers." Wheat, 46 U.S. at 159. Thus, even if a defendant waives the right to conflict-free representation, the presumption in favor of defendant's counsel of choice "may be overcome not only by a demonstration of actual conflict but also by a showing of a serious potential for conflict." Wheat, 486 U.S. at 163–64.

As the D.C. Circuit explained in United States v. Lopesierra–Gutierrez, 708 F.3d 193, 199–200 (D.C. Cir. 2013), "a defendant's counsel-of-choice right may sometimes be trumped by a conflict of interest." This is because "where a defendant's chosen counsel suffers from a conflict of interest, . . . the court's own institutional interests" are implicated. Id. Guaranteeing conflict-free counsel protects not just defendants' rights, but also the "'[f]ederal courts['] ... independent interest in ensuring that criminal trials are conducted within the ethical standards of the [legal] profession and that legal proceedings appear fair to all who observe them.'" *Id.* (alterations in original) (quoting *Wheat*, 486 U.S. at 161).

Since the Court has an independent interest in investigating potential conflicts, *see Wheat*, 486 U.S. at 161, the Court retains "substantial latitude in refusing waivers of conflicts of interest not only in those rare cases where an actual conflict may be demonstrated before trial, but in the more common cases where a potential for conflict exists which may or may not burgeon into an actual conflict as the trial progresses." *Id.* at 163. Accordingly, "[i]f in the context of a particular case the district court believes a conflict is intolerable, it may decline to accept a defendant's waiver." *Lopesierra–Gutierrez*, 708 F.3d at 202. "In making this determination, a court balances the defendant's right to choose his representative against both the defendant's countervailing right to conflict-free representation and the court's independent interest in the integrity of criminal proceedings." *Id.* at 200 (emphasis in original). The key inquiry in this analysis is the "nature and extent of the conflict." *Id.*

Discussion

The Government respectfully requests that the Court inquire concerning the following issues that may give rise to potential conflicts of interest with regard to Latham's current representation of the defendant:

I. Latham's Prior Representations in the Special Counsel's Investigation
   A. Latham's Prior Representation of Law Firm-1 and Campaign Lawyer-1 in This Investigation

From approximately July 2020 through approximately July 2021, Latham represented three separate clients – the defendant, Law Firm-1, and Campaign Lawyer-1 – in connection with the Special Counsel's investigation.[1] As part of its representations, Latham communicated and met with the Special Counsel's Office and other DOJ officials on behalf of each of these clients. As noted above, the Indictment alleges that Tech Executive-1 conferred and consulted with both the defendant and Campaign Lawyer-1 on multiple occasions in connection with the Russian Bank-1 allegations. As a result, the Government expects that testimony at trial will address factual issues concerning, among other things, (i) the extent to which the defendant did or did not inform Campaign Lawyer-1 and Law Firm-1 that he was billing work on the Russian Bank-1 allegations to the Clinton Campaign, (ii) the extent to which the defendant did or did not inform or receive instructions from Campaign Lawyer-1 and Law Firm-1 regarding his billing of the Clinton Campaign and his meeting with the FBI General Counsel, and (iii) the defendant's potential motives to mislead the FBI concerning whether he was working with or on behalf of the Clinton Campaign, Campaign Lawyer-1, and Tech Executive-1. In each of these areas, the defendant's interests may diverge from those of Campaign Lawyer-1 and Law Firm-1. In addition, to the extent that the defendant's factual accounts might differ from those of Campaign Lawyer-1 and Law Firm-1 on these issues, Latham may already have gained privileged insights to any such differences from their prior, confidential attorney-client communications. *Cf. United States v. Gotti*, 9 F. Supp. 2d 320, 323–25 (S.D.N.Y. 1998) ("attorney-client relationship with the witness or co-defendant gave rise to continuing obligations of loyalty and confidentiality that may be breached when the confidences are required to be exploited in, for example, cross examining [a] former client"); *cf. also United States v. Weaver*, 265 F.3d 1]074, 1075–77 (D.C. Cir. 2001) (holding that counsel's representation of a client and a potential witness against the client created a conflict of interest).

Moreover, it is possible that the defendant, having recently resigned from his partnership at Law Firm-1, is currently or will become in an adversarial posture with his former employer. Latham – through its prior representation of Law Firm-1 – likely possesses confidential knowledge about Law Firm-1's role in, and views concerning, the defendant's past activities. Accordingly, the Government believes that potential conflicts of interest may exist or arise from Latham's prior representations of Campaign Lawyer-1 and Law Firm-1 in this investigation.

---

[1] One of the Latham attorneys who represented the defendant during this time period is now serving at the U.S. Department of Justice. It is the understanding of the Special Counsel's Office that this attorney expeditiously and appropriately recused himself from any involvement in the Special Counsel's investigation and these proceedings.

B. Law Firm-1's Representation of the Clinton Campaign and Another Political Organization

Potential conflicts of interest might also arise from the fact that during the time period when Latham represented all three of the aforementioned clients, one of those clients, Law Firm-1, was representing both the Clinton Campaign and a related political organization ("Political Organization-1") in the Special Counsel's investigation. Law Firm-1's representations of those clients began in approximately May 2021 and ended in approximately July 2021. The Government believes that Law Firm-1's prior representations of these entities may give rise to potential conflicts of interest because it is possible that Law Firm-1 shared confidential facts and/or communications concerning its representation of those clients with its then-counsel, Latham. In addition, to the extent the Government offers documents and other evidence at trial that it obtained from the Clinton Campaign and/or Political Organization-1, Latham's duties to its former client (Law Firm-1) might cause its interests to diverge from those of the defendant in connection with such evidence and/or the cross examination of witnesses. Accordingly, the Government respectfully requests that theCourt inquire into any potential conflicts, including an examination of whether Law Firm-1's own representations of the Clinton Campaign and Political Organization-1 may contribute to or amplify such conflicts. Gotti, 9 F Supp. 2d at 323-25.

II. Latham's Other Representations in Related Matters

In addition to the above representations, Latham also has represented the defendant, Law Firm-1, and Campaign Lawyer-1 in other matters that predated the existence of the Special Counsel's investigation but which are likely relevant to these proceedings. In particular, the Government is aware of the following:

I. Latham's Representation of the Defendant in his December 2017 Congressional Testimony

Latham served as counsel to the defendant and Law Firm-1 in connection with the defendant's December 2017 testimony before the House Permanent Subcommittee on Intelligence. That testimony addressed the Russian Bank-1 allegations and other matters. At numerous times during the defendant's testimony, attorneys from Latham interjected to clarify and/or address issues relating to attorney-client privilege and other topics.[2] In his testimony, the defendant acknowledged bringing the Russian Bank-1 allegations to the FBI General Counsel and to Agency-2 on behalf of a specific client, namely, Tech Executive-1 (whom the defendant did not identify by name). The Government expects to offer this testimony at trial to prove that the defendant knowingly and intentionally lied when he stated to the FBI General Counsel in September 2016 that he was not acting on behalf of "any client." The Government also may seek to establish that the defendant's Congressional testimony itself was knowingly and intentionally misleading insofar as it failed to disclose that the defendant billed work on the Russian Bank-1 allegations to the Clinton Campaign. Because Latham attorneys played a role in, and were witnesses to, this testimony and related conversations, it is possible that their past advice might give rise to a potential conflict of interest. For example, it is possible that motion practice surrounding the admissibility of this testimony may require consideration of issues such as the appropriate boundaries of the attorney-client privilege, the potential waiver of such privilege by the defendant or Tech Executive-1 and the Clinton Campaign, and/or the potential applicability of an advice of counsel defense. Because Latham attorneys witnessed the defendant's testimony and advised both the defendant and his employer in connection therewith, it is possible that conflicts of interest would arise in connection with these matters. Gotti, 9 F. Supp. 2d at 324 ("An attorney may be disqualified if he has first-hand knowledge of events that may be part of the government's proof at trial.")

II. Latham's Advice to Law Firm-1 in Connection with Public Statements in 2018

In 2018, Latham also advised Law Firm-1 concerning the drafting and issuance of statements to the media that Law Firm-1 made concerning the defendant's October 2016 meeting with the FBI General Counsel. Those statements – which the defendant appears to have reviewed or assisted in drafting – were at least partially inaccurate and/or misleading. The Government therefore may seek to offer these statements at trial pursuant to Rule 404(b) or other provisions of law. The two statements are, in pertinent part, as follows:

---

[2] Both of the Latham attorneys who were present for the defendant's testimony (one of whom is the Department of Justice employee referenced above) have since left the firm.

- On or about October 12, 2018, Law Firm-1 issued a statement to multiple media outlets in which the firm stated, in part: "When Sussmann met with [the FBI General Counsel] on behalf of a client, it was not connected to the firm's representation of the Hillary Clinton Campaign, the DNC or any Political Law Group client."
- On or about October 18, 2018, the then-Managing Partner of Law Firm-1 wrote a letter to the editor of a major newspaper in which he asserted, in part, "Mr. Sussmann's meeting with the FBI General Counsel James Baker was on behalf of a client with no connections to either the Clinton campaign, the DNC or any other Political Law Group client."

Privilege logs and redacted emails obtained from Law Firm-1 in this investigation reflect that in the days before the issuance of these statements, Latham attorneys sent, received, and/or were copied on correspondence relating to the drafting and dissemination of the statements. (Much of the substance of those emails was redacted and withheld from the Special Counsel's Office pursuant to Law Firm-1's assertion of attorney-client privilege and attorney work product protections). Because the defendant was aware of and/or reviewed these media statements, the Government may seek to offer them as evidence pursuant to Rule 404(b) or other provisions of law to establish that the defendant sought to conceal the Clinton Campaign's ties to the Russian Bank-1 allegations from the FBI and others.[3] Latham's advice concerning these statements therefore may become at issue in motions *in limine*, trial testimony, or other aspects of these proceedings. Accordingly, Latham may encounter potential conflicts of interest in advising the defendant concerning past events in which Latham played a significant role.

III. Defense Counsel's Prior Interactions with Witnesses or Potential Witnesses

Based on its review of documents in its investigation and other information, the Special Counsel's Office also has learned that one of the members of the defendant's current defense team ("Defense Team Member-1") previously worked as Special Counsel to the then-FBI Director from 2013

---

[3] According to counsel for Law Firm-1, the attorneys at Law Firm-1 and Latham who participated in drafting and/or reviewing these statements were unaware at the time that the defendant had billed work on the Russian Bank-1 allegations to the Clinton Campaign.

to 2014. In connection with that work, Defense Team Member-1 developed professional and/or personal relationships with several individuals who later were involved with and/or knowledgeable of the FBI's investigation of the Russian Bank-1 allegations. For example, Defense Team Member-1 appears to have developed a professional relationship with the former FBI General Counsel to whom the defendant made his alleged false statement and who will likely be a central witness at trial.[4] While it is unlikely that these past interactions and activities will give rise to an actual conflict of interest, the Government respectfully requests in an abundance of caution that the Court inquire with the defense concerning whether Defense Team Member-1's relationships with persons and entities who might be witnesses in this case could give rise to a potential conflict or appearance issue and, if so, whether the defendant waives any such conflict. See Lyle v. Artuz, No 03-CV-5155 (CBA), 2006 WL 1517750 at *20 (E.D.N.Y. May 31, 2006) (examining whether defense counsel's relationship with a trial witness gave rise to a conflict of interest).

Conclusion

For the foregoing reasons, the Court should inquire regarding the potential conflicts of interest set forth above.

Respectfully submitted,
JOHN H. DURHAM
Special Counsel By:
/s/ Andrew J. DeFilippis

Jonathan E. Algor
Assistant Special Counsel jonathan.algor@usdoj.gov

---

[4] Following his employment at the FBI, Defense Team Member-1 worked from 2014 to early 2017 as an attorney in the EOP which, as noted above, was involved in certain factual issues that the Government expects will be relevant at trial and any sentencing proceedings. Latham has represented to the Government that while employed at the EOP, Defense Team Member-1 had no role in the aforementioned events or arrangements involving Tech Executive-1, Internet Company- 1, and/or allegations involving the purported use of Russian-made phones. The Government similarly has not seen evidence to suggest that Defense Team Member-1 had any role in, or direct knowledge of, the Russian Bank-1 allegations or the FBI's ensuing investigation.

Andrew J. DeFilippis
Assistant Special Counsel andrew.defilippis@usdoj.gov
Michael T. Keilty Assistant Special Counsel michael.keilty@usdoj.gov

Clinton campaign paid to 'infiltrate' Trump Tower, White House servers to link Trump to Russia, Durham finds

'Tech Executive-1 and his associates exploited this arrangement by mining the EOP's DNS traffic and other data for the purpose of gathering derogatory information about Donald Trump.'

By Brooke Singman Fox News
Published February 12, 2022 5:02pm EST

Two men indicted by Durham will go on trial in 2022

Former Federal Prosecutor James Trusty details what to expect in 2022 as two men have been indicted as a result of the Durham probe into the roots of the Trump-Russia investigation First on Fox: Lawyers for the Clinton campaign paid a technology company to "infiltrate" servers belonging to Trump Tower, and later the White House, in order to establish an "inference" and "narrative" to bring to government agencies linking Donald Trump to Russia, a filing from Special Counsel John Durham found.

Durham filed a motion on Feb. 11 focused on potential conflicts of interest related to the representation of former Clinton campaign lawyer Michael Sussmann, who has been charged with making a false statement to a federal agent. Sussmann has pleaded not guilty.

The indictment against Sussmann, says he told then-FBI General Counsel James Baker in September 2016, less than two months before the 2016 presidential election, that he was not doing work "for any client" when he requested and held a meeting in which he presented "purported data and 'white papers' that allegedly demonstrated a covert communications channel" between the Trump Organization and Alfa Bank, which has ties to the Kremlin.

Declassified Trump-Russia Probe Docs to Date: What to Know

But Durham's filing on Feb. 11, in a section titled "Factual Background," reveals that Sussmann "had assembled and conveyed the allegations to the FBI on behalf of at least two specific clients, including a technology executive (Tech Executive 1) at a U.S.-based internet company (Internet Company 1) and the Clinton campaign."

Durham's filing said Sussmann's "billing records reflect" that he "repeatedly billed the Clinton Campaign for his work on the Russian Bank-1 allegations."

Special Counsel John H. Durham.

The filing revealed that Sussmann and the Tech Executive had met and communicated with another law partner, who was serving as General Counsel to the Clinton campaign. Sources told Fox News that lawyer is Marc Elias, who worked at the law firm Perkins Coie.

Durham's filing states that in July 2016, the tech executive worked with Sussmann, a U.S. investigative firm retained by Law Firm 1 on behalf of the Clinton campaign, numerous cyber researchers and employees at multiple internet companies to "assemble the purported data and white papers."

"In connection with these efforts, Tech Executive-1 exploited his access to non-public and/or proprietary Internet data," the filing states. "Tech Executive-1 also enlisted the assistance of researchers at a U.S.-based university who were receiving and analyzing large amounts of Internet data in connection with a pending federal government cybersecurity research contract."

"Tech Executive-1 tasked these researchers to mine Internet data to establish 'an inference' and 'narrative' tying then-candidate Trump to Russia,"

Durham states. "In doing so, Tech Executive-1 indicated that he was seeking to please certain 'VIPs,' referring to individuals at Law Firm-1 and the Clinton campaign."

Former U.S. President Bill Clinton and First Lady Hillary Clinton arrive for the Presidential Inauguration of Trump at the U.S. Capitol in Washington, D.C., U.S., January 20, 2017. (REUTERS/Saul Loeb/Pool).

Durham also writes that during Sussmann's trial, the government will establish that among the Internet data Tech Executive-1 and his associates exploited was domain name system (DNS) internet traffic pertaining to "(i) a particular healthcare provider, (ii) Trump Tower, (iii) Donald Trump's Central Park West apartment building, and (iv) the Executive Office of the President of the United States (EOP)."

Special Counsel John Durham 'Still In Action,' Garland Says

Durham states that the internet company that Tech Executive-1 worked for "had come to access and maintain dedicated servers" for the Executive Office of the President as "part of a sensitive arrangement whereby it provided DNS resolution services to the EOP."

"Tech Executive-1 and his associates exploited this arrangement by mining the EOP's DNS traffic and other data for the purpose of gathering derogatory information about Donald Trump," Durham states.

The filing also reveals that Sussmann provided "an updated set of allegations" including the Russian bank data, and additional allegations relating to Trump "to a second agency of the U.S. government" in 2017.

Durham says the allegations "relied, in part, on the purported DNS traffic" that Tech Executive-1 and others "had assembled pertaining to Trump Tower, Donald Trump's New York City apartment building, the EOP, and the aforementioned healthcare provider."

In Sussmann's meeting with the second U.S. government agency, Durham says he "provided data which he claimed reflected purportedly suspicious DNS lookups by these entities of internet protocol (IP) addresses affiliated with a Russian mobile phone provider," and claimed that the lookups "demonstrated Trump and/or his associates were using supposedly rare, Russian-made wireless phones in the vicinity of the White House and other locations."

Pedestrians pass the Trump Tower building, Tuesday, July 7, 2020, in New York. (AP Photo/Frank Franklin II).

"The Special Counsel's Office has identified no support for these allegations," Durham wrote, adding that the "lookups were far from rare in the United States."

"For example, the more complete data that Tech Executive-1 and his associates gathered--but did not provide to Agency 2--reflected that between approximately 2014 and 2017, there were a total of more than 3 million lookups of Russian Phone-Prover 1 IP addresses that originated with U.S.-

based IP addresses," Durham wrote. "Fewer than 1,000 of these lookups originated with IP addresses affiliated with Trump Tower."

Durham added that data collected by Tech Executive-1 also found that lookups began as early as 2014, during the Obama administration and years before Trump took office, which he said, is "another fact which the allegations omitted."

Durham Targets Clinton Campaign Law Firm in Fresh Round of Subpoenas

"In his meeting with Agency-2 employees, the defendant also made a substantially similar false statement as he made to the FBI General Counsel," Durham wrote. "In particular, the defendant asserted that he was not representing a particular client in conveying the above allegations."

"In truth and in fact, the defendant was representing Tech Executive-1--a fact the defendant subsequently acknowledged under oath in December 2017 testimony before Congress, without identifying the client by name," Durham wrote.

Former President Trump reacted to the filing on Saturday evening, saying Durham's filing "provides indisputable evidence that my campaign and presidency were spied on by operatives paid by the Hillary Clinton Campaign in an effort to develop a completely fabricated connection to Russia."

"This is a scandal far greater in scope and magnitude than Watergate and those who were involved in and knew about this spying operation should be subject to criminal prosecution," Trump said. "In a stronger period of time in our country, this crime would have been punishable by death."

Trump added: "In addition, reparations should be paid to those in our country who have been damaged by this."

Former chief investigator of the Trump-Russia probe for the House Intelligence Committee under then-Rep. Devin Nunes, R-Calif., Kash Patel, said the filing "definitively shows that the Hillary Clinton campaign directly funded and ordered its lawyers at Perkins Coie to orchestrate a criminal enterprise to fabricate a connection between President Trump and Russia."

"Per Durham, this arrangement was put in motion in July of 2016, meaning the Hillary Clinton campaign and her lawyers masterminded the most intricate and coordinated conspiracy against Trump when he was both a candidate and later President of the United States while simultaneously perpetuating the bogus Steele Dossier hoax," Patel told Fox News, adding that the lawyers worked to "infiltrate" Trump Tower and White House servers.

The anti-Trump dossier, authored by ex-British intelligence officer Christopher Steele, commissioned by opposition research firm Fusion GPS, was funded by the Democratic National Committee and Hillary Clinton's campaign through Elia's law firm, Perkins Coie.

Patel added that Sussmann relayed the "false narrative" to U.S. government agencies "in the hopes of having them launch investigations of President Trump."

Sussmann's indictment is the second prosecution to come out of Durham's probe.

Sussman pic: Perkins Coie (Perkins Coie).

In November 2021, Durham also charged Russian national Igor Danchenko of making false statements. Danchenko, who pleaded not guilty, is accused of lying about the source of information that he provided to Christopher Steele for his "dossier" on Trump.

In 2020, Durham charged former FBI lawyer Kevin Clinesmith with making a false statement – the first criminal case arising from his probe. Clinesmith was referred for potential prosecution by the Justice Department's inspector general's office, which conducted its own review of the Russia investigation.

Specifically, the inspector general accused Clinesmith, though not by name, of altering an email about Page to say that he was "not a source" for another government agency. Page has said he was a source for the CIA. The DOJ relied on that assertion as it submitted a third and final renewal application in 2017 to eavesdrop on Trump campaign aide Carter Page under the Foreign Intelligence Surveillance Act (FISA).

Former Attorney General Bill Barr appointed Durham, then the U.S. attorney from Connecticut, in 2019 to investigate the origins of the FBI's original Russia probe, or Crossfire Hurricane, which began in July 2016, through the appointment of Special Counsel Robert Mueller in May 2017 shortly after Mueller completed his years long investigation into whether Trump's campaign colluded or coordinated with the Russians to influence the 2016 presidential election.

Mueller's investigation found no evidence of illegal or criminal coordination between Trump or the Trump campaign and Russia in 2016.

Barr, in December 2020, before leaving the Trump administration, tapped Durham as special counsel to continue his investigation through the Biden administration.

Get the Fox News App Here

In the scope order, Barr stated that Durham "is authorized to investigate whether any federal official, employee, or any other person or entity violated the law in connection with the intelligence, counter-intelligence, or law-enforcement activities directed at the 2016 presidential campaigns, individuals associated with those campaigns, and individuals associated with the administration of President Donald J. Trump, including but not limited to Crossfire Hurricane and the investigation of Special Counsel Robert S. Mueller, III."

Under U.S. code, the special counsel would produce a "confidential report" and is ordered to "submit to the Attorney General a final report, and such interim reports as he deems appropriate in a form that will permit public dissemination."

Brooke Singman is a political correspondent and reporter for Fox News Digital, Fox News Channel and FOX Business.

Index

Q

R

S

T

U

V

W

Y